JACK DOYLE: THE GORGEOUS GAEL

MICHAEL TAUB was born in Hillingdon, Middlesex, and has three grown-up children. He is the author of two published books: *Jack Doyle: Fighting For Love* and *Danoli: The People's Champion*. He began his career in journalism at seventeen with five years at *Boxing News*. He was Assistant Press Secretary at the old, twin-towered Wembley Stadium and has held executive editorial positions with the *Sunday Express* and *Daily Mirror*, where he was respectively Deputy Sports Editor and Night Sports Editor. As a sideline, he staged rock-music concerts and professional boxing tournaments. He is married and lives in Berkshire, England.

For Martha, Kevin, Vanessa and Siobhan, who have suffered my preoccupation with Jack Doyle with patience and good humour.

MICHAEL TAUB

THE LILLIPUT PRESS
DUBLIN

Published 2007 by
THE LILLIPUT PRESS
62–63 Sitric Road, Arbour Hill,
Dublin 7, Ireland
www.lilliputpress.ie

First published 1990 by
STANLEY PAUL & CO. LTD
An imprint of RANDOM CENTURY GROUP LTD

A CIP record for this title is available from the British Library.

1 3 5 7 9 8 6 4 2

ISBN 978 1 84351 123 6

Set in Ehrhardt
Printed in England by Athenaeum Press Ltd, Tyne and Wear

Contents

Book III JACK AND MOVITA

Book IV NANCY – AND AFTER

Foreword

We all love a hero but we tend to love a flawed hero even more. George Best springs immediately to mind.

Before World War II another young Irishman, a practitioner in an unrelated sport, was the George Best of the pre-television age. He was Jack Doyle, a giant of a man in every way, a heavyweight boxer with a knockout punch who would have become world champion had his dedication matched his self-promotion.

The charmer from Cobh in County Cork stood 6 foot 5 inches, had the looks of a movie star and a lilting tenor voice. He married the Mexican film actress and beauty Movita, later to become the wife of Marlon Brando.

Jack was a playboy, a libertine and, eventually, a drunk who, at the time of his death in the late 1970s, was a virtual down-and-out.

The book is a labour of love by Michael Taub. When it was first released a few years ago I wrote in a Sunday newspaper that it was the best sports book I had read in an age. Revisiting it now has been a joy all over again and if the name Jack Doyle has not yet registered with you, it certainly will after reading this riveting account of his life.

Too talented in so many ways for his own good, Jack could not live up to his billing; but then, how many of us can? In his character and the perceptive telling of his story, you will probably find a little of yourself. Your first problem, though, will be ever to put this book down.

This is an outstanding tale of fame, fortune and failure, beautifully written by an author with a love and understanding for his subject without ever avoiding the harsh realities of Jack's darker side.

DESMOND LYNAM, *2007*

Acknowledgements

There are many to whom I owe a debt of gratitude. Foremost among them is Helen Doyle, whose husband Bill was the one person privy to the truth about his famous brother. He was Jack's famous aide and companion in London and the United States from the age of fifteen and knew all there was to know about his fighting and his loving. He had turned down several would-be biographers and only after being prompted by Helen did he agree to meet me. He and Helen stuck loyally by me when his help was further requested. My biggest regret is that he did not live to see the completion of the book. Since his death Helen has given me every possible assistance, including access to their treasured photo album of Jack. Some of those pictures appear in the book.

Other members of the Doyle family were equally helpful in laying bare the details of Jack's life, wherever it might lead me and whatever hurt it might cause them. It takes a special kind of courage and a special kind of trust. I would like particularly to thank Ted Doyle, Tim Doyle, Bella Doyle and Bridie Gibbard (née Doyle), all since deceased, and Mick Doyle.

A book of this nature cannot be produced without the backing and encouragement of a whole host of people. I wish to pay tribute to my agent, Jonathan Williams, and the MD at publishers The Lilliput Press, Antony Farrell. Also my original editors Jeff Cloves and Dominique Shead.

The following helped greatly in locating people and documentation:

In the United States: Movita, the late Keith McConnell, Philip Paul.

In Ireland: Morgan O'Sullivan, Patrick Myler, Tim Cadogan, Sr Margaret McFadden, the late Denis Morrison, Dave Guiney, Spike McCormack, Peter Barry and John McGinn.

In France: The late Jacques Descamps, Robert Papon.

In Australia: David Jack, Caroline Shone.

In the United Kingdom: John Morris, Lt. Morgan O'Neill and Colour Sergeant Brian Hazard BEM (Irish Guards), Peggy and Velimir Stimac, Dr Richard Agius, Martha Taub, Madeleine Smalley, Alex Toner, the Notting Hill friends of Jack Doyle; the late Gilbert Odd, Ron Olver, Frank Duffett, Jim Doherty, Tony Ross, Vic Hardwicke and Siggy Jacobsen.

It is not possible to name the numerous others who assisted in small yet important ways, but I am no less grateful to them all.

The quest: An introduction to the Lilliput edition

The date: 12 November 1981. The time: nine-thirty in the morning, GMT. Christine Cromwell was calling from her Florida hotel suite, drunk and in tears. She had endured a night of torment distilling the news in my letter: Jack Doyle was dead.

She poured out her heart: 'My darling Jack, my baby; I can't believe it. He was the love of my life.'

The daughter of the late Delphine Dodge confirmed with that emphatic last sentence precisely what I had always suspected: she had carnal knowledge of the man she affectionately called Mr Blarney, having pursued him lustily from the age of fourteen. It had been difficult to dismiss her heartless goading of her immensely wealthy but emotionally insecure mother – 'You'll never marry Jack; he likes me more than you!' – as childish infatuation. Her missives to Jack, written in 1965 when in her early forties, and which I had stumbled upon purely by chance, proved it had been anything but.

'I'll tell you about that place in Windsor,' she cried. 'Horace Junior had prostitutes there; it was a den of vice, pure and simple.' I said I would drop everything and fly out to see her. She was elated, offering even to pay my airfare. I booked up and faxed her my itinerary: I would be with her in Coral Gables in forty-eight hours. I could hardly wait to get the low-down on her love affair with Jack and the secrets contained within the walls of the mansion the Dodge family had provided rent-free to US ambassador Joseph Kennedy during World War II.

On the very eve of departure, while working at my job in Fleet Street, my family relayed to me an urgent message: Christine Cromwell's attorney had forbidden her to see or even speak to me. I was devastated. Having finally homed in on one of two remaining Dodge divas privy to the peccadilloes and sexual excesses of one of the richest families on the planet, I was effectively being warned off.

I had a simple decision to make: either to accept the situation or jump on the plane and attempt to force the issue. Buoyed by a sense of purpose and even destiny, I chose to take the leap of faith that, lawyer or no lawyer, I might yet get an opportunity to confront her. I sent a defiant message saying it was too late to cancel and that I would be 'flying into Miami as arranged'.

If all was lost, I reasoned, I had the address and telephone number of former Ziegfeld beauty Martha 'Mickey' Devine, the third and evidently most alluring of Horace Dodge Jnr.'s quintet of wives (all of whom would take him for a fortune), although by August 1943 – by which time Mickey was suing for divorce – his feelings toward her had turned from lifelong love and devotion to insidious loathing, to the extent that he burst into her Park Avenue apartment and ripped every piece of jewellery from her body.

I had dismissed as fanciful the promise of a consolation prize from Christine: she would press the president of Columbia Pictures to produce a movie from the book. It was a tough call on my part, and possibly a foolhardy one. Christine, I knew, would be incredibly well connected and yet I considered it some kind of ploy, a sop she had thought I would be unable to resist. She was wrong. I had also by this time made contact with Movita, who, to my surprise and delight, would willingly testify to her turbulent years with Jack. Before leaving London, I confirmed she was available for interview.

There was no one at Miami International Airport to meet me. I felt lonely and dispirited. Christine had told me of her personal assistant, Alan DeJohn, a Virgin Islander she had befriended and was putting through business school. She also had a 'very able' male secretary, a Mr Sol Hershman. They would be tough nuts to crack.

I took a taxi to the David William Hotel and booked myself a room. I picked up the phone and asked for Miss Cromwell, who occupied the sumptuous tenth-floor suite. Alan DeJohn answered. I told him who I was and that I had checked into the hotel. He asked for my room number and said he'd be in touch. Half an hour later, there was a knock on my door. I was confronted by a big, strapping, black man in his early twenties, well dressed and wearing expensive-looking silver-framed glasses. He announced himself as Alan DeJohn and I invited him in. He stated apologetically that Miss Cromwell was 'out of town' and that only that morning he had taken her to the airport, pushing her in a wheelchair through vast crowds of people and placing her on a plane destined for one of the small islands off Miami, the name of which he could not recall. Her son, he said, was going through a particularly painful divorce and she 'just had to be with him'.

He sounded earnest and convincing and I had no reason to doubt him. He asked what my plans would be now that I was unable to meet Miss Cromwell. I said that after a good night's sleep I would hire a car and travel upstate to Jupiter Island, where I hoped to see Mickey Devine, after which I would fly across to Los Angeles to meet with Movita. He again apologised for Miss Cromwell's absence and said he would call in to see me before my departure next morning.

I awoke with a start, the realisation dawning that the story fed to me by Mr DeJohn was a work of fiction. I was incensed that I should have been regarded as a soft touch. I resolved to prove otherwise.

Mr DeJohn appeared at my door bright and early, kitted out head to toe in dazzling white tennis gear. He explained he was going for a lesson and had called to say goodbye. He once more expressed regret at the 'mix-up' over Miss Cromwell and wished me the 'very best of luck' in my quest.

I watched him leave the building and took the lift to the tenth floor. I knew I had an hour at most and must make every second count. I tapped gently on the door just to the left of where I had exited the lift. A Spanish maid half-opened it, peering out suspiciously. 'Ah, yes,' I said with supreme self-confidence (and legs of jelly). 'I've called to see Miss Cromwell.'

She held her hands to the side of her face, inclined her head slightly and said: 'Mees Cromwell, she is a-sleepeeng.' At that precise moment I knew my instincts had been correct: Christine Cromwell was indeed here in the hotel and I had to act smartly if I was to see her. I moved to the door to prevent the maid closing it, explaining reassuringly that 'Miss Cromwell knows I'm in town and wouldn't mind, I'm sure, if I came in and waited for her.' With those words I eased my way into the huge room, gestured toward the settee and said, 'I'll sit here quietly until she wakes up.' The maid was wary but at the same time relieved that I did not appear to pose a threat. She was placing implicit trust in me, a total stranger.

Five minutes passed: I had counted every one of them. I had to make a move before this huge man arrived back in his tennis gear and threw me from the window to a vain and inglorious death, as I imagined he might. I got up from the settee, my eyes fixed firmly on the maid. I backed my way slowly into the short passageway leading to the bedroom, holding up my hands and saying, 'I'm going to wake Miss Cromwell. Don't be alarmed. I know she won't mind.'

Christine was sound asleep and looking pretty much as I remembered her from a photograph taken nearly twenty years earlier with her banker-turned-diplomat father James, though perhaps a little old for her years (she was then in her late fifties). Walking frames were propped up against a wall and I realised she must be crippled with arthritis or some other such debilitating disease, resonating strongly with Alan DeJohn's account, albeit fictitious, of him pushing her in a wheelchair through the crowded concourse at Miami International Airport.

I tapped her gently on the hand. Her eyes opened. I spoke barely above a whisper: 'Christine, it's Michael. I knew you were here and I had to see you.' She displayed not the slightest sign of distress. 'Alright, Michael,' she said, calm as you like. 'Wait out there in the lounge – I'll be with you shortly.'

I did as I was asked. I heard the shower going. 'Hurry, hurry,' I was saying to myself. She did not hurry enough. In walked a casually dressed man I assumed at once to be the redoubtable Sol Hershman. He was small and slight and bespectacled and not at all the imposing figure I had envisaged. He smiled and bade me a cheery 'Good morning.' I returned his greeting, feeling obliged to mention that I was 'just waiting for Miss Cromwell'.

'Sure, fine,' he said, before disappearing toward Christine's bedroom. A minute or so later he re-emerged, brusque and businesslike. 'Michael, you have to go. Miss Cromwell does not want to see you.' I tried my best to brazen it out: 'Miss Cromwell has just said she *would* see me. I'm going nowhere.' He became agitated, threatening: 'If you don't go right now, I'll call the cops.'

It was tough conceding defeat, particularly after a journey of 4000 miles, but there was the dubious satisfaction of having given the undertaking my all. I left her a piece of pricey Wedgwood pottery I had brought from England as a gift; and was at pains to absolve the maid of blame for my having been able to enter the inner sanctum of a Dodge family member virtually unchallenged. Touchingly, she appeared to appreciate what I was saying: she told me with her sad brown eyes.

The armed security guards at Traverse Circle were, paradoxically, the quintessence of charm and civility. Every few minutes, they insisted on ringing the home of Mrs Martha Gerlach (Mickey Devine as was). 'Maybe she's shopping; maybe she's away.' I hung around for a couple of hours before heading off for a quick bite to eat. During my absence of all of twenty minutes, Mickey – wouldn't you know it? – had arrived back. 'We'll ring her for you right away.' My heart was pounding as I took the phone and duly introduced myself, outlining my mission and wondering if she 'might spare the time to talk'. Her answer was an uncompromising 'No.' I pleaded and cajoled and remonstrated but nothing would convince her to change her mind. This was one tough cookie, evidenced by the fact she once socked 6ft-8in. Primo Carnera on the jaw in a Paris nightclub.

I felt I had better change tack: 'In a spirit of friendship, let me at least come and see you. I won't ask questions. A quick cup of tea and I'll be on my way.' Even that failed to move her. Finally, I said that my research had revealed a physical liaison between her and Jack Doyle: 'I'm giving you the opportunity to put your side of the story. Otherwise, I'll go with what I've got.' That did it. 'Write what you like,' she said before banging down the receiver.

From Florida I flew on to Los Angeles, where my faith in human nature was restored by a warm and gracious greeting from Movita, looking incredibly young and glamorous at sixty-four. She and the tall, fair-haired, fifty-something Keith McConnell, though not living together, had maintained the friendship formed in Dublin toward the end of the war. Out of the blue, she asked: 'Why don't you try and see Marlon? I know he's in town – I was with him only yesterday.'

It was pitch black as Keith and I headed off in his huge black Mercedes. On the way he told me what 'an absolute bastard' Brando had been during the remaking of *Mutiny On The Bounty* in 1962, in which Keith himself had a bit-part role. 'He was so objectionable, the shooting of the movie became a nightmare for the whole crew. The director, Carol Reed, quit in disgust.'

Keith glided to a halt directly opposite the Brando residence on Mulholland Drive. As he did so, a car was entering through the automatic gate. Keith revved the Merc's engine: 'I'm going in right on its coat-tails.' He careered across the road but screeched to a halt as the gate began its descent. We cursed our luck. I got out of the car and asked through the intercom to speak to Brando. 'He ain't home,' was the response of a spaced-out young lady, in all probability tragic daughter Cheyenne. I scribbled a note and placed it in the mailbox. Brando never got back to me but, as it turned out, I wouldn't need him. My interviews with Movita produced more than ten hours of taped testimony while Keith provided not only magnificent quotes and a compelling critique of Jack but documentary evidence relating to the darkest days of the marriage. Sadly, he has since died but Movita, as I write, is still going strong at ninety.

Next on my list was the much-married Judith Allen, who had been divorced from husband number seven by the time we met. I had been trying for years to locate her whereabouts and succeeded only by virtue of the efforts of a long-time friend in New York, Philip Paul, working in conjunction with a police chief cum movie buff from North Carolina.

By then in her seventies and in delicate health, she was trading as The Revd Judith Rucker, which explained the difficulty in tracing her. She was based at the Institute of Mentalphysics in Joshua Tree, California, part of the Yucca Valley region of the Mojave Desert, where scorpions and rattlesnakes abound. I stayed more than a week in the bungalow adjacent to Judith's, spending entire days and evenings in her company. She was a wonderful host and willing at the drop of a hat to discuss virtually anything about herself, including the most intimate details of her marriage to world champion all-in wrestler Gus (Cannonball) Sonnenberg, news of which had shocked even hardened Hollywood sceptics and resulted in the mercurial Cecil B. deMille tearing up her movie contract.

> Gus was so enormous, I couldn't have intercourse with him; it was just too painful. On our wedding night I was torn to shreds: I couldn't walk for days. He was booked on a wrestling tour and my mother had to get me to the hospital. The doctor there was appalled; he said my husband should be locked up and that I had to leave him immediately. But he had it all wrong. Gus wasn't a brute in the bedroom: he was a gentle and considerate lover. It's just he was way too big.

The brief and pain-racked union with Sonnenberg, whom she had wed at nineteen, might reasonably have been expected to turn her off sex for life; but far from it dimming her ardour, she admitted she had struggled throughout her career to control her libido, as a consequence of which Gary Cooper and Jack Doyle would appear to have been the main beneficiaries. Of all her many husbands and lovers, she maintained that Jack was 'the best, absolutely'.

Visits to the United States had become almost de rigueur. There were, in addition, numerous trips to Ireland and to various destinations in the UK, notably to Lynton in Devon to interview the quixotic Sir Atholl Oakeley. I headed, too, to France in the hope of tracking down Jacques and Denise Descamps, whose once-famous father, François, had attempted in 1933 to transform Jack into 'the new Carpentier'.

On arrival at the village of La Guerche-sur-l'Aubois, some 150 miles south of Paris, I was reduced to asking a woman in the street in halting phrase-book French if she knew the whereabouts of the Descamps family. She popped into a doctor's surgery and emerged with the receptionist, to whom I repeated my request and who, in no time at all, was surrounded by a group of a dozen or so women, young and old, big and small, and all of them babbling excitedly. Finally, the receptionist hopped in her car and returned with a local schoolteacher, M. Robert Papon, who spoke the most perfect English. He invited me to visit him that evening.

In the meantime I managed to locate the street named after the great manager – *rue François Descamps* – and the former Descamps family residence, where Jack had been based during his two-month tutorial. I visited also the local graveyard where generations of the Descamps family are entombed. At M. Papon's house I was introduced to Madame Paulette Desphilippons, aged ninety-one and a prosperous former market fruiterer, who revealed that Jacques and Denise were resident in Paris. She provided me with an address for Jacques in the Saint Germain district of the city.

I turned up unannounced at his apartment to explain that I was writing a book on Jack Doyle, whom he remembered with affection, and that I had travelled from London via La Guerche to see him. He wiped away a tear when I mentioned Jack's sparring partners of the day, Maurice Griselle and Marcel Moret, saying: 'No one in France today would have heard of them and yet you, an Englishman, arrive on my doorstep and start to speak of them.' He explained that Denise was unwell and unable to receive visitors, which saddened me more than he would know. Unusually for me, I accepted the situation without question for fear of offending this decent and kindly former French war hero. We corresponded after my visit and then I heard nothing more from him. Shortly afterwards, I learned he had died.

As I believe I have illustrated, the task of bringing to completion the biography of Jack Doyle was about very much more than writing. It required patience and persistence, the skill and cunning of a detective, a skin as impenetrable as a rhinoceros hide and, above all, passion. It took seven years to identify and track down the major players in Jack's life, one contact often leading to another. The search for the real Jack Doyle had turned from being a fascinating job of work into a magnificent obsession.

And so, seventeen years after the book was first published in September 1990 as *Jack Doyle: Fighting For Love*, we have a new edition with a new subtitle and a new audience. My hope is that it will prove richly entertaining and informative for you, the reader, and final arbiter.

MICHAEL TAUB
Berkshire, England, September 2007

Jack Doyle

Some think he might have won the crown
That now to Brown Joe's head seems glued
But he got tangled in the gown
Of Venus waiting as she would
For the handsome boy who comes to town

Patrick Kavanagh

Hollywood, 1938

'Hi Movita! It's me. Alex.'

'Who?'

'Alex – Alex D'Arcy.'

'Oh Alex! Sorry, I've just come from the studio – I'm not thinking straight.'

'Listen, never mind that – guess who's come to town?'

'I've no idea. Surprise me.'

'JACK DOYLE!'

'Jack Doyle – wow. The guy in jail?'

'You got it.'

'What about him?'

'Well, he's out of the slammer. I'm throwing a party for him on Saturday. And get this! He wants to meet you.'

'Me?'

'Yeah honey, you. I've told him all about you.'

'I'd love to be there. I saw his picture in the paper. He's some guy. But I've got a weekend date with Howard.'

'Where's he taking you?'

'Palm Springs – in his private plane.'

'Damn! Jack's dying to meet you.'

'But Alex, Howard's got first claim on me.'

'Aw, screw Howard Hughes. This Doyle's a *real* man. Listen – you two are just made for each other.'

'Don't get me wrong – I'm dying to meet him. But what can I do about Howard?'

'Are you crazy? This guy boxes, sings, acts, gets slung in jail – the whole town's talking about him. He's dynamite. Come on! Ditch Howard. He's a bore.'

'Okay, Alex – you've sweet-talked me into it. I'll find a way out. I'll meet him.

'Movita, you're a doll. You won't regret it – I promise.'

Book 1
JACK

Chapter 1

The Holy Ground

He was almost too young to be a hero, this boy of 19 whom fame had beckoned. Even heroes are allowed to catch their breath, and he had not quite counted on the whole harbour town of Cobh* turning out to greet him. Nor had he imagined that a pipe-band would be waiting to parade him along the waterfront and out to the Holy Ground, where he was born. He was shaken by the magnitude of the welcome as he waved to the hundreds who lined the route, many of them hanging from upstairs windows. All were anxious to catch a glimpse of the handsome *buachaill* who had grown up in their midst and whose fighting deeds had given them cause for rejoicing. He was their local boy made good, their chieftain returning from glorious battle.

His brother Bill, then 15, recalled:

> 'He jumped up on to the sea wall and made an impromptu speech: "My next aim is Jack Petersen and the British title. Then I'll be after Larry Gains and the Empire title. And after that it will be full speed ahead to the championship of the world." A mighty roar went up and someone asked him to give them a song. He sang *Mother Machree* just for Mum and you could have heard a pin drop. People were crying, so beautifully did he sing it. Afterwards they shouted things like, "We love you Joe. We're proud of you." He had them all in the palm of his hand and he knew it. He was a majestic figure.'

Sadly for 'Joe' it could be only a fleeting visit. Brigadier-General Critchley had wasted no time in arranging his next contest. It was to be at the Royal Albert Hall in just three weeks' time and, against a Frenchman whose name he could not even pronounce. He had not wanted to fight again so quickly. Already he'd had eight bouts in his first six months as a professional boxer and he needed a break. He would have preferred a little time to savour his success – to get the feel of being famous. But he had no option other than to go through with the contest, if only to appease his new master. The Brigadier had a reputation for

* *Cobh* (Cove), in Co. Cork, was a British garrison town. It had been renamed Queenstown in honour of Queen Victoria's visit to Ireland in 1849, but later reverted to its original title.

being as prickly as the thin moustache that lined his upper lip.

Before heading back to London, he decided to steal a few days to renew old friendships. He would step back from the present and remind himself how life had been just a few short years earlier, before his sudden rise to fame.

*

It had all started on August 31, 1913 – hardly an auspicious date in early 20th century Irish history, but one that would hold some significance for the world at large.

Doc O'Connor could scarcely believe it. The baby boy he had just brought into the world at 12 Queen's Street* was the biggest he had delivered. A hefty 14-pounder.

The child was the second born to merchant seaman Michael Doyle and his wife Anastasia and they called him Joe. They already had a daughter, Bridie, and four more children were to follow – Betty, Bill, Mick and Tim.

Michael Doyle was tall, upright and God-fearing, a Cork man born and bred. He had married the tiny Stacia in 1910 when he was 41 and she just 18, a slip of a girl who, in common with her contemporaries, had nurtured one abiding ambition in life: to settle down and raise a family.

In those unpretentious days it was considered an honourable, even admirable, aspiration. Apart from the uneasy expediency of emigration, there was little other prospect for girls like her, brought up as they were to observe the time-honoured virtues of love and obedience and schooled skilfully by their mothers in the domestic requirements of sewing, knitting and cooking.

Michael was naturally proud of his children. Like many well-intentioned fathers, he hoped to see in his eldest son some of the qualities that might enable him to fulfil a frustrated ambition – to rebuild a broken dream. He remembered how, as a small boy, he had listened awestruck to his father's tales of the dashing exploits of the Doyles of old, who, reputedly, had helped King Brian Boru banish the Danes from Ireland at the Battle of Clontarf in 1014. He had heard also of a fearless uncle, said to be a boxing champion of the British Navy, who thought nothing of taking on several men on a foreign quayside to rescue one of his mates from trouble.

Fuelled with the desire to continue the family's fighting traditions, Michael once tried his luck in the boxing ring. Having received some painful indications that his fists would never be his fortune, he toyed

* *Queen's Street* has since been renamed Connolly Street.

with the idea of entering the priesthood – an ambition cloaked more in fantasy than hard realism and which eventually came to nothing. But being both a devout Catholic and a proud Irishman, he vowed that if any child of his grew up to be a priest or a champion boxer, he would call a truce with his Maker and ask for nothing more in his prayers.

So when with a piercing cry the infant Joe announced his entry into the world, Michael could have been forgiven for thinking that his latent hopes and dreams would be realised. They had, in a sense, been reborn.

Little Joe was barely out of the cradle before it became obvious to one and all that he would never achieve the high calling of the priesthood. With a fighting pedigree stretching back 900 years to Brian Boru, it was perhaps pre-ordained that his qualities would be more pugnacious than spiritual. The inheritance would stand him in good stead. The Holy Ground was a tough nursery where the children played, or more often fought, in bare feet.

Ireland was in the grip of grinding poverty and the Doyles, like countless other families, were forced to make the best of it. Their plight could be considered worse than most after two appalling accidents left Michael permanently disabled. First, he was invalided out of the Navy after injuring his right leg in a fall from the rigging. Then, after obtaining employment in a quarry, he was blinded in the left eye when struck by a fragment of splintered limestone. He had to be fitted with a false eye and for a time thereafter was cruelly, but predictably, referred to around town as 'Nelson'.

With her crippled, half-blind husband unable to contribute to the family budget, it fell to the spirited Stacia to take over as bread-winner. It was an onerous responsibility, but she set about it with her customary zeal and always seemed able to find some job or other that would supplement the weekly parish relief of ten shillings allocated by the local Catholic church.

She worked for a time on the farm of the town butcher, Tim McCarthy, who held the lucrative contract for the supply of meat to the British forces of occupation. McCarthy was a huge man, standing at more than six feet and weighing in the region of 20 stones. Formerly a renowned athlete and wrestler, he owned racehorses that ran under the Galtee prefix (in honour of the Galtee Mountains in his native Tipperary) and lived in a mansion called Mount Eaton, situated high up on the East Hill overlooking the harbour.

A dapper dresser in bowler hat and dark suit, and with a gold watch-and-chain dangling from his waistcoat pocket, he took a great shine to the busy Stacia – perhaps for no better reason than that she, too, hailed from Tipperary – and often helped her out with provisions for the

Doyle dinner-table. He first got to know Joe when Stacia brought him with her to the farm each day, placing him on a blanket in the field while she went about her work – gathering the crops, potato-picking and the like. Tim loved the little fellow from the start and was forever sounding forth in the expansive tones that befitted a man of his stature, 'Mark my words, Stacia, that boy will amount to something in life.'

The ruddy-faced Dr. John O'Connor was another trusty friend to the Doyles. Like Tim McCarthy he was a big man with a heart to match, his innate kindness evident in his custom of passing on clothes that his own daughter had outgrown. He held a particular admiration for Stacia and her iron constitution in the face of adversity: she was invariably bright and cheerful and never burdened others with her troubles. In private, Stacia's stoicism sometimes faltered. On one occasion, daughter Bridie chanced upon her sitting alone in the kitchen, head in hands and tears streaming down her face. 'Mum was desperate with worry because we were so poor. I remember her saying she didn't know how we were going to manage.'

But manage she did and in any manner she could devise. She took on a variety of jobs, including scrubbing out the huge assembly hall in the town – a daunting task for which she enlisted the aid of Bridie. There were other, less legitimate methods of adding to the family income, such as pilfering coal from the horse-drawn cart that trundled slowly up the hill from the docks to Steve Moynihan's coal-yard. Stacia would deposit the coal into bags and later sell it – an action perpetrated in the cause of necessity and which depleted the coal stocks by such a minute extent that the deficiency was never noticed.

In spite of their impoverished circumstances, the Doyles were a contented and close-knit family: Michael a mild-mannered man with an easy attitude to life and Stacia the family hustler, always beavering away at some task or other and gently but firmly cajoling the children to action.

Home was one of the huge tenement houses that fronted the water's edge in the heart of the Holy Ground. They were cold and uninviting but the families that lived there – three or four of them to each house – were happy just to have a roof over their heads. The Doyles' small, cramped living accommodation on the third floor of 11 Queen's Street, into which they had moved from No. 12 next door, was sparsely furnished but spotlessly clean. The focal point was the kitchen, in the middle of which stood a large table that Stacia, a stickler for hygiene, insisted on scrubbing meticulously, kitted out in a starched white apron. The kitchen, which served also as dining room and lounge, contained a huge, open hearth on which were hung pots and pans and all the paraphernalia of day-to-day living.

There were two bedrooms, the larger of which was divided by a curtain. Bridie and Betty slept on one side and the boys on the other. The beds were the old-fashioned iron type, the mattresses home-made and filled with straw. The one lavatory, shared by all the occupants of No. 11, was situated outside and access to it involved a lengthy descent of three flights of stairs followed by an unwelcome walk to the back of the yard. Small wonder, then, that chamber-pots were always readily to hand at night.

With money in such short supply, the family had to make do with the barest of necessities. Most days the children ate at the convent opposite the town's magnificent Gothic-style cathedral, St Colman's, completed in 1919 after 51 years and standing proudly on a hill above the harbour. The convent, a refuge for the sick and needy, was known locally as the 'Penny Dinners' and for just such a sum the saintly Bon Secours* nuns served piping hot soup and a chunk of bread to warm up frail, undernourished young bodies in the chill of winter.

The local St Vincent de Paul Society, a Catholic charitable organisation, also helped out hard-up families like the Doyles by providing plimsolls for the children to wear during Mass. It would have been considered disrespectful, even irreverent, for them to be seen approaching the altar rail barefoot for Holy Communion. Though times were hard, faith in God and in the Church never wavered. Everyone attended Mass on Sundays and holy days. Cobh's Catholic community was like one enormous family, its individual members going about their separate business during the week but unfailingly coming together for a powerful, prayerful, sacramental reunion on Sundays. They may have been poor, but they were upstanding and devout.

Happiness, at least, cost nothing and neither did entertainment: the Doyles provided their own. During cold winter evenings they would sit huddled round the fire in the kitchen that offered some protection from the biting winds whipped in from the Atlantic while Michael sang and played his beloved melodeon. His favourite songs were traditional ballads such as *Valley of Slieve-na-Mon*, *Carrigdhoun* and the Cork song *Bells of Shandon*. Stacia was also a beguiling songstress and from an early age the children were encouraged to contribute to the family musical evenings. Often, one or more of them would sit astride their father's stiff leg as he sang and played. 'We'd also take out his glass eye and clean it for him,' recalled Bill Doyle, smiling at the memory. 'It was just a game to us then, but later the very thought of it made me shudder.'

Michael and Stacia were delighted to discover that Joe had music as

* *The Congregation of the Sisters of Bon Secours:* an international nursing and teaching order devoted to the poor. Founded in Paris in 1824.

well as fighting in his blood. He developed a fine soprano voice and quickly mastered the melodeon and the mouth organ. He grew to be a big, strapping lad and became a popular figure around town – a boy the others could look up to in more ways than one. He seemed always to be the centre of attraction, the leader of the gang, the practical joker who would do anything for a dare.

In those distant days, children had to devise their own amusement. One of the most cherished pastimes in the Holy Ground was a game of pitch-and-toss under the gaslamps; another was alleys, a game similar to skittles. The boys would play till late at night and there was great consternation whenever Joe cheekily tried to trick them out of their stakes.

Joe's pals never ceased to be amazed at his antics and often he would perform outlandish feats with little purpose other than to watch the startled expressions on their faces. On one occasion he devoured six raw turnips while the gang looked on in disbelief.

At home, too, Joe liked to cause something of a stir, particularly when it came to displaying a touch of bravado. He delighted in drinking straight from the bottle the dose of cod-liver oil that Stacia, wise in the ways of motherhood, insisted on her children taking daily. As the rest watched with a certain incredulity, for they could barely stomach the stuff, he would gulp down a huge mouthful and then grin defiantly. Joe certainly knew what was good for him: he also made regular sorties to the yard, where he would climb the ladder to the hen-house, crack open an egg and swallow it raw.

His favourite haunt in the town was the Soldiers' Home and Sailors' Rest, where his Uncle Joe worked. The chief attraction there was the delicious Chester cakes that were baked on the premises. The cakes were a kind of currant pudding known more commonly as soldier's duff and they made a tasty and filling feed for hungry young bellies. Joe always went in with a halfpenny and asked for some Soldier's Duff, whereupon his uncle – with a wink, a smile and well-practised sleight of hand – would invariably slip three or four huge chunks into a bag for the price of one. Joe could cheerfully have scofffed the lot with his huge appetite, but the cakes were always shared with the rest of the gang, rather in the manner of a general enduring the same hardships as his men when times were tough.

The devious side to Joe's nature did not endear him to the local shop traders. One of his fondest ploys was to enter Kelly's store armed with a stick, protruding from the end of which was a long nail which he had hammered into the shape of a hook. He would ask the proprietress, known by her nickname Moll Dooneen, for a drink of raspberry juice.

While she was out at the back of the shop attending to his request, he would produce the stick from behind his back and spike cakes, packs of cigarettes and any other sundry items within reach, which he then stuffed quickly into his pockets and up his jumper before the unsuspecting Moll returned with his drink.

On other occasions, the boys would play follow-the-leader through the town, the idea being to discover who could leap highest and touch the tin shop-signs swaying gently in the breeze. 'Joe was always last to go,' remembered Bill Doyle. 'He was taller than the rest of us and could generate more height. But once, when we got to Bunny Harris's grocery store, he made a huge running jump and snatched a joint of smoked ham that had been hanging up on display. He tucked it inside his coat and we all ran like hell.'

Joe received his education, what little there was of it, from the Presentation Brothers who taught at St Joseph's school for boys on the outskirts of town. He cut a comical figure as he trundled off to lessons each morning barefoot and wearing patched-up clothing, but times were such that Stacia had to be a genius with the needle-and-thread.

Joe disliked school intensely. He tried his best to be a diligent pupil, but the discipline administered by the Brothers was strict, the lessons dull and the confinement of the classroom restrictive. There were other, more exciting things for a robust and energetic boy to do and going 'on the lang' proved an infinitely more attractive proposition. Several times he was threatened with expulsion for absenteeism, but always Stacia's intervention saved the day. She could melt the hardest of hearts and the Brothers proved no match for her.

Stacia, a fierce protector of the family reputation, also went to work on the local magistrates after Joe had been accused of killing a couple of ducks. It was an offence punishable by a spell in a reformatory, but he was let off with a warning following a tearful submission from Stacia.

Joe may not have been the most popular boy in town with those in authority, but his standing with his school-mates was of the highest order. To them he was a hero to whom they turned in times of trouble, a match for the bullies who had wronged them. Most of the disputes between the lads in Cobh were decided in a disused quarry directly opposite the school. Referred to locally as 'The Arena', it was a place where old scores were settled and new ones nurtured. It was an unlikely gladiatorial venue, ringed as it was by dozens of pig-pens and with a blacksmith's forge situated in one corner. Whenever a fight broke out the smithy, Dinny Connell, would douse down his fire, remove his apron and rush across to restore order. But there were times when peace-maker Dinny got caught up in the excitement of it all and ensured fair play by taking on the role of referee.

Joe had his share of fights in the quarry but, as his reputation grew, few boys were brave enough to take him on. 'No one dared pick a fight with him,' recalled an old school pal. 'He was so big and strong that he could handle two or three at a time.'

Gang fights, too, were commonplace, especially in the Holy Ground, where Joe learned quickly that the art of survival owed much to striking first and striking hard. Yet fists were not the only weapons of war: rocks were hurled and catapults fired as rival groups fought for supremacy. The Holy Ground was no place for the faint-hearted. The boys who lived there spoke tough, acted tough and for the most part were tough. But according to those who were around at the time, none was tougher than big Joe Doyle.

During school holidays, when Joe could legitimately be seen out and about during daytime hours, he worked in a bicycle shop owned by a character called Floaty O'Keeffe, who hired out his bikes on a daily basis. The boys rarely returned them on time and Mr O'Keeffe earned his nickname by 'floating' round town on one of his bicycles, resplendent in plus-fours, searching for the culprits.

In the heat of summer Joe and his pals would go swimming in the sea at picturesque Cuskinny, just outside town. It was a mud-flat at low tide, necessitating a walk of a couple of hundred yards or so in order to reach the water. This presented a problem for the boys, none of whom possessed bathing trunks; it meant they had to leave their clothes by the shore and walk naked out to sea. One afternoon, when they had finished their swim and were heading back across the mud-flat, they could see in the distance a group of girls who had chanced upon their clothing.

A member of the gang, Jim Doherty, remembered:

> 'The girls were standing around waiting for us to return. As we got nearer, we covered out private parts with our hands and the girls started giggling. Joe decided to forget his modesty and have some fun with them. He uncovered his shaft and started waving it around. The girls were so shocked, they ran for their lives.'

Joe's great penchant for exhibitionism, which would become outrageously evident in later life, concealed an almost intense puritanical streak that served to make him an unpredictable, even enigmatic, character. One instance was his professed abhorrence of foul language in the presence of girls; another was the unlikely choice of his Confirmation name, Alphonsus, which he was proud to adopt and then project as his middle name, the suspicion being that it provided an aura of intellectualism which acted as cover for his lack of basic education.

His schooling had ended abruptly and in somewhat dramatic fashion at the age of 12. He was by that time more man than boy, standing 5ft 10in tall and weighing around 11 stones, and his boredom with scholastic studies had resulted in his days on the lang becoming more frequent than his attendance in the classroom.

One morning he, Jim Doherty and another friend, Sharkey Griffin, decided to give lessons a miss in favour of a day's scrumping at French's orchard, a secluded spot on a private estate some two miles out of town. The boys gathered a plentiful supply of apples, which they then stuffed inside their jumpers, and climbed up into what was termed the langing tree – a huge, leafy oak where they would be hidden safely from view while they munched their apples and shared a joke or two.

When they emerged from the tree, Joe was cradling a young crow he had caught and which in his boyish naivety he was considering keeping as a pet. But as the three boys headed back to town they were intercepted by Jim Ahearne, a vigilant and much-feared school board inspector, and marched unceremoniously off to St Joseph's.

'What have you under that coat, Doyle?' demanded Joe's form-master Willie Murphy, a small, bespectacled lay-teacher who, in common with all who shared his surname, was referred to disparagingly as 'Spud'.

Joe was in truculent mood and felt disinclined to answer. Murphy, a fluent speaker of the Gaelic language and a man renowned for his fierce temper, decided to waste no more words on him, whether in English or Irish; instead he selected one of six willowy canes he kept for just such a contingency and moved menacingly toward him. At that moment Joe opened his jacket and out flew the startled crow which, to the delight of the rest of the boys, circled the classroom at a rapid rate of knots before disappearing through an open window and taking to the skies.

Murphy was furious and began immediately to administer a beating, striking Joe with reckless abandon across the arms, chest and shoulders with his cane. But Spud was in for a further surprise when Joe, upset at losing the bird he had so recently befriended, grabbed him by the lapels of his coat, lifted him off his feet and shook him so hard that he resembled a puppet being jerked uncontrollably on the end of its strings. Joe then turned indignantly on his heels and walked out of the school, never to return. The incident earned him the nickname 'Crow' Doyle.

Children were permitted to leave school at the age of 12, provided they had a job to go to and their families were deemed to be in need of an additional wage-earner. The Doyles certainly fell into that category, having been forced to move to larger premises at No. 8 Cottrell's Row*, a two-storey cottage which they secured from the owner, Mrs Flanagan, for five shillings a week. Mrs Flanagan, a kindly soul, lived in the house next door and Stacia used to 'do' for her, cleaning, dusting and polishing and the like in return for a modest recompense.

The authorities made several attempts at luring Joe back to school, but having made the break he was determined to resist their efforts. All he was interested in doing now was finding work and proving himself a man. As the eldest son he considered it his duty to provide for his parents a measure of comfort and security after the long, wearying years of struggle that had made them old before their time. He could sense that poverty was a strait-jacket of despair which sapped the spirit and undermined the will. He could see it in his father, an outwardly happy man who accepted the cruel blows that fate had dealt him, but inwardly resented the fact that his physical disabilities had forced the unnatural role of bread-winner on to his wife. Joe was not yet old enough to fully understand such things, but subconsciously his father's sense of futility came through to him. He resolved to take on the responsibility of providing a decent standard of living for his family, though at that moment he knew not how.

Jobs were scarce for boys of Joe's age but eventually he got fixed up courtesy of Tim McCarthy, who took him on at a wage of 12 shillings a week on the farm where he had romped around happily as a toddler while his mother worked the land.

After a time he became restless and decided to try his luck on the coal boats that sailed into Cobh. The lure of the waterfront was strong: big money could be earned there by a tough lad with a broad back and a zest for hard work. He became a quay labourer, unloading the coal vessels, and was delighted to discover he could shift as much coal as men twice his age.

The boats had to be unloaded in 48 hours or incur a punitive Harbour Board tariff. Eight men at a time worked ceaselessly from six in the morning till seven at night to clear the 350-ton cargos. There was no slacking: if you couldn't do it, you were out. Joe's job was to go down into the collier's hold and fill two huge containers, which were then heaved up on a winch and their contents loaded on carts for delivery to the coal yards. It was back-breaking work down in that dark

* No. 8 has since been demolished. Only remnants of Cottrell's Row now remain.

and dusty hold, but the rewards were high: as much as £3 could be earned for two days' work.

Sister Bridie recalled:

> 'Joe would come home worn out, his face, neck, arms and vest covered with soot. He would clean himself up in an old zinc bath in front of the fire and Mum used to scrub his back for him. Most of the money he earned he gave to her – and he also liked to buy her little gifts. I remember his first present was a purse. He was always promising that one day, when he was rich, he would buy her a fur coat.'

Unfortunately for Joe, work on the coal boats was irregular. With just two shipments a week, there were plenty of men willing and able to bare their backs for the chance of earning a decent wage. Between times, he helped carry the luggage of visiting Americans from the docks to the town's numerous hotels and guest-houses. It was an exercise that earned him healthy sums in tips and afforded the opportunity of making a favourable impression on any attractive young lady who might take his fancy. He would target a family group that included a likely candidate, offer to act as porter and then attempt to engage the object of his desire in conversation as he humped the baggage into town.

His success rate was high. The friendly and impressionable Yankee girls, invariably a good deal older than himself, were captivated by his freckle-faced good looks, his mop of black curly hair and an original line in blarney that would prove irresistible to women in the years to come. Joe was to consider such relationships a more important, and certainly more enjoyable, aspect of his education than anything he could have learned at school; to him, it was an invaluable part of growing up. Yet though he seemed able to sweet-talk his way into the affections of total strangers, Joe rarely enjoyed similar success with the local girls. They were mostly good Catholics and on their guard against red-blooded youths seeking to prove their manliness.

By the age of 14, Joe's massive build made his jacket appear as if it had shrunk in the wash. Other boys, puny by comparison, were suspicious of his fine physique and jealously accused him of wearing padding. Joe did not take offence at these jibes; instead, he capitalised on their doubts by taking wagers on it. Bets struck, he then delighted in removing his jacket and shirt to reveal a torso of which any grown man would have been proud.

It was around this time that Joe came across an instructional book on boxing – *How to Box* by Jack Dempsey, one of the roughest, toughest fighters in the history of the heavyweight division. Dempsey had recently lost his world championship to Gene Tunney but his hold on the title in the seven years from 1919–26 was of such destructive and explosive dimensions that it would secure his immortality in a boxing sense and earn him a place at or near the top of anyone's list of all-time greats. Quite what technical qualities Dempsey felt he possessed that qualified him to write a treatise on boxing would have been lost on those who saw him only as a heavyweight of primitive power and savagery who scorned defensive postures and whose fighting style displayed not an atom of skill or subtlety. However, to anyone unconcerned with the niceties of the sport, and intent only on learning how best to club an opponent to the canvas in the shortest possible time, there could have been no finer tutor.

Dempsey's inspirational words had a profound effect on Joe's fertile young mind. He read each page with wide-eyed amazement, and from that moment his destiny was shaped. He vowed there and then that he would one day win the world heavyweight championship for Ireland. He would become the Irish Jack Dempsey, he affirmed to himself over and over again. It was an ambition that was to transform his character and personality. He even decided he would adopt the same forename as his hero when the time came to commence his career as a fighter, in much the same way as he sought to project Alphonsus as his middle name.

Each night as he looked from his bedroom window across the harbour to the naval depot on Haulbowline Island and then let his gaze wander across to the Army barracks on neighbouring Spike Island, where once convicts were interned before being shipped off to Australia, he dreamed of the day he would find fame and fortune as the new Dempsey. The part of the book that particularly fired his imagination was the description of the famous Dempsey knockout punch. He delivered it repeatedly into the empty air as he shadow-boxed with an imaginary opponent, the simulated roar of the crowd reaching a deafening crescendo as his rival took the count.

Along with his regular shadow-boxing routines, Joe toughened up his hands by punching, bare-fisted, the walls and door-frames of the house in Cottrell's Row, with its little parlour downstairs and three rooms up, its doorways so low that he had to duck his head on entering each room.

Soon there were to be opportunities to practise the punch for real. 'He put a fellow out on the beach for using bad language in my presence,' recalled Bridie. 'He injured his thumb when he hit him, but told Mum he hurt it carrying suitcases from the boats. He would not have liked her to know he had been fighting.'

On another occasion, Joe became embroiled in an argument with the notoriously tough Woods brothers during a game of brag on the deep-water quay, where numerous card-schools flourished. Johnny Woods, a hardy fisherman then in his thirties, had accused Joe of cheating – and whether he was right or wrong, it was a slur that could not pass unchallenged. A fight developed and a crowd quickly gathered to encircle the combatants lest they toppled into the swirling grey waters below. Bill Doyle recalled:

> 'The big fellow connected with his right hand and knocked Johnny cold. He went out like a light. Everyone thought he was dead. We became scared and made a bolt for it.'

Happily, Johnny Woods recovered and was none the worse for his ordeal, but another opponent did not fare so well after insulting Joe's father. Sullivan was his name and he had a formidable reputation as a boxer, having reputedly won the heavyweight championship of the Free State Army. But reputations did not worry young Joe. He sought out Sullivan and gave him such a beating that the poor chap ended up in hospital. Then, filled with remorse, Joe half expected to be arrested for murder if the man died. Thankfully, he did not.

According to the late Bill Hughes, a native of Cobh and father of international stage and TV star Finola Hughes, Joe's swift demolition of Johnny Woods was not the only time he was forced to defend himself over a game of cards. Neither was his set-to with Sullivan his only confrontation with a soldier:

> 'Joe just used to cheat for devilment, really, but not everybody appreciated it. I remember that during a game of cards on Lynch's quay, where the coal boats tied up, a fellow known as Danny Dick and someone else accused him. Joe wasn't frightened in the least, although he was only 14 and the others grown men. He offered to fight the two of them. Danny Dick said to his mate: "I'll go first. I know his style." There was a big audience and everyone stood back. Joe hit Danny Dick and knocked his teeth out. Danny's mate didn't fancy it after that. He scarpered.'

The incident with the soldier remembered by Bill Hughes occurred during a game of pitch-and-toss. He recalled:

> 'A British soldier stationed at Spike accused Joe of cheating and they squared up. Joe hit out and the man fell back against a shed and collapsed. He never moved.'

Joe was proving a match for any waterfront braggart or brawler. Anyone in or out of uniform who sought to slap him down would find him more than willing to prove himself their equal. He never went looking for trouble, but neither was he the type to turn away from it when an opportunity presented itself. And yet, surprisingly in view of his fast-developing physique – he now stood more than 6ft and weighed 13 stones – and his even faster-growing reputation, there seemed to be no lack of volunteers willing to take him on.

Bullying types he had fought and beaten would scour the district in an effort to find a well-built lad who might prove to be his master. Someone he had never seen before would suddenly stand out in the road, shake his fist and throw down his coat. Joe knew what this meant – it was another tough of the town eager to make a name for himself. He began to welcome these street fights. They gave him the opportunity to develop his knockout punch. He never lost. Always and without exception, he sent his rivals crashing.

It was an incident far removed from fighting that convinced Joe he had finally perfected the potency of his Dempsey-style right hand. It concerned an ill-tempered old donkey in a field which all the boys were attempting to ride but which invariably bucked and sent them sprawling. When Joe, too, took a tumble, he was far from pleased at being laughed at by his pals. 'Give the beast a thump, Joe,' joked one of the older lads. He did so, but with far more force than intended, and it toppled over as if struck by lightning. Joe was instantly concerned at the plight of the animal as he helped it back to its feet, but his compassion was coupled with a feeling of elation at the realisation of his devastating power of punch. Thereafter the donkey always retained a special place in his affections, though he never again risked riding it.

Joe was yearning for an opportunity to set foot on the first rung of the boxing ladder which he was convinced would take him step by step to stardom and the fulfilment of his cherished Dempsey dream. His problem was that there was no organised boxing in Cobh. Impatient to make his name, he asked Tim McCarthy to use his influence and get him some 'proper' boxing contests in England.

McCarthy remembered the prediction he had made when Joe was an infant, and nothing had happened since to make him change his mind. He knew of Joe's reputation around town and was eager to be of help now the boy had decided what course his life should take. He dressed him in football shorts and plimsolls, dug out a pair of old boxing gloves and took a photo of him in fighting pose. He sent it off to the boxing correspondent of the *Daily Mail* in Fleet Street, Geoffrey Simpson, together with a letter extolling the fighting prowess of 'this future champion we have here in Cork'. He wrote also to the promoters of a heavyweight competition to be staged at London's Crystal Palace arena, waxing lyrical about 'this young lad of 15 who is knocking out all the champions of Queenstown'. They wrote back stating he was too young.

There was now only one thing for it, to Joe's way of thinking: he would join the Army. People had long been saying what a fine soldier he would make and how good he would look in uniform, being so tall and upright. He was not slow to realise that a year or two of military service would provide him with the platform to fashion a career as a boxer. He made application to join the Irish Free State Army, telling the recruiting officer he was 18, but was turned down when it was discovered he was only 16. 'Come back in two years, son,' they said.

Undeterred, he turned his attention to the British Army and the one regiment he would wish to join above all others: the Irish Guards. He loved the idea of being a guardsman, but even more he relished the prospect of being based in England, where his opportunities of making the grade as a boxer would be distinctly greater than if he stayed at home in Ireland. Guardsman Doyle! How wonderful it sounded as he pictured himself marching proudly in a smart new uniform, his lively mind conjuring up visions of adventure and excitement in another land. He decided he would make the crossing to the British mainland and take a chance on being accepted.

Often he had watched with boyish longing down at the docks as his compatriots boarded the tenders that would take them out to the ocean liners waiting in the deep, ready to transport them to a new life in the United States. 'Every mother's son aboard the tender is following out his fortune,' he would think to himself at such moments. Now his own time had come. He was ready to set sail for the journey of his dreams.

Accompanied by his mother and brother Bill, he boarded the train for the short ride to the city. From there he would be ferried across the Irish Sea on the first stage of his trip to stardom. At the quayside, the distraught Stacia bade a tearful farewell to her eldest son. Joe fought hard to disguise his own sense of sadness, but he knew better than to indulge in emotional outpourings that would serve only to make his mother feel worse than she already did. Instead, he offered words of comfort to soften her sorrow at the parting:

> 'Don't worry, mother. I'm a big boy now. I'll take good care of myself. And soon I'll be famous, you'll see.'

With that he marched boldly on to the ship, battered suitcase in hand. He was a firm believer in fate and was about to follow the course he felt had been charted for him.

In the scheme of things, Joseph Alphonsus (alias Jack) Doyle was off to keep an appointment with fame and fortune.

Chapter 2

Soldier of fortune

It was late September, 1930, when the *Innisfallen* rounded Passage West on its leisurely journey to the open sea. Joe searched keenly from the deck for a glimpse of his home near the shore, fearing he might fail to recognise it from a distance. He need not have worried: there could have been no mistaking Stacia's huge white tablecloth being waved frantically from an upstairs window. 'Make sure you watch out for it,' his family had told him. 'And don't forget to wave back.' Joe did wave back, and for all he was worth; but soon he tired of doing so, doubting anyway that they could see his handkerchief fluttering in the breeze. Instead he settled for one last, lingering look at the old town of Cobh nestling snugly in the autumn sunset, taking in the familiar sights that had been so much a part of his boyhood. Once out in the deep, his musings gave way to a more buoyant mood as he looked forward to the exciting new life that would unfold before him.

Almost before he knew it, the *Innisfallen* had docked at Pembroke. Joe could not believe he was in Wales. All those busy porters on the quayside sounded as if they came from Cork! He was bemused by the hustle and bustle and not a little worried: he had just two shillings in his pocket after paying his passage, and no return ticket. He felt like a lost being on another planet and wondered for a fleeting moment whether he had not erred in his great quest for adventure. He was now all alone in the world, without friends or family to help and guide him. It was a step into the unknown and the thought filled him with chilling uncertainty. Then, his mind flashed back to the tales of his ancestors that had been handed down to him by his father, as they had by his father before him. He was, he remembered being told, a lineal descendant of those doughty fighting Doyles who had battled manfully side by side with Brian Boru. Fact or fancy he did not at that instant care to question, for the passions the stories aroused acted as a catalyst in stirring his soul. Come what may, this was no time for doubts or fears: he had to show himself as a warrior, a brave soldier of fortune like the Doyles of old.

He took a deep breath and sought out the Irish Guards recruiting officer at Pembroke Dock. Not wishing to run the risk of being put aboard the first boat back to Cork if he revealed his true age (he had just turned 17), he gave his date of birth as June 30, 1912 – making himself out to be 14 months older than he actually was – and explained that he had forgotten his birth certificate. It seemed to matter not. He was told he could be accepted without verification of age. He gave a huge sigh of relief. He was in.

After being medically examined, weighed and measured, he swore the Oath of Allegiance and signed on for three years. His personal particulars were recorded thus:

Name	Joseph Doyle
Apparent age	18 years 3 months
Height	6ft 3½in
Weight	184lbs (13st 2lbs)
Chest	41in
Complexion	Dark
Eyes	Brown
Hair	Black
Religion	Roman Catholic
Distinguishing marks	Small tattoo scar on left hand*

Next day Recruit Doyle No. 2717222 was packed off to the Brigade of Guards depot at Caterham, in Surrey, for training. His pay was to be five shillings a week – hardly an encouraging remuneration for one who in just two years' time was destined to have a fortune at his fingertips, but it was a start.

Joe was delighted to discover his fellow recruits – a bedraggled collection of English, Irish, Scots and Welsh – were a jolly, boisterous bunch just like himself. He had felt slightly self-conscious in an ill-fitting suit bought for him by Tim McCarthy, but soon he was standing proud and erect in a brand new guardsman's uniform.

Any illusions he may have harboured about Army life were quickly dispelled. He may have been used to hard work on the coal boats back home in Cobh, but the rigid 16-hours-a-day discipline that confronted him at Caterham caught him totally unawares. He was to discover, after just a couple of days, that the making of a soldier was a harsh and physically demanding experience in which the normal pleasantries and courtesies he had been brought up to observe since childhood were patently non-evident. When ordered to attend to some chore or other, he had to jump to it smartly or risk the consequences. He also learned

* The remnant of a star-shaped tattoo Joe had scratched on his hand between the base of the thumb and the index finger.

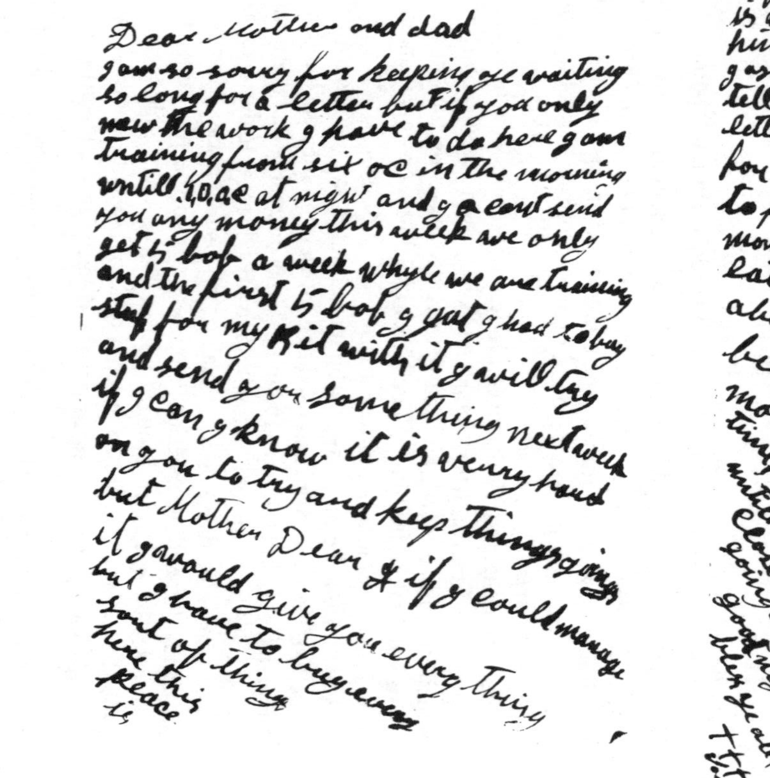
Dear Mother and dad
I am so sorry for keeping ye waiting
so long for a letter but if you only
new the work I have to do here I am
training from six oc in the morning
untill 10 oc at night and I cant send
you any money this week we only
get 5 bob a week whyle we are training
and the first 5 bob I got I had to buy
stuf for my kit with it I will try
and send you some thing next week
if I can I know it is verry hard
on you to try and keep things going
but Mother Dear & if I could manage
it I would give you every thing
but I have to buy every
sort of thing
here this
place
is,

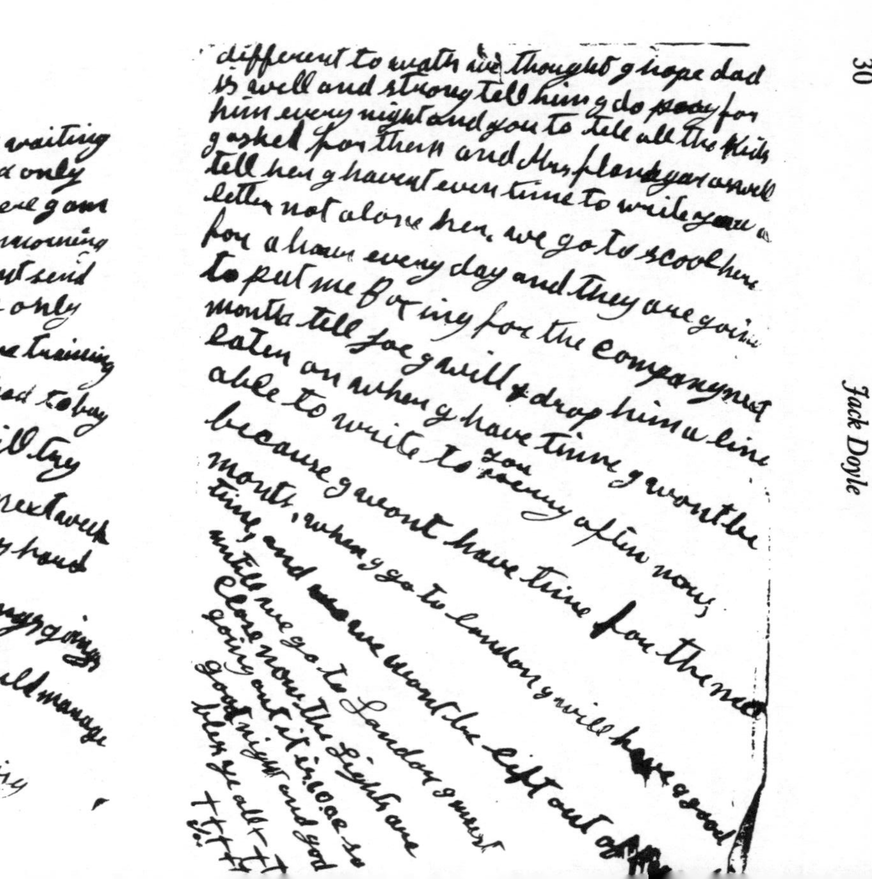
different to what we thought I hope dad
is well and strong tell him I do pray for
him every night and you to tell all the kids
I asked for them and Mrs flanagan as well
tell her I havent even time to write you a
letter not alone her, we go to scool here
for a hour every day and they are going
to put me for ing for the company next
month tell Joe I will + drop him a line
later on when I have time I wont be
able to write to you verry after now,
because I wont have time for the next
month, when I go to london I will have a good
time, and we wont be lift out of
untill we go to London I must
close now the Lights are
going out it is 10 oc so
good night and god
bless ye all

that four-letter words were held in common usage by superiors in order to accentuate a point.

Indeed, so busy was Joe during that first traumatic week at Caterham, and such was the shock to his system, that he scarcely had time to gather his wits. The letter he had promised to send home immediately on arrival remained unwritten. He was well into his second week before his family received word from him.

The letter, which was undated, is reproduced as written on page 30. It was penned in child-like scrawl, with the lines running almost diagonally from the top left to bottom right-hand corner of the page, and served to illustrate just how limited had been his formal education. Army schooling would later improve him somewhat in that respect.

What the letter did reveal about Joe was his deep love of his family and an overriding concern for their well-being. It was this warm feeling for them and his intense desire to improve their circumstances that was to drive him on in relentless pursuit of his Dempsey dream.

He had told his new pals to call him Jack, for he wished from the very start to be known by the name with which he was convinced he would be achieving a similar immortality to that attained by his hero.

Three weeks after enlistment, 'Jack' was pleasantly surprised to observe a fellow-townsman among a group of new recruits. George Patterson had been brought up in Harbour Row, not far from the Holy Ground, and had served for a time in the Free State Army before deciding to seek his fortune on the other side of the Irish Sea. Patterson remembered:

> 'It was only my second day at Caterham. I had come down from my billet for breakfast and, quite suddenly, someone grabbed me by the hand. I looked up and it was the big fellah. I was quite a bit older than him, but he was certainly glad to see me. I noticed over breakfast that everyone was calling him Jack, so I said, "His name's not bloody Jack, it's Joe." But later he told me he wanted to be known as Jack and I soon got used to it. I discovered his billet on the landing was directly opposite mine, so we decided to pal around together.'

The recruits were given a tough military baptism. They had to be up at six each morning to scrub out their quarters and were on the go all day until six in the evening. From then until lights out at ten most of the time would be employed in a kit-cleaning ceremony known as Shining Parade, during which they were supervised by trained soldiers. Strict silence had to be observed during Shining Parade but eventually permission was sought, and given, for Jack to entertain his colleagues with renditions of the haunting Irish ballads he had learned as a boy. He had regularly broken into song in an effort to cheer himself up and lighten the load of his daily duties, but was at first hesitant when requested to sing before what amounted to a captive audience. Young guardsmen could be cruelly, wickedly offensive when they had mind to be and Jack did not relish being held as an object of derision, the butt of sly winks and nudges.

He fretted needlessly. His fellow recruits, especially the Irish among them, were close to tears as this huge man sang deceptively sweetly and tenderly of the land of his birth. His favourite song then, according to George Patterson, was the soft and lilting, *How Do You Buy Killarney?*

Jack's light tenor voice, his natural feel for a song and the heart-rending simplicity of his delivery belied an impudent humour and immense bodily strength. His new Army pals had by this time already experienced to their cost his skill as a card-sharp, fashioned so expertly on the deep-water quay in Cobh, where the rules according to Hoyle might more aptly have been described as the rules according to Doyle.

His physical prowess also was soon to be demonstrated in spectacular style when, at long last, he was presented with the opportunity to put to legitimate use the Dempsey knockout punch he had practised so painstakingly. It came during his initial workout in the depot gymnasium, the prospect of which had filled him with keen anticipation since he had first set foot in England.

The mystery of the boxing ring loomed invitingly as he pulled on the gloves for the first time. Yet, almost as soon as he had climbed through the ropes, the feeling of excitement and exhilaration that till then had pervaded his consciousness was coupled with an underlying sense of unease. Perhaps he had been waiting so keenly and so long for this emotionally-charged moment that, when it arrived, the reality did not measure up to the dream. The confining area of engagement, the strange feel of the canvas beneath his feet, the lack of atmosphere in the gym and the fact his blood was not up – as it had to be if he was to engage in one-to-one combat – could all have been contributory factors. His fellow recruits were clearly expecting to see something special in view of the innumerable occasions he had unwisely boasted to them of his outstanding ability as a fighter. Now he was in utter dread of becoming a laughing stock among his colleagues – a state of affairs that would always have been a source of acute embarrassment to him. Finally, he came to terms with the situation by convincing himself that the great Dempsey must have made just such a modest start to his career.

The instructor's face bore a look of bewildered amusement at the sight of the gangling figure that stood before him. Jack, fresh of face, his handsome features sharp and refined, was a most unlikely pupil of pugilism as he ambled around awkwardly, his gloved hands reaching down almost to his knees. When told to shape up he felt strangely ill-at-ease: this was not how he had imagined it at all. Back home, where bare fists had been the order of the day, all he'd had to do was stand there and fight; but now that he was being asked to jab and move, he was dismayed to discover there was no co-ordination between mind and muscle. He was ungainly on his feet, with the result that he found himself off-balance whenever he attempted to push out a tentative left jab. He felt peculiar and uncertain, and to such a degree that he doubted even his ability to connect with his pet right-hand punch. Finally the instructor, frustrated in his efforts to find even a modicum of ability in this bumbling buffoon of a recruit, decided to let him do things his own way.

'Hit me, hit me,' he urged repeatedly, but Jack found he could not do so. He had become so anxious that his shoulder muscles had tightened and his long legs felt as if they had taken root in the canvas, giving him more the appearance of a sculptor's model in statuesque pose than the man he hitherto had fancied himself to be: a young giant with a punch that could fell an ox, to say nothing of a donkey.

The instructor, his patience exhausted, decided as a last resort to adopt a different tactic: he delivered a few stinging left jabs to the tyro's face, all the while continuing to taunt, 'Come on hit me, hit me. You *can't* hit me.'

That did it for, by now, Jack was fighting mad. As the adrenalin started to course through his veins he found he was no longer confused and hesitant, his muscle-bound body responding at last to the promptings of his mind. His only thought now was to make the man pay dearly for his arrogance. He moved forward, swung his right hand and down went his tormentor in a heap.

The instructor sat up, exercised his jaw to make sure it was still in place and climbed to his feet – smiling. His psychology had worked, and to a greater degree than he had dared to hope. He then suggested Jack should take lessons from a fellow instructor – but there was a glint in his eye as he cautioned him to hit the chap when told if he did not want to take a hiding.

The new trainer in question was Lance-Sergeant Paddy Peters,* a talented welterweight, who, apart from being the star of the Irish

* *Patrick Bowden Peters* was born in Aston, Birmingham, on June 24, 1908, and joined the Irish Guards as a drummer boy at the age of 15. His boxing skills gained him three Army titles and, in 1933, a coveted Amateur Boxing Association (ABA) Championship. He later boxed professionally, but retired to take up an appointment as coach to the RAF boxing team. He was killed in 1938 when a plane carrying members of the RAF and South African Air Force teams came down near the Limpopo River on the Rhodesia–South Africa border.

Guards team in tournament boxing, acted also as instructor to the novices. Peters was casual in his manner, nonchalant almost, when he stepped in the ring. As an experienced boxer some five years older than Jack, he had seen it all before – or so he thought. But he had been given no intimation of Jack's punching power by his colleague, on whose face was a knowing smile of anticipation as Peters barked: 'Right, son. Let's see what you're made of.'

In spite of the warning he had been given, Jack held back. This time he was not in the least nervous, merely in awe of a man he considered must have forgotten more about boxing than he would ever know. But in response to several choice adjectives shot at him from several directions, he decided to cast caution aside. He thought of Dempsey, unloaded his big right hand and Peters, smaller and some three stones lighter, collapsed to the canvas.

And so a bright new boxing career was born. Jack Doyle had proved to his superiors that he was equipped to compete in the toughest of all sporting arenas, the boxing ring. He was raw as a new-laid egg when it came to the finer points of the game, but the Guards' instructors considered they had a champion in the making if ways could be found to improve his footwork and harness some semblance of skill to his undoubted power of punch. They quickly discovered, however, that the technical side of the sport held little appeal for him. Jack felt his best form of defence was a total dependence on his right-hand punch, which he considered potent enough to end all arguments. He was scornful of all defensive measures that might blunt his natural aggression and leave him in a no-man's land of mediocrity. He would be a fighter in the Dempsey mould or not at all, a decision he had taken at the age of 14 and by which he was determined to abide, whatever any well-intentioned tutor might advise to the contrary. He saw no merit in being a cagey boxer well versed in the arts of jabbing, feinting and evading punches like some slippery eel. Such method-boxing would never find favour with a boy whose heart was stirred by the heat of battle, who considered all-out attack to be the only pathway to victory and who would come to view a referee as one whose sole qualification for the job was an ability to count from one to ten. Small wonder, then, that Peters concluded it would be unwise to interfere too much with the forces of nature, but rather to let him rely totally on his inborn assets of brute strength and punching power.

Jack's love of a rough-house was never better illustrated than by his enthusiasm for what was termed the Milling Competition, a virtual free-for-all in which the recruits at Caterham – including George Patterson – engaged:

'We were all gloved up outside the ring and then placed in twos. The idea was that when the whistle went, each pair of boxers in turn had to rush into the ring and batter the hell out of each other. If you managed to get there before your opponent, you could prevent him getting in the ring by walloping him as he attempted to climb through the ropes. Jack really loved it; he was in his element. He was so big and strong that the other lads were terrified of being drawn against him. They knew he really would put them through the mill. He could flatten anyone.'

Jack's first taste of boxing under official amateur rules came on November 12, 1930 – seven weeks to the day after his arrival at Caterham – when he represented the Irish Guards in an inter-depot tournament for the Mayor of Canterbury Cup. He looked forward eagerly to his debut and trained hard for it. It was his big chance and he was determined to start on a winning note. All his waking hours were filled with the anticipation of glory in the boxing ring – and some of his sleeping hours, too. On the eve of the tournament, the vision of Dempsey as ever in the forefront of his mind, he had a dream in which he saw his opponent stretched out on the canvas, with his colleagues in the audience cheering wildly.

Next day the dream came vividly to life as Jack went into action like a threshing machine on Tim McCarthy's farm, battering his opponent, Recruit Brown of the Scots Guards, to a stunning second-round knockout defeat that secured the Cup for the jubilant Irish Guards. Jack experienced his first taste of hero worship on that heady night at Caterham. The contest had assumed for him the importance of a world title fight and he had won it in magnificent style. As he basked in the warm after-glow of victory, graciously accepting the congratulations being showered on him by his team-mates, he could look ahead confidently in the certain knowledge that his future, literally, was in his own lethal hands. Gone was the uncertainty that had surrounded him when he sat down to write that first lonely letter home to his parents shortly after enlistment; banished to the four winds were any doubts that may have served to undermine his ability to control his destiny. Jack Doyle was his own man at last, ready to make life do his bidding.

His exquisitely-proportioned body was displayed for all to see on open days at Caterham each Sunday, when friends and relatives of the recruits came to visit. George Patterson recalled:

'A big crowd would gather in the gym just to watch Jack going through his paces. They stood around admiring his physique. Jack loved an audience. He always put on a show for them.'

Patterson also remembered Jack putting on a big show for women, although such performances were not always confined to gymnasium workouts:

'Whenever we went out on the prowl, Jack would suck in air through his teeth if he set eyes on anyone he fancied. He carried around pictures of himself in fighting pose, which he would show to the girls and say, "That's me, Jack Doyle, future British heavyweight champion." He had a great line in chat and it never failed. He could pull anyone. I remember once we picked up two girls at Caterham railway station and took them to a nearby graveyard. We never saw them again. It was love 'em and leave 'em in those days. Jack had a prick like a pony – I don't know how any girl could take it.'

On completion of his training at Caterham in the spring of 1931, Jack was transferred to Windsor, where the Irish Guards, commonly known as the Micks, were acting as the Castle guard. He was assigned to No. 1 company, reserved for the tallest men in the regiment.

His reputation had preceded him to the extent that his arrival at the Victoria Barracks was awaited with the kind of anticipation normally reserved for a visit from royalty itself. The Micks were delighted to have among their ranks a young heavyweight of such prowess. It was a boost to morale, a focal point of discussion that gave these earnest but warm-hearted Irishmen something other than nostalgic thoughts of home on which to centre their off-duty attention. The vast majority of them welcomed Jack like a long-lost brother, eager to make his acquaintance and to hear all the news concerning him. But as is often the case in such matters, there were one or two who held no respect for reputations and Jack was forced to put them in their place.

On the first occasion he was singing to piano accompaniment at a public house in the town. A fellow-soldier, a huge man by the name of Tierney, walked over and requested an opportunity to sing, but in terms that indicated clearly to Jack what would happen if he refused to vacate the platform. George Patterson, who transferred to Windsor shortly after Jack, witnessed what followed:

'He was reluctant to let Tierney sing. He was having a joke with the chap, really, but a fight developed and the place was wrecked. Even the landlady got a black eye trying to separate them. The fight continued in the yard outside, but it didn't last long. Tierney was a big bloke and he must have fancied his chances. But once Jack connected cleanly with his right hand, it was all over. Christ, he could hit.'

The second incident occurred after Jack had returned to his billet following a spell of sentry duty at the Castle. He lay down on his bunk for a nap but discovered when he awoke that his purse, containing £1, had been cut from his webbed belt. Ex-Irish Guardsman Tim Sullivan served with Jack in No. 1 Company at Windsor and recalled:

> 'Jack was furious, because a pound was a lot of money in those days. He had a shrewd idea who was responsible and marched off to the Windsor Castle pub to confront him. A punch-up followed, the police were called and the two of them got slung out. After that, the pub was declared out of bounds.'

Jack was making quite a name for himself in Windsor, both in and out of the ring. He became a well-known figure in the town, especially at the Star and Garter, a famous centuries-old hostelry frequented mainly by The Fancy. The inn was situated at the back of Windsor railway station in Peascod Street, on the site now occupied by the Marks & Spencer department store. It had a cobbled forecourt, livery stables for up to a dozen horses and a boxing gymnasium that attracted some of the leading professionals of the day. The proprietor, Frank Godfrey, was a small, plump Pickwickian character who gave the place a certain atmosphere by dressing for the most part in jodhpurs, snazzy waistcoat and bowler hat.

On hearing that the great Len Harvey* was training at the Star and Garter, and considering himself ready for bigger and better things, Jack decided to make his presence known to the champion. He turned up at one of Harvey's training sessions and sought permission to spar with him. 'I'm in the Irish Guards and unbeaten as a boxer,' he stated proudly. His request was met with characteristic disdain by Harvey, who, when the occasion demanded, could be as much a master of the verbal put-down as he was an undoubted master of the boxing ring. He appeared to regard the young soldier as little more than an impudent upstart.

Undeterred, Jack repeated his request until he was urged by Harvey's aides, and in language as strong as any he had heard in the barracks, to make himself scarce. But Jack didn't frighten easily; though barely old enough to grow whiskers on his chin, he had already been in enough scrapes to know that he could handle himself in just about any situation, and those tough boxing types did not worry him. He repeated his request after each round of Harvey's sparring session until at last he relented. 'Okay,' sighed Harvey wearily. 'Bring your kit with you tomorrow. I'll spar with you then.'

'But I've got it with me now, sir,' replied Jack smartly, fearing that unless he acted promptly the chance would be lost. His persistence

* Len Harvey made six successful defences of the British and Empire middleweight titles. He also became British and Empire champion at cruiserweight and heavyweight and fought for the world middle and cruiserweight crowns.

brought its reward. Harvey agreed to accommodate him there and then, more out of a feeling of exasperation than for reasons of artistic merit.

Jack donned trunks and plimsolls and climbed confidently into the ring, determined to prove he could compete on equal terms even with a boxer as skilled and experienced as Harvey. He was in for a surprise. Harvey, as befitted one of Britain's finest exponents of the noble art, treated him just like a toy soldier, twisting and turning him, holding him and placing him precisely where he wanted him, all the while slipping and parrying his clubbing punches with effortless ease. Jack appeared completely unruffled, however. He was searching keenly for an opening and suddenly it presented itself. Over came that big right hand, an audible gasp went up and it was clear Harvey was in trouble. As he clung to Jack in an effort to clear his head, the bell conveniently sounded to end the session.

Harvey watched with interest as the cheerful, cocky young guardsman left the gym. The sparring session had been a breeze until that sledge-hammer blow had scattered his senses. He had noted also the power of the wayward punches that had landed on his arms and shoulders. He considered that, with careful handling and diligent application to his trade, Jack could become a champion. Already Harvey reckoned he would prove too strong and powerful for many of Britain's professional heavyweights.

He decided to contact his manager, Dan Sullivan. The two men were not then on the best of terms, according to Harvey's widow Florence. Harvey had only recently returned from a disastrous trip to the United States, where he lost all three of his fights in dubious circumstances* and was given the run-around over his purse money. Florence Harvey recalled:

> 'Len told Sullivan that although he would shortly be leaving him, he would be wise to come and see this young Irishman box.'

Sullivan, an illiterate but street-wise cockney of Italian descent, was impressed by Harvey's glowing testimonial. He also received enthusiastic reports on Jack from Frank Godfrey, the useful Slough heavyweight Gunner Bennett and a racehorse trainer friend, Captain Percy Whitaker. He proceeded to make some discreet enquiries concerning Jack. He learned he was unbeaten as a boxer in the Guards,

* Sullivan did not accompany Harvey to America. Instead he appointed an American, Walter Friedman, to represent him. Harvey was outpointed by Vince Dundee (twice) and by Ben Jeby. The three fights were over 12 rounds in New York and a disgruntled Harvey felt he won each of them comfortably.

that indeed he was a dynamic puncher and, music to his ears, the boy was anxious to pursue a career as a professional.

What he did not know at the time was that Jack had made application to leave the Army on compassionate grounds, an action prompted by his increasing concern for his family in Cobh. His parents still had no regular income apart from the weekly ten shillings they were receiving in parish relief – a fact verified for the Army by their priest, Fr. William Walsh – and Jack had decided he would be able to help them better by leaving the Guards and obtaining more lucrative employment while awaiting an opportunity to join the professional boxing ranks.

His commanding officer, Lt. Col. the Lord Gough, thought differently. He issued a report on June 9, 1931, recommending that the application for discharge be turned down, observing, 'As Doyle was only a casual labourer before enlistment, it would appear that he would serve his family effectively by staying in the Army and making an allotment.'

Gough's recommendation was rubber-stamped by the regimental big-wig, Colonel Pollok. 'Application *not* approved,' he scribbled beneath Gough's missive, adding, 'There has been no material change in the condition of Guardsman Doyle's family, and there is no guarantee whatever that he will get employment if this application is approved.'

The only option open to Jack was to buy himself out. Whatever the cost, he could have had little prospect of raising it. He faced an agonising predicament. Apart from the modest amount he dutifully sent home to his parents – his Army pay had now risen to 14 shillings a week – he was unable to help them. He was desperate to turn his talents to the professional ring, where fame and fortune awaited him. After just nine months in uniform, the novelty of soldiering had begun to wear painfully thin. He was anxious to get ahead, to become the great benefactor who provided for his loved ones a new and better life far removed from their present dire circumstances. He considered he had to find a way in which to free himself from the shackles of Army life.

Fate, as he was always inclined to believe, was about to play its part. Dan Sullivan, anxious to know what all the fuss was about concerning this young fellow Doyle, had quietly arrange to see his next contest at the Victoria Barracks. Trilby hat perched precariously on his bald head and regulation seven-inch cigar clamped firmly between his teeth, he paid his admission money at the door and stood quietly, though hardly anonymously among what was mainly a military audience, at the back of the hall.

Sullivan, whose long, pointed nose gave him the appearance somewhat of a middle-aged Pinocchio, was a knowledgeable and experienced fight trader who ran the promotions at South London's hot-bed of boxing, the Blackfriars Ring. He knew precisely what he was looking for in a fighter and, though he had never learned to read or write, there was nothing wrong with his arithmetic where money was concerned.

Sharp and observant, he liked the look of the dashing guardsman making his way confidently to the ring and noted well the buzz of excitement that went round the packed hall as he climbed through the ropes. This must be the man he had come to see – unmistakably so. The MC's announcement in clipped, military tones confirmed it: 'In the red corner, J. Doyle, Irish Guards.'

Sullivan's blood-pressure really soared as Jack, dispensing with the usual niceties of a customary exchange of left jabs, sailed straight into his opponent and clubbed him to the canvas, where he lay stretched out and motionless as the count tolled over him. Sullivan was highly impressed. He sensed that Jack possessed the two most priceless assets available to any heavyweight boxer: power of punch and that intangible quality called charisma. He decided to act speedily for fear of letting such an exciting young prospect slip through his fingers, and so hung around impatiently afterwards to see him. 'If you're properly looked after, you'll make a champion,' he told him with that worldly-wise air of authority so commonly exuded by boxing managers.

Jack, naive and inexperienced, was flattered that the manager of the great Len Harvey was willing to take him on. He recognised that this well-known fight figure held the pull and the sway to get him to the top, but explained almost by way of apology that he had signed on in the Army for three years and that an indeterminate sum of money would be required to secure his release. Sullivan impressed on him that he need not worry his head about such things. He explained that the money was no problem, that he would be pleased to pay it and that Jack could reimburse him from the earnings of his first professional engagement. 'In the meantime,' he cautioned him, 'get as much experience as you can under your belt. You're only 17, son, and professional boxing is a tough business.'

Like most managers, Sullivan was something of an actor. He was adept at playing many roles in life and the performance he had just put on for Jack's benefit was pure theatre. Act one had been a deliberate attempt to build up Jack's hopes by openly declaring his interest; act two was a portrayal of studied aloofness designed to make Jack think he was in no hurry to sign him. In reality, the reverse was true. Sullivan was so smitten that he could not resist taking another look at him – but this time it would be a closer inspection, well away from the confines of Jack's cloistered Army environment.

He arranged to give him a secret workout at a private gym in London and asked Alf Hewitt, a trainer whose judgement he respected, to be in attendance. Sullivan wanted Hewitt to run an experienced eye over Jack, as if to reinforce his own opinion of him as a heavyweight of extraordinary promise. Jack was put to work on the swing-ball, an unwieldy contraption where the ball is suspended at chin height by elasticated straps that stretch from floor to ceiling and the like of which he had never seen before. It did not take the two men long to receive confirmation of what Sullivan had already sensed at the Victoria Barracks: that this was a youngster of truly exceptional punching power. Instead of the usual practice of working up a rhythm by letting the leather ball swing in unison with the punches, Jack drew back his right hand and thumped it so fiercely that the straps snapped and the ball was sent bouncing around the floor of the gymnasium. Sullivan and Hewitt were astounded. They realised at once that in their midst was a rare breed of fighter who, when unleashed, would take the professional fight game by storm.

Sullivan's next stop was to call on Geoffrey Simpson to inform him of a 'new heavyweight sensation' he had discovered. The name rang a boxing bell in Simpson's mind. He remembered Jack as the boy he had heard about two years earlier from Tim McCarthy. He had been unable to help him then, but now Sullivan had rekindled his interest. He travelled to Windsor to see him and ran a story in the *Daily Mail* saying, 'Doyle is big enough to beat any man in the world. He is naturally a fighter and thoroughly in love with boxing.' The article must have gone down well with Lord Gough: shortly after its publication, Jack was promoted to lance-corporal for the honour he was bringing the regiment.

Simpson's astonishing eulogy caught his fellow scribes off guard. None had even heard the name Jack Doyle, still less seen him fight. Now they were hot on his trail. They turned up in droves for his next contest at Windsor, where he was competing in what was misleadingly labelled the Guards Novices' Championships. Jack was still very much a novice, of course, but his opponent, Guardsman Murphy, a 15-stone former Brigade of Guards champion, clearly was not. According to George Patterson and others, Murphy had already left the Army at this time, but was brought back and beefed up with the sole intention of providing Jack with some noteworthy opposition. These claims are borne out by an obscure reference to the contest in the Autumn 1931 edition of the Household Brigade Magazine, where it was stated: 'Lance-Corporal Doyle, a newcomer to the battalion, met *ex*-Guardsman Murphy, of Brigade heavyweight fame.' It went on to report with equal brevity that, 'Lance-Corporal Doyle was a much stronger man with a terrific punch, so Murphy was put out for the count in the second round.'

In fact Jack, celebrating the completion of his first year in uniform, struck so hard and often that Murphy was floored four times before being sent crashing through the ropes and almost into Lord Gough's lap. It had been his sternest test as a boxer and he had come through it in impressive fashion. Geoffrey Simpson was lavish in his praise, saying, 'In two years Doyle may learn enough to beat any man in the world. Even now he would be too destructive a puncher for some of our [professional] heavyweights.'

Sullivan considered the time had come for Jack to be launched on a professional career that would make him a household name throughout Britain. He regarded him as the most dynamic puncher he had seen and potentially the biggest money spinner in the history of British boxing. Apart from his undoubted attributes as a fighter, there was an additional highly-marketable quality about him that Sullivan felt was ripe for exploitation: a film-star profile. Indeed, so striking were Jack's looks and so magnificently fit and lean his body that Sullivan could picture him as a kind of Valentino of the ring, even if this Valentino did speak with the broad, unmistakable accent of his native County Cork. But that, too, could be turned to advantage, for fight managers have long been preoccupied with the great Irish heavyweight dream, knowing as they do that in the United States a dollar-laden trial awaits any robust son of Erin who aspires to the greatest prize in all sport.

Arrangements were speedily put in hand for Jack's departure from the Army. He applied for discharge on payment, both he and Sullivan hoping for an early release date. But each had reckoned without the stubborn resistance of Lord Gough, who, true to his nature, was mortified at the thought of losing the star of the regiment.

Gough had been among the first batch of soldiers to be awarded the Military Cross in the First World War. He had lost his left arm at the Battle of the Aisne in September, 1914. An enemy bullet struck him just below the shoulder, gangrene set in and the arm had to be amputated. A hero on the battlefield, the Irish-born, Eton and Oxford-educated Gough liked to see the same brave, fighting qualities in the men under his command. To his way of thinking they were never more perfectly exemplified than by the irrepressible Doyle in the boxing ring: fearless, full of spirit, taking the fight to, and finally crushing, the enemy.

Gough was all for the honour of the regiment and Jack was his pride and joy. He made every effort to get him to stay on in the Army, where he considered lay his best prospect of advancement. At the same time, being a man of integrity, he did not wish to hinder the lad's progress as a boxer; he was aware that with his immense height and mighty punch, Jack was destined for a career of glorious conquest as a professional.

A compromise was reached. Gough persuaded Jack to stay on and represent the battalion in the Household Brigade Championships. It was the most prestigious event in the military boxing calendar and one in which rivalry between the regiments always took on a fierce intensity. Gough was eager for his 1st Battalion Irish Guards to capture the Inter-Unit Team Challenge Cup. And with Jack's magnetic presence acting as a spur to the rest of the boys, he felt certain they could pull it off.

Agreement having been reached, Jack settled down reluctantly to a further stint of soldiering. Now at least, having set his mind on leaving directly the championships were over, he could count the days to freedom. There were consolations, of course, such as being excused duties to enable him to concentrate on his training. 'His soldiering was virtually nil,' admitted George Patterson. 'The Army wanted him only for his boxing.'

One duty not even Jack could escape was the regulation twice-weekly return run to the Copper Horse in Windsor Great Park that was part of every guardsman's physical training. The distance varied from six to ten miles, according to the route taken, but Jack rarely, if ever, completed the course. Instead he devised a ploy that would enable him to appear to have run the full distance while in effect expending only a minimum of time and effort.

As the mass of runners set off at what seemed to Jack like breakneck speed, he would lag along at the back searching keenly for some place of refuge. At a convenient point along the route he would duck adroitly behind a hedge or bush and remain hidden until the runners returned on the homeward-stretch. At that point he would then rejoin the pack, overtaking many of his tired companions in the final few hundred yards to finish fresh and full of running.

By the time the Irish Guards had been transferred from Windsor to Wellington Barracks in London in the October of 1931, Jack's intentions on the boxing front were well known. Dan Sullivan had announced officially that he would be signing him to a long-term contract, to which the national newspapers had responded by giving Jack the star treatment. 'The boy with the punch of a Carnera,' said one. 'The boy who is big enough to beat the world,' said another. 'Faultlessly proportioned – a goldmine,' trumpeted a third. By any standard, it was an extraordinary build-up for a novice whose proving ground thus far had been a few explosive contests in an Army ring, a sparring session with Len Harvey and a couple of unofficial bouts in Windsor pubs. But newsmen who had seen him in action were convinced he was a champion of the future.

Jack was delighted to be based in London. He had fallen for the place during weekend leave from Windsor, when he and his companions, resplendent in their smart red tunics, attracted many pretty admirers around the Marble Arch and Hyde Park area. Then he had slept at the Union Jack club in Waterloo, where it cost ninepence for a bed, before travelling back to Berkshire. Now that he was stationed in the very heart of the capital, he was to consider what little soldiering he had to do no longer irksome but more a positive pleasure. Perhaps his new attitude was prompted by the realisation that soon he would be leaving the military life far behind. Seeing for himself the wonderful places which previously he had only heard or read about had opened his eyes to the glamour and excitement of London. There were the colourful ceremonials at Buckingham Palace, just across the road from Wellington Barracks; the State Opening of Parliament, at which he was on duty in November 1931; the Prime Minister's residence at 10 Downing Street; Whitehall, The Mall – all inspired in him a feeling of great awe.

Then there was St James's Palace at Westminster, over which, in company with others in his regiment, he had occasion to stand guard. He watched enthralled as the Prince of Wales – the future king – and his beautiful companion of the day, Thelma Furness, swanned in and out of Marlborough House, so obviously in love. In later years he was to relate a scabrous story to friends about 'the night I saw the Prince put his hand up Lady Thelma's skirt'. What he did not know at the time was that before too long, during his rapid rise to fame, he would become one of David Windsor and Lady Thelma's favourite sporting sons. We can be certain that he never had the nerve to tell them then what he claimed to have seen as a young guardsman on duty outside Marlborough House.

London's Edgware Road, just off Marble Arch, was the popular off-duty haunt of the Irish Guards during their tenure at Wellington Barracks. True to their heritage, the Micks were good drinkers to a man and Jack was no exception, though his love of a pint of porter was no more excessive than that of any other hot-blooded soldier in his regiment.

On one occasion, which still lives vividly in the memories of those who witnessed it, a fight broke out in the King's Head pub between soldiers from the Grenadier Guards, known commonly as the Bill Browns, and a small battalion of Micks. The Bill Browns were disliked intensely, apparently for no better reason than that they were the senior regiment. The ensuing battle was reminiscent of a bar-room brawl in a Wild West movie as men from the rival regiments, most of them the worse for drink, went at each other with such ferocity that beer glasses were sent flying and a table was hurled through a window. The Micks were getting the worst of it, so a couple of them retreated behind enemy lines in search of reinforcements. Their luck was in. Who should be striding out along the Edgware Road but Jack Doyle.

Tim Sullivan (no relation to boxing manager Dan) was at the battle zone:

> 'The boys told Jack the Bill Browns were giving the Micks a going-over in the King's Head. The big fellow's eyes lit up. He rushed inside and waded straight into the Grenadiers. He knocked out two men with successive punches and the rest ran for their lives. The Micks weren't far behind them, either, once they learned the police were on their way. I had always been struck by Jack's enormous size. He was one of the biggest men I've ever known. But that night he looked like a giant.'

The time was fast approaching when Jack would have to concentrate his mind on the forthcoming championships. He was concerned that the publicity he had received might rebound on him in dramatic fashion. Having been described in such grandiose terms in the newspapers meant he had a lot to live up to. As the big day drew near, his well-meaning colleagues unwittingly made matters worse by betting he would knock out every man he met. It would be no easy task carrying the money of the regiment.

He was now a man apart, pampered by his pals, permitted extra rations and given as much free time as he needed for training. Coldstreamers, Grenadiers, Scots, Welsh and Irish – all were entering their top men for the great event.

The vision of Dempsey that had become such a strong motivating force was again alive in Jack's mind on the first day of the championships as opponent after opponent fell before his flailing fists. 'Doyle is the winner,' was being repeated over and over again. The question on everyone's lips was: Can the Irish Guards capture the team trophy for the first time in 18 years?

It seemed the whole battalion had crammed into the London-Scottish Drill Hall for the semi-finals and finals. They saw Jack's first opponent go the same way as all the others – crashing to first-round defeat. Then, that same night, the finals . . .

Excitement is at fever pitch as the heavyweights enter the ring. It has been a long day, with boys' and novices' finals as well as the meatier senior bouts, and this is the last contest on the bill. The battle between the Irish Guards and their arch-enemies, the Grenadiers, has been a close one. In all the pandemonium, no one is quite sure which will carry off the coveted Inter-Unit Challenge Cup. One thing is certain: the heavyweights will provide an explosive finale.

Jack looks across at his rival in the opposite corner. He is Guardsman Brown of the Scots Guards, the man he had smashed to defeat in the depot championships just seven weeks after enlistment. It had been Jack's first bout in the Army and now fate has decreed he will be meeting the same opponent in what is to be his last. Both have come a long way since the day when, as a couple of raw recruits, they had tossed hopeful punches at each other without knowing what it was all about. Now they have survived the tough preliminaries, beating all-comers along the way, and are faced with the supreme test: the heavyweight final, the blue riband event of the championships.

The noise is deafening as the referee brings the boxers together in the centre of the ring. There is no dramatic eyeball-to-eyeball confrontation, no snarls or grimaces in a bid to outpsyche each other; instead, just an old-fashioned two-gloved handshake and almost whispered words of 'Good luck,' coupled with half smiles that suggest there will be no hard feelings whatever the result.

As they return to their corners, Jack's supporters are in a state of high excitement bordering on hysteria, shouting their encouragement and urging him to finish it quick. Then, just as suddenly, the huge hall is hushed as the opening bell calls the protagonists to action.

Jack realises what is expected of him. The honour of the regiment is at stake. The fight has become a cause. Come what may, he must not fail. He wastes no time sizing up his man. He knows only one way to proceed and that is going forward, willing himself on and trusting his body to respond. It does. He wades into his adversary, pinning him against the ropes and crashing home lefts and rights with all the power he can muster. The unfortunate Brown is again no match for him; he topples like a felled tree in the first round and Jack is declared the winner amid scenes of great jubilation. Now it is not only the Irish who are cheering. This is a Guards night and all the men in the packed arena join in the acclaim, irrespective of regiment.

Jack's delighted comrades, their wagers won, charge at their hero. They hoist him high on their shoulders and carry him off to the dressing-room, where hearty handshakes and back-slaps are the order of the day. A battalion party follows back at the barracks and the officers look in. Jack is the star of that little gathering, too. He sings Mother Machree *and* Old-Fashioned Town in the Old County Down. *The boxer has turned balladeer – the tiger is really just a pussy-cat. Jack Doyle is learning that his voice can hold an audience spellbound. He feels a strange power in the silence that descends when he sings, a power even more awesome than that which grips him when an opponent is at his mercy in the ring. He does not understand this power. He is too young to contemplate it. All he knows is that he feels it.*

Lord Gough, the old one-armed war-horse, is beaming with pride, despite his disappointment. His troops have failed by just one point to lift the trophy, beaten 57 points to 56 by the Grenadiers. But this is no time to let his disappointment show. He is proud of all of his men. They have fought their hearts out for him and he appreciates it. He shakes each of them by the hand and there are warm words of praise for Jack. Gough knows he has kept faith with him and his comrades and he is grateful. He wishes him well . . .

Four days later, on February 23, 1932, Jack Doyle was officially discharged from the Army. He departed with an unbeaten record as a boxer – 28 fights, 28 wins, an incredible 27 of them by knockouts* – and the following testimonial from Lord Gough:

'A smart, clean, sober, hard-working and promising young NCO, he holds a third-class certificate of education. In 1932, he was heavyweight boxing champion of the Brigade of Guards. Military conduct: Very good during his 1 year and five months' service.'

As Jack left Wellington Barracks for the last time in company with Dan Sullivan, the man to whom he was entrusting his future, he reflected that Army life had taught him many priceless lessons, not the least of which was the value of comradeship. The Guards had made a man of him and it was an experience for which he would always be grateful. But now he had worn their uniform for the last time. That part of his life was over and done with forever.

He was ready to strike out once more along the road to his date with destiny.

*

Little more than a year later, Tim Sullivan was walking through Hyde Park with a couple of soldier pals. They stopped to admire the handsome young toff dressed in top hat and tails, a white scarf hanging loosely from his neck, as he emerged from a Park Lane hotel with a glamorous woman at his side.

They watched with interest as the couple's chauffeur-driven car sped off into the night. The young man had shot no more than a cursory glance in their direction. His former buddies were out of uniform and in the darkness he had failed to recognise them.

Jack Doyle was now living in a different world.

* There is no precise record of Jack Doyle's amateur career. An Irish policeman, Garda Mulligan, is thought to have been the only man to have survived to the final bell.

Chapter 3

Pretty Phiddy's bird in a gilded cage

Jack can scarcely contain his excitement: he is a professional fighter at last. He is about to enter a dangerous, physically demanding trade bolstered by an apprenticeship of dubious merit. He has not fought in the top bracket of the amateurs – in Army and ABA championships and on the international circuit. His fame has been built on his reputation as king of the Guards and on the lofty words of sports journalists who have found him irresistible. They made him a star before he even stepped out of uniform.

His debut at London's Crystal Palace arena, a scheduled ten-rounder, is attracting such vast numbers that thousands will be turned away. It is a crazy phenomenon destined to re-occur whenever and wherever he fights. It is beyond comprehension that such hysteria can surround a boxer who has yet to make his debut as a professional, more especially one who has never been exposed to public scrutiny.

He has held on to his dream and it is materialising sooner than he dared imagine. The Irish Jack Dempsey has developed the punch of his hero. He is fast gaining the popularity of his hero. Now he must match the fighting deeds of his hero all the way to the world heavyweight championship. It is a long, tough, arduous assignment that will require dedication and staying power.

He needs to fight like a man, but at 18 he is still a boy at heart. He imagines himself as a story-book hero like Jack in *Jack and the Beanstalk*. He is about to climb to the enchanted realms. Once there he will bestride them like a colossus, in the manner of his beloved Dempsey.

He is already on a high. He has been working in a furniture shop in Victoria, not far from Wellington Barracks. The heavy lifting has strengthened his arms and his stomach muscles, just as intended. Alf Hewitt, a short, thick-set ex-wrestler, has been putting him through his paces at the Guy's Hospital gym at Maze Pond. He is in peak condition and primed for action.

It is April 4, 1932. The man targeted to give him his first critical examination as a professional is Chris Goulding, a colliery worker from Barnsley who thus far has failed to mine a rich seam in the boxing ring. They call Chris the Yorkshire Carnera because of his height and his punch. He is the perfect test for a much-vaunted debutant.

Jack is bullishly confident, his destiny imprinted like some invisible badge on the knuckles of his right hand. His determination to commence his career on a memorable note is channelled into a powerful right cross that floors Goulding seconds after the opening bell. Chris struggles bravely to his feet, but is again upended by a booming right that explodes on to his chin. The count is a formality. It is all over in 30 seconds.

Jack follows his impressive debut with another knockout victory at Crystal Palace. This time the victim is Arthur Evans, who also takes a first-round journey to oblivion. There is a similar summary dismissal for Jack's third opponent, Bill Partridge, who is floored three times and stopped in the opening round at Holborn Stadium.

During training for his next fight, Jack is admonished for pulling his punches. It is a practice Hewitt and co-trainer Fred Duffett consider he might unwittingly repeat when fighting for real. Jack responds by knocking out three men in quick succession and Hewitt and Duffett get the message: unless Jack *does* pull his punches, he will run out of sparring partners.

Jack is all out to maintain his sequence of quick wins against experienced Guardsman Gater at Wimbledon Stadium; but he has to settle for victory in the second round after the bell saves Gater from a knockout in the first.

Scottish champion Bobby Shields, a daunting test for a four-fight novice, can do no better than the rest. He is dispatched in the first round by a scything right uppercut at Anfield, the home of Liverpool Football Club.

Five fights, five wins. Jack is hurtling onward and upward to the fulfilment of his dream. He has won each contest in splendid style and already the newspapers are describing him in glowing terms as a future world champion. The acclaim is wildly premature, but Jack is generating excitement on an unprecedented scale. Though he has still to face anyone of true note, the vanquished quintet have, in boxing parlance, 'been around': they can handle themselves. Gater and Shields, for example, each lasted three rounds with Walter Neusel, a capable, big-hitting German destined to become one of the world's top heavyweights.

Such is Jack's popularity, and so rapidly has his fame spread, that fans are beating a steady path to Dan Sullivan's front door in Clapham. Jack often returns after a day's work and an evening in the gym to find a stack of autograph books for him to sign.

Sullivan senses the time is right to show Jack off around London's West End, where he can meet the right people and be photographed in high-class clubs and restaurants. They also make regular visits to Jack Bloomfield's* fashionable pub in Bear Street, in the heart of theatre-land, where boxing and racing people meet. Sullivan introduces him to his racing friends – bookmakers, trainers and top jockeys like Steve Donoghue and Charlie Elliott. Jack learned to ride almost before he could walk – his fall from that obdurate donkey not withstanding – and he delights in being in the company of his heroes of the turf. He strikes up a friendship with Donoghue, despite a difference of some 30 years in their ages. They seem always to be roped in by well-meaning priests and nuns to assist at the same fetes and bazaars, a happy-go-lucky pair united by their love of sport, their Irishness and their Catholicism. Whenever Jack sees Steve coming he bellows with all his might, 'Come on, Steve!'

Jack cannot help but notice the barely-disguised looks of admiration he is receiving from pretty society types. Whenever he enters the expensive Mayfair establishments he has started to frequent – places like the Café de Paris and the Café d'Anglais, Murray's and the Kit-Kat – the eating and drinking stop as people stare at him in astonishment, utterly taken by his enormous height and devastating presence. They begin seeking out this young Irishman who is being hailed as a world-beater, anxious to shake his hand and be seen in his company.

Jack's table-manners have improved somewhat since his days as a guardsman. Sullivan had first been shocked and then faintly amused on finding when he took him to lunch that he quickly wolfed down everything in sight, including a whole bunch of bananas that had been placed in front of him after the meal.

Jack delights in being recognized and feted, and the bright lights fast become an irresistible lure – so much so that Sullivan begins to get worried. His plan to make Jack the darling of the smart set is succeeding a little too well for his liking. This is brought home to him one night when Jack fails to return after an evening out. Sullivan sits up waiting for him until four in the morning before deciding to turn in. Jack arrives at nine, explaining by way of apology that he has been visiting his old Army pals at Aldershot. His unit has been transferred there since his

* Jack Bloomfield held the British and Empire cruiserweight titles in the early twenties.

discharge from service and he had missed the last train back to town. Sullivan learns later that Jack was seen in the West End at three in the morning.

Now that he has a regular income of decent proportions and is becoming so immensely popular, Jack clearly hankers after some excitement. No longer is he the shy, modest young lad who was happy, as in those first uncertain weeks after leaving the Army, just to sing and play his melodeon at home with the Sullivans. He is beginning to regard himself as unbeatable in the ring and irresistible in the salons of high society.

Inevitably, Jack moves to the West End – there, it is said, to become ensconced with one of the most sought-after and glamorous women of the thirties.

*

Phyllis Kempton's pictures adorned the pages of leading fashion and society magazines. She was a late twenties and early thirties version of Jean Shrimpton – only rich and upper-crust.

They called her Pretty Phiddy, this winsome woman with the dark auburn hair, porcelain features and sylph-like figure. Her father, Reuen O'Neill, was a well-to-do London merchant and she had been brought up to be a lady of refinement and social esteem. She was a formidable horsewoman, well known in the hunting field.

Pretty Phiddy and her husband, Arundel H. Kempton, were a celebrated sporting couple who owned a string of horses and greyhounds, including the legendary Mick The Miller.* Kempton was immensely wealthy. He dealt in property, owned a company that supplied the gaslamps for the whole of London and the south of England and was a Freeman of the City of London. He was vice-chairman of Wimbledon greyhound stadium – described at the time as the 'bijou château' of dog racing – and a director of several commercial and shipping companies. His elder brother, Andrew, was a Surrey cricketer.

Pretty Phiddy had married Kempton in 1926 – 'I was 19 and green as grass' – and they lived in a magnificent nine-bedroomed house in fashionable Wimbledon Park. He was 17 years older and, she would discover, a playboy and philanderer:

* *Mick The Miller* won every classic of the track, including two Derbys, and earned a (then) phenomenal £7 000 in prize-money in three seasons before going to stud. His effort to land a third Derby was foiled when he was beaten in a re-run after winning the original race. The Kemptons had purchased him for a record £2 000.

'My parents had been in favour of the marriage because Arundel was something of a father-figure. But I soon found out what he was really like. Jack Doyle had nothing on my husband as a womaniser, I can tell you.'

Her most treasured possession was a wedding gift from the Surrey and England cricketer Jack Hobbs – the bat with which he beat W. G. Grace's record of centuries. Kempton and Hobbs were great friends and together organised charity events for hospitals and the local poor, assisted by their many well-known society, business and sporting acquaintances.

Pretty Phiddy was strikingly attractive. She was a social lioness. And she was in big demand as a personality in her own right. She opened Selfridges' Roof Garden in company with Mick The Miller and presented Lonsdale Belts and cups and trophies in the boxing ring. She was glamour, class, wealth and breeding all rolled into one.

For the idle rich and the pleasure-seekers, these were the days of casino gambling and golf at Le Touquet, of high-spending shopping expeditions to Fortnum & Mason and Harrod's, of matinées and of twice-weekly visits to the Embassy Club and the Café de Paris:

'The Embassy was the in-place. The food was delicious and you could hear all the gossip. It was a wonderfully glamorous time. The women's clothes and jewellery were amazing – very swish. I must admit we were lazy bitches. We didn't have a thought about anything else.'

Pretty Phiddy is commonly credited, or more accurately debited, with leading Jack into a life of debauchery, of giving this innocent abroad a taste of and for the erotic. It is said she was a bird of prey who got her talons into Jack when he was 18 and she 24 and made him her Mayfair pet, putting him up in her smart flat and treating him as a plaything – someone she could amuse herself with while husband Arundel was occupied with his own hedonistic pursuits. She is held to be the first of those society women who refused to let little things like divisions of class and upbringing stand in the way of a physical affair with Jack.

Pretty Phiddy admitted she knew Jack and she was several times in his company. But she denies any romantic involvement with him:

'I was very interested in boxing and used to go to all the fights. I knew the Prince of Wales well and we used to engage in long conversations at the ringside. I found him handsome and charming. But an affair with Doyle? I think it's hilarious. I wouldn't have touched him with a barge-pole. He was just a thick Irish peasant when I knew him. I remember Dan Sullivan saying he hoped Doyle would do well because he ate three steaks for breakfast. He was big and brawny and may possibly have appealed to some society women with their puny husbands. But I honestly don't think he had the kind of personality to attract them. Being a handsome hunk was not enough. Afterwards it may have been different – I just don't know. He obviously acquired some superficial knowledge.'

Former professional gambler Albert Deacon, a well-known thirties fringe figure in boxing and racing circles, told a different story. According to him, Pretty Phiddy's disparaging comments are at odds with the truth. He maintained that she could not resist Jack and started him 'on the downward slope' by using her wealth and position to snatch him from the cradle:

'Mrs Kempton had a luxury flat in Bury Street, just off Piccadilly. She invited Jack to move in with her and they lived together for a time. She absolutely showered money on him. He used to sing from the window: "I'm only a bird in a gilded cage." He was just a kid – innocent.'

*

Dan Sullivan knew he'd overdone it. All his scheming and manoeuvring had backfired on him in dramatic fashion. He had wanted nothing more than for Jack to enjoy celebrity status among the elite of London, but sexual escapades with whichever plum-voiced woman happened to take a fancy to him had not been on the agenda. Now it was too late. Jack was hooked on the high life. There was an ever-present danger that training in night clubs and bedrooms instead of in the gym would begin to have an adverse effect on his career.

The only solution was to choose an opponent for Jack's next fight possessed of the durability to stand up to his big punch and make him understand professional boxing was a tough business which demanded 100 per cent dedication. The Press had inadvertently come to his aid by suggesting that stronger opposition should be found for Jack. Sullivan took the hint and lined up George Slack, known for obvious reasons as the Doncaster Iron Man. Slack had twice gone the distance with Len Harvey and had lasted five rounds with the newly-crowned British champion Jack Petersen. He was battle-hardened enough to shock Jack into the realisation that total commitment was required if his Dempsey dream was not to fade and die on some society beauty's satin pillow.

A crowd of 17,000 flocked to see the fight at the St Helen's rugby ground in Swansea – a record for a boxing contest in Wales. The huge attendance bore testimony to the extent to which Jack had captured the public imagination in just five fights that had lasted a total of six uncompleted rounds. The fans sensed they were about to witness something special and they did not go away disappointed. Jack, paying scant regard to his opponent's iron-man tag and confident that anything Petersen had done he could do quicker and better, smashed the startled Slack to the canvas four times and put him out for the count in the second round. It was a performance of pure majesty, of raw, unadulterated power. An opponent who had been expected to extend Jack fully, and possibly to take him the distance, was crushed by a two-fisted bombardment which left the fervent Welsh audience in no doubt that they had seen a boy with the punch to conquer the world.

Jack considered Slack the toughest man he had fought. He admired his bravery and his sportsmanship and invited him to become his sparring partner. It was a magnanimous gesture, rather in the manner of a bully who feels guilty about blacking someone's eye and offers to make restitution. In the event Slack readily agreed to act as sparring partner, though Jack had to promise not to hit him as hard in training.

Jack's earnings had been growing as fast as his fame. For his first professional engagement he had been paid £50 – a significant sum in the depression days of the early thirties, when a skilled worker was lucky to take home £3 a week. Now, less than six months later, Sullivan was being offered a massive £750 to let him loose on Jack Pettifer, another unbeaten young prospect being heralded in some quarters as a budding champion. The financial inducement must have been a huge temptation to Sullivan and yet, in spite of his renowned love of the folding stuff, he thought long and hard about accepting the match. Although he had decided the wraps should come off as far as Jack was concerned, the useful Pettifer was one fighter who had not figured in his list of possible future opponents. Sullivan recognised that the gangling giant who had been dubbed the Great White Hope of British boxing possessed the skill and the power to expose Jack as little more than a crude novice with more ambition than ability.

There was one person who entertained no doubts as to the advisability of taking the fight, nor of its outcome. With all of the refreshing, unswerving faith that accompanies youthful aspiration and endeavour, Jack Doyle was by this time certain of his destiny in the prize ring. He remembered Pettifer as the man who had won the heavyweight competition he had been refused permission to enter at the age of 15 and wanted him badly – so badly that he could hardly sleep nights. The pressure he exerted was such that Sullivan relented and completed negotiations for the contest. It was to take place at the Crystal Palace arena, where Pettifer had first caught the eye and where Jack had launched his professional career on such a spectacular note.

Sullivan, his calculating brain working overtime, felt it prudent to arrange a warm-up bout against an opponent who might present Jack with the kind of problems he was certain to encounter against Pettifer. An experienced Belgian, Gerard Ghesquiere, was imported and the fight arranged far from the capital's critical gaze in Grimsby, a town noted more for its fishing trawlers than for big-time boxing. That was the way Sullivan wanted it – no fuss, no fanfare, no massive media attention.

Pitching Jack in against a seasoned Continental just seven days before the Pettifer fight was a high-risk venture so fraught with danger that few managers would have contemplated such brinkmanship. A cut eye, a hand injury or even defeat, however unlikely or controversial, would have placed the Pettifer fight in considerable jeopardy. But these possibilities were not a serious consideration as far as Sullivan was concerned. The need for Jack to gain the vital experience he lacked was the overriding factor and he felt that even three or four rounds against an opponent as ringwise as Ghesquiere would prove inestimably beneficial.

His hopes were dashed, just as they had been with George Slack. Jack ignored his manager's advice to pace himself and set about the job with such headstrong enthusiasm that the Belgian was blasted to defeat after just 1min 40sec of the first round. Ghesquiere, in fact, was so completely gone that he had to be carried back to his corner.

Jack had trained for the fight at the Star and Garter in Windsor, where first he had sparred with Len Harvey, and he returned there to complete his preparation for the showdown with Pettifer. He was now famous in his own right but, having flown the cage, the Irish Nightingale was to come up against the resentment of Sullivan's other fighters.

Chapter 4

Battle of the giants

Charlie Smith, a leading Sullivan heavyweight, had been a British title contender in 1931.* He, too, trained for a time at the Star and Garter and remembered how Jack was disliked by his stablemates. They thought he was a joke. They reckoned that because he could sing, he couldn't fight. They tried to turn him over.

The truth is they were jealous: of his looks, of his earning power, of his pulling power. Charlie reckoned Jack's sex appeal was as devastating as his punch:

> 'Women worshipped him. They flocked to the Star and Garter in droves just to catch a glimpse of him. They'd go up to him and run their hands over his shoulders and down his chest. They'd say things like, "You big, strong, silent man." Jack loved it all – he was absolutely woman crazy. I remember going to his room once to wake him for his early morning run. I was an early riser and used to wake all Sullivan's fighters, one by one. "I'm up," said Len Harvey. "I'm up," said Gipsy Daniels. When I knocked on Jack's door, there was no answer. So I opened it, thinking he must still be asleep. There he was, naked on the bed with one of the chambermaids. I was disgusted and told him so. Jack just smiled and said, "We're only having a bit of fun." He must have thought me a prude.'

Florence Harvey was a regular visitor to the Star and Garter to watch her husband train:

> 'Almost from the start Jack had been receiving tremendous publicity and earning big money, while the rest were training twice as hard for comparative peanuts. To them boxing was their trade and their livelihood, but to Doyle it was nothing of the kind. He rarely trained hard because he felt he had no need to with his big punch. And he would never take advice, from Len or anybody else. But I must admit Jack was a very handsome young man and extremely courteous, particularly to women. They were mad about him and I think this also got under the skins of the other boxers.'

Charlie Smith confirmed the accuracy of Florence Harvey's testimony and recalled the first time he sparred with Jack at Windsor:

* Charlie Smith fought Reggie Meen for the vacant British heavyweight title at Leicester on November 16, 1931. He was outpointed over 15 rounds.

'He came at me throwing big right hands and I went pop, pop, pop with my straight left into his face. I was rebuked by Dan Sullivan for trying to make a monkey of him. None of the boxers cared too much for Jack because he was so big-headed. He was Sullivan's pride and joy and that rankled with the rest of us. Dan truly believed he had discovered a future world champion. But Jack didn't have much ability. All he had was that big right-hand punch.'

Charlie told how jealousy had surfaced when Gipsy Daniels*, the former British cruiserweight champion, first sparred with Jack at the Star and Garter:

'Jack tore in determined to impress, but Gipsy ducked, hit him with a right and Jack was out cold. Sullivan had a fit. "Close those bloody doors," he screamed. He had to pay the Press to keep quiet about it. He actually bribed them so that nothing about the incident would appear in the newspapers. Daniels couldn't stand Jack and neither could Len Harvey. I remember Harvey saying to him: "If I ever get you in the ring, I'll absolutely cut you to ribbons." '

Gipsy Daniels was an accomplished fighter and had proved it in no uncertain manner by knocking out Max Schmeling in Germany. That a man of his championship pedigree, experience and undoubted hitting power should have taken it upon himself to smash a teenaged novice to the canvas in a sparring session was a callous misuse of the tools of his trade. To have done so in front of an audience of newspapermen with the sole purpose of destroying a reputation was little short of an outrage. The reason was glaringly obvious. Jack had come fresh from the Army with little to recommend him apart from a big punch and yet, almost immediately, had superseded top-liners like Daniels, Harvey and Smith as the star of the Dan Sullivan stable. In that respect Daniels' behaviour, however reprehensible, could at least be understood.

Harvey's almost intense dislike of Jack is harder to explain. Having played no small part in his discovery, it was reasonable to assume he would have derived immense pleasure from his romantic rise to eminence. Yet it appears he harboured bitter resentment when Jack began attracting the kind of hero worship he had always craved. The gifted Harvey was rightly held in high esteem by the sport's *aficionados* and purists who recognised and appreciated his outstanding ability. But Jack Doyle was done down because he appealed to a far wider audience – the great British public at large. He was a celebrity in the truest sense

* Billy (Gipsy) Daniels was born in Newport, Gwent, in February 1902. Won the British cruiserweight title at the National Sporting Club in London on April 25, 1927, by outpointing champion Tom Berry over 20 rounds. Knocked out Max Schmeling in the first round in Frankfurt (February 25, 1928). Retired from boxing in 1938. Died June 1967 in Plymouth.

of the word. It was something Harvey could not stomach.

There was, of course, a chance that Jack would suffer for his cavalier attitude to training and his sexual indiscretions. He'd have to be in top shape to beat Jack Pettifer of King's Cross – a man even bigger and heavier at 6ft 7in and 17 stones and also unbeaten as a pro.

The fight had captured the public imagination like none other in recent times. The two men, walking skyscrapers both, had set the boxing world buzzing. Large parties made the crossing from Ireland. There was a big contingent up from Brighton, where Pettifer had completed his training. Sydney Hulls, the promoter, claimed he could have sold each seat twice over. He wasn't exaggerating. Newspapers estimated the attendance to be in excess of 20 000 – a capacity 12 000 crammed inside the centre transept of the glass-domed arena and almost as many again locked outside. Cars jammed the approach roads to the stadium. Police sent for reinforcements in an attempt to control the crowds.

Women were prominent among the fans – office and factory girls, housewives who had talked husbands into taking them along, wealthy society types draped in furs and dripping with jewellery. No longer was boxing solely a male preserve: Irish Jack Doyle had opened the floodgates to a new and enquiring audience. London was not the only city gripped by big-fight fever. Jack's native Cork also teemed with activity. Thousands packed the square outside the *Cork Examiner* offices waiting for the result to come through. A green light was to be shown if he won, a red light if he lost.

Inside the Crystal Palace dressing-room, Jack was suffering from a more literal fever. He had felt unwell at Windsor on the eve of the fight. A doctor summoned urgently by Sullivan diagnosed 'flu symptoms. You can catch a nasty chill lying on a bed with no clothes on.

He was advised not to box, but it was unthinkable: the 'boys' had made the journey and he could not disappoint them. Now, with the bout only minutes away, he was doubting the wisdom of that decision. He faced the biggest challenge of his sporting life – both in terms of Pettifer's size and the importance of the contest – but felt lousy and drowsy. Dosed up with medication, he was barely able to summon the will or the energy to go out and fight.

A roar of expectancy greeted him as he made his way to ringside. Normally the ear-splitting din acted on him like a battle hymn; this time it might as well have been a funeral dirge. It was not the thought of defeat which bothered him now, catastrophic though that would be. It was more the sense of shame he would feel if unable to make a fight of it.

That seemed to be the way of things in the first round. Dazzled by

Pettifer's skills, he was punched all round the ring. He took such a hammering that he was in real danger of being knocked out. It was the very outcome he had been dreading, but he was unable to do anything about it. His limbs were heavy and lifeless; he was too weak to call the shots. Only through a combination of Irish heart and magnificent bodily strength did he manage to survive.

Pettifer was cool and confident. He strutted back to his corner to be told by jubilant handlers that he was heading for the greatest triumph of his career. Jack could only stagger back to his corner, eyes glazed, for a much-needed respite. Drastic action was called for and fortunately for him Dan Sullivan was a manager who did not mind bending the rules when disaster threatened. The alternative was to see his big-money dreams go up along with the cigar-smoke that permeated the ringside. With all the guile of a magician conjuring a rabbit from a top hat, he produced a small flask of brandy from the pocket of his white corner-man's coat and, under cover of the water-bottle, tipped a generous quantity down Jack's throat. Its effect was immediate.

The dramatic second round provoked some purple prose from *London Evening Standard* fight reporter Ben Bennison:

> 'The bell sounded for the resumption of hostilities and the buzzing audience was suddenly hushed into an eerie silence.
>
> Then, to a shout of delight from the crowd, Doyle sprang to his feet as if restored to life by black magic. "Wait!" bawled Sullivan, who had forgotten to replace his gumshield, but, unheeding, Doyle rushed at his surprised opponent, who was slow to leave his stool, like a man possessed.
>
> Pettifer was taken by storm. Crash, bang did Doyle send his thudding fists into the neighbourhood of his jaw to rock him and cause him to clinch.
>
> Poor Pettifer; a hurricane now raged against him as Doyle forced his huge frame against the ropes. He tried in vain to hold off the Irishman by means of his left hand or by erecting a guard with his right in an attempt to nullify the full weight of the punches that were being rained upon him.
>
> A fighting monster now was Doyle, his teeth clenched and his eyes awesome in the viciousness they portrayed. The crowd was on its feet and the noise deafening as he smashed to smithereens the last semblance of defence Pettifer was able to offer.
>
> Then, with a left and a right, he dropped his man to land him almost in the auditorium. There Pettifer lay, his eyes staring at the roof, the last ounce of his fighting power beaten out of him.'

There was bedlam in the huge arena. The fans went wild, quite unable to believe the unexpected turn-round in fortunes. They had been elevated to a pitch of uncontrollable excitement by the transformation of Jack Doyle from battered and beaten fighter in the first round to cold-eyed killer in the second. The women in the audience – 'Many were crying with joy' – had been caught up in the emotion of it all. They barred his path back to the dressing-room. Some tossed flowers. Others attempted to reach out and touch him. Those close enough to pierce his cordon of police and handlers threw their arms round him and kissed him. Several hung around afterwards waiting for him to emerge, most wanting autographs, some desiring a more tangible token of remembrance.

But Jack for once was in no mood for the company of adoring females. He spent the night alone in a Turkish baths.

*

Next day his head was still swimming – this time in a tide of euphoria as a glance at the morning papers confirmed his celebrity status on both sides of the Irish sea. At home the result of the fight had been greeted by a tumultuous roar from the faithful massed outside the *Cork Examiner*. But not only in his native county was he a hero. There was jubilation in every pub and bar and household the length and breadth of Ireland. His destruction of Pettifer had stirred the hearts of the people; it was as if a national day of rejoicing had been declared. Even in the Irish parliament, politics were forgotten for a day as opposing politicians for once found themselves in full accord. At long last they could agree about something: Jack Doyle's mighty punch would bring the heavyweight crown to Ireland.

On the mainland, too, the atmosphere was one of unfettered enthusiasm. The win over Pettifer earned him lavish praise, particularly from Geoffrey Simpson – the first to have drawn attention to his magnificent potential. Simpson was justifiably proud that his initial faith in Jack – when he had written about him in glowing terms without knowing how good he really was – had been so sensationally vindicated. His post-fight verdict: 'Not for years have we possessed a heavyweight with the magnetic appeal of this Irish novice – and it has all been built up in eight fights.'

Jack was big news. There were dozens of messages and cables hailing his triumph, among them a telegram from his parents saying simply: 'CONGRATULATIONS TO OUR DARLING SON.' The tears streamed down his face as he read and re-read it and realised how much he had missed his family back home. He'd sent them every penny he could since first leaving home to join the British Army and been as generous as circumstances had permitted. But he did not delude himself. His letters of late had been few. The demands of increasing fame had diverted his attention from his family, who always waited in great expectation for word from him and pored eagerly over every line. It was brought home to him, as he held their telegram in bruised and tender hands, just how much he had neglected them.

Two years had elapsed since he sailed off with the promise to his tearful mother: 'I'll soon be famous, you'll see.' He recollected that those words had been uttered more by way of reassurance than with total conviction, but now fame had arrived, as if by decree, at the age of 19. In just six months as a professional, his explosive punching power and matinée idol looks had made him the sporting heart-throb of the 'thirties.

Yet what good was success, he reasoned, if it could not be shared with his loved ones? He wanted to be part of the celebrations in his honour, to return in triumphal procession through the streets of his native Cobh. He could not resist the thought of it and made up his mind to go immediately, sending advance notice of his imminent arrival with all the theatrical aplomb of an actor stage-managing his own encore.

Jack's happy preparation for the visit to his homeland was shattered by unexpected news that soured the pleasant aftertaste of victory. It came in an announcement by the chairman of London's White City Stadium, Brigadier General A. C. Critchley, stating that his company had acquired Jack's management contract and would be undertaking responsibility for his future as a boxer. Critchley coupled the statement with his strongly-held view that, 'Doyle carries the greatest punch since Georges Carpentier's early days.'

Jack received the news calmly enough. Dan Sullivan had broken it to him gently, assuring him it was in his best interests to have the powerful and influential Critchley wheeling and dealing on his behalf. It could only help his career, he was advised, and accentuate his climb to the world championship. His fears were further allayed when Sullivan confirmed he had reached an agreement with Critchley that would enable him to continue as manager in the accepted sense. He would, where necessary, retain the power of veto over opponents and attend to all the duties normally associated with the management of a professional fighter.

Within hours of the announcement, Jack was dismayed to discover that Sullivan had collected 5 000 guineas for signing over the contract to White City. It was an enormous sum and reflected Jack's unique box-office appeal.

The shock of being bought and sold like a racehorse made him sense he had been betrayed by a man in whom he had placed his total trust and faith – a man he had come to regard more as a father-figure than manager.

He could not help the feeling that he had been used as a pawn in a deal which had given Sullivan the opportunity to pocket a fortune with one swish of his pen while he was not entitled to receive, nor indeed did receive, one penny piece. For a boy who had been brought up in abject poverty, it was a tougher blow than any he had taken in the ring.

His relationship with Sullivan would never be the same again.

Chapter 5

Tricks of the trade

'Advance bookings are bigger than for any tournament I have ever staged,' declared proud promoter Jefferson Davis Dickson from his Cecil Court offices, just off London's Charing Cross Road. It was some claim, but the man was no small operator. And he had style.

Dickson was a wealthy American entrepreneur with a financial interest in films and the theatre. He was a sophisticated, educated, travelled, society figure – 'Attractive and a real charmer,' according to Pretty Phiddy Kempton. So what was he doing in this most unsophisticated of sports where the in-fighting between promoters and managers can often elevate blue language to the level of an art form? It appears that, like many before him blessed with the crusading zeal of throwing good money after bad, he had fallen head over heels in love with the unique atmosphere generated by boxing and its roguish characters. He was previously based in Paris, where he had staged big-time boxing and where, presumably, he had learned to swear quite fluently in French.

A certain Gallic flavour could be evidenced in the alliance between Dickson and Jack's new guiding light, the Carpentier devotee General Critchley. It came as no surprise, therefore, that Jack's first opponent after the drama of his win over Jack Pettifer was to be a Frenchman – in this case the dynamic-punching Moise Bouquillon, a winner by knockout of each of his two previous fights in England.

As Dickson's excited announcement had indicated, the Royal Albert Hall concert arena was packed to baroque bursting point as the burly Bouquillon ducked under the ropes. His appearance was followed by Jack's almost gladiatorial entrance, a smile splitting his features from ear to ear as the removal of his emerald-green dressing-gown brought gasps of admiration from the women at ringside.

The brief interlude in Ireland following the Pettifer fight meant that Jack's preparation had left a lot to be desired, and the huge smile was soon to be wiped from his face. As the swarthy Frenchman moved menacingly within striking distance of Jack's jaw-line to find the range for his powerful short-arm punches, everyone in the arena seemed to sense what was coming – everyone, that is, except Jack himself. Suddenly, over came a vicious right and down he went with a crash.

There was a startled yell from the crowd and an even more startled look on Jack's face as he climbed unsteadily to his feet. Worse was to come. His defence was non-existent and again he presented an invitingly open target as the crouching Bouquillon bobbed and weaved his way forward to smash home another right to the chin. This time Jack dropped like a stone to the canvas, where he lay helpless on his back. It seemed to be all over there and then. The spectators, loyally and solidly behind Jack to a man, and a woman, screamed hysterically; his seconds banged frantically on the canvas in an attempt to rouse him. The timekeeper counted dispassionately: 'Six, seven, eight . . .'

With a despairing heave, Jack hauled himself back to his feet. Lusty cheers greeted his brave effort and a supporter dashed to the corner of the ring shouting, 'Hold him, Jack, hold him.' Jack needed no telling. He held the Frenchman all right, and so tightly that even his celebrated compatriot, the great Houdini, could not have freed him. Almost unconscious, Jack lay on Bouquillon as the referee, former world flyweight champion Jimmy Wilde – who was dwarfed by both men – made valiant efforts to pull them apart. But before he could manage to do so, and much to Jack's relief, the bell sounded to end the first round.

Jack was helped back to his corner, where he sat in a state of some shock before his senses were restored by a spurt of cold water from the sponge that had been squeezed over his curly head. As he gathered his wits, the realisation dawned that it would be curtains for him if Bouquillon managed to connect again with one of his powerful right-hand punches. Jack had been warned beforehand by Dan Sullivan in no-nonsense cockney vernacular that 'This Frog can really dig' and if he doubted it then he most certainly had been given good cause to believe it now. He quickly resolved to deal with the problem in the only way he knew: by taking the fight to the Frenchman. Bouquillon could dish it out, but could he take it? Jack bit hard on his gumshield and decided to find out.

To everyone's amazement he came up fresh for the start of the second round, though this time there had been no liberal intake of the brandy which fortified him against Pettifer. He took the initiative immediately by sailing straight into the surprised Frenchman and connecting solidly with a crashing right almost before the sound of the bell had died away. It was just as Jack had thought: Bouquillon did not relish being on the receiving end himself. His knees began to unhinge and he sank slowly to the canvas. As he did so, Jack hastened his slow-motion slide from the perpendicular to the horizontal by hammering him on top of the head in the manner of a percussionist pounding the kettle-drum during Last Night of the Proms. Jack was in such a frenzy that he did not much care where the blows landed, with the result that many of his wayward punches strayed to the back of Bouquillon's bull neck.

The Frenchman lay writhing, clutching the back of his neck as if guillotined and appealing for a disqualification. Referee Wilde would have none of it and with great reluctance Bouquillon rose at 'eight'. There was to be no stay of execution. Another explosive right-hander, another downward stream of punches as he fell and the fight was over amid the greatest scenes of clapping, stamping and cheering ever witnessed at the Albert Hall.

The verbal punch-up after the fight was as fast and furious as the hectic action that preceded it. Bouquillon, apoplectic with rage, insisted that a two-inch laceration on the back of his neck be examined by a doctor, who ventured the opinion that the injury had been caused by a lace on Jack's glove. The Frenchman claimed Jack should have been disqualified for 'persistent holding and hugging, five rabbit punches [blows delivered to the back of the neck] and for hitting me while I was on the floor.' He flew back to Paris complaining about the injustice of it all and, further, demanding that the verdict be reversed.

Jack was relieved, for the second fight in succession, to have turned near disaster into triumph. This time he had cause to be grateful for some of the more questionable lessons learned during his formative years in the Holy Ground. The circumstances had demanded rough-house tactics and he had not hesitated to use them, just as his hero Dempsey had not always been particular where his punches had landed when charged with the task of turning imminent defeat into sensational victory.

Jack's win over Bouquillon carried with it an undercurrent of suspicion, according to former fighter and manager, the late Tommy Daly. The theory he advanced is that Sullivan, of whom it is said that money was his only god, had paid Bouquillon to lose but that the Frenchman rewrote the script in that incredible first round, when he had Jack down twice and tottering like a drunk at a wedding party.

Daly cited Sullivan's close connection with the Sabini brothers*,

* *Charles (Darby) Sabini* and his brothers Harry and Joseph emerged from Saffron Hill, then known as London's Italian quarter. They controlled prostitutes and operated a bookmakers' 'protection' racket at South of England racecourses in the twenties and thirties. (From *Britain's Gangland,* by Norman Lucas, W.H. Allen.)

whose chilling gangland exploits had earned them the title 'London's Mafia'. He described how the Sabinis wielded a powerful influence in the sport and claimed they 'put the frighteners' on Bouquillon, inducing him to take a dive:

> 'At the end of the first round the Sabini brothers got up from their seats and went over to Bouquillon's corner, where they made a number of threats and gestures. Bouquillon may not have understood the lingo, but he certainly got the message. Then, lo and behold, after bashing Doyle from pillar to post in the first round, he comes out for the second and gets himself knocked out. I know it's true because I was there and saw what happened with my own eyes.'

Daly suspected also that many of the early victims of Jack's professional career were either paid to lose or petrified into submission by the presence of the gangster element surrounding Sullivan, whom he claimed had been unable to believe his good fortune when he first set eyes on Jack and resolved to market him in such a way that the Press would be raving about him, the public falling over themselves in the rush to see him and women drooling at the very mention of his name. He certainly succeeded beyond his wildest expectations, but the suggestion that Jack's spectacular string of victories had been achieved by virtue of a Dan Sullivan Dirty Tricks Campaign cannot be substantiated. Every old-time fighter and manager consulted on the matter regarded the claim as ludicrous. Yet Daly maintained that such was the case, saying:

> 'It was very cleverly done. Nothing was ever said to Doyle's opponents, but a cold, hard stare from one of the Sabini brothers in the dressing-room before the fight was enough. It would scare any boxer out of his wits. Everyone knew of the Sabinis' reputation and no one in his right mind would attempt to cross them. Jack knew nothing about it, of course. He thought it was all genuine when he was knocking them over like ninepins.'

If Jack's opponents had indeed been frozen with fear through that kind of intimidation, something would surely have been revealed at the time. Or at least it would have become common knowledge among the fight fraternity. Sullivan's collaboration with the Sabinis related exclusively to horse-racing and it remains unlikely that the brothers exerted any influence over Jack's career.

It must be accepted that Pettifer and Bouquillon were in deadly earnest in attempting to knock him out. That both had come within an ace of doing so would appear to ridicule any suggestion that they then suddenly took a dive and denied themselves the kudos that victory over Jack would undoubtedly have brought. Though Sullivan was the Artful Dodger of the fight game, with few scruples where money was concerned, there would have been no need for him to adopt dubious tactics in order to build up Jack's reputation.

Jack's performance against Bouquillon, which had brought the Albert Hall audience to such a pitch of noisy excitement, failed to impress the one man who mattered – his new boss General Critchley, who was dismayed by his appalling ignorance of the finer points of the game. Critchley had just seen his company's 5 000 guineas investment almost vanish overnight, like shares on the Stock Exchange when a public company suddenly goes bust. He called an urgent post-fight conference with Sullivan and Dickson to discuss the future of the most prized asset in British heavyweight boxing. White City's stake in Jack was not as rock-solid as he had imagined and he proposed to do something about it.

He ventured the opinion that Jack must be taught a modicum of skill and defensive strategy and suggested he be sent to France to train under the guidance of François Descamps, the manager who had piloted the General's beloved Carpentier to the world light-heavyweight title in 1920. But whenever Critchley ventured an opinion, it was usually delivered in the form of a *fait accompli*; he was not a man to be trifled with and Sullivan tamely acquiesced when the General stated that, at the end of one month's tuition, Descamps would report on the progress made and give a forthright appraisal of Jack's ability.

It was no surprise to Jack that he had not been consulted. The first he learned about it was when he was told a decision had been taken to send him to France for instruction under Descamps and that all arrangements had been made. He did not like it one little bit. He was beginning to tire of having to do as he was told without question; it was just like being in the Army all over again, especially with a no-nonsense military type like Critchley in charge of his affairs. He wondered how he had allowed himself to be manipulated in such a way as to be given no say over how his career should progress. He considered he knew better than anyone what was best for him, but nobody was really interested in what he had to say; he was told he was there to do the fighting and advised that other matters should not concern him. Yet he had no desire to become a new Carpentier: he was a fighter, a born fighter in the Dempsey mould and he did not wish to change. The fact that Dempsey had destroyed Carpentier in a world heavyweight title fight in Jersey City eleven years earlier, in 1921, was enough to convince him that a good fighter with a punch and plenty of heart would always emerge victorious over a more skilful adversary even if that adversary, as in the case of Carpentier, was a brilliant boxer who possessed a block-busting punch himself. Dempsey had taken all Carpentier could throw at him, walked fearlessly through it and then smashed the Frenchman to defeat in the fourth round. It was soul-stirring stuff to Jack, whose passions were inevitably roused by the heat of battle. He resolved to stay loyal and true to the style of his hero.

He expressed his misgivings to Sullivan, who surprised him by confiding that he also entertained doubts as to the wisdom of the move. 'But,' he reassured him, 'General Critchley is a sportsman. He has explained that it is only in the nature of an experiment and that you can come back if it does not suit you.'

The thought of weeks of monotonous boxing tuition in some drab French village was not the most alluring of prospects, for by this time Jack had taken premises in fashionable Mayfair Court in company with brother Bill. He considered it would be both uplifting and much to his social advantage to have his own residence in the heart of the West End. It was all part of his education, and he had a lot of lost time to make up.

He engaged a valet, appropriately named James, who, according to Bill Doyle, acted also as secretary. Jack's fan-mail had, by this time, grown to quite staggering proportions. Jack liked to answer every letter, the vast majority of which were from women. He dictated his replies to his faithful James, who then typed them out.

James, middle-aged, well educated and immaculately groomed, became a trusted aide to a boy who aspired to greater things than his limited academic learning had allowed. Jack abhorred the image of the archetypal pug – all brawn and no brain – and perhaps this explains in part the animosity of other boxers toward him. He was sensitive to a greater degree than people imagined. The biggest dread he harboured was that he might be considered a thick Irishman, and he took pains to present himself in a far different light. As his growing fame brought him increasingly into contact with the upper classes, he wanted to be sure he could handle himself in their presence. It was this desire for acceptance as a gentleman boxer who could hob-nob with the rich and the titled that was occupying his lively young mind. Very shortly he would be armed with the social graces and etiquette that would adequately equip him for the task, for he now wished to take the best from life, to meet the right people and impress them. In the past he had bared his back to the humblest of tasks and he hoped he might be forgiven for thinking that part of his life was done with forever.

From his invaluable James he learned the social graces of correct diction and impeccable behaviour. He was introduced to a new world of learning that held a strange fascination for him, and he thirsted after knowledge in a way which the Presentation Brothers back home in

Cobh would have found impossible to believe. He discovered that the writings of philosophers and poets contained the wisdom of the ages. They added a new dimension to his life – one of elevated thought and expression.

Kipling's *If* had almost as profound an effect on him as the Dempsey book he had latched on to as a lad. He read and re-read it until he could recite it by heart, identifying with it so strongly that the poem was to become for him a kind of personal anthem.

The third verse particularly was one with which he felt a powerful affinity:

> 'If you can make one heap of all your winnings
> And risk it on one turn of pitch-and-toss,
> And lose, and start again at your beginnings
> And never breathe a word about your loss;
> If you can force your heart and nerve and sinew
> To serve your turn long after they are gone,
> And so hold on when there is nothing in you
> Except the Will which says to them: "Hold on!"'

He remembered how, as a boy, he had risked his 'all' – then just a halfpenny or so – on games of pitch-and-toss in the Holy Ground. He never moaned then, and he would never complain now, if fate dealt him a rotten hand; he would merely reshuffle the pack and start all over again. He would never be a Cautious Harry, for life was a gamble in which he was playing for high stakes. Fortune favoured the brave, a sentiment he had proved to his own satisfaction in the boxing ring. As for money, he would spend it freely on himself and others and never worry about the consequences. He remembered that old Irish saying, 'A generous man never went to hell.' Hell to Jack would mean living a life of constraint, hoarding up money like a miser and being unable to enjoy the fruits of his labours.

As to holding on 'when there is nothing in you except the Will which says . . . "Hold on!"' – hadn't he done precisely that against Pettifer and Bouquillon? Perhaps it was the power of the Spirit that carried him through when all had seemed lost. Perhaps. But he had to concede it was more the power of an alcoholic spirit which had aided him against Pettifer than any act of divine intervention.

The obsessional Dempsey dream that had motivated Jack so strongly since boyhood had not been obscured by his new thinking. It remained still bright and vivid but, unquestionably, it had taken on a new, diluted form. No longer was the desire to emulate Dempsey his *sole* purpose in life.

At 19, Jack had awoken to the realisation that a boxer's career was a short one and felt it prudent to expand his talents in other directions. He had been blessed with such a fine voice that he began to picture himself as a budding singer in the mould of Ireland's world-renowned tenor Count John McCormack,* whose songs he played for hours on end in his London flat. Bill Doyle recalled:

> 'Jack would sometimes sit around in his dressing-gown listening to McCormack records all day long. As each song ended, he would say to me, "Put another one on, Bill." He was in a world of his own – a kind of dream world – when McCormack was singing. He was completely enchanted by the man's voice and his songs.'

There were other distractions, the biggest among them being women. Invitations to parties were pouring in and Jack accepted them eagerly. He gazed in admiration at girls with beautiful figures – strikingly accentuated by low-cut dresses – drinking, dancing and making whoopee. He became a social lion in Mayfair, living a life that contrasted sharply with the monastic discipline required of a boxer. Flush with money from his earnings in the ring, he splashed out recklessly on expensive clothes. He purchased morning suits, evening suits, lounge suits, sports jackets, smoking and riding jackets, silk shirts, silk pyjamas, silk underwear and more pairs of shoes than he would need in a lifetime. The suits, costing from £10 to £25, were made by a fashionable and expensive Savile Row tailor. His shirts, each with his monogram embroidered on the breast pocket, and his size 13 shoes, were also hand-made. The underwear and pyjamas were a needless expense. He was uncomfortable in both and rarely wore them – a consequence of his parents having been unable to afford them for him as a child.

Jack liked nothing more than dressing up and going out on the town. He would usually start the day horse-riding with an early-morning canter in The Row adjoining Hyde Park, followed by a singing lesson

* *Count John McCormack* was the last tenor to be simultaneously both popular idol and great opera singer. Before the age of radio and mass travel, his was the first English-speaking voice heard throughout the world via the medium of his records. When he died in 1964 at the age of 61, his wife found that he had written in a diary: 'Now, like the old Irish minstrels, I have hung up my harp.' It was a fitting epitaph, for he was one of the finest minstrels of the century – an artist who brought the magic of music and poetry to the people. Though he was a much-acclaimed opera star he was a poor actor and by the early twenties had abandoned the stage for the concert platform. By doing so he brought pleasure to millions, singing with superb technique and artistry, and in a voice that combined sweetness and purity, anything from opera to folk songs – and earned him the then phenomenal riches of some £200,000 a year. (Taken from *My Music* by Peter Dacre, *Sunday Express*).

from Welsh maestro Gwynne Davies at his studio just off Baker Street. Then would come lunch at The Ritz, an afternoon matinée, cocktails and a visit to a party or fashionable club or restaurant.

'An ex-guardsman is bred to this love of a good cut,' he explained when asked for his reaction to being described as one of the best-dressed men in London. 'A man of exceptional build needs an exceptional tailor and it is good for mind and body that a fellow should have the feel of looking well.'

It had been literally wine, women and song all the way for Jack since the Bouquillon fight, for which he had received £759–17s after payment of management commission and expenses. At the time it was a huge sum to have been earned by a nine-fight novice and considerably more than could have been commanded by his contemporaries – champions excepted. Before long, as his drawing power continued to gather pace, his fight earnings would dwarf that figure.

In the meantime, he was enjoying his money and his initial taste of fame. He was like a child having his first ride on a merry-go-round and being reluctant to get off. It was the predictable behaviour of a young man who felt he had made the jump from rags to riches. The sudden, exciting social whirl in which he had been caught up presented him with an additional reason for not wanting to go to France. He had put it off for some two months in the hope that Critchley would forget all about the idea, and indeed he thought he had until one day he was summoned to the General's office in Pall Mall and told, 'Here are your plane tickets and passport. You will be leaving for France in the morning. Monsieur Descamps is expecting you.'

Jack returned to his flat to pack his boxing gear and what other belongings he felt he might need. Then he called up some friends and asked them round for a sing-song and a game of cards. He would not be seeing them again for some time and wished to bid them a fond farewell.

Finally, he climbed into bed in the early hours, pondering with heavy heart his reluctant exile to a foreign land just as he was beginning a life-long love affair with London.

Chapter 6

Lost in France

If Jack's mood had acted as a barometer for the kind of weather he would experience in France, then the outlook was indeed bleak. It had been cold, wet and windy when he took off for Paris. But if blustery conditions alone were not enough to make a man feel slightly nervous at the thought of his first flight, the equally disconcerting date – January 13, 1933 – mocked at him cruelly.

Ironically enough, there were occasions when the plane was thrown about in the sky with enough force to evoke unwelcome visions of a crippled craft ditching dramatically into the Channel below. Once the plane had landed safely and his sense of relief became wholly apparent, he realised how foolish he had been to doubt the wonders of modern technology and the skills of a pilot trained to fly in all weathers.

He was met at the airport and driven 150 miles south through rural towns and villages so quaint and isolated that they reminded him of home. As the French countryside flashed by, he began to experience a feeling of unease not dissimilar to that which usually surfaced in the dressing-room just before a fight, but which then would disappear as the mighty roar of the crowd engulfed him. Yet this discomfort was quite unconnected with the nervous excitement that grips boxers when battle is imminent; it was more a hollow sensation symptomatic of a deep despondency he knew would not abate. At journey's end there would be no welcoming crowds, no familiar faces, no hearty back-slaps. He would be a stranger among strangers again, just as when he had first set foot in Wales after crossing from Cork. Then he had been bursting with ambition and a sense of adventure that had served to conquer his fears and his uncertainty. Try as he may, he could not summon the same enthusiasm now.

He realised, only too well, that Monsieur Descamps would be hugely disappointed once he had put the gloves on him and discovered what little technical expertise he possessed; in fact, he doubted whether the French maestro could benefit him at all. But he knew he had to give it a try: he was honour-bound to do so, not least because the operation had been mounted at considerable cost and the whole of Britain and Ireland would be expecting to see a considerable improvement in him on his return to the ring. He resolved to put a brave face on it all as the car finally reached the village of La Guerche-sur-l'Aubois and swung through the iron gates that fronted the large, high-walled house in which the Descamps family resided.

François Descamps was smaller than Jack had imagined, slightly stooped and with a shock of thick grey hair brushed back purposefully from a noticeably low forehead. The features had a strangely Mongolian appearance, but the way the man's eyes danced revealed him as a lively person of considerable mental prowess. Descamps had decided against making the journey to Paris because of failing health, but Jack recognised him at once as a warm, good-natured individual who, on first setting eyes on him and perhaps mindful of the presence of a couple of English newspapermen who had made the trip, threw his hands to the heavens and exclaimed in fractured English: 'My beloved Georges as a boxer ees no more, but 'ere I 'ave a boy – ees name, what you call eem? It makes no matter – whom I, François Descamps, weel turn into a champion of ze world.' Jack was quick to identify this as a touch of French blarney, but it was, nonetheless, an exceedingly generous and expansive gesture, even if the greeting had fallen a bit flat when Descamps momentarily forgot his name.

Jack surprised himself by taking an instant shine to Descamps and the feeling was clearly reciprocated. A mutual bond of affection was forged between tutor and tyro that would prevail through the difficulties of language and the tricky interpretation of the training methods Descamps would be seeking to introduce. To Jack, it quickly became apparent how this charismatic figure had managed to fashion Georges Carpentier into a world champion. For although Descamps was now an ailing 57-year-old with little more than a year left to live, he was a remarkable man whose life history had been one long chapter of success and achievement.

Descamps had always possessed great physical and mental dexterity, the former enabling him to become champion French gymnast in 1899 at the age of 24 and the latter becoming internationally evident as he steered Carpentier to triumph after triumph in the boxing ring. He was said to possess occult powers and was famous for his so-called hypnotic eye, with which he apparently unnerved Carpentier's opponents.

His interest in boxing had been triggered in an unlikely way during a gymnastics tour of schools in Northern France. A blond kid caught his eye – one who was athletic and sturdy but blessed with quick movements and reflexes. Descamps, who had an uncanny knack of being able to walk up and down ladders on his hands with his back straight and his legs and feet projecting skywards, recognised that the youngster was endowed with rare natural talent that would enable him to reach the top in any sport. He met the lad's parents and asked if he could take him under his wing; he was sure he could make something of him, he told them. The Carpentiers were poor country people and welcomed this opportunity for their son Georges, feeling instinctively that Descamps was a man they could trust. That trust would not be misplaced.

Descamps took Georges home with him to La Guerche. He nurtured him and disciplined him and trained him to such a high degree that Carpentier acquired the fighting qualities which would make him a legend throughout France. Descamps guided him to a remarkable quartet of European championships, all at different weights, followed by a challenge for the world cruiserweight title, which Carpentier won in 1920 with a fourth-round knockout of Battling Levinsky in New York. Carpentier failed in his bid to lift the world heavyweight crown, when, giving away weight, he himself was dispatched in four rounds by Jack Dempsey. The fight, at Boyle's Thirty Acres in Jersey City in 1921, attracted the sport's first million-dollar gate. He defended his cruiserweight crown successfully with a first-round knockout win over Britain's Ted (Kid) Lewis before losing it to Battling Siki in Paris in September 1922. Carpentier was known as 'The Orchid Man' and he became hugely popular throughout Europe and in the United States. According to George Bernard Shaw, he was a reincarnation of Charles XII.

Descamps' extraordinary feat in taking a youngster not yet in his teens and moulding and shaping him into a champion of the world, when possessed of no previous experience in the exacting trade to which he had turned his attention, must rank as one of boxing's most incredible management achievements. In addition, the level of trust that existed between the pair was such that they never drew up a formal contract.

François had experienced tragedy as well as triumph at a relatively young age. His second wife Gilberte – 'Very pretty,' according to 91-year-old Paulette Desphilippons, one of the few remaining people in the village old enough to have remembered her – died from influenza in 1918 at the age of 26, leaving two young children, Jacques and Denise, to be brought up by their father and Gilberte's elderly mother, Marthe Vanhaellebroucq.

Jacques Descamps was 18 and Denise 17 when Jack arrived amid much excitement at the house in La Guerche. Jacques, a member of the

French Resistance during World War II and decorated for bravery, retained vivid memories of the young Irishman's stay at his home:

> 'Doyle was beautiful-looking, too much so to be a boxer – very tall and slim, with fine features. I remember his first night at La Guerche. Perhaps it was superstition, but he put a sprig of something in a glass of water near his bed and sprinkled it around the bedroom, like a priest does with holy water. I thought it must have been some kind of Irish custom.'

For years boxers had been coming and going at the Descamps residence. The villagers had grown accustomed to seeing strangers in their midst from time to time, young men of athletic persuasion. They were known to be boxers in the care of the respected Monsieur Descamps and, apart from the great Carpentier, were paid little attention. He had always been treated with special reverence, with huge crowds flocking round him whenever he rode out on horseback. But now several years had passed since his retirement and Descamps had long ceased to concern himself with the management of fighters. It came, therefore, as something of a surprise to the locals when Jack appeared as if from nowhere. Friends and acquaintances of Descamps were told the reason for his presence in La Guerche but, as is often the case in such matters, the message became somewhat distorted and word soon got round that Jack was a veritable world champion – a new Carpentier.

So much time had elapsed since the village was last alive with boxers that a stranger was a unique event – especially one of Jack's massive proportions backed up by a big fighting reputation. At 6ft 5in, he stood literally head and shoulders above anyone else. He was studied with such intensity that he began to feel like a prize exhibit in a museum as people gathered in small groups on the street, discussing him earnestly and pointing toward him. Even at Mass on Sundays it was he, and not the priest, who was the focus of attention. He became aware that the congregation around him was staying silent during the responses just to listen to his voice. And, whenever his mind wandered from his prayers, he would glance round furtively to find several pairs of French eyes fixing him with unabashed curiosity.

'Monsieur Jacques', as he became known, was the only bit of excitement in the village, apart from a weekly dance at the local hall, the Tivoli. Since demolished, it was situated near the railway station and most of the boxers liked to show off their nimble footwork there, to say nothing of their ability in the clinches. Jack had no difficulty in finding pretty partners at the dance, much to the chagrin of the local swains, who stood around giving him menacing looks and were no doubt longing for a crack at him.

For the most part, Jack was lonely and dispirited in France. Apart from the dance he rarely ventured out, except to do his roadwork and get his hair cut at M. Pierre Dureau's salon. André Petit, now in his eighties and still living in La Guerche, used to attend to him. He remembered:

> 'Jack was always elegantly dressed. He didn't speak, but made signs to show me how he wanted his hair cut. In those days everyone put their tips in a box placed there for that purpose, so I don't know if he was generous or not. Sometimes he came alone, sometimes with other boxers who were training with him. I recall the local girls being interested in Doyle, but then they were interested in all the boxers because they were stars.'

The French language was the biggest problem for Jack to overcome. He had great difficulty making himself understood and contented himself mainly with just a nod and a smile. He grew more homesick by the day and it was with a certain heaviness of heart that he opened the stack of letters which arrived daily from England.

During the early part of his stay he had a visit from a *Daily Express* reporter, Pembroke Stephens, who noted the look of relief on Jack's face as he greeted him with a huge smile and the cordial words, 'Thank you for coming, sir. I'm very pleased to meet you.' Jack expressed to Stephens his delight at being able to converse freely in English once again and confided how lonely he felt so far from home. Stephens observed that Jack's bedroom was 'littered with fan-mail, most of it from women and schoolgirls, others from sportswriters and would-be managers and promoters.'

Jack's frustration was perhaps best summed up in a correspondence he had with the late James Butler, boxing writer of the now defunct *Daily Herald*. He expressed himself in a manner which showed clearly how his literacy had improved since that touching letter he sent home to his parents shortly after enlisting in the Army:

> 'It's filthy weather for training in the south of France: tons of sleet and rain and bitterly cold winds. This is the quietest village I have ever known – no cinemas and the nearest town Nevers. I'd sooner winter in London.'

Indeed, so depressing was the weather that Jack had little option but to spend most of his days in the house. Time was heavy on his hands and he whiled away the hours studying from an English-French phrase book. He tried hard to make progress under his new mentor, applying himself diligently in the gymnasium (a hut at the bottom of Descamps' rose garden) and sparring countless rounds with former European title contender Maurice Griselle and another top French heavyweight, Marcel Moret, who had been recruited to put him through his paces.

Jack found his sparring partners slow and the crab-like style of French boxing somewhat artificial. Descamps had taught Carpentier how to box defensively out of a crouch and then to strike with the speed and venom of a viper, but such guile and subtlety were lost on Jack. To compound the problem, Descamps possessed only a smattering of English. His instructions were passed on to Jack by an interpreter, and somewhat imperfectly at that.

Jacques Descamps confirmed that Jack was palpably unable to carry out his father's instructions:

> 'He was a good student and tried very hard, but he was just no good. He was not a fighter. Never. I think his period of instruction under my father was arranged for publicity, because Doyle was an Irish heavyweight. He was just too good-looking and too nice to hit anyone.'

Touching though Jacques Descamps' testimony is, Jack's nine professional opponents to date – and especially his most recent victims, Pettifer and Bouquillon – would certainly have taken issue with that statement.

Jack steadfastly refused to let his despondency show in spite of his inability to adapt to the new methods being taught him. He regarded Descamps as a caring and sympathetic host for whom no request was too much trouble, even in ill health. Jack would not have hurt his feelings for the world and took great pains to hide his unhappiness, always putting on a cheerful face and tackling his training with apparent gusto.

He sought and found solace in the company of Descamps' delightful daughter Denise, a dark, piquant young lady with a figure so fulsome and striking that it set off even simple clothes to advantage. Jack spent most evenings standing beside her as she played the piano, singing softly to her in his light tenor voice. He attempted to teach her songs like *The Mountains of Mourne* and *You Are My Heart's Desire*; she responded by teaching him *Parlez Moi d'Amour* and the *Marseillaise*. They were tender moments of shared musical expression and proved the most memorable aspect of Jack's stay at La Guerche. It is said a voice is given to a pretty French girl to speak and sing of love, and Jack considered Denise did both delightfully. The language barrier prompted them to communicate with each other in mime and their somewhat inept efforts usually ended with them both laughing uproariously. There is no doubt

Jack and Denise were infatuated with each other but, according to Jacques Descamps, the relationship was entirely innocent and proper.

Denise, now living in a fashionable part of Paris, cast her mind back 57 years and confirmed that she had a powerful romantic attachment to Jack:

> 'He was a nice boy and, of course, I was attracted to him. Any girl of my age would have been. He was so handsome.'

There had been little chance of a physical liaison, for the young couple were never left alone: Denise's grandmother was always there, acting as a kind of unofficial chaperone. Even when she started to nod off under the influence of some lilting melody, they had the absurd feeling she was watching over them in her sleep.

Far from resenting her constant vigilance, Jack took a great liking to the old lady. She was charming and gracious, full of fun and a willing victim when frequently he played courtier to her. He loved her little scream of delighted surprise when he brought her a small tribute of flowers plucked from nearby woods, or marched across the lawn playing the *Marseillaise* on his mouth-organ. He would bow to her with all the elegance of a Beau Brummel and intone with great vehemence, '*Bien*!' or '*Voilà*!', to which she would respond by raising her hands and eyebrows in a gesture of mock surprise. She was especially fond of the song *Carrigdhoun*, which had been such a favourite in Jack's home as a boy. It describes the lament of the girl left behind when her man goes off to become an Irish soldier of fortune. The chorus goes:

> 'Tis but a chance –
> He's gone to France
> To wear the fleur-de-lis!'

Jack had sung it for his friends the night before he left London for La Guerche and he sang it again and again for Denise and her grandmother, who, failing to comprehend the rest of the words, cried with enthusiastic understanding, '*Ah, la fleur-de-lis*.' So he always repeated the chorus a few times, just for her.

On some evenings, Denise and her 'Beeg Irish' danced to radio music from London while Jack's sparring partners – huge, heavy and sinister-looking men, according to Pembroke Stephens – sat silently, and possibly a trifle enviously, in a corner of the room. Afterwards, Jack would sing to Mademoiselle's piano accompaniment and play his great favourite, *The Minstrel Boy*, on the mouth-organ. The proceedings invariably ended abruptly, just as he was getting into his stride. 'Ten o'clock, Jacques. Time for bed,' would say the strict but fatherly François Descamps.

Those pleasant evenings of music and laughter reminded Jack of his formative years in Cobh and served also to provide a pleasant interlude to the drudgery of training, which increasingly he was finding frustrating and unrewarding. His progress in adapting to the new techniques being taught him was so laboriously slow that one month had ground monotonously into two before finally, and much to Jack's relief, Descamps informed General Critchley in London that he had made sufficient improvement to be able to return to the ring.

Never could anyone have packed their bags so quickly and eagerly as did Jack on the eve of his departure. The word quickly went round that he was leaving, and next day the whole village turned out to bid him *au revoir*. Everyone seemed sorry to see him go, except perhaps the local swains. There were tears from Denise, and people came running from their fields and their gardens and kitchens. Kisses were blown and dainty handkerchiefs waved as the car set off for Paris. One last hand-clasp, one more glance backwards, and so farewell.

Adieu, my pretty ones. *Adieu, ma jeunesse.*

Exit Monsieur Jacques.

Chapter 7

Petersen and perdition

The return to London was everything Jack could have hoped for after the loneliness of La Guerche. It felt good to be in the spotlight once more as he faced reporters eager to record his impressions of France and his progress under the tutelage of François Descamps. Pens and notebooks at the ready, they hung on his every word as if he were a Prime Minister about to pronounce on the parlous state of the economy and the measures being taken to put it right. But this was no Stanley Baldwin: this was a boy whose business was boxing and whose celebrity was such that he commanded a Press coverage as big as any political leader.

Jack chose his words carefully. He knew it would be an enormous insult to a generous and charming host if he admitted he had been bored out of his mind in La Guerche and had achieved so little in the way of improvement that the whole exercise had been a waste of time and money. Instead, he came out with fighting talk calculated to attract maximum publicity and make a championship showdown with Jack Petersen an irresistible proposition.

'I have come back to challenge Petersen for the British title,' he announced grandly. Then, cleverly, he fuelled the hopes and expectations of all who had been waiting in anticipation of his exciting raw talent being fashioned into something resembling the perfect fighting machine when he claimed: 'I have found the punch that will win me the world title.'

Petersen's swift response paid due heed to the fact he could earn considerably more for a title defence against this cocky, precocious Irishman than any other challenger. 'I want £5 000 to fight Doyle – win, lose or draw,' he said, sharpening still further the public appetite for a fight that was rapidly becoming Britain's most sought-after sporting confrontation.

Jack, in turn, felt he could take the unbeaten Welshman apart, not by employing the strategy so patiently and persistently taught him by Descamps, but by reverting to the old-style Dempsey power punching that had brought him to the brink of a huge fortune in the prize-ring.

General Critchley, suitably impressed by Jack's diligent application to his training as outlined in a glowing testimonial from Descamps, was keen to match him with Petersen in a bonanza open-air promotion at White City. Having splashed out 5 000 guineas for Jack's management contract and a further substantial sum in fees and expenses for his tuition in La Guerche, it was time to balance the books.

In a bid to bring public interest in the fight to the boil, a two-point plan was hatched out between Critchley and Sullivan. Part one involved a warm-up bout as proof that Jack's recent French lessons had equipped him with the body language necessary to present him as a credible contender for Petersen's crown. An experienced Belgian, Jack Humbeeck*, was selected to be the fall-guy in a scheduled 15-rounder at London's Olympia. Humbeeck was well known in British rings, having acquitted himself with distinction back in 1924 when taking the up-and-coming Phil Scott, the body-beautiful, to a 10-round points decision. But the bloom of youth had long since faded from old Jack's jowls. He had failed to last a round in 1931 against another future British champion, Reggie Meen, who had since been dethroned by Petersen. On that basis he appeared to Critchley and Sullivan to be the right man for the job.

As was now his custom, Jack set up his training camp in Windsor – 'More serious, more of a man than the playful youth he was before he went to France,' according to one observer. His uncharacteristically solemn demeanour owed less to a growing maturity than to the fact he was feeling distinctly uneasy about the contest. The opponent, Humbeeck, was not the cause of his concern; it was a nagging fear that the fans and the media would be anticipating a marked improvement in his boxing and judge him accordingly. But the pilgrim path had taken him to La Guerche, not Lourdes, and anyone hoping for a miraculous transformation would be sadly disillusioned.

Nevertheless, come the fight, he did his best to apply the lessons taught him in France, tucking in his chin and jabbing out left hands in an attempt to force an opening for his crushing right. Descamps had instructed him to bring the right hand back quickly to protect his own chin in the event of a countering left from his opponent – a manoeuvre that had the effect of restricting him from following through properly with the punch and robbing it of its destructive power. This drastic departure from his normal fighting style may have been all very well when sparring with a couple of ponderous Frenchmen in a hut at the bottom of Monsieur Descamps' delightful rose garden, but making a fool of himself in front of his adoring public back in London was a

* Alternatively spelt Humbeck or Humbeek.

different matter entirely. He concluded that unless he changed course quickly, he stood more chance of sending his audience to sleep than Humbeeck.

In the second round he dispensed with probing patiently for an opening and unleashed his right hand with all its former venom, swinging it round in its customary wide arc from somewhere down around the hip and following through with the full force of his powerful shoulders behind it. Ungainly, yes, but devastatingly effective. Humbeeck crashed to the canvas and lay motionless while the referee counted him out.

Once again Jack had followed the boxing gospel according to Dempsey and come out an easy winner. The reformation preached by Descamps had prove a false doctrine and he wanted nothing more to do with it. One newspaper report questioned whether the lessons learned in La Guerche had robbed Jack of his punch, but there were no major inquests. Instead the Press and the public began clamouring for him to be given his chance at the championship.

The time was now ripe for part two of the Critchley–Sullivan plan. The object on this occasion was to mount a huge publicity build-up based on Jack's growing popularity as a singer. Sullivan remembered how Jack often sang and played the mouth-organ and melodeon at his home in Clapham before getting big ideas about himself and taking off for the ritzy world of the West End. He had considered then that his young protégé possessed a voice that could bring him as much acclaim on stage as his fists had in the boxing ring – an opinion since reinforced by the esteem in which Jack was held in society circles, where his McCormack-style tenor had made him the darling of the smart set.

In an article in the Sunday newspaper *The People* in 1954, Sullivan told how he invented a story that Jack had signed up for a month of singing engagements in theatres around the country at a staggering £750 a week. He claimed he produced a fake contract in order to 'validate' his claim and boasted that the newspapers 'fell for it'.

Sullivan said that next day, armed with a bundle of Press cuttings, he called to see London Palladium impresario George Black – a friend of some years' standing – and arranged for Jack to make a guest appearance in the highly-popular Crazy Gang show that was destined to become something of a show-business legend. Each morning for a week Jack sang and rehearsed a routine with Crazy Gang comics Bud Flanagan and Teddy Knox. By the time the big day arrived his performing technique was polished and professional.

His reception when Flanagan conveniently spotted him in the audience and called him up from his seat in the stalls to, 'Give us a song or two, Jack', was rapturous. Sullivan claimed he had seen to that by securing £50-worth of tickets in advance and stationing people at various points around the famous theatre. Jack's performance was the predictable knockout; his tear-jerking rendition of *Mother Machree* brought such sustained applause that he was forced to do an encore – seemingly spontaneous but in fact very well rehearsed – during which he sang a duet and exchanged gags with Flanagan. The audience loved it and so did the music business. Afterwards Jack was besieged by agents and offered enough work to keep him on stage full-time for the foreseeable future. Presumably acting on prior instructions from Sullivan, he turned them all down flat. 'Tis a fighting man I am,' he said, emphasising his Irishness. 'I sign no contracts till I fight for the championship.'

The Palladium appearance was a master stroke – and stroke is the operative word if Sullivan's account of the lead-up to it is to be believed. Yet there is no evidence of publicity in connection with a Jack Doyle singing tour at that time, phantom or otherwise. Sullivan's claim that he visited George Black 'armed with a bundle of Press cuttings' has to be taken with a pinch of salt, as must his assertion that he hired a *claque*. It seems more probable, and certainly more plausible, that Jack was offered what was termed a 'surprise guest' spot on the bill and the news then deliberately leaked to stimulate box-office activity. As things turned out, the rush for tickets when the story broke caused such a sensation that the Palladium could have been filled many times over.

The publicity value emanating from the Palladium appearance was immense, with Jack depicted as a man who had turned down the chance of a fortune on the stage to pursue his first and only real love. This added strongly to his appeal as a fighter. His image was enhanced by his refusal to compromise his boyhood dream of glory in the ring for the rich and easy pickings of a singing career that were his for the taking.

Jack did agree to an offer from recording company executives that would enable him to maximise his appeal as a singer off-stage. On May 28, 1933, just two days after his Palladium performance, he made his first record at the Decca studios in London. On the 'A' side was his show-stopper *Mother Machree* and on the flip side another native ballad rich in sentiment, *My Irish Song of Songs*. In those days of unsophisticated recording techniques there were no lengthy rehearsals with a band, no multitudinous backing tracks superimposed on one master tape. Jack was in and out of the recording studio in a day, having performed with solitary piano accompaniment. The record, the first of eleven with Decca, was released the following month. It was followed quickly by another featuring two more Irish favourites, *Little Town in the Old County Down* and *Where the River Shannon Flows*.

Sales figures for these and subsequent Jack Doyle records in the 1930s no longer exist. Likewise there is no information on Jack's earnings from them, though they are thought by Decca to have been 'considerable'.

The timing of the first two records was an all-important consideration as far as the Petersen fight was concerned. It was vital that Jack's soft tenor tones would be wafting over the air-waves and into people's living-rooms in the weeks and days leading up to the championship showdown at White City.

Jeff Dickson had been called in to promote the big fight, his brief being to negotiate with the champion's father and manager, Jack 'Pa' Petersen, over the Welshman's purse. The bargaining was tough, with the Petersens demanding and eventually getting the £5 000 they had originally sought.

Having secured Petersen's signature, there came the apparently minor detail of reaching an agreement on Jack's fee for the fight – and in that regard it was assumed he would be grateful, as challenger, to accept a comparative pittance just to get his chance. But Jack was growing up fast. He realised he was the one who would be bringing the public through the turnstiles; he knew also that in addition to collecting a 25 per cent management commission from his earnings, White City would profit from the gate receipts.

The situation was further complicated by the fact that Sullivan, whose financial interest in Jack should have ended when he collected 5 000 guineas for his contract, considered himself still entitled to a 25 per cent management stipend. Jack insisted on receiving a sum similar to that agreed with the Petersen camp, and it was a measure of his growing disillusionment with Critchley and Sullivan that he conducted his own negotiations in a bid to pinpoint the precise amount. That he should have found it necessary to by-pass his managers *and* the promoter and talk terms with a third party in an effort to secure what he saw as a fair deal was a unique occurrence in British boxing.

His intermediary was White City director Frank Gentle, with whom he agreed a sum of £3 000 net. He asked Gentle to put it in writing and Gentle did so. The date of his letter – June 29, 1933 – shows there was less than a fortnight to go to the big fight on July 12, suggesting that some tough in-fighting had taken place before the figure was fixed. Gentle wrote as follows:

> 'Dear Jack,
>
> Please confirm our conversation that the terms of the fight with Petersen are that you are to receive £3 000. This is of course clear to you and exclusive of personal and training expenses. Best of luck in your training.'

Jack's reply, dated July 3, read:

'Dear Mr Gentle,

Thank you for your letter agreeing that I am to receive £3 000 win, lose or draw for the Petersen fight, clear of training expenses and commission. Hoping you are well and to see you soon.

Yours truly,
Jack Doyle.'

Apart from the money, there was another compelling reason behind Jack's desire to get written confirmation from White City. The key to it lies in the words '£3 000 *win, lose or draw* . . .' Jack wanted to be certain of receiving his purse in full whatever the outcome of the fight because he feared not only that he *would* lose, but that he would do so in sensational circumstances. The plain, unpalatable truth is that he had contracted a venereal disease, the symptoms of which – according to ex-fighter Billy Barnham, who fought George Daly (Tommy's brother) on the same White City bill – he had first noticed shortly after a visit to Murray's Club in London's West End. Jack had become slightly drunk after being plied with drinks by a host of well-to-do people. There were glamorous women in attendance, one of whom foisted her attentions on him. He did not know her, but she was pretty, well-formed and available. The drinks had gone to his head and he spent the night with her. Now he could hardly recall what she looked like, least of all remember her name. But she had certainly left her mark. Indelibly so.

Jack confided to Barnham, one of three boxing brothers and now an octogenarian London taxi driver, that he had been 'running rotten' with the disease; but he did not reveal to him its precise nature, whether gonorrhoea or syphilis. Barnham also learned of his absolute conviction that he had been set up – that the girl was a moll who had got him into bed with the express purpose of passing the complaint on to him.

At first Jack had failed to recognise the symptoms and their significance: he thought the irritation would quickly abate and consequently neglected to seek medical opinion.* However, as the days went by he was left in no doubt as to what was wrong. The pain, especially when passing water, was excruciating and, with insufficient time available for treatment, his mind was in turmoil. In the thirties, before the advent of penicillin and antibiotics, no advanced method of dealing successfully with venereal diseases was available and it would take several weeks to effect a cure.†

* Symptoms can manifest within a week of infection.

† Treatment in pre-penicillin days consisted of irrigating the infected area with chemicals and applying antiseptic ointments. In the case of syphilis, doses of arsenic (Salvarsan) and bismuth were administered intravenously.

The fight had originally been scheduled for June, but White City announced a postponement to enable Jack to undergo treatment. The excuse given was that he had injured his back in training. But even after receiving the requisite medication, Jack was still in no fit state to enter the ring by the new date of July 12. This was brought home to him during training at the Dumb-Bell Hotel in Taplow, just a short route march from his old stamping ground at Windsor. He felt uncommonly listless as he went through the motions of sparring, shadow-boxing and exercising in the well-equipped gymnasium of the hotel, whose facilities had been provided free of charge in the knowledge that Jack's presence would draw the public there in droves. Each day the hotel was besieged by hundreds of admirers, the vast majority of them women. They cheered and applauded and shrieked and giggled as they sat on the hotel lawn watching a bare-chested Jack indulging in a leisurely game of tennis. Jack ignored all advice to shield himself from the sun; he was doing what came entirely naturally to him: playing to the gallery. Despite his physical malaise he felt it would have been churlish not to put on a show for his fans, some of whom had obviously travelled long distances to see him. But, had they required any close-quarter contact, he would have been unable to oblige.

The Doyle party travelled up to London by train on the morning of the fight. There had been a sing-song and a game of cards the night before and Jack had sensibly retired to bed at 9.30 p.m. He *appeared* relaxed and carefree as he played a game of snooker with Sullivan before tucking into a hearty luncheon of boiled chicken. After the formality of the weigh-in he was driven to his manager's home, where he slept soundly till 6.30 p.m.

There was great excitement in London town, where the big fight had captured everyone's imagination. The betting slightly favoured the champion and the newspapers, in the main, were tipping Petersen to retain his title. One published the wording of a telegram purporting to come from Jack Dempsey and which read:

'BEST WISHES AND GOOD LUCK TO DOYLE THE IRISH BOY. TELL HIM WE EXPECT GREAT THINGS FROM HIM AND HOPE TO SEE HIM IN AMERICA SOON.'

It was a wonderful thrill for Jack to learn of his hero's support for him in his bid for glory. He hoped and prayed he would not let him down.

The tape-measure proved that Jack had filled out more than a little since being sized up for Army duty almost three years earlier:

Height	6ft 5in
Weight	15st 31bs
Neck	16¼in
Chest (Normal)	42½in
Chest (Expanded)	47in
Waist	33in
Thigh	24in
Calf	16in
Ankle	11in
Biceps	16¼in
Forearm	13¼in
Reach	80in

The capital was at a standstill on the evening of the fight. All roads leading to the magnificent White City Stadium, with its imposing concrete edifice and huge banks of terracing, were jammed by long lines of cars and taxis and awash with crowds of people who had spilled from the pavements. There was chaos as police attempted to control the traffic and the heaving masses.

Jack and his entourage were forced to run the gauntlet after deciding to abandon their taxi half a mile from the stadium. Star-struck admirers could not believe their luck; they besieged him with such animated fervour that at one stage he was in danger of disappearing beneath a sea of well-wishers. Sullivan, trainers Alf Hewitt and Fred Duffett and the ever-vigilant Bill Doyle had the tough and at times hazardous job of fighting off the fans. One woman armed with a pair of scissors attempted to cut off a lock of Jack's hair.

Once inside the sanctuary of the dressing-room, Jack's behaviour – high on nervousness and dread – entered the realms of the outrageous. 'He started playing the role of court-jester,' recalled Bill Doyle. 'He began laughing, joking and singing. No one would have believed there was a big fight ahead.' He ignored Sullivan's exhortation to, 'Relax, Jack, lie down and rest.' Instead he engaged those around him in light-hearted banter as he pored over the dozens of telegrams that had arrived and took stock of several quite elaborate bouquets. Only when his hands had been bandaged in preparation for gloving-up did Jack finally manage to compose himself. He stretched out and closed his eyes for a few minutes, seemingly oblivious to those around him as, inwardly, he summoned help to aid him in the heat of championship battle.

Jack knew he would need some kind of miracle, an infusion of supernatural strength, to enable him to wrench the title from Petersen's grasp. His biggest worry was that in the event of his failing to finish the job early, he would be punched senseless by the educated fists of ex-public schoolboy Petersen and become a laughing stock, a figure of fun, a boy who could sing but could not fight. Jack feared the spectre of humiliation like most people fear death. His phobia had its roots in his austere upbringing in the Holy Ground, when it was humiliation enough to have been brought up in poverty. That was something over which he'd had no control: he had been born into it. But it fostered in him a resolve that he would never be a victim of circumstance in the areas of his life he *could* control. This is what spurred him to become such a formidable fighter. The thought of defeat was anathema to him. From his earliest scraps in the quarry in Queenstown, through his waterfront battles with men twice his age, to the pulsating punch-ups with Pettifer and Bouquillon, in which he had turned imminent first-round disaster into stunning second-round victory, the sense of shame he would have felt in defeat was the crucial motivating factor.

Though yet to be beaten in any contest, he could be forgiven for thinking his run was about to end. He doubted with a deep sense of foreboding that his appeal to Providence would be answered. He had always been a good Catholic as a boy but, since his rise to fame, he had allowed himself to be diverted from regular attendance at Mass and from saying the night and morning prayers that had always been such a comfort to him, especially during his first days in England. Because he was now turning to prayer more or less as a last resort, he was uncertain as to its efficacy. A spurned God might not help him at all. Or, worse, punish him by making sure he lost!

What a dilemma he faced. His championship challenge was the realisation of all the hopes and dreams he had nurtured since boyhood. Victory over Petersen, two years older and unbeaten in 23 fights, would put him within reach of the world crown that had been worn with such distinction by Jack Dempsey. In normal circumstances he would have been ecstatic that his big opportunity had arrived and brashly confident that his power of punch would prove too much for anything the more skilful Petersen could produce. Now he was having to ponder near-certain defeat before he had even thrown a punch in anger.

As before the Pettifer fight, he was bitterly regretting his decision not to pull out. He had got away with it then by virtue of Dan Sullivan's swift intervention and a do-or-die effort in which he had discovered unknown reserves of strength. But a touch of 'flu was nothing compared with the illness he was suffering from now and, short of blasting Petersen to defeat in the opening rounds, he feared that nothing would save him.

Jack had half considered acquainting the Board of Control doctor with the facts during his routine pre-fight medical, but thought better of it in the light of what might have been printed in the newspapers. Even so, he was amazed the doctor did not suspect anything during an almost cursory examination of his genitals. Now, as he lay waiting for the call to action, he was in a state of acute agitation. A dose of the clap would have been bad enough in any circumstances, but the thought of having to fight possibly 15 championship rounds against a man as fit and formidable as Petersen was alarming.

A resounding roar went up when he appeared in the arena and began making his way to ringside, his outwardly jaunty demeanour contrasting dramatically with the unrest within. An even mightier cheer rang out as he climbed through the ropes resplendent in a dressing-gown of emerald green, which he removed to reveal a sun-tanned torso. His green satin shorts with white waistband had his initials and a shamrock embroidered in gold on either leg. The green, white and gold of Ireland symbolised what Jack Doyle stood for that night at White City. He was the first native of Eire to challenge for the heavyweight championship of Great Britain – permitted to do so because his country had been under British rule when he was born in 1913, just 19 years and 315 days earlier.

The spectators packed into the arena craned their necks as he bowed like an actor to the audience and blew kisses to the women at ringside, many of whom he obviously knew. He then engaged those around him, including the MC, in cheerful conversation while awaiting the entry of the champion, who had captured the title a year earlier to the day by knocking out Reggie Meen at Wimbledon.

The seconds ticked by, but there was no sign of Petersen. The seconds turned to minutes and still Petersen had not put in an appearance. The agonising delay succeeded in heightening the tension and excitement and the atmosphere was electric as it began to dawn on Jack that he had suffered his first setback before a punch had been thrown. He had been duped by the oldest trick in the boxing book: that of champion cleverly keeping challenger waiting in a bid to unnerve him. The tactic had worked, but surely not in the way Petersen and his father-manager had hoped. Instead of Jack being reduced to a feeble bundle of nerves, the champion's waiting game had served to bring a slight flush to his cheeks. His calm exterior began to give way to a look of anger. Any trepidation he had felt beneath the surface during his theatrical, gladiatorial entrance had been superseded in the interim by a feeling of contempt for Petersen.

Jack's brown eyes flashed ominously at the Welshman as the referee, Cecil 'Pickles' Douglas, brought them together in the centre of the ring to deliver a pronounced lecture on what he expected of both men. Petersen nodded in acquiescence but Jack paid not the slightest attention, jigging about on his toes and impatient for the bell to ring. He was so keyed up that he went out for the first round in a blinding temper. The huge crowd roaring him on, he steamed into Petersen aiming blows in all directions, disregarding the referee's warnings and apparently oblivious to the consequences as punch after punch thudded home below the belt.

Petersen, rocked back on his heels by the onslaught, at first attempted to box his way clear of trouble. When this proved unsuccessful, he unleashed his heaviest blows in a bid to stem the wayward tide of punches that was threatening to engulf him. But Jack appeared impervious to Petersen's punches and the round ended with the two men slugging it out toe-to-toe in the centre of the ring.

Referee Douglas, a fussy, no-nonsense official, visited Jack's corner before the start of the second round to warn him that any further transgression of the rules would result in instant disqualification; but so great was the din from the crowd, even during the one-minute interval, it is doubtful if Jack even heard him.

The champion began the second session on his toes while Jack, with a faint trace of a smile, again went straight for the kill. Petersen dodged a vicious right that would have torn his head from his shoulders, then stabbed a left to the body. The two men went to close-quarters. 'Break!' bawled Douglas and his command was obeyed. According to ringside reports Jack then again caught Petersen low, whereupon Douglas called a halt and, beckoning dramatically to the MC, indicated he had been disqualified.

Irish Jack at once offered his hand to Welsh Jack in a token gesture of sportsmanship, tossing back his head in defiance as he did so. In this manner he was acknowledging the outcome while at the same time indicating that he did not accept Petersen was the better man.

Recalling the fight in *Boxing News* more than 13 years later, Peter Varley wrote:

> 'Immediately Doyle was disqualified the storm broke and in the whole of my life I have never heard such an uproar.
>
> The majority of the spectators in the far-away seats had not been aware of Jack's transgression of the rules and were utterly dismayed to realise the contest had been ended.
>
> They booed everyone out of the ring, they booed the next pair of fighters that entered and they booed continually throughout every round and every interval. They were still booing when finally they had to leave the arena.'

The fight had lasted just 213 seconds, each one of them filled with drama. The crowd had been unable to believe that a contest so rich in promise had finished in such ignominy. They had been robbed of the spectacular ending that the previous fast and furious action had suggested was only seconds away.

As the enormous throng spilled from the stadium to make their way home, their anger gave way to an almost funereal solemnity. There was an air of bewilderment. The fans were at a loss to understand why the fight had been stopped. From their various vantage points around the cavernous arena it had been impossible to notice that a number of Jack's punches had strayed below the champion's waistline. Only those close up at ringside could detect the illegality of the blows. Even then it was difficult to tell. If Petersen had fallen writhing in agony, *à la* Bouquillon, perhaps the crowd would have been able to understand; but the fact he had shown no noticeable signs of distress gave rise to the inevitable conclusion that Jack had been robbed, or at the very least harshly treated, and this opinion still exists today. The feeling among many old-timers is that, having got away with dubious tactics against Bouquillon, Jack was made to pay in full measure against Petersen when he scarcely deserved it.

In Ireland, where they had become convinced of Jack's invincibility after his heroic display against Pettifer, the result was received with profound disbelief. The massive crowd that filled the square outside the offices of the *Cork Examiner* was grief-stricken, as if news of some great national tragedy had just filtered through. Gradually, the numbing sense of shock gave way to indignation. The feeling was that Jack must have been robbed – disqualified by an anti-Irish referee when seemingly well on the way to victory.

Morale was also at an all-time low in Jack's dressing-room. It was under siege as, voice choking with emotion, he related his version of the events that had turned his boyhood dream into an adult nightmare. Barely pausing for breath, the shock of defeat making him sound almost delirious, he babbled:

> 'I just sailed right in, knowing so many of the folks from Ireland were watching me, and said to myself, "I'll finish it quick." I suppose I did hit low, because everyone says I did, but it will never happen again.'

Then, as if to convince himself the defeat was just a temporary hiccup in his quest for greatness, he declared:

> 'I was disqualified because I am so young and inexperienced, but I can beat anyone alive and one day I shall be champion of the world.'

They were defiant words spoken from the heart – a broken heart. Jack was down and he was trying to pick himself up. To salvage some pride.

Respected fight historian Gilbert Odd, formerly editor of *Boxing News*, is convinced that if the referee had been anyone other than Pickles Douglas, Jack would not have been disqualified:

> 'Doyle was a bit unfortunate in that respect. He just happened to have the wrong ref. Douglas had obviously taken after his father, John Douglas, who was the strictest and fussiest referee I have ever seen. He would think nothing of disqualifying a fighter in the last seconds of a 20-rounder.'*

Petersen was in no doubt that the frequency with which Jack's powerful fists pounded his nether regions made it extremely unlikely they were stray blows delivered in the heat of the moment. Aged 79 and president of the British Boxing Board of Control when he died in 1990, he said:

> 'Doyle must have hit me low 14 times in all, and the punches put a huge dent in my protector. Had I not been wearing it, I would never have fought again. He could have crippled me for life. The fight itself I can only describe as an absolute farce. It was a disaster as far as British boxing was concerned.'

The fact is that Petersen walked away from the fight as champion – and £5 000 the richer. It was Jack Doyle who had to deal with disaster.

* *Pickles Douglas* came from a sporting family. His elder brother, J. W. H. T. Douglas, was an England cricketer. As might be expected, considering the mentality of his brother and father, J. W. H. T. was a stone-waller as a batsman. This, and his elongated initials, led to him being dubbed 'Johnny Won't Hit Today' Douglas.

Chapter 8
The fight for justice

If Jack had thought the disgrace of disqualification was the end of the matter, he would be sadly disillusioned. His entire £3 000 purse was withheld pending an investigation. This took place a week later and was considered the most momentous ever undertaken by boxing's governing body. The portents were ominous for Jack. He could sense the mood was one of outright hostility toward him.

The Board of Control's stewards* first considered the report of the referee, their fellow-steward Pickles Douglas, a London timber merchant by profession. It read:

> 'I wish to confirm my verbal report to you [Board of Control secretary Charles Donmall] on the disqualification of Jack Doyle in his contest with Jack Petersen for the heavyweight championship of Great Britain, in which I told you I was called on to caution Doyle twice in the first round for hitting low and of one occasion on which I also cautioned him for holding, and just before the bell was rung for the termination of the round he hit low again. During the interval I again cautioned him for hitting low, which warning I told him would be definitely the last. Immediately after the resumption of the second round, in my opinion he hit Petersen low again twice, which brought about his disqualification.
>
> I consider his offence rather a serious one and *was caused by Doyle completely and totally losing his head.* Such an offence is more serious owing to it being a contest for the heavyweight championship of Great Britain.'

Any chance Jack had of escaping with a small fine or a reprimand was destroyed by Douglas's damning account of the fight which, if the stewards were to uphold, compelled them to take a tough course of action.

Jack explained to them that his mother and father depended on him totally for financial support, that since turning professional he had dutifully sent home £8 each week and that he had recently provided a

*The stewards sitting in judgment on Jack Doyle were: Col. R.E. Myddelton (chairman), Charles Donmall (secretary), Lord Tweedmouth (vice-president), Sir William Bass, Jack Onslow Fane, Dr T. Marlin, C.H. Douglas (referee), P.J. Moss, E. Horace Holme, Dr R. Melville Hilley and the Board's solicitor G.R. Ellis Danvers.

comfortable home for them at 65 College Road, Cork. He expressed his sincere regret about hitting Petersen low and pleaded that any financial penalty would place an intolerable burden on his family.

The stewards listened solemnly to Jack's almost tearful submission – then sent him outside while they debated the issue. He had felt more like a prisoner in the dock than a boxer who had infringed the Board's rules and it made him fear they were about to make an example of him. After an agonising wait he was recalled to be informed of the verdict, which was delivered in tones of such gravity that it was as if he was shortly to be marched off to the gallows.

The penalty the Board decided to impose was vicious in the extreme. It suspended him for six months and ruled he should forfeit £2 740 of his £3 000 purse. The balance of £260, they decreed, was to be divided equally between Jack and his mother and paid at the rate of £5 a week each for the duration of the ban. The stewards, mindful of the fact that Jack was his parents' sole means of support, were attempting to minimise the financial hardship they would suffer.

Jack was incensed by both the fine and the suspension, and announced immediately that legal action was to follow. He stood dejected outside the Board's West End offices and talked of 'this very heavy burden on a young man's shoulders'. Fresh yellow rose in the button-hole of his brown-chequered suit, he spoke sadly of being 'knocked out for the first time in my life' and added:

> 'I am not accepting any part of their ruling and nor am I looking for charity. I ask only for justice and my legal rights, and I intend to press for them. I am going to test the legality of the Board's decision.'

Jack had every right to feel aggrieved. In its determination to exact retribution, the Board's action can today be seen in its most appalling light. In spite of abundant inflation in the 57 years since, no boxer disqualified in a British title fight (and there have been many) has been fined a remotely equivalent sum. For instance, Eddie Phillips, whom Jack was later to meet in two short, explosive and sensational fights, was fined just £100 when disqualified against Len Harvey in 1938. Johnny Sullivan escaped a fine when disqualified against Pat McAteer in 1955, Terry Downes was fined £100 when ruled out against John (Cowboy) McCormack in 1959, John (Young) McCormack was fined £25 when disqualified against Eddie Avoth in 1970 and John H. Stracey merely cautioned after being disqualified against Bobby Arthur in 1972.

Blackpool's Brian London is possibly the best post-war example of a boxer incurring the Board's wrath, not through disqualification, but for defying their edict that he was an unsuitable world heavyweight title challenger in 1959. Believing he *was* good enough, and not wishing to pass up the opportunity of the biggest purse of his career, London went to Indianapolis and proceeded to prove the Board right by getting himself knocked out by Floyd Patterson. London was fined £1 000 and suspended for six months on his return to England. He considered this penalty monstrous and most everybody agreed the Board had been hard on him. London's purse was reported to have been £20 000, though he claimed it was £12 000. Whatever the correct figure, the fine was, by comparison with what was meted out to Jack Doyle in 1933, an extremely lenient one.

Jack Petersen was in full accord with the stewards' treatment of his challenger and the punishment they handed him:

> 'I thought they were quite right. They were good stewards and extremely fair. Doyle deserved what he got. It was a very important fight and it drew more people than any other contest I can recall. There must have been 90 000 there.'

Perhaps, in the opinion of the stewards, Jack had been getting too big for boxing. There is reason for believing they felt dismayed that a 19-year-old eleven-fight novice could cream off such a huge sum in prize-money and eagerly took the opportunity to divest him of it, thus in their eyes restoring some sense of sanity. Yet they had signally failed to take into account his youth and the veneer of his sophistication: he was in reality just a simple Irish lad attempting to fulfil a dream and provide a better way of life for himself and his family. That he had become so hugely popular should have been a cause for great rejoicing in official circles, since the Board – which receives a percentage of the takings from professional tournaments – was enjoying increased financial benefits because of the crowds he attracted like a magnet. Jack had established his right to become one of British boxing's biggest earners, and indeed he enabled Petersen to earn a sum of money far in excess of that which he could have commanded as a personality in his own right. Any doubts about this were dispelled by Gilbert Odd, who confirmed that Petersen was never a great attraction, and by a reference to the fight that appeared in *The Bystander* of April 26, 1933, when the bidding for Petersen had risen to £4 000:

> 'If the size of the purse is determined by the drawing power of the boxers there is no question that Doyle should be receiving the £4 000 and not Petersen, for Doyle is the man who attracts the spectators.'

The admirable James Butler was one of those convinced Jack had been treated unfairly. He noted that Walter Neusel had not even been required to appear before the Board's stewards to explain the circumstances of his disqualification against Don McCorkindale at the Royal Albert Hall six weeks earlier. Butler continued: 'No information was forthcoming on whether Adrian Anneet was asked to explain why he was disqualified for low hitting when opposing Jack Hood for the British welterweight title a couple of months ago. And I have yet to learn that Al Brown appeared before the Stewards when he was disqualified for striking Johnny Cuthbert below the belt.'

Small wonder, then, that Jack was feeling down. He had given the sport the kiss of life and in return boxing's rulers had given him the kiss of death. The folly of having gone through with the fight in the first place had become plainly apparent, the more so when he learned that General Critchley would lend neither moral support nor financial assistance toward his appeal. 'The Board have made their decision and we must abide by it,' he said curtly.

Critchley's attitude served to sour their relationship still further. Jack decided to ignore the General's urgent summonses to his office in Pall Mall, where he would always talk down to him like an officer addressing a subordinate. Notwithstanding their own official figures, White City had made a huge profit on the fight* and Jack felt he deserved support. Yet now, in the hour of his greatest need, the General had turned his back on him.

The fact that Critchley and Sullivan had known Jack was unfit to go through with the contest is apparent from his comments six years later in the *Sunday Pictorial,* forerunner of today's *Sunday Mirror:*

> 'I fouled Petersen in the first round. I admit that now, freely. I was warned that I should be disqualified if I persisted. I did persist. I fouled him again in the second round, more than once. I was ordered back to my corner, disqualified and disgraced.
>
> Why did I do it? Why did I ignore the warning I got? The plain honest fact of the matter is that I was ill, so ill I should never have been in the ring. But nobody stopped the fight before it started. I could have refused flatly to go in the ring at all. I put the public first. I did not want to disappoint the tens of thousands who were waiting for the "match of the century", not just the huge crowd who watched, remember, but the peoples of Britain and Ireland.
>
> So I fought. I knew I had only one chance. A knockout in the first two rounds. My strength would not last beyond that. At all costs, I must knock Petersen out in six minutes. A colossal task when you consider the strength and determination of Petersen. So, my nerves on edge through being kept

* Astonishingly, White City's official figures put the attendance at a mere 24 622, with receipts of £15 768-12s.6d. As already stated by Jack Petersen, the crowd appeared to be substantially bigger – certainly three or four times greater than that recorded by White City – and with correspondingly higher receipts. Gilbert Odd, who was at ringside, confirms the crowd was so huge that thousands were unable to get in.

waiting in the ring nearly ten minutes before the fight, I left my corner reckless and desperate, my mind obsessed by just one thought – I must hit and keep on hitting. In this way I became fighting mad. I did not know what I was doing. I saw red. "Hit and keep on hitting" drummed through my dazed mind. And not until I had been forced back to my corner did I realise what I had done. And that was one of the bitterest moments of my life.

Why should a fighter be ill before the fight of his life? That's a question you are entitled to ask. I am prepared to answer it frankly – I had not looked after myself. My real training for the fight had been in society circles in the West End of London. There had been women. Champagne. Late parties, luxury and licence. Night clubs. I had slipped into it all so easily. I was young. I was handsome. I had a natural, pleasing Irish personality. I could talk well and people said I could sing well. I had money from my previous fights, money I spent cheerfully on others as well as myself. So, long before the Petersen fight, I became a social lion in Mayfair. Invitations to parties poured in. I met more and more people, got more and more invitations. I was idolised by women, admired by men. I liked it. I felt on top of the world. I was only nineteen, remember .... Once I got in the smart set it was difficult to break clear, though I knew myself that I ought to give it up and keep fit for the fight with Petersen. I thought that I could win with one punch. And but for my unexpected illness, I think I should have done.'

Jack did not name the illness and few outside his inner circle were privy to the truth. The key sentences were: *'But nobody stopped the fight before it started. I could have refused flatly to go in the ring at all.'* It suggests he was under pressure to go ahead with the fight in order to save the promotion.

Now Jack had been left to pick up the pieces of his shattered career. He felt resentful toward Sullivan and Critchley,* whom he felt had let him down badly, and resolved to take matters into his own hands in an effort to seek the justice he felt had been denied him.

He made no attempt to conceal his scathing contempt for officialdom. He regarded the Board's offer as an insult which wounded pride and a sense of outrage would not permit him to accept. When he received his first £5 cheque, with the request that he notify the Board of his mother's address in order that a similar sum could be forwarded to her, he returned it via his lawyer, Edmund O'Connor.

Jack instructed O'Connor to fight the Board's controversial ruling in the High Court. In the meantime, deprived of the means of earning a living with his fists, he decided to employ his other gifts – his looks and his voice – during the period of his suspension. He considered fate had

* *General Critchley,* now deceased, made no mention of the fight in his autobiography *Critch*, published in 1961 after he had been afflicted with blindness. Oddly, there was not a single reference to Jack Doyle in the entire book.

played a part, for his singing lessons had equipped him for the role in life he now had to play. He had been taking them in preparation for the day he would have to quit boxing, but his chance had come earlier than expected. It had been forced on him and he was ready to grasp it eagerly.

He engaged an Irish comedian of his acquaintance to act as his theatrical manager. Fred Curran (real name Conway) was a stand-up comic in the Tommy Trinder mould. He had been born in Galway but brought up in Manchester, where his parents had settled when he was a child. Jack loved Curran's droll, almost impish humour and greatly respected his knowledge of vaudeville. Fred may never have succeeded in hitting the big-time but, after appearances in theatres all over Britain and Ireland, he knew everything there was to know about the business. It was to him that Jack entrusted his immediate future at this time of crisis in his young life.

Curran, outwardly a mild, almost timid figure, nevertheless proved himself a shrewd entrepreneurial operator, quickly realising that the best way to project Jack on stage was to accentuate the duality of his talents as singer and boxer. This he did by devising a programme in which Jack would first sing a selection of his favourite songs before disappearing into the wings and re-emerging for a series of exercises and shadow-boxing routines to musical accompaniment in a ring hastily erected on stage. In this way, he considered Jack would be identifying with his by then oft-stated public persona – that of the man who sang like John McCormack and fought like Jack Dempsey.

It was astute tactical awareness on the part of Curran. He had arranged for the tour to commence in Ireland, where Jack's popularity, far from diminishing in the aftermath of the Petersen debacle, had risen to new heights on a wave of sympathy fuelled by what was considered to be the rough justice meted out to him in England. That he was held in the same high esteem as any noble figure of Irish republicanism who had been martyred by the British was evident from the reception he received at Dublin's 3 600-seater Theatre Royal, at that time the biggest in Europe.

The demand for tickets for his twice-daily performances broke all known box-office records. Jack was on a percentage of the gate and his earnings averaged around £600 a week during the show's extended four-week run. His voice was a captivating blend of Doyle soprano and McCormack tenor. His material struck a perfect balance between pure schmaltz and acceptable sentimentality, and his delivery, as in the boxing ring, was executed with a perfect sense of the dramatic. He set up his audiences perfectly with perennial favourites like *The Hills of*

Donegal and *The Rose of Tralee* and then knocked them cold with his emotional rendering of *Mother Machree.*

Then it was exit McCormack to the wings, a quick change from white tie and tails to full boxing strip, and enter Dempsey. Having been held spellbound by The Voice, the fans were now to be transfixed by The Torso as Jack pushed his massive frame through a series of callisthenics and shadow-boxing routines. The physical side to the show was designed not only to keep Jack in fighting trim during his enforced absence from the ring, but also to arouse the women in the audience. In both respects it succeeded admirably. Off stage, too, Jack attracted devoted hordes, who thronged the streets whenever he so much as took a stroll.

Similar scenes greeted him when the show moved on to his native Cork, where he was appearing at the famous Opera House. It was September, 1933 – just three years after he had set sail for mainland Britain. Now, despite the disqualification against Petersen, he was the country's favourite sporting son – the fetish of the hour. And the welcome he received shook him like nothing before in his life.

Thousands lined the route as he was paraded in a jaunting car through the streets. The band played and the city throbbed. He looked down from his carriage at the fresh-faced young boys who reminded him of the cheeky lad he once was and in his mind's eye could picture himself as an onlooker at the great procession. It was hero-worship on a scale he had never experienced, not even in London. And it overshadowed even the ecstatic reception he had received in Dublin. He thanked the God of his heart for the warmth and generosity of his own Irish people, pondering as he did so the irony of his deliverance from humiliation and disgrace in England to unparalleled adulation in his own country.

He delighted in the obvious pleasure of his parents and family. His money and his fame were theirs to share. They had been forced to rough it all their lives and now the constraints had been removed, he hoped forever. But no one who has suffered the appalling indignity of poverty ever forgets: the harrowing memory of it leaves a permanent imprint on the mind that acts as insurance against complacency. According to Bill Doyle, his father gave Jack a timely piece of advice.

'A fool and his money are soon parted, son,' warned Michael Doyle, alarmed at the way Jack had been spending his money on everything from wardrobes of fashionable new clothes to expensive racing greyhounds. 'If you're not careful you'll end up in the gutter.' Jack had always respected his father, but could not resist chiding him for his apparent caution as he repeated his favourite saying: 'A generous man never went to hell.'

The warning had gone unheeded. Jack Doyle was top of the bill. He was above taking advice. He had resolved to listen to no one. And that included his own father.

*

In the New Year of 1934 – his suspension from the ring nearing its end – Jack's mind was still far from his comeback. Instead, it was again focused on the big fight outside the ring – his battle of litigation with the Board of Control.

Edmund O'Connor had engaged the eminent KC Serjeant Sullivan* to fight the case. The surname was an unfortunate coincidence in view of Jack's now less than harmonious relationship with his manager and so was the fact that this Sullivan had been unsuccessful in his defence of another famous Irish rebel, Roger Casement,† on a charge of high treason in 1916. Casement was executed.

Jack's action to contest the legality of the Board's decision to fine and suspend him was heard in the King's Bench Division of the High Court before Justice MacKinnon. Being a minor Jack was suing through a Cork man of his acquaintance, Patrick Sheehan, described for legal purposes as his 'next best friend'.

Sullivan, tall and bearded, told the court that the claim was to recover £3 000 from one or other of the defendants, namely the Administrative Stewards of the Board and White City Stadium Ltd. The money, he said, was agreed to be paid to the plaintiff for engaging in the contest with Petersen for the heavyweight championship of Great Britain.

White City's defence was that if they made the contract sued upon, they

***Alexander Martin Sullivan (1871–1959)*. Born in Dublin and educated at Trinity College. Called to the Irish bar in 1892 and to the English bar in 1899. Was third King's Serjeant in Ireland (1912), second Serjeant (1913) and first Serjeant (1920), the last to hold office, and continued to use the title by courtesy after leaving Ireland to practise exclusively in England. Said to have made brave defence of Casement in 1916, which he had undertaken out of a sense of duty although personally strongly opposed to him. Escaped an attempt on his life in 1920 when shots were fired at his railway carriage in Tralee. Sullivan figures in a painting of the Casement trial by Sir John Lavery which hangs in the Irish President's residence in Phoenix Park, Dublin. Died at his home in Beckenham, Kent.

†*Roger David Casement (1864–1916)*. Born in Kingstown (now Dun Laoghaire) and educated at the Academy, Ballymena. Born into an Ulster Protestant family, but eventually turned Catholic. British consular official. Knighted in 1911 after many years of valuable and conspicuous public work. Degraded and hanged in Pentonville prison for high treason, having been arrested on landing in Ireland from a German submarine to head the Sinn Fein rebellion. Had in the meantime attempted to deter action. Wrote the controversial *Black Diaries*, revealing his homosexual activities. They were finally published in 1960 after long suppression.

made it not as principals but only as agents for the promoter, Jeff Dickson, or his company. The Board maintained that under their rules, which they claimed were binding on Doyle, the money had been received in circumstances that entitled them to do what they liked with it.

Sullivan outlined Jack's case with impressive clarity and brevity:

'Doyle was born in August 1913 in Cork, Ireland. He enlisted in the Irish Guards, developed a taste for boxing and was bought out of the Guards as a result and put into training as a professional boxer. On March 8, 1932, he obtained his licence from the Board of Control. The Board purports to control boxing like the Jockey Club purports to control racing. That is to say, all persons connected professionally with boxing are practically compelled to take out a licence with that body.

The fight in question took place on July 12 last year at White City. Doyle was warned for striking low and when he did it again the referee, Mr Douglas, who had much experience, disqualified him for a foul. There is no allegation that Doyle intentionally or dishonestly attempted foul play. As Mr Douglas says in his report: "Doyle had totally and completely lost his head."

Doyle is only a boy and there was played on him what I believe is a well-known trick. The challenger had to go in to the ring first, and when Doyle went there Peterson was kept out of the ring for a long time by his manager so that Doyle's nerves would be upset by the long wait for the contest to come on. In all events, Doyle did completely lose his head.

He refused to accept the Board's adjudication when he appeared before the Stewards on July 19, that his licence be suspended for six months, that the Board pay £5 to him and £5 to his mother for six months and the balance of the purse money be forfeited. I contend that the contract with Doyle was one made with a minor and that therefore the regulations of the Board were not binding on him.'

Justice MacKinnon was sympathetic: 'I think the proper course is to amend the claim with the words: "If there was such a contract, then the defendants were not entitled to rely upon it by reason of the infancy of the plaintiff at the time it was effected." '

The Board had considered the case of sufficient importance to warrant their engaging the services of one of the country's leading experts on the law of contract, Mr D.N. Pritt, KC,* a man renowned for

* *Dennis Nowell (Johnny) Pritt*. Born in Willesden, London, in 1887 and educated at Winchester. Self-taught as a lawyer and called to the bar in 1909. Made a study of every case in Sir William Anson's *The Principles of the English Law of Contract* (1879). Was variously a member of the Conservative, Liberal and Labour parties. Elected Labour member for Hammersmith North in 1935, he was expelled from the party after writing a book defending the Soviet attack on Finland. Independent Socialist MP for Hammersmith from 1945–50. Prolific writer. Three volumes of his autobiography were published in *The Times* following his death in May 1972.

his inexhaustible mental energy – he could go 24 hours a day without sleep – and phenomenally retentive memory.

However, for all Jack's youth and comparative lack of intellect, he proved he could look after himself when cornered by a skilled interrogator in court. He appeared not in the least overawed by Pritt's formidable reputation and dealt competently with his probing questions.

In answer to the portly, bespectacled Pritt, he agreed that the control of the Board had been a good thing for boxers.

Pritt: You have no complaint about your treatment by the stewards?
Jack: I thought they were severe. There is quite a lot I could tell you which I think was unfair. For instance, I was not treated fairly financially.
Pritt: That is because you did not get the money?
Jack: Yes. I was surprised they did not give it to me.

Jeff Dickson told the court that three minutes after the contest he was ordered by Lord Tweedmouth, one of the administrative stewards, to send Doyle's £3 000 to the Board, and that he forwarded a cheque for that amount. The two letters that had passed between Jack and White City director Frank Gentle before the contest were then read in evidence and the hearing adjourned.

Chapter 9

Grand larceny

The date is March 8, 1934. Jack is stretched out on a table in the gymnasium that has been specially constructed for him by the millionaire builder and developer Eugene O'Sullivan. He has just run six miles through Kentish lanes in a thick heavy sweater and now one of his trainers, Alf Denhart, is massaging his leg muscles. A telephone shrills and the message it brings spreads like wildfire through the gym. Jack springs from the table and does a jig of joy. 'I've got my three thousand pounds,' he cries. 'I've got my three thousand.' He does not dance for long, for even such eagerly awaited news cannot be permitted to interfere with a fighter's preparation. Denhart, feigning the role of the ultra-strict trainer, orders him to be seized and brought back to the table, where he proceeds to give him the best massage he has ever had.

Over in County Cork, Stacia Doyle is delighted. 'I never doubted he would win,' she says. 'I have always had faith in Jack. My husband is an invalid and Jack is our sole support. There is no finer son in all the world.'

That Justice MacKinnon* had ruled against the Board of Control was not altogether surprising. Though having to operate within a strict legal framework in which complete impartiality underpinned the whole of the judicial system, he had been quite unable to conceal his keen admiration of Jack, paying tribute to his fine physique and noting wryly that his purse for one fight was more than a judge earned in a year.

MacKinnon revealed in his summing-up that there was no contract for the Doyle–Petersen fight in existence, despite the Board's elaborate rules. He said the plaintiff had relied on oral contact with Mr. Gentle, as evidenced by the letters of June 29 and July 3, but ruled that Gentle

**The Right Hon. Sir Frank Douglas MacKinnon*. Born in 1871 and educated at Highgate School and Trinity College, Oxford. Became a barrister at the Inner Temple in 1897 and a King's Counsellor in 1914. Was a judge in the King's Bench Division of the High Court from 1924, when he was also knighted, until 1937, when he became a Lord Justice of Appeal and Privy Councillor. Wrote several books, including *The Murder in the Temple* (1935) and *Grand Larceny* (1937), the latter title perhaps unconsciously reflecting his feelings on the Boxing Board's bid to relieve Jack Doyle of his £3 000 purse. Died in 1946.

was merely informing Doyle of terms agreed between manager Sullivan and promoter Dickson on his behalf.

The judge could not accept the referee's assertion that because he had warned Jack twice, the punches must have been deliberate. 'Doyle was not charged at the inquiry with committing a deliberate foul and the money was not forfeited on that ground,' he said. MacKinnon decreed that Doyle was bound by the Board's rules that were supplied to him when the licence was granted, including one that stated a boxer's money would be stopped only when he was disqualified for committing a deliberate foul. In June, 1932, that regulation was amended to provide that, in the case of disqualification, boxers were entitled to receive only their expenses pending the decision of the Board on the circumstances of the case, when the Board might deal with the money as it thought fit. The plaintiff was bound by the rules supplied to him when the licence was granted, but not by rules of which he had no knowledge.

He said he accepted Doyle's evidence that he knew nothing about the new rule, had never received a copy of it and had received no notification of the alteration. He contended that the Board acted under the power of the amended rule when dealing with Doyle, but held that the Board had made no effort to call evidence that any amended rules or notice of alteration was ever sent to the plaintiff. In those circumstances, he concluded, the plaintiff would have been bound by the old form of Paragraph 16 of Regulation 20, but was not contractually bound by the new form of that paragraph. Judgement was for the plaintiff against the Board for £3 000, with costs, and also for White City Stadium Ltd, with costs.

The Board's stewards immediately served notice of appeal, as was their right in law; but the fact that they were not prepared to accept his verdict clearly rankled with MacKinnon. Concerned that Jack would have to wait some further considerable time before receiving the £3 000 he had deemed was rightfully his, he took the unusual step of allowing the sum of £500 to be paid to him immediately.

Jack was not unduly worried that an appeal had been lodged. His name and reputation had been vindicated in the High Court and the full purse from the Petersen fight would be coming to him after a time; he preferred to believe it had been merely deferred. That comforting thought did not stop him feeling bitter toward the boxing authorities. They had had their noses bloodied in public by Justice MacKinnon, yet were unwilling to take their defeat in the sporting and gracious manner they expected of their licensed boxers. He deplored the double standards by which on the one hand this autocratic – even aristocratic – body projected itself as the epitome of justice and fair play while on the other they were attempting to hang on to his £3 000 by overturning a judicial ruling.

Jack could ill afford to waste valuable nervous energy pondering the matter. He had another, more pressing confrontation to concern him, this time inside the ring where he had made his name. His comeback fight was to be at the Royal Albert Hall on March 19 against Frank Borrington of Derby. Jack was hardly relishing the prospect, for of late he had done nothing more strenuous than confer with lawyers and make a couple of records for Decca – *Ireland I Love You, Acushla Machree/I'm Away in Killarney With You* and *Thank God for a Garden/ My Home by the Wicklow Hills*, to be released in April and May respectively.

He had gone soft in his eight months out of the ring and now was trying to get fit in a fortnight. His new training establishment in St Mary Cray hardly lent itself to Spartan preparation. There was no tumble-down shack miles from civilisation; no red meat to feed on; no monastic discipline. Instead he was staying at Orpington Garden Village, with an elaborately-equipped gymnasium for his exclusive use three miles away and his own high-powered chauffeur-driven Buick in which to do his travelling. Often he was accompanied by beautiful and glamorous women. Ned Morrissey, coincidentally later to become secretary to Eugene O'Sullivan, recalled:

> 'I was coming home from school with my sister when an open-topped American car drew up alongside us. It was Jack Doyle and he had a lovely female companion with him – a brunette. He said: "Do you know who I am?" I replied: "I should think everyone in England knows who you are." He gave me a huge smile, said "Bye-bye then" and the car drove off. I don't know why he stopped, really. It could have been a bit of ego on his part. He must have wanted to know if we'd recognise him.'

O'Sullivan had created a summer training camp for Jack around the Blue Lagoon swimming pool, the finest in the south of England and which Jack, in company with the glamorous Cochran girls, had opened the previous year, in 1933. O'Sullivan, whose father hailed from Cork, was then in his early forties and considered himself Jack's number one fan. He constructed a roofed, open-air ring and indoor gym for him in a secluded wooded area adjacent to the pool, tennis court and putting green. No world champion ever had such magnificent arrangements for his training, according to one critic. Not even Carpentier, when he was preparing to meet Dempsey for the world title, could boast of finer quarters.*

Ex-boilermaker Borrington, on the other hand, was training in London. When he finished his workouts, he would board a tramcar and go back to his lodgings. Such were the contrasting fortunes of star performer and bit-player on the boxing stage.

The disparity between the two men was further accentuated when Jack made his entrance in the oval concert arena at 9.45 on the night of the fight, decked out in his now familiar emerald-green dressing gown. In customary style he bowed graciously to the crowd – 'Never was there a more handsome fighter' – and then came Borrington wrapped in red-and-white towelling. His few supporters in the vast audience cheered, but not a smile of acknowledgement flickered across his pale face.

'Go right in and have a do,' was the heavily-accented advice given to Borrington by his handlers, who must have suspected his only chance would be to catch Jack unawares before he had a chance to plant his big punches flush on Frank's whiskers.

To his credit, the bold Borrington did go right in and 'have a do'. He immediately smashed home a full-blooded right to the chin, but his heart sank to his boots as Jack took the shot without so much as blinking. There was a gleam in Jack's eye seconds later when he narrowly missed the referee with a punch as he started to unleash his heavy artillery. He crashed in lefts and rights that had his full weight behind them and then, with a blow that travelled no more than a few inches, dropped Borrington to the floor, where he lay stretched out and helpless as the seconds were ticked off by the time-keeper. 'Ten' was bawled and Jack sportingly hastened to Borrington's aid. Then, with long arm held aloft, he did a few circles of joy and saluted a chorus of appreciation for his victory.

The raw, naked aggression that belied Jack's gentle nature out of the ring had now enabled him to smash eleven of his twelve opponents into a state of sleepy oblivion in a career in which no fight had gone beyond the second round. So swift, so stunning and so spectacular had been his 83-second destruction of the hapless Borrington that his career on canvas was now set for a great renaissance. A return championship contest with Petersen was his for the asking. Once more this man of so many compelling contradictions had fired the imagination of the country; once again he stood on the threshold of glory, his Dempsey

**The Blue Lagoon* camp was utilised as the training headquarters for Britain's 1936 Olympic boxing team. A housing estate now stands on the site.

dream having been rekindled by a High Court judgment and the anaesthetising power of his right-hand punch.

Tragically Jack's comeback was to fall as flat as Borrington had done when at the mercy of his lethal fists, counted out by the ruthless opportunism of his manager and the heavy hand of officialdom. The most exciting home-grown heavyweight fighter of the century would not be seen again in a British ring for close on three years.

Jack had reached the point of no return with Dan Sullivan. He claimed that Sullivan was continuing to press for a slice of his boxing earnings, despite having pocketed £5 000 guineas for his contract and collecting a previously-agreed percentage from White City. According to Jack, Sullivan had insisted on receiving 25 per cent of his £1 000 purse for the Borrington fight and he had refused to agree. It had created an impasse between the two men and Jack found himself with no room for manoeuvre. He was bound contractually to Sullivan and White City, which meant he could engage nobody else to act as his manager. The only alternative as far as he was concerned was to stay out of the ring altogether.

Ordinarily a boxer might have accepted the situation, albeit reluctantly, and continued with his career in the knowledge that it was the only means by which he could build a life of prosperity. Jack was no ordinary boxer: he possessed other gifts, other talents. These would not only keep him at the forefront of attention but would earn him substantially more than he could secure in the roped arena that up to now had been his principal stage and where every nerve and sinew, every last ounce of bodily strength and motive power had to be employed to gain victory.

It was a different matter on the real stage, where huge public acclaim and no small fortune awaited him in return for little more than a gentle exercising of his larynx. It was an effortless, painless way to enjoy the massive popularity to which he had grown accustomed and which he now craved. And so Jack took the conscious decision to turn his back on boxing – his first and true love – just at a time when his presence in a ring would inevitably have sparked repeats of the astonishing scenes of queues forming on the mornings of his fights and of hysterical fans smashing down huge stadium gates and barriers in an effort to see him. The over-used word charisma is applied liberally to popular sports stars, but none had it in such large measure as the young Jack Doyle: not Mike Tyson, not Muhammad Ali, not Henry Cooper, not Frank Bruno, not even Ireland's much-loved latter-day hero Barry McGuigan. Speak of Jack in the same breath as Elvis Presley and The Beatles in terms of live performances and the comparison is more realistic, although as far as record sales went it was another day and another era.

Jack's first engagement was to be at London's Alhambra (now the Leicester Square Odeon), which was reopening as a music hall. The fact he had been engaged to top the bill on this prestigious occasion in preference to every leading singer and variety performer in the country bears testimony to his unique pulling power. The appearances could not have been better timed: his latest recording, *I'm Away in Killarney With You*, was proving a big success on radio request programmes.

Jack was 'a wow' at the Alhambra. His performances followed closely the routine that had proved so successful in Ireland. To quote one newspaper of the day:

> 'He opened with *Where the River Shannon Flows*, followed by *No Rose in All the World*. The audience nearly took the count when he sang *I'm Away in Killarney With You*. Then came the famous, high-kicking Cochran girls before punishing his shadow to the *Blue Danube* waltz. Then Irish jig and enter girls . . .'

The show was so successful that it toured all over the country, with full houses at every venue. According to variety agents and promoters of the day, Jack attracted girls like bees round a honeypot. He never chased after them because he never had to: they were always there at the stage door, dozens of them, clamouring for his autograph.

His boxing career had, temporarily at least, been placed on hold. The greatest pity was that a return contest with the giant Jack Pettifer – which had been in the offing as a prelude to another championship clash with Petersen – eventually fell by the wayside. The thought of him meeting Pettifer and Petersen again was enough to send a tingle down the spine. The fans would have smashed down the gates and everything else to see those two return contests, and at one stage there was still an outside chance of it all happening. However, Jack could not be persuaded to abandon the music hall for the boxing arena. He had had enough, for the time being, of being dictated to by managers, trainers and officials, and was enjoying what he considered to be a pleasant intermission. It was not to last.

On July 10, the Board's appeal against the award of £3 000 to Jack was heard. The three appeal judges – the Master of the Rolls, Lord Hanworth, and Lord Justices Romer and Slesser – first criticised Justice MacKinnon for allowing £500 to be paid to Jack. His stipulation that it should not be returnable in any event had thus reduced the right of appeal to £2 500. They then referred to the application for a professional boxing licence signed by Jack and which said: 'I hereby apply for a licence as a boxer, and if the licence is granted me I declare to adhere strictly to the rules of the BBB of C (1929), as printed, and abide by any further rules and alterations to existing rules as may be passed.'

The Master of the Rolls found that the agreement as a whole was for the benefit of the infant and that Jack could not escape his obligations under the rules on the ground of his infancy. Further, he stated, there was no ground for implying the proviso that the plaintiff should have notice of any change in the rules before the new rules became binding on him. The Board's appeal was therefore allowed and a cross-appeal by Jack (claiming that as an infant he was not bound by the regulations and was entitled to judgment on that ground also) dismissed.

It is hard to refute the conclusion of the law lords that, having been willing to apply for his licence as a minor and box under the Board's jurisdiction as such, Jack could hardly then claim the Board's rules and regulations were not binding on him. It would appear Jack was badly or wrongly advised by Serjeant Sullivan in that respect. The question of his infancy at the time his licence was granted seemed an irrelevant side-issue and should never have been pursued, even though Justice MacKinnon found in his favour on that score. Where Jack's case did appear to rest on solid ground was in relation to the fact that he had not been charged at the inquiry into the Petersen fight with having committed a *deliberate* foul. Indeed, referee Douglas's report stated the offence had been 'caused by Doyle completely and totally losing his head'. If it was conceded that the misdemeanours had not been intentional, what possible justification could the Board have had in banning him for six months and seeking to withhold all but £260 of his purse of £3 000? Jack's defence should have proceeded solely along those lines.

The appeal court's decision* plunged him into a mood of black despair. The shock to his system was such that it bred in him a hatred of officialdom that would last the rest of his life. It is difficult not to sympathise with the way he felt at the loss of the outstanding £2 500 or his decision to resurrect his boxing career in the United States. 'I am finished with England,' he said. 'I have had enough. They shan't have the chance to take my money from me again.' He wanted to hit back at the heartless boxing authorities who had accomplished what no opponent had yet succeeded in doing: they had forced him to throw in

* *Doyle v White City Stadium Ltd.* is mentioned at length as a test case in *Anson's Law of Contract* (1964), in the section dealing with contracts beneficial to infants.

the towel. Suddenly, his anger at the cruel jibes he had endured from within the sport came gushing to the surface:

> 'People are jealous of me just because I like to dress nicely, to keep myself clean and meet nice people – and nice women, too. They think that because I wash myself and dance and drink very little that I am soft and they blame all that for my bad luck as a boxer. I turned music-hall performer because it has been making me up to £400 a week for months past. I make more in a fortnight as top-of-the-bill than I've ever made from any of the fights I've had to wait months for. I am saying all this because I know that many years will pass before I put on the gloves again in this country.'

He said he would start at the bottom in the States and fight his way up. Then, characteristically, he contradicted himself by saying he wanted to fight the great Max Baer in Irish-American New York city, where Catholic Doyle versus Jewish Baer would ensure a million-dollar gate. He said a lot of things, much of it emotional invective uttered in the heat of the moment. But of one thing no one was in any doubt: he had been deeply wounded by his treatment by the Board of Control and the three appeal judges, who between them had effectively forced him into boxing exile. In the process they had robbed the country of its greatest showman and crowd-puller.

Jeff Dickson said at the time: 'I do not think Doyle will fight again.' Geoffrey Simpson, supportive as always, urged him in the *Daily Mail* to resume boxing – for his own sake. The whole country began to wake up to what it would be missing. Advice came from all quarters pleading with him to continue. Jack would have none of it; he had meant what he said and was determined to stand by it.

In August 1934 came an announcement that meant Jack's American mission would have to wait. He was signed by British International Pictures to feature in *Radio Parade of 1935* – his first movie – but BIP had a change of plan after tests at Elstree. The takes were excellent and they signed Jack immediately to play the lead role in *McGlusky the Sea Rover*, an adventure film based on the novel by A. G. Hales.

Shooting was scheduled to start in Devon, in England's West Country, later in the year. Jack was delighted to have been chosen for the swashbuckling role of McGlusky, a stowaway who becomes involved with gun-runners and falls in love with an Arab girl, Flame, to be played by the beautiful Russian-born Tamara Desni.* The role would project precisely the image he wished to portray: that of a roguish

* *Tamara Desni.* Born 1913. British-resident leading lady. Films: *Jack Ahoy* (1934), *McGlusky the Sea Rover* (1935), *Fire over England* (1936), *The Squeaker* (1937), *Traitor Spy* (1940), *Send for Paul Temple* (1946), *Dick Barton At Bay* (1950).

buccaneer of the high seas who emerges both as fearsome fighter and robust lover. Just one thing served to dampen the enthusiasm with which he viewed his screen debut. McGlusky was supposed to be a Scot and Jack would have to work hard perfecting a dialect that was as foreign to him as the French language he had failed to master after two months in La Guerche.

It was a problem he decided to put to the back of his mind until after his twenty-first birthday party celebrations in Cork at the end of August. He would then have a full month in which to adapt to Scottish vowels and consonants and grow the beard the producers were insisting was necessary for the part.

Although deprived of his purse from the Petersen fight, he could still well afford to put on a show for the folks back home. He would make it the biggest and grandest coming-of-age party ever seen in Ireland. It would provide the perfect platform for the announcement of his plan to conquer America and the world.

Chapter 10

Birthday bhoy

The cost of the great feast would be £500 – the very sum the Board of Control had forfeited by virtue of Justice MacKinnon's magnanimity. It would be money wonderfully well spent.

On the morning of the banquet Jack smiled as he examined the dinner menu: *hors d'oeuvres, turtle soup, sole, spaghetti à l'Italienne* – all to be washed down with gallons of champagne. 'There's no meat, you see,' he said to newsmen, 'but it's good Catholics we all are in Cork, and today is Friday.'

A circle of home-town friends in the ornate Imperial Hotel listened respectfully as he opened the celebrations early with a selection of his *own* gramophone records. In the adjoining banqueting hall, dozens of waiters dashed to and fro laying covers for the 300 guests. His father stood with the many remarking on the poise and assurance his son had acquired in the four years he had been in England. 'So he has, so he has,' said Michael Doyle in proud agreement.

Meanwhile, Stacia Doyle was flustered at the thought of the festivities that evening. She chased off reporters who had interrupted her busy schedule:

> 'I have to get dressed for Jack's party. And I must look after little Tim and Mick, who are only ten and fourteen and see they don't shame their mother. Then I must look to the two girls, and I haven't a moment, anyhow.'

The party exceeded even Jack's wildest expectations. It seemed the whole city had converged on the hotel in an attempt to catch sight of him and to witness the comings and goings of the glittering event. Jack looked resplendent in full evening dress as he stood arm-in-arm with Stacia at the top of the red-carpeted staircase while his guests trooped up one by one to shake his hand. Waiters scurried round with anxious looks, but their discreet signals went unheeded. Dinner could wait, for this was the food of life to Jack. They were eating out of his hand and they pumped their young king's arm with all the earnestness of a washer-woman drawing water from a well.

The protracted introductions finally at an end, dinner started an hour and a half late – as garnished and overdone as the formalities that had preceded it. Jack was seated at the head of the long table in the huge banqueting hall. When the elaborate birthday cake with its 21 lighted candles was placed before him, he rose majestically from his chair. With an almost audible hush descending over the proceedings he took in a deep breath and, using his huge lungs like a bellows, extinguished the whole bunch with one mighty puff – a good omen in Irish eyes and evidently a feat of such great moment that it was greeted with a near-hysterical burst of whooping and cheering.

Two elderly men were unexpectedly toasted at the dinner. One was Tim McCarthy, to whom Jack owed so much for putting him on the path to fame and fortune. The other was Cork's own Packey Mahoney, a half-forgotten old-timer who had fought a bruising, losing battle with Bombadier Billy Wells for the British heavyweight title in 1913, the year of Jack's birth. Both were close to tears as all assembled rose and drank their health. It was a generous gesture on the part of Jack, who had realised how much the simple honour of recognition would mean to them.

It was said that dozens of Cork's most beautiful girls footed it merrily at the party – but Jack, ever the dutiful son, took to the floor with his mother as his first partner, so he did. Then he strolled out to show himself to the crowds thronging the streets. The whole city must have heard them cheer.

The party was hailed as the greatest social gathering Cork had known and, as such, it proved a tremendous triumph for Jack. Though a huge star in England, the homage of his own people was important to him, particularly at this time of uncertainty in his life. He needed their approbation and their support, and he received both in large measure when making the announcement that he would be heading for America to win the world heavyweight title for Ireland.

First, he was destined to go into a few clinches on the film set with Tamara Desni. The love scenes, tame by modern standards, presented Jack with little difficulty. They were second nature to him. But he was in trouble with the Scottish accent he was meant to have perfected for the part of McGlusky. In the end, after much exasperation, the producers gave it up as a bad job and McGlusky the Sea Rover from the Clyde became McGlusky the Sea Rover from County Cork.

The film was made at Elstree and shot mainly on location in Devon. A low-budget Certificate 'A' picture of 58 minutes' duration, it failed to set any cinema box-office records when released in July 1935. It was later also put out on general release in the United States under the more eye-catching title *Hell's Cargo*, but again met with little success.

Though it was clear Jack would never become an Oscar-winning actor, there was a definable animal magnetism about him on screen. His unshaven features and unkempt, almost raffish appearance lent him a handsome ruggedness that was utterly compelling. The one thing that detracted from his performance was the tone of his voice; thanks to elocution lessons he spoke too haltingly and deliberately, as did most actors and actresses of the era.

Yet sartorial elegance and correct diction had proved far from a hindrance to Jack off-screen. Just the opposite, in fact. He had been mixing socially as well as professionally with stage and film people for some time – established stars like Gertrude Lawrence, Dorothy Dickson, Evelyn Laye, Jessie Matthews, and emerging stars like the lovely Ida Lupino.*

Ida was tall and sensuous, with a deep, husky voice. She had been introduced to Jack by her father, Stanley Lupino, and there was an instant chemistry between them. They were virtually inseparable for a time, seen frequently at dance-halls, the theatre and boxing tournaments. 'She was the prettiest, most gorgeous thing I'd ever seen,' said boxer Eddie Phillips, who had caught sight of them together at the Royal Albert Hall.

Ida lived a reclusive life in Los Angeles up to her death in 1995. She remembered Jack with great affection:

> 'He was awfully good-looking. There was nothing cheap or common about him and he had great charm. My father liked him very much and I remember them both teaching me how to punch. Jack demonstrated that for maximum effect you had to hit opponents to the side of the jaw and not on the point of the chin.
>
> Jack was a heck of a good fighter. He used to take me dancing and always behaved like a perfect gentleman. For a tough boxer, it was a nice side to him. He never tried to take advantage of me.'

There was no way Jack wanted to take advantage of BIP, either. They had an option on him for a further two films, but the problem lay in finding the right parts for him. The uncertainty proved irritating to

* *Ida Lupino* was born in London on February 4, 1918, the daughter of celebrated British revue and film comedian Stanley Lupino and actress Connie Emerald and descendant of a theatrical family dating back to the 17th century. She made her film debut at 14 when American director Allen Dwan was looking for an actress to play a Lolita type in his British film *Her First Affaire*. A casting agent sent Connie Emerald but Dwan showed more interest in her 5ft 6in daughter, who accompanied her on audition. Ida got the role. She went to Hollywood in 1934 and made numerous films, among the best known of which were *They Drive By Night*, *High Sierra*, *Ladies In Retirement*, *The Hard Way*, *Devotion* (as Emily Bronte) and *Roadhouse*. In 1948, she turned to directing.

Jack, who by now was impatient to cross the Atlantic and take America by storm, as Ida Lupino had hoped to do when setting off for the States just a short while earlier.

He had signed a contract with a well-known US fight trader, Walter Friedman, who liked to describe himself as a business associate of Jack Dempsey. In reality he was a business associate of the Liverpool-born gangster and racketeer Owney Madden, though John Lardner in his obituary on Friedman in *Newsweek* magazine in June 1954 emphasised he 'was not a hoodlum, or a gunman, or in any way a man of wrath.' Friedman had acted as agent for Len Harvey in the US, but left him high and dry when he mysteriously disappeared after being indicted on charges of income tax evasion. He had made a killing with 6ft 8in Primo Carnera,* but since the Italian had just been relieved of the world heavyweight title by Max Baer, he was looking for another European giant to replace him. He regarded Jack – 6ft 5in and 16 stones of prime Irish beef – as his new meal-ticket and travelled to London to complete negotiations. Jack had Fred Curran acting for him, but the pair were no match for the street-wise Friedman. They were naively steam-rollered into signing a contract guaranteeing him – and presumably Madden – an extortionate 50 per cent of Jack's earnings in the United States.

After his unfortunate experiences with Sullivan and Critchley – to whom he was still legally bound – it would have made sense for Jack not to have rushed into signing up with someone he was having to take largely on trust. Yet he seemed satisfied with the credentials of Friedman, who had hit this innocent young man with the perfect weapon – the magic name of Dempsey. He had told Jack all about 'Dempsey's ranch in the west', where he would be installed in his own gymnasium with a hand-picked team of sparring partners. The plan, according to Friedman, was for Dempsey to act as tutor and trainer while he looked after the managerial side. Further, Friedman revealed he had already booked a series of fights for Jack, the first to take place in Chicago.

In announcing the deal to the English Press, Friedman waxed lyrical about the way in which he and Dempsey would 'take Doyle along the right road and land him at the top'. He continued:

> 'If any man can handle Doyle, it is Dempsey. Like some Irishmen the boy is a bit headstrong, but there is not a heavyweight in the world who hits harder than Doyle – and don't forget he's Irish. That means a lot in the States.'

* Walter Friedman had paid off Primo Carnera's French manager, Léon See, and transported Carnera to America, where he was managed by Bill Duffy and Louis Soresi. But the real behind-the-scenes manager was Owney Madden. Friedman received a cut from Carnera's earnings.

Friedman, small, bespectacled and Jewish, had more the appearance of a hick-town storekeeper than a fight mogul, but he could certainly talk a good fight. Too good, in fact, for his pronouncement drew a challenge of possible legal action from General Critchley, who declared that White City was determined to test its rights under its contract with Jack by legal means if necessary.

Jack dismissed Critchley's warning contemptuously. He had long since refused to have anything to do with him or Dan Sullivan. Let them sue. He did not care any more. The United States was where he had set his sights for the fulfilment of his Dempsey dream and no amount of finger-wagging or threat of court proceedings from a man he had come to despise was going to stop him. He was eager to get to America early in the new year of 1935 – as eager as he had ever been as a boy in Cobh watching young men and women sail off on that great voyage of self-discovery. He remembered always being slightly envious of them, but the fires of ambition that burned fiercely inside him then were raging no less fiercely now. He needed to feel excitement, to taste adventure, to conquer new frontiers. It was part of his make-up and he would never be any different.

He hoped BIP would not take up its option. He was itching to make himself as much a household name in the States as in Britain and Ireland. He would be the Dempsey of the ring, the McCormack of the air waves and, perhaps more ambitiously, the Douglas Fairbanks of the silver screen.

Having completed McGlusky and divested himself of his whiskers, he took himself off for a winter skiing holiday in St Moritz. It was the fashionable thing to do, and doing the fashionable thing was important to Jack. The crisp, white snows of Switzerland were good for mind and body after monotonous weeks of filming; he needed to get fit and skiing, he said, would be good for his footwork. In fact, he fell so many times during his first lesson that he was more bruised than he had been after any of his fights.

Lady Thelma Furness was with Jack in St Moritz. Her romance with the Prince of Wales had been broken by the Aly Khan's relentless pursuit of her and the appearance in the Prince's life of Wallis Simpson – formerly her best friend. Jack was attracted to Thelma, but not for her beauty and her wealth alone. There had been many a pretty young society butterfly flush with money who had pursued him in Mayfair but Thelma, twin sister of Gloria Vanderbilt, was in a different league.

The notion of bedding the Prince of Wales's ex-lover appealed to Jack immensely. Just four years earlier, as a guardsman on duty outside St James's Palace, he had seen the couple, or so he claimed, in various stages of tender embrace. Now he was on friendly terms with them; he had been in their company several times at fights, at parties and at some of London's top night-spots. David Windsor was a boxing buff and he was especially fond of Jack. Thelma Furness was no less fond. In St Moritz, the highly-publicised trauma of her parting from the man destined to be king for 326 days behind her, she found Jack's company refreshing. He was dazzlingly handsome and manly, but with an Irish charm and courtesy that immediately put a woman at her ease. It was a brief but pleasant interlude, during which they were photographed together in a group of celebrities that included husband-and-wife solo fliers Jim Mollison and Amy Johnson, both good friends of Jack's.

The question as to whether Jack and Thelma Furness were lovers cannot be answered conclusively. The only clue is provided by Bill Doyle. He had accompanied Jack to St Moritz and he suggested that his brother had been successful. 'Not many got past him!' was his blunt comment.

If Jack had indeed been willing Thelma Furness into bed with him, he had also been just as earnestly willing BIP to pass up the option on his contract. On that particular point, we can be absolutely certain of the outcome. BIP decided not to pursue it.

Jack was free to head for the United States.

Chapter 11

El Dorado

It is mid-January, 1935. Walter Friedman sails from New York aboard the liner *Deutschland* en route to Ireland. His mission: to escort to the United States the man Jack Dempsey will mould in his own image and likeness as heavyweight champion of the world.

He travels alone. Dempsey is detained in New York by the imminent opening of his restaurant on a former car lot opposite Madison Square Garden.

Friedman arrives in Ireland shooting from the lip: 'They say Doyle's pretty – not a fighter but a lady-killer. He's gonna show the wise guys.' He uses words economically and makes each one count, delivering them in clipped, staccato bursts like an assassin spraying bullets from a machine-gun.

Jack stands tall and proud on the balcony of the Atlantic Hotel, ready to fire some parting shots of his own. Unlike Friedman, whom he dwarfs, he is positively effusive:

> 'In three years of my career to date I have made £25 000 between boxing, film work and stage appearances. I have signed contracts with a US film company and expect to make £50 000 from those films within the next year. I will treble my £25 000 within 18 months and be world heavyweight champion within that time. I will not return to Ireland until I am champion. When I become champion, I will not retire immediately. I will defend my title a few times and at the end of five years retire. Then I'll find a sweet Irish girl to marry and settle down in Ireland.'

The punch-line was carefully constructed – even calculated. Its execution was timed as sweetly as any knockout blow he had delivered in the ring. Having got his audience on the ropes, he went straight for the kill with a highly-charged rendition, not for once of *Mother Machree* but *Ireland I Love You, Acushla Machree,** another song rich in sentiment and which he had recorded for Decca a year earlier. He sang it with Stacia at his side, a huge arm round her tiny frame as he gazed down at her, the epitome of the loving son who, for all his wealth and fame, loved

* *Acushla Machree* means 'Darling of My Heart.'

his mother more than anyone else on earth. The cool night air hung heavy with emotion as his voice rang out around the square, the great excitement over his quest for the world title tinged with a certain sadness at the parting of the ways.

McCormack himself could not have received a greater ovation. No hero of Irish nationhood had been accorded a more spectacular send-off than that which the town of Cobh was about to give its favourite fighting son. The band played, the vast crowd cheered and bonfires were lit on the hills and high ground around town as Jack and his entourage – Friedman, Fred Curran and brother Bill – boarded the tender that would take them out to the liner *Washington* waiting in the deep. The sheer majesty of the occasion overwhelmed even the cynical, hard-nosed Friedman, who confessed he had seen nothing to equal it.

It was late evening as the *Washington* sailed out of the harbour bound for New York. The crowd continued to wave and cheer, the band played on and the sea-port of Cobh was ablaze, as if countless flares had been fired heavenward to light up the sky.

Chin nestling snugly on arms that were folded over the ship's railings, Jack was oblivious to those around him. Lost in profound thought, he watched until the town had merged with the still blackness of the night and the huge bonfires resembled dozens of flickering candles. He knew not when he would return to the place and the people he would always hold dear, but hoped it would be soon. He had promised to bring back the world heavyweight championship, but that bold vow made to the rapturous townsfolk only minutes earlier had now come back to catch him in less buoyant mood. The fierce wind that was biting ever harder as the ship left the shelter of the harbour and sailed out to sea seemed suddenly to match his mood, raising doubts as to whether he could indeed capture the prize that would immortalise his name. Words were cheap. He had been caught up in the emotion of the moment and told the people what he knew they had wanted to hear. Just as the beacons that burned all round Cobh in tribute to him had receded into the distance, the fires that had been ablaze within him were beginning to cool. He needed to stoke them up with renewed enthusiasm, to fuel them with fresh fighting passion. Far better to sink to the depths of the icy Atlantic than to return to his homeland a fighter in disgrace.

Soon all his misgivings vanished as a new tide of optimism swept over him, just as when he had first set sail for stardom four years earlier with a tattered suitcase in his hand and a dream in his heart. That dream was now tantalisingly close to reality. It was no longer on a distant horizon. It was something so tangible he could almost reach out and touch it.

There was a new world to explore, a new world to conquer.

*

Jack arrived in New York to find he was already something of a celebrity. There were dozens of telegrams awaiting him, including one from his parents and another from Dempsey. American scribes were out in force to greet him – or maybe to eat him.

He wanted headlines and he knew how to get them. He threw the newshounds some red meat, saying he'd had a raw deal in England but expected a fair deal in the States. 'My sole ambition and intention is to win the heavyweight championship of the world,' he announced without a hint of prevarication. America welcomed winners and this Irish kid knew where he was going – right to the top.

Next day there was a Press dinner in his honour at the Waldorf-Astoria. 'Get the boys on your side. Give 'em a song,' Freidman had counselled. Jack knew instinctively the right number for New York. He sang *When Irish Eyes Are Smiling* and 'the boys' could hardly believe it. 'If only he can fight like he sings,' cracked one reporter.

The surface signs were encouraging, but they disguised disturbing undercurrents. Bill Doyle recalled how he and Fred Curran were taken aside and advised that Friedman was associated with gangsters:

> 'I didn't know the identities of the people who told us, but they obviously had our interests at heart. They tipped us off that Friedman was no good – that he was mixed up with a bad bunch. They said Jack would end up being fleeced if he didn't get rid of him.'

The presence at the reception of several shady underworld characters, including Owney Madden,* lent the warning a sinister touch of realism. Bill and Fred were gripped by fear. They were innocents abroad to whom the word gangster conjured up unthinkable possibilities, from shootings in the street to being thrown from the top of skyscrapers. It had been brought home to them in somewhat stark fashion that gangsters were real flesh-and-blood people and not just characters in books and films and people's imaginations. It made them think that everything they had heard about boxing in the States was true: it was a sport run by hoodlums.

* *Owen (Owney) Madden*. Speakeasy operator, bootlegger and gangster. At one time had the dubious distinction of being Public Enemy No. 1.

Jack was singularly unperturbed. He ignored Curran's advice to sack Friedman. Contractual considerations apart, he was already receiving more publicity in America than he had imagined possible. Offers were said to be 'flooding in' for him to broadcast and appear in films. Friedman's intention was to turn Jack into a marketable commodity and in that respect he appeared to be succeeding. 'The fighting can come later,' he had told Jack. 'First we've got to make you a big name – get you noticed around town. You've got to be seen in all the right places, kid.'

Jack was the celebrity guest at an ice hockey match at Madison Square Garden, where he started the game by throwing in the puck. The singing fighter was hot news and soon he was attending the best restaurants and night-spots on Broadway – always with Friedman in tow. Flush with money from his fights, his stage appearances and his film work – Bill Doyle revealed that he had taken £3 000 with him to the United States – he was spending it like there was no tomorrow. Friedman, renowned for his love of the high life, was acting true to his reputation. Not for nothing was he known as Goodtime Charlie.

Jack was delighted to have found fame in another country and on another continent. In effect he was paying in hard cash for his own publicity, though it never occurred to him at the time: he thought it was all part of the show. He was the Great White Hope on the Great White Way, singing his Irish songs and shaking so many hands that he felt more like a US Presidential candidate than a big-time fighter and would-be screen idol. He met so many 'important' people during those early days in New York that he had difficulty in even recalling their names, still less in attaching any significance to the relevance they were supposed to have had to his career.

The image of himself he wished to project was apparent from a full-page feature article in the *New York World-Telegram*, in which he talked to staff writer Geraldine Sartain about his preoccupation with women. He told her: 'I can't get along without the beautiful creatures . . . I adore them. I love all women. I simply must have them around me all the time.' His stated preference was for blondes and he burst lyrically into French, proving at least that not everything learned in La Guerche had been forgotten. 'Ah, *cherchez la blonde*,' he said. He closed his eyes and added: '*Oui*. It is *les blondes*.' It was clear he possessed only a smattering of phrase-book French, but it did suggest a certain suavity. When asked to describe the kind of blonde that appealed to him, he did not skimp on detail:

> 'My ideal girl is tall, beautiful, not too slim, but very graceful as to figure – on the lines of Carole Lombard and with a face not unlike hers. It is very

fortunate for me that Carole is not married now. Maybe she will wait for me? [He laughed]. When I get to Hollywood I would like to make a picture with her.'

His fascination with Lombard was intriguing in view of the events that would unfold when eventually they met. As regards blondes, he had wasted little time in selecting one for intimate pleasures. Almost as soon as he set foot in America he was canoodling with a New York socialite named Peggy Joyce, whose description as an 'international charmer' sounded suspiciously like another way of saying she was a high-class hooker. Peggy was older than Jack and equipped to teach him plenty, as evidenced by his comment: 'A very sweet girl; a very sweet girl indeed. A young man needs a bit of sophistication, an experienced woman. I am only 21, you know.'

After a couple of weeks he began to tire of Broadway night-spots and being seen everywhere fashionable people went. He had dragged himself round as many as three or four in an evening. Even for Jack Doyle, that was some going. He had spent lavishly at Friedman's behest and now realised how his new manager had earned his Goodtime Charlie tag. Friedman was fond of a good time all right, but always at Jack's expense. Bill Doyle recalled:

'Goodtime Charlie was continually asking Jack for money. He told him he had to square this person or that person for services rendered. Jack did not know who they were half the time, but he was forever slipping him 20-dollar bills. He thought this was the way things were done in America. Wherever he went, he always ended up paying. He did not mind at first because of the publicity; he thought it would all pay off. But after a time he realised his money was disappearing and there was nothing coming back.'

The fact that he had yet to meet Dempsey did not bother Jack unduly, but it did concern Bill:

'The Dempsey connection was bosh. Friedman had led Jack to believe that Dempsey would be playing a major role in the development of his career, but it was not the case. Of course Dempsey was interested in Jack and prepared to give him advice, but in reality he was too busy running his new restaurant.'

The inoffensive Fred Curran, pushed into the background by the brash Friedman and unable to countenance a lifestyle of night-clubbing and making whoopee, had become disenchanted and sailed home to England. Jack was sorry to see him go, but could permit himself no pangs of remorse; he was totally in the hands of Goodtime Charlie, who decreed that the circus must keep rolling. Roll on it did – to Hollywood, 3 000 miles away. There, Jack found he had to court publicity in the same manner by paying his own way and making outlandish statements in a bid to attract attention.

He had by this time become a master of self-projection. He realised his best line of attack would be on the one hand to accentuate his appeal as a fighter by actively pursuing his ambition of a tilt at the world heavyweight title, while on the other making it known he was amenable to offers that might lead to a career in the movies. 'I will meet Max Baer in the ring or at a game of hearts – and I'll beat him at both,' he said as he toyed with a late breakfast at the Knickerbocker Hotel. 'I'll be ready to take on Baer in a year from now and poor old Max won't know what hit him.'

Cleverly, Jack had thrown down the gauntlet. He had fuelled interest in himself as a heavyweight contender by issuing a cheeky challenge to the world champion and at the same time, with an eye to a possible film contract, had emphasised with his taunting 'game of hearts' jibe his wide appeal to women. It was tongue-in-cheek Baer-baiting, but it had the desired effect. Everyone knew Jack Doyle was in town.

He also pronounced on the screen offers allegedly received by Friedman – 'I should be foolish not to accept them' – and revealed he would be perfectly willing to play leading roles opposite the likes of Marlene Dietrich, Joan Crawford and Anna Sten. 'It makes no difference to me which one it is,' he said, as if to indicate that the pleasure and the privilege would be theirs. Oddly, he neglected to mention Carole Lombard. Perhaps she was ripe for romance but not nearly a big enough name to star with him on screen.

Hollywood hardly knew what to make of this impudent young Irishman. Whether he could fight or act made little difference; he could talk a good fight, he could act out the part off-screen and he had a film-star profile. Before long, screen tests were being lined up and a chauffeur-driven limousine put at his disposal.

Of course, no one in the film capital had seen clips of Jack's best-forgotten non-epic, *McGlusky the Sea Rover*. It had yet to be released in the States – and it was just as well. The movie-makers would have observed that Jack had magnificent screen presence and a certain magnetism, but they would also have been certain to note that he 'could not act his way out of a paper bag'. This opinion, held by Tamara Desni, was passed on some years later to Jack's younger brother Mick when he was her juvenile lead in the musical *Moscow Belle*.

Hollywood still could not make up its mind about Jack. He was in constant demand from radio producers – 'Those boys want me to sing night and day' – but it was the film producers he was more anxious to impress. There were rumours that M-G-M wanted to cast him opposite

Maureen O'Sullivan in a film about Ireland titled *Faraway Hills*, but nothing came of it. Film tests confirmed that while Jack was the predictable knockout in front of the cameras, he found difficulty in acting to a script. With his profile and build, studio chiefs felt he might be best suited to Westerns. They saw him as a kind of singing Gary Cooper, but therein lay another problem: rough, tough cowboys out on the trail just did not sing in soft tenor. Neither did they speak with a refined, if cultivated, English accent.

Though boxing was his business, Jack felt he could adjust quite easily to the life of a film actor. It would be an infinitely more pleasant existence than sweating blood in some seedy gymnasium, risking life and limb in the roped arena and then having your purse money confiscated after attracting half of London through the turnstiles.

Another consideration was that he had fallen for an actress. Her name was Judith Allen, a honey blonde discovery of one of Hollywood's greatest star-makers, Cecil B. de Mille. Judith – real name Marie Elliot – was born in Chatham, New York, on January 28, 1913, but brought up in Boston. Her father John, a department store executive, spoiled her to distraction but was unable to come to terms with the idea of his precious daughter entering the theatre, which he considered no fit place for a lady. However, Marie proved a determined and resourceful young woman. She attended the prestigious Leland Powers finishing and dramatic school in Boston, working her way through by baby-sitting for 25 cents an hour. Whilst at Leland Powers she was employed by the Walter Thornton Agency, which listed her as an 'innocent, unmarried-looking young woman, five-three, blue eyes, beautiful bust, etc.' The training she received enabled her to take parts with a small New England stock company and these led to the screen test that sparked her Hollywood career. Then known as Marie Colman, her looks and potential were such that she was one of only two actresses signed from a total of 1 500 auditioned by Paramount. The other was Elizabeth Young.

Judith was heralded by de Mille as his new star discovery for *This Day and Age*, her first big film role in 1933. 'She has the intellect of Bernhardt, the beauty of Russell [Lillian] and the dramatic appeal of Duse [Eleonara, a star of the 1880s],' was his extravagant description of her. The imaginative de Mille had previously taken Judith's breath away when he told her: 'If you can make love on the screen the way you can freeze a man in real life, you'll be a glorious actress.' She could have been forgiven for thinking that all the hopes and dreams she had entertained while scraping her way through drama school were about to materialise on the grand scale. Having received a build-up as fantastic as some of de Mille's screen epics, she might have been expected to become screen goddess of the century, and indeed she went on to play successive leads in de Mille's *Too Much Harmony* (opposite Bing Crosby) and *Hell and High Water*. But her subsequent roles did not justify such lavish praise and she was to wind up playing in low-budget melodramas and Westerns.

Perhaps she had only herself to blame. When someone is as interested in you as de Mille – and if you value your career prospects – you don't run off and marry virtually the first man to throw his hat into the ring. But Judith could be excused. There she was, a stranger in Hollywood – lonely, vulnerable and slightly awed by it all. Enter world heavyweight wrestling champion Gus (Cannonball) Sonnenberg, a former pro footballer credited with introducing the flying tackle and head-butt to professional wrestling.

Sonnenberg was something of an organic write-off, but he was rich. He weighed 16st 6lb (230lbs), had two cauliflower ears, a twisted nose and several dents in his head; he had also suffered many broken bones and internal injuries during his career. But Judith was not put off by mere incidentals such as physical flaws and imperfections. She flipped over Sonnenberg and married him in 1932, when she was 19 and he 32. She wed in secret for fear of harming her career, but after a few months the news broke and caused something of a sensation. Beauty and the Beast wasn't in it, and the age gap didn't help. The film world could hardly believe it.

The couple made their home at Newton, near Boston, but Judith was based mainly in Hollywood. Gus showered her with gifts and, as in the wrestling ring, he did not do things by halves. He bought her $20 000 worth of jewellery, including rings and necklaces, watches and bracelets. One necklace, her favourite, reputedly contained 4 000 pearls. But Judith's film career put a strain on the marriage and Gus became jealous of the attention she was receiving. In particular, he did not care for the titbits in Hollywood gossip columns linking her romantically with Gary Cooper.

Inevitably, Judith split with Sonnenberg and the pair were divorced in 1934. She was granted a decree *nisi* on the ground of extreme mental cruelty after alleging that Sonnenberg* tried to prevent her continuing her film career. But Judith promptly substituted one piece of brawn for another when she picked up with Max Baer, then being feted the length and breadth of America after relieving Primo Carnera of the world heavyweight championship †.

* *Sonnenberg* died of leukemia in 1944, at the age of 44.

† The fight was on June 14, 1934, in Long Island City, New York. Baer had Carnera down a record 11 times but could not keep him down. The referee stopped it in the 11th round.

Enter Jack Doyle. In order to back up his 'game of hearts' jibe, he had already deliberately robbed Baer of Mary Kirk Brown, a former movie actress and much-married playgirl. Now he was about to lure away the current love of his life – though on this occasion it would be an unintentional steal. It happened when Jack was invited to a party being thrown by Kay Francis, then one of Hollywood's biggest and highest paid stars at $200 000 a year and Bette Davis's predecessor in the Warner megastar hierarchy.

Kay was noted for throwing lavish annual parties which always had a novel twist and, on this occasion, she had turned Hollywood's Vendome Restaurant into a ship. Guests had to enter by sliding down a chute. It was a magnificent theatrical touch and one typical of Kay's great penchant for the unusual. But Jack needed no lessons in the art of theatrics. He dressed slowly and arrived at the Vendome after most of the others had put in their appearance. He could hear the laughter and the merry-making as he climbed the steps to an upstairs floor and was guided to the top of the chute. He took in a deep breath, slid helter-skelter to the bottom and landed unceremoniously on the floor of the private ballroom, which was packed with guests. A slight flush of embarrassment reddened his cheeks as a glamorous woman rushed over to help him to his feet. He recognised her immediately from her films as Kay Francis. The only trouble was, she did not recognise him.

As Jack straightened out his jacket, bowed and bade her a respectful 'Good evening', she asked in tones of some amusement: 'Who are you? A crasher?' 'I'm no crasher. I'm Jack Doyle,' he replied with a ring of indignation.

Suddenly the whole room erupted with a burst of clapping and cheering, and Jack knew he was welcome among a congregation of Hollywood's most famous names. Kay Francis took his hand and introduced him to each of her guests in turn: James Cagney, Pat O'Brien, Anna Sten and dozens more whose faces were familiar even if their names were not.

Eventually she got round to Judith Allen. As Kay Francis brought her forward to speak to him, Jack was captivated by the sight of 'the most beautiful woman I had ever seen.' For once he was speechless, unable to utter even a single word. He could sense she had something other than beauty of feature and form: there was character and an 'element of sweet simplicity' behind her physical loveliness. 'At that moment, though we had only just met, I loved her more than I had ever loved a woman before.'

The electricity between them was so highly-charged that everyone in the huge ballroom could feel it, none more so than Judith: 'I knew I loved him the first moment I saw him.'

Once Jack had recovered his poise they went over to Judith's table, where he at once demonstrated the art of letting a woman know who's boss by picking up her brandy and tipping it out. 'You don't need that.'

He was huge, handsome, masterful. 'I tell you, he could have knocked me down with a left,' said Judith. 'You don't know what he does to a girl. And he had a great line in blarney.'

He certainly had. His confidence increased as they sipped champagne and he responded to Judith's request to tell her all about his home and his family. They sat out several dances as the orchestra played romantic music, the lighting cleverly subdued and shadowy. Jack knew he had won Judith's heart when she put her dainty hand in his and begged him to tell her more about 'your little home in Ireland.'

By the end of the evening she was weak at the knees and he felt as if he had won a million dollars. The satisfaction of getting another one over on Max Baer did not enter into it, although he would not have minded if Max hated him enough to give him a shot at the title. He was in love and as out of touch with reality as if the vengeful champion had just come up and hit him on the chin.

Next morning he spent $20 on flowers for Judith and from then on they saw each other every day. She was fully occupied at the studios, but on her days off they went to the races. They partied nearly every night and, in her company, Jack met all the film stars worth knowing in Hollywood. They had a glorious time together and each day their love grew stronger. It all cost money, of course, and plenty of it – and Jack's problem was that he was earning none. Some of the film tests he had been given were highly satisfactory, but when it came to discussing a possible deal there were problems over his association with Friedman. The studios explained there could be no question of a film contract until his management complications were cleared up.

Jack was fast running out of readies. The £3 000 he had brought with him to the States had virtually gone, most of it frittered away during his first heady days on Broadway – where he had come to be regarded as more of a romancing bard than a top-line fighter – and more recently playing the Hollywood game. Now, having received the thumbs-down from the film people, he had only one option: to get his boxing career moving.

On returning to New York, he learned from Goodtime Charlie that there had been a delay over the granting of his licence. The hold-up had been caused by the British Board of Control, who had informed the National Boxing Association of America – with whom it had a working agreement – that Jack's licence had expired and that he owed £781 in England as a result of the lawsuit following the Petersen fight.

However, the NBA decided that since, technically, he had no licence, they had no reason to refuse him one in the United States.

Having received the all-clear, Goodtime Charlie opened negotiations for Jack's first fight – a ten-rounder against Stanley Poreda in Boston on April 8 – and installed him in a magnificent training camp at Pompton Lakes, New Jersey. It saddened Jack to part from Judith, but he had to be fit and in the right frame of mind. Poreda had gone the distance with Primo Carnera in 1932 but had since been smashed to first-round defeat by the up-and-coming Joe Louis. It was no disgrace. Louis was battering the majority of his opponents into early submission and Jack could not dismiss Poreda lightly.

There was an air of excitement and not a little curiosity surrounding Jack now that his boxing career was set for take-off. Radio programmes played his songs and the newspapers gave him a tremendous build-up. They said he overshadowed Max Baer as a killer: a lady-killer. And they christened him variously 'Heart-Smashing Doyle', 'Battling Beauty', 'Lover with a Left', 'Gentleman Jack' and the 'Hibernian Mocking Bird'. Doyle-mania had begun in the United States.

Dozens of girls invaded the camp each day hoping to get to close-quarters with Jack. Some even broke in at night. Wisely, he'd decided to keep himself celibate. He had thoughts only for Judith back in Hollywood and would do nothing that might jeopardise their future happiness or cause him to blow his big chance in the States. He had good reason to remember what happened to him before the Petersen fight and had learned the lesson, but it sure was tough fighting off all those lusty young Americans. Discretion played no part in their vocabulary and their mode of dress left little to the imagination. They were Doyle groupies on a scale that made his legion of fans in England appear almost virtuous by comparison.

As in England, Jack found that fellow pugs resented the huge publicity he attracted and, still more, his appeal to women. Numerous boxers arrived at the camp offering to spar with him but it was soon apparent that their intention was to give him a going-over. However, the man the newspapers had depicted as 'pretty' and a 'singing boxer' was pretty useful when it came to a rough-house: many took the first train home and did not return.

Jack Dempsey took time out from running his restaurant to visit the camp and see what all the fuss was about. He had been given the low-down on the kid by Goodtime Charlie and now it was time to judge for himself. He took charge of some of Jack's training sessions and offered him priceless advice.

Jack was thrilled to have met his boyhood idol at last. He told him earnestly: 'I want to fight like you and sing like Count McCormack.' Dempsey, who loved a joke, is reputed to have replied: 'Wouldn't it be just too bad if you could only sing like me and fight like Count McCormack?' It was to become an immortal line in boxing folk-lore and a perennial thorn in Jack's side in later years. McCormack, who on occasions had given Jack singing lessons and been favourably impressed with his voice, was said to have been in hysterics when told.

Any notion that Jack was a joke figure must have been dispelled on the eve of the Poreda fight when he called off the contest, claiming that promises to pay him in advance had been broken. In view of the purgatory he had endured in England in the wake of the Petersen fight, he had resolved never to fight again unless his money was paid up front. That way, in the event of disqualification, the authorities would be powerless to penalise him financially even if they saw fit to ban him or revoke his licence.

Jack's decision to pull out signalled the end of his brief association with Goodtime Charlie. It had finally dawned on him that the Dempsey connection on which Friedman had based almost his entire sales pitch was a tenuous one and he could not trust the man. In addition the film offers spoken of so enthusiastically had signally failed to materialise, to say nothing of the vast amounts of money Jack had been forced to dispense since his arrival in the States. Goodtime Charlie's failure to secure his fight fee in advance as previously agreed was the final ignominy. It was time for Jack to cut his losses.

The stubborn stand on the matter put him in a fix. Holding fast to your principles can prove highly expensive and this little episode had cost him a packet, besides proving a considerable let-down after the vast publicity the fight had generated. He travelled back to Hollywood flat broke and immediately asked Judith to marry him. An uncharitable view would be that it was not Judith but her cash with which Jack was in love. Judith did not see it that way. She was filled with sympathy when he explained how he had been bad-timed by Goodtime Charlie. Though her star had waned since de Mille's premature immortalisation of her, Judith was earning a hefty $1 500 dollars a week from her film work and it guaranteed a period of gracious living until Jack managed to sort out his career.

Jack and Judith acted with almost indecent haste. Aglow with mutual passion, they travelled immediately to Agua Caliente, the resort of the stars in mid-Mexico, where they were joined in matrimony on April 28, 1935. Marriage is supposed to be for ever, but straight after the ceremony the Mexican judge who had sealed their love handed Judith a card inscribed: 'Legal Mexican divorces quickly secured. See ———, Lawyer.' The humour of the situation was not lost on her, but had

Judith realised that Agua Caliente means 'Hot Water', she might well have had some misgivings.

With one failed marriage already behind her, she decided to concentrate all her efforts on making the new union a success. She unselfishly abandoned her film career in order to assist Jack fully in his quest for the world title. It was the supreme sacrifice and she gave it not a second thought. That she had appeared in four films released in 1935 and would feature in only one 1936 release, *Burning Gold* – to which she was already committed – was proof of her desire to put love and marriage before personal ambition.

Jack spent his last $1 000 dollars on an ermine coat which he presented to Judith as a wedding gift – an act of generosity which served only to strengthen the deep feelings she undoubtedly had for him.

At first the couple were blissfully happy. Judith helped Jack negotiate a new fight contract with a pair of wealthy Irish-American brothers from Brooklyn, Tom and Andy McGovern, reputable men of integrity who fancied they could steer Jack to the greatest prize in sport. Tom had the Irish heavyweight dream particularly badly and undertook the major management role. His initial move was to free Jack from Goodtime Charlie's clutches. He paid an unspecified sum to Friedman, put Jack into training on a farm in New Jersey and engaged veteran fight-wise trainer Dan Morgan – known as Dumb Dan because he never stopped talking – to supervise his training.

Jack was delighted to be rid of Friedman and to have some stability in his private and professional life. He was like a child with a new toy: the toy was Judith, more than a foot shorter but dazzlingly attractive and full of bounce. She was a good influence on him, according to Bill Doyle, who lived with them. Far from resenting the 17-year-old's presence, Judith pampered Bill and made sure he felt at home with them. 'She was very sweet to me always,' he recalled. 'I must admit I really liked her.'

The marriage appeared to bring Jack peace of mind. He resolved to finish playing the wild rover as the first weeks of wedded bliss washed over him, bathing him in a kind of easy euphoria. He was in bed by nine every night and spent most mornings hiking or running up and down hills close to the farm in preparation for the series of fights McGovern was attempting to arrange. But the cancellation of the contest with Poreda had left the media united in scepticism. Most observers were convinced he was not serious about his boxing.

'All the pointers are that he is heading for a film and singing career,' said Britain's *Daily Mail*. The US newspapers ran stories that suggested Jack could sing but not fight. He was stung to the quick, but had only himself to blame for giving the impression he was more interested in hitting the top as a vocalist than hitting a top title contender. When reporters visited the happy couple six weeks after the wedding, he insisted on playing them McCormack's *Bird Songs at Eventide* and then singing it himself to prove how his voice measured up to that of the Count. It did, and very well, but the only count American boxing scribes wanted to hear was the referee tolling one to ten over a Doyle opponent.

They were soon to get their opportunity when McGovern announced he had lined up a fight against Phil Donato at New York's Dyckman Oval. Jack trained like never before for a scheduled ten-rounder against a man billed as an iron-hard fighter who would thoroughly test his famous right-hand punch. In reality Donato did not warrant a mention in American record books. However, after being out of the ring for 15 months and having never travelled beyond two rounds as a pro, Jack needed a soft touch to set his US career in motion.

He was disturbed when he received word from Judith stating she was on her way to see the fight. He had requested her not to attend, fearing he might make a fool of himself after such a long period of inactivity. Would that old dread of humiliation never leave him?

The intensity of having to co-ordinate mind and muscle to an unusually high degree insulates fighters against the distractions of sight and sound, and normally Jack never saw or heard anybody in the crowd during the heat of battle. But as the bell rang to start the fight, he happened to glance down and see the lovely Judith sitting radiant in a front-row seat.

'Come on Jack,' she almost pleaded, her distinctive voice full of encouragement for him to do well. It was a lover's call that, from the beginning of time, has enabled man to conjure up reserves of strength and power he never knew he possessed. Jack reacted by rushing fearlessly from his corner like some latter-day General Custer mounting a do-or-die cavalry charge. He was made to pay for his lack of caution when Donato caught him with a clubbing left to the head but, fortified by his determination to please his lady, he responded immediately with a salvo of punches that dropped his man for nine. Donato climbed unsteadily to his feet, but Jack put him straight back down again with a left to the jaw followed by a magnificent right. This time Donato did not get up: he was flat on his back and out to the world. It was all over in a whirlwind 66 seconds.

Jack may have delighted his new wife, who embraced him with such fervour that she proved a bigger danger than Donato, but the Americans who mattered were unmoved. The New York State Athletic Commission clearly regarded Donato as little more than a pushover and stated that in future Jack would be expected to fight worthier opponents if they were to sanction further engagements. One name put forward was that of former world heavyweight champion Jack Sharkey, who showed what he thought of the suggestion by turning down a $10 000 offer to come out of retirement.

Jack was eager to make up for lost time as far as his boxing career was concerned. It needed to continue apace in order to maintain the momentum that this first victory on American soil had brought and McGovern recognised the fact by arranging two further fights in quick succession.

The first was to be against Jack Redmond, a tough black whose suitability and fitness were not in question. Redmond had lasted the full ten rounds with former world light-heavyweight champion Maxie Rosenbloom and had just completed a stint as sparring partner to Primo Carnera for the Italian's disastrous encounter with Joe Louis in New York, when he was smashed to defeat in the sixth round.

Judith sat proud and excited in her ringside seat at the Meadowbrook Field in Newark, New Jersey, as Jack ducked under the ropes. He was in splendid condition thanks to Dumb Dan Morgan – even if he did have earache from Dan's incessant nagging. He took time to settle as Redmond set the pace in the first two rounds and kept him guessing by adopting a peculiar crouching stance. Supremely confident, Redmond outfoxed him by boring in with two-fisted assaults to the head and body and succeeded also in unnerving Jack by laughing contemptuously at his efforts to land.

By the third round, Jack was beginning to find his way. Angered by Redmond's taunts, he charged from his corner and immediately began to pummel away with both fists to the body. The American stood up well to the barrage and proved he was no quitter by coming back strongly toward the end of the round, scoring with rights to the rib-cage.

Jack decided on an all-out effort in the fourth. He launched a concerted attack during which he managed to connect cleanly for the first time with his powerhouse right. Redmond was sent crashing to the canvas. Though hurt, he somehow clambered to his feet at the count of four, his brain scrambled and that cynical sneer wiped clean from his face. Redmond was finished now, his will to win, his energy and his arrogance having been destroyed by one punch. Jack was transformed into a fighting fury, his uncertainty cast aside. He rushed Redmond to the ropes, battering him until he was halfway through them and hanging limply over the middle strand like a broken doll. He then let fly a terrific left that sent Redmond toppling into the laps of ringside reporters, whose frantic efforts to push him back were to no avail. Redmond was counted out.

Jack had won his second fight on US soil – and proved he could go more than two rounds if the need arose. Redmond had been a tricky opponent, but the end had come quickly and cleanly once Jack found his range.

There was to be no let-up in McGovern's crusade to produce an Irish world heavyweight champion. Just 15 days later Jack was in action against another black fighter, Bob Norton. The contest took place in Elizabeth, New Jersey, at a small open-air arena packed to capacity by a crowd numbering several thousand – an attendance that bore testimony to Jack's growing reputation in the States.

The venue was surrounded by slum dwellings whose raucous tenants were hanging out of the windows for a grandstand view of the action. The unlikely setting was matched only by the unique dressing-room facilities provided for the occasion. Jack used a nearby tavern, while Norton changed alongside a funeral hearse in an old barn. Bill Doyle recalled:

> 'We had never experienced anything like it. The whole atmosphere could only be described as frightening. There was a genuine element of fear. For some reason the crowd was fiercely antagonistic. It made my blood run cold, but it must have been even worse for Jack. They shouted abuse at him and there was nothing good-natured or humorous about it. We just wanted to get out of the place as quickly as possible while we were still in one piece.'

Fists were waved under Jack's nose and he was subjected to all manner of vile insults as he climbed the steps to the ring apron. One rabble-rouser yelled up at him: 'If you don't win, we'll come up there and beat the shit out of you.' The remark was greeted by guttural laughter from those within earshot, but Jack was not amused. He looked across at Norton – big, black and scowling like a caged panther – and knew he had to tame him, to beat every ounce of fighting life out of him, for that was the way of it. He was trapped and enslaved just as surely as the menacing Norton.

Shortly before the start, he noticed Judith seated among a bellicose mob that resembled little more than a lynching party. He began to fear for her safety. He wished she had taken his advice and stayed in the comfort of the tavern until the fight was over, rather than having to witness the indignity of her husband being ridiculed and reviled.

The bell went and Jack could have no mercy in his heart for Norton, no pity or remorse for what he was about to do. He went straight on the attack and handed out such a first-round hiding that he wondered how the fellow was still standing. When the round ended, he realised with a sense of relief that the unruly spectators who minutes earlier were baying for his blood had gone peculiarly quiet. They had been made to realise he could fight, and fight like a man, in complete contrast to the figure of fun they had obviously imagined him to be.

In the second round, Jack carried on where he had left off in the first. He delivered a peach of a right that sent Norton clean through the ropes. The American climbed back, but received a merciless pounding from Jack's bludgeoning fists. Blood streaming from a cut over his left eye, he was unable to withstand the onslaught and sank slowly to his hands and knees, where he was counted out.

The end had come after 2min. 18sec. of the round and the previously hostile crowd crammed in and around the arena cheered Jack to the echo. He was in no mood to acknowledge their plaudits or even to take the customary winner's bow. Jumping down from the ring, he grabbed Judith by the hand and, still attired in boxing kit, drove off without giving newsmen a chance to interview him. It must qualify as the most unusual exit ever effected in the long history of boxing and one that is scarcely likely to be repeated.

With three sensational wins under his belt, it was time for Jack to step into the big league. Critics who had scoffed at his ability and written him off as a two-bit fighter were now being forced to revise their opinions. Their words had been stuffed back down their throats.

McGovern had rearranged a bout for him against dangerous Leo 'One-Punch' Williams at Miller Field, New Jersey, on August 9. It had previously been scheduled five days before the Norton fight, but rain had forced a postponement. Now Madison Square Garden matchmaker Jimmy Johnston was pitching to match him with Max Baer's unbeaten 17-stone kid brother Buddy, who had built a big reputation with a string of 20 successive knockouts. Jack would rather have been fighting Max, but was assured that victory over the highly-touted Buddy would put him among the contenders for the title.

There was one problem: the Williams fight. Johnston knew that if Jack walked into one from Williams, he could kiss goodbye to his plans of a 22 000-gate at the outdoor Garden Bowl. He advised McGovern to pull him out and he duly did so, claiming Jack had injured an arm in training. McGovern refused to let him be examined by a doctor for the very good reason that the injury was non-existent. As a result Jack was banned in New Jersey and 37 other States, though thankfully not New York. He was not unduly bothered by the ban, which he had been told would be rescinded once he had beaten Baer and established himself as a top-notcher. The showdown with Buddy attracted such widespread media attention that it appeared more like a world title fight than the six-rounder it had to be because of an outdated New York State

Athletic Commission ruling that a minor – Baer was 20 – should not fight beyond that distance. In effect, nobody was seriously concerned about the scheduled number of rounds. The fight was not expected to go beyond the second.

Jack's training camp at Kingston, high up in the Catskill Mountains, was an extraordinary place packed with holiday-makers and run by a bouncy black Methodist woman, who attracted a huge crowd each evening as she stomped away at the piano and belted out hot gospel songs. Jack and Judith joined in enthusiastically, but the showman in him could never leave it at that. He loved nothing better than an audience and took the opportunity to regale the assembled gathering with a selection of his McCormack-inspired ballads, with Judith providing piano accompaniment.

Judith's live-in presence at the camp shocked fight-hardened Americans, who considered no woman should be allowed within touching distance of a boxer preparing for an important contest. In spite of the fact it was Jack's make-or-break fight in the United States and that victory over Baer would enable him virtually to name his own terms for future engagements, she insisted on being with him. So intensely jealous was Judith, according to Bill Doyle, that she was reluctant to let Jack out of her sight. She could not trust him to keep his hands to himself in the company of adoring females and even insisted on sharing the same bed with him lest he fell victim to the camp followers who monitored his every move.

Bill sensed Jack had erred in not banning Judith from the camp:

> 'It didn't seem right for them to be sleeping together and having sex in the days leading up to a big fight. Jack must have known he needed to store up every ounce of his energy, but he went along with what Judith wanted.'

The irony of the situation was not lost on Judith's former boy-friend Max Baer. He weighed in with a barbed comment declaring himself in favour of a 'wifeless' training camp. Judith must have been hurt by such remarks, but it was her own doing. Her enthusiasm for Jack even extended to directing his training routines, much to the chagrin of Dumb Dan Morgan, who quit in protest.

The one occasion on which Judith could not be by Jack's side was during his morning training runs. These usually commenced at 9.30 and were followed by a light luncheon, afternoon training, a swim, a sing-song and then bed. Highly-strung and, in spite of her film star status, distinctly vulnerable in the presence of so many Doyle groupies, she always insisted on waiting for him to return from his run and re-entering the camp with him. One day Jack did not arrive back at the usual time; in fact, he did not return until late afternoon. He had elected to spend the day high up in the Catskills in the company of an attractive holiday-maker, who had joined him at a remote, pre- arranged meeting place. Bill Doyle had an uncanny awareness of his brother's eye for women and had not failed to notice the build-up to this extra-marital fling. Judith's suffocating mother-love influence had the effect of producing in Jack a strong desire to break free on occasions and enjoy the company of less possessive women. Bill recalled that Judith became extremely agitated when Jack failed to return on time and that her histrionics increased by the hour:

> 'When eventually he did arrive back, she threw her arms round him in relief. Jack acted as if nothing untoward had occurred and made some excuse to her that apparently explained his absence. It must have been a good one, because she soon calmed down.'

Jack was reported to have impressed in his training despite the presence of Judith and the absence of Dan Morgan, who had been replaced by Tom Broaders. His chief sparring partners were Willie McGee and Mickey McAvoy, a New Jersey heavyweight whom he treated with scant regard, flashing lefts and rights to the head and body. Judith cheered each 'hit' scored by Jack. Even his heavy bag-punching sessions under a blistering sun were accompanied by her shouts of encouragement.

Buddy Baer was training at nearby Speculator. He had the benefit of working out with Max, who had lost his world crown to boxing's 'Cinderella Man', James J. Braddock, and was now in training for a September bout with Joe Louis, which he would lose in four torrid rounds.

The 6ft 6in Buddy was in confident, even cocky mood, hardly able to contain himself at the prospect of spanking the Irish charmer who had upstaged his brother so comprehensively. The scorching New York summer had given Buddy the appearance of a Red Indian and the city's boxing scribes were favouring him to take Jack's scalp in a fight described as being for the Crooning Championship of the World. Jibes like this upset Jack, who wanted more than anything to be taken seriously as a fighter. He became depressed when a freak rain-storm caused the fight at Long Island Bowl to be postponed for a week and switched to the smaller indoor Madison Square Garden. He had been fit and keyed up for the contest and feared the delay might blunt his fighting edge, but he quickly recovered his poise and could be heard singing cheerfully each morning at the Kingston camp.

The famous Garden was packed for a fight that promised to be every bit as uncompromising as the build-up that had preceded it. 'Doyle will be knee-deep in dollars if he whips Baer's hide,' was one amusing but accurate assessment of the big money Jack could expect to command in the event of victory. 'He who strikes first will strike gold,' was another snappy newspaper comment that brought into focus both the explosive nature of the contest and the riches awaiting the winner.

In the event it was Jack who landed the first telling blow, but Baer's youth and magnificent bodily strength enabled him to absorb it. Jack followed up with another tremendous right to the jaw and this time Baer was shaken to his boot-laces. He wobbled but did not topple and, like a wild beast at its most dangerous when hurt, came charging in furiously. His first effort was a thudding right which caught Jack low, causing him to collapse in Baer's corner with a ringing cry of 'Foul'. He was in a bad way, but foolishly climbed to his feet before a count could begin. Baer then mounted a fresh attack that drove Jack across the ring and sent him to the floor for a count of three. He arose with a determined look on his face, but Baer smashed home a right cross and a left hook that put him down again. Though up at six, Jack was groggy now and Baer caught him once more before the fight was stopped. Jack thought the bell had sounded to end the round and seemed surprised when it was announced that referee Billy Kavanaugh had stepped in after just 2min. 38sec. and awarded victory to Baer on a technical knockout.*

Poor Judith, who visited the dressing-room before the fight to deliver a good-luck kiss, had fainted before the finish and was carried from the arena. The sight of blood pouring from Jack's face and the shock of seeing him reeling drunkenly round the ring had proved too much for her.

Jack was dismayed at the way the fight had been handled. He claimed Baer fouled him deliberately and that the referee not only turned a blind eye to it but stopped the bout prematurely, thus robbing him of his chance of glory. Baer's booming punch, with the full weight of his 17 stones behind it, had produced a massive purple bruise in his groin. The effect of the blow had paralysed his legs and left him with little resistance to offer when Baer subsequently turned on the pressure. Yet he was sure he could have lasted out the remaining 22 seconds to the end of the round, when his handlers would have worked to restore the use of his legs. Then he'd have gone out and blasted Baer to defeat, just as he had Pettifer and Bouquillon after taking similar first-round hidings. He was heart-broken as he sat forlornly in his dressing-room, his hopes of a world title challenge and the big money that went with it

* Jack's sparring partner Willie McGee fought on the undercard. He was outpointed by the up-and-coming Tony Galento.

having been dealt a savage setback. He considered professional boxing in America to be little more than a racket and said so – a view reinforced by the faithful Judith, who claimed she had overheard beforehand exactly how the fight would finish.

Jack vowed to turn his back on the fight game for good. He wanted nothing more to do with it, in spite of the fact the American Press had warmed to him over the brave manner in which he had stood up to Baer after being blatantly fouled. The *New York Times* said: 'Doyle exhibited unusual courage and gave evidence that his right hand carried plenty of power.' Other Press comments were equally complimentary. 'Doyle was no quitter, though it would have been easy and not at all unreasonable,' said Hugh Bradley in the *New York Post.* The *New York Journal*'s Bill Corum observed: 'Doyle showed courage and was made of stern enough stuff to stagger to his feet while plainly helpless.' The *Herald Tribune* commented rather matter-of-factly: 'Doyle the game Irishman refused to leave his feet and lost the fight erect.'

At last Jack had the American fight critics on his side, although ironically it had taken a losing fight to achieve the kind of recognition he felt he should have been accorded from the start. Jimmy Johnston promised him a return with Baer, but Jack rejected it out of hand. He suspected that Baer, having felt the power of his venomous right hand, had quickly realised the only way he could win was to produce a damaging low punch. What was more, he had been allowed to get away with it. Jack could be forgiven for feeling a sense of outrage, especially when comparing Baer's good fortune with his own fate after fouling Jack Petersen in London two years earlier, when he lost both the fight and his prize-money. Where Jack Doyle was concerned, there seemed to be little justice in this toughest of all sporting trades.

Judith was an influential ally in Jack's decision to quit the ring. Though she, too, had been incensed by the manner of his defeat, her thinking was directed more toward keeping her husband to herself. She did not mind if he was no longer to be a high-profile public figure, for at least then he would cease to be the target of other women. Or so she thought.

Jack and Judith returned to California and took a house in fashionable Santa Monica, complete with servants. A luxury limousine transported her to and from the studios in nearby Hollywood each day while all Jack had to do was a little light training in order to keep himself in trim and console himself by counting his and Judith's money. It was a recipe for disaster.

The problem was that having just turned 22, he was too young to go to seed. He needed ambition and fulfilment and there was nothing on the horizon. He would have been better served staying in New York and continuing his career now that he had achieved some acclaim and more than a little sympathy as a result of the Baer fight. The boxing people were beginning to take him seriously at last and three wins in four fights in the States was a good foundation on which to build. His only loss had been suffered in highly unsatisfactory circumstances and he could have taken his pick of world-rated opponents. He was handsome, famous and far from discredited and boxing had plenty of room at the top for his punching power and box-office charisma. Instead, he allowed the flame of his Dempsey dream to flicker and die. He permitted the circumstances of his defeat against Baer to turn to disillusionment rather than accept it for what it was: a setback that, far from eroding his chances of success, had opened the door of real opportunity for him in the US.

Jack quickly became bored kicking his heels and admiring the California coastline. Hollywood night clubs and parties beckoned. There were scurrilous stories about his hard drinking and philandering and, inevitably, these reached Judith's offended ears. Rows and discord followed. The relationship became strained.

In a rare moment of mutual forgiveness, the couple decided to set about mending the marriage. They hit on the idea of doing a variety tour of the United States. It necessitated Judith again abandoning her film career, but she felt it would be worthwhile if Jack could be removed from the decadent influence of Hollywood. They rehearsed a double act in which Jack sang and Judith did a dramatic scene from one of her pictures. It closed with a short dialogue they had written between them.

Their tour did not bring about the hoped-for metamorphosis. Instead, it foundered on the suspicion, jealousy and resentment that now existed between them. Judith objected to Jack even dancing with other girls and her possessiveness drove a further wedge between them. Jack continued to flaunt his attractiveness to women; he could not resist doing so and his behaviour began to break down Judith's defences. Though she was mentally tough and resilient, each betrayal of trust was like a dagger wound to the heart. No sooner had the healing process begun with a profession of Jack's love than the scars would be re-opened by his drinking and womanising.

The spirited Judith was determined to preserve her marriage at all costs. She and Jack made a New Year resolution to start afresh in 1936 by taking their act to England and then across to Ireland, where she would meet Jack's family and see the sights about which he had talked so fondly when they held hands and gazed lovingly into each other's eyes at Kay Francis's party.

Chapter 12

Punch and Judy

Judith was fully aware of Jack's huge popularity in Britain, but even she was astounded at the scenes that greeted them on their arrival from New York. Countless newspapermen, photographers and a newsreel camera crew jostled for position. The public were his adoring subjects and the media the faithful recorders of his every word. He spoke in youthful, high-pitched tones, and so faultlessly that any unenlightened onlooker might have thought he had graduated from Eton and Oxford rather than a state school in Ireland which he had left at the age of 12.

With the petite Judith standing proudly at his side, he took obvious delight in relating some of his American experiences. He smiled as he recalled the memory of his first sparring sessions there, and added:

> 'I rather thought my welcome back to England might be cold and frigid, and for Judith's sake I hoped and prayed there might be a show of warmth. But we have been met with nothing but handshakes and welcomes and a show of loyalty I shall do a lot to repay. For myself I would not have cared, but for her I care a lot.'

Jack wisely renewed his association with Fred Curran, who, though he had been out of his depth in the United States, knew everything there was to know about the music-hall in Britain. He had been weaned on it since he was knee-high to a chorus girl and that knowledge and experience was put to good use on Jack and Judith's behalf. He dubbed their act Punch and Judy and packaged a variety tour that was to last a marathon 18 weeks. Besides being a clever title, Punch and Judy reflected accurately the relationship that existed between Jack and Judith. They did not exactly beat each other with sticks as in a seaside show-booth, but they squabbled constantly and usually Jack was to blame.

The New Year resolution to put their previous problems behind them and start afresh was beginning to weaken under the weight of Jack's extra-marital activities. Judith was deeply troubled, but her wounded pride and obvious displeasure were tempered by a touching understanding of the forces that drove him:

'Jack was so beautiful and he knew it. He could not resist sharing himself. Yet afterwards he was always contrite, and indeed he'd frequently cry like a little boy. At such times he'd promise to be good, but would keep his word only as long as it took him to start all over again.'

His tears and his remorse were as much a manifestation of Catholic guilt over his having committed the *sin* of adultery as for his betrayal of Judith. His private acts of contrition were admirable for their humility and undoubted sincerity, but he was unable to sustain his good behaviour beyond the next good-looking woman who presented herself.

Judith recalled – in somewhat theatrical fashion – what happened when they were staying at a charming little English inn near a river, where they went bathing each afternoon. One day she had a bad headache and Jack went alone:

'I woke up with a start and for some strange reason feared something terrible had happened to Jack. He'd been gone so long.'

She ran toward the river in a frenzy, along a path they had often taken together. It wound its way to a stile, through which they never passed without kissing, and then took an abrupt turn to the river bank:

'My feet flew and as I was about to pass over the stile, my heart was stabbed by the pain of seeing a girl in Jack's arms, tenderly returning his kisses. I was riveted to the spot. Since his back was to me, it was the girl who first looked up with a start.

"Hello honey," he said as he turned to follow her puzzled glance. "I want you to meet a friend of Bill's." Then, back at the inn, he denied the witness of my own eyes.'

Incidents of that nature were not the only torment Judith had to endure. There was worse to follow when the tour took in Ireland in the middle of March – and for once, it had nothing to do with Jack's womanising. Instead, it had everything to do with his relationship with Judith. He had suspected public opinion in Catholic Ireland would be strongly opposed to his union with a divorced woman, but he had underestimated the degree of hostility that would be directed at them.

The sense of outrage that gripped Ireland over the marriage has to be understood in the context of the country's then intransigent attitude, not so much toward marriages between Catholics and non-Catholics as to divorce, which was considered completely unacceptable. Jack was a revered public figure who, by taking a divorcee for a wife, had set the worst possible kind of example and one that undermined the structure of the Church and its teachings.

Ireland's vehement condemnation was first made manifest from the pulpits, where he was lambasted by bishops and priests for openly 'living in sin'. Jack's liaison with 'the Allen woman' was considered an adulterous one that could not be condoned. Feelings were running so high that he became an outcast in his own country, ostracised and disgraced.

The variety show Jack and Judith were due to stage at Dublin's Theatre Royal – where just two years earlier he had been cheered to the echo – had to be called off. A large notice outside the theatre stated the performance was cancelled because Miss Allen was unwell. It fooled nobody. The previous evening, when an announcement was made from the stage of the Theatre Royal that they would not be appearing the following night as advertised, there were hisses, catcalls and shouts of, 'We don't want him here.' So violent was the outburst from all parts of the theatre, and so long did it continue, that the announcer was clearly embarrassed and could hardly make himself heard above the din.

Clearly, Jack no longer had a future in Ireland while he stayed married to Judith. He had been disowned and dishonoured for having the temerity to marry the woman he loved. Yet he felt no sense of shame and had planned to stand defiantly on stage and profess his love for Judith, despite being advised that mobs were planning to wreck the theatre and that injury to either or both of them might result. In the end it was Judith who decided they would be wiser to call the whole thing off and head back to England.

Jack's young brother Mick was living in the Dublin suburb of Raheny at the time and remembers meeting Jack and Judith at the Shelbourne Hotel about a week before the rumpus surfaced. Then aged 15, he joined them for breakfast. It was the first time he had met Judith:

> 'She was very sweet and asked me what I would like to have. I was just speechless. She ordered for herself thick hunks of beautiful Irish grilled ham and piled them high with marmalade – it was the most incredible thing I'd ever seen. She saw the look of astonishment on my face, smiled and stuffed some ham in my mouth. She was then under contract to Paramount and receiving $200 a week whether she worked or not. Jack usually stayed at the Gresham, but was obviously not welcome there at that time. When all the fuss blew up, he took it extremely badly. He was hurt deep down inside.'

Judith was no less hurt. She had been longing for the day she could set foot in Ireland after hearing Jack's many wonderful stories about the land of his birth.

It was ironic that Jack's ardent fan David Windsor, who had become the uncrowned King Edward VIII following the death of his father, George V, would be the target of a similar moral crusade in

England when seeking to marry the divorced Wallis Simpson. Later in 1936 he would be forced to abdicate and live in exile in Paris. Jack's own exile from Ireland, in similar distressing circumstances, caused him to identify closely with the mental pain and anguish of his royal friend.

Jack and Judith returned to continue their variety tour in England, where they were fully booked for eight weeks. Fred Curran had also arranged boxing and training exhibitions for Jack which inevitably fuelled within him the desire to return to the ring. Judith was dead set against it, but Jack had grown tired of the music-hall circuit. The money was good, the format enjoyable and simple and he and Judith were in big demand. But he had no sense of purpose; life was tame and he missed the glamour and excitement of the boxing ring. He was certain he could beat Petersen – who had since been stopped twice by the powerful Walter Neusel – and also fancied his chances with Len Harvey, who had made a monkey of him when he was a raw, ambitious guardsman. Petersen was still champion, Harvey still a top-line fighter. Both contests would generate massive interest at the box-office.

He visited the Board of Control secretary, Charles Donmall, stating that he wished to let bygones be bygones and clear up any financial difficulty that stood in the way of his reinstatement as a boxer. He owed £700 to the Board and £400 to White City in costs as a result of their successful appeal to the High Court, and quite why he did not settle these sums immediately and resume his career is a mystery. He certainly had the money, but instead asked for his licence to be renewed on the understanding that 25 per cent of his future boxing earnings should go to the Board until both claims were satisfied. He threatened that if the Board did not agree, he would hang up his gloves for good. The conclusion must be that he could not bring himself to pay out a further £1 100 in addition to the £2 500 he had already forfeited. He was willing to have the sum deducted in stages from the purses of his fights because in that way he would not be handing over the money; they would be taking it before it reached him.

Jack made an impassioned appeal in the newspapers for his licence to be re-issued:

> 'I do enough exercise twice nightly on the stage to keep myself fit. Though I am booked up for several weeks ahead, I am seeking to avoid making further arrangements in the hope that by that time I will need to go into strenuous training for a really big fight. Litigation and tribulation are no good for a boxer's nerves. I left them behind me when I went to America and, although I am not yet clear of this old legacy of trouble, I am confident that the fair-

mindedness of the British sportsman will allow me to make a fresh start in the game that is nearest my heart.'

Predictably, the Board's stewards were unmoved. Until he repaid what he owed in legal costs, there was nothing doing. When finally this sank in, Jack decided to quit the variety circuit and head back to America. He and Judith tried to leave secretly and without even a word to Fred Curran, who had done so much to help them. They boarded the liner *President Harding* at Southampton, but a news reporter from the now defunct *Daily Sketch* caught up with them. When he called at their cabin before the ship left, Jack opened the door barely two inches and said: 'I am going with my wife to visit relatives in Queensland.' When it was pointed out that he had a quota visa for the United States he admitted he was bound for America, but he declined to say which part of the United States and for what purpose.

The disappointed Curran explained:

'Though Doyle and his wife have been earning about £200 a week in variety, he was fed up. He wanted to box and often said the fact he could not do so was breaking his heart. I don't think he will ever come back to this country. He confided to me that he intended becoming a naturalised American. I am hurt that he should have gone and not said a word to me. I had some good offers of work for him.'

Back in California, Judith decided to continue with her movie career. She even managed to get Jack a part in *Navy Spy*, a Certificate 'A' picture starring Conrad Nagel and Eleanor Hunt. The film was billed as a US Navy thriller, but turned out to be more of a yawn. Jack played the part of a Lieutenant Carrington, who, after inventing an undetectable poison gas, is lured ashore by a letter from a pretty girl and kidnapped. But after getting waylaid in the first reel by sinister types seeking to discover his secret, he does not show up again until the last.

The film, produced by George A. Hirliman for Grand National Pictures and directed by Crane Wilbur, was released the following year (1937). The *New York Times* reviewed it at the city's Central Theatre where, said their critic, 'an afternoon audience displayed no noticeable manifestations, pro or con.' The British Film Institute *Monthly Bulletin* commented:

'The plot is more suited to a boys' magazine than to adult entertainment. It is acted throughout as if neither actors nor director were very interested, so it is hardly surprising if the audience, too, finds it dull.'

It had been an inauspicious US screen debut for Jack and he had not particularly enjoyed his work on the film. The irksome hours of delay between takes, the monotonous rehearsing of lines and movements – though his were comparatively few – and the strict discipline required of an actor were all too tedious for a man who much preferred living dangerously.

With filming over, he let off steam by pitching into Hollywood's social whirl. His closest friends – according to Bill Doyle – were two of Hollywood's greatest hell-raisers, Errol Flynn and Clark Gable: 'The three of them palled around together, competing with each other for birds and booze.' Flynn and Gable saw in Jack a man after their own hearts, a soul-mate who roused in them the challenge to prove their virility. There were wild drinking sessions and sex parties at Flynn's home in the Hollywood Hills. They were attended by bit-part actresses, impressionable starlets and other sundry adornments, all of them willing to sacrifice their honour, their pride and just about everything else in the hope of being handed a ticket to the big-time. Of course, the big-time would never come for the pretty young things who were almost tearing off their clothes in the rush to be laid by a star; they were just so much bedroom fodder, like those who went before them and those who would come after them. However, there is no reason to suppose they were too disappointed. They were doing what it pleased them to do – playing the Hollywood Fame Game. As Gable himself might have said: If nothing came of it, what the heck? They had seen some action.

Jack's association with Flynn and Gable would last several months. And in the ensuing years he would enjoy the companionship of many more members of the Hollywood star hierarchy, including James Cagney and Pat O'Brien – whom he first met at Kay Francis's party – Johnny Weissmuller, Fredric March, Brian Aherne and Bing Crosby. Weissmuller, the original multi-muscled Tarzan, and O'Brien, perhaps to become best known for his portrayal of a priest in the Cagney classic *Angels with Dirty Faces*, were to become particularly close friends.

Flynn and Gable were screen tough-guys who liked to live up to their movie images in real life. If Gable, then in his mid-30s, was regarded as the uncrowned King of Hollywood, then Flynn, in his mid-20s, was his pretender. He had arrived in Hollywood shortly before Jack and wed his first wife, Lili Damita, in May 1935. But Flynn's incessant philandering meant he would be married in name only. As he once said: 'Women won't let me stay single and I won't let myself stay married.'

Gable was no less a philanderer. His second marriage – to the wealthy socialite Rhea* Langham, 17 years his senior – was virtually at an end. According to Larry Swindell in his biography of Carole Lombard, *Screwball*, Gable was 'sleeping around more or less openly,

* Alternatively spelt Ria.

without recrimination from Rhea, who understood his needs and was resigned to them.' Swindell quotes an M-G-M casting director, Billy Grady, as saying, 'Clark was the least selective lover in the hemisphere. He'd screw anything – a girl didn't have to be pretty or even clean.'

It all leaves little to the imagination in visualising what Gable, Flynn and Jack Doyle got up to together. It was well known that Gable liked to keep a mental, aptly-named *score*card, and the competitive instincts of Flynn and Doyle doubtless enabled both to keep pace. The aggregate must have run into the hundreds, to say nothing of the alcohol they consumed.

Lombard had felt no guilt when she took up with Gable in the early part of 1936. She was not the type to be worried by accusations of husband-stealer and whore. Since the demise of her marriage to the debonair William Powell she had been squired by several eligible Hollywood suitors. Among them were singer, songwriter and band-leader Russ Columbo – the one-time violin prodigy whose voice had matured into a 'silken high baritone' before he died in 1934 – screenwriter Robert Riskin, gangster actor George Raft and Latin-American leading man Cesar Romero. She had starred with Gable in *No Man of Her Own* (1932), but was married to Powell at the time and out of bounds. According to Larry Swindell, their romance was triggered by the Mayfair Club Ball* at Victor Hugo's in Beverly Hills. Gable arrived with Eadie Adams and Lombard with Cesar Romero. They are said to have disappeared together for a time during the evening and to have become lovers shortly afterwards.

The emancipated Lombard was lovely and lively, with an outrageous sense of humour which manifested in myriad ways. She could swear like a trooper and frequently did, especially at important social functions. In his description of that year's Mayfair Ball, David Niven revealed in *Bring On The Empty Horses* that a tacit agreement between the women to wear white was broken when Norma Shearer, wife of M-G-M's boy wonder film producer Irving Thalberg and the studio's biggest star, turned up in eye-catching red. The stir she caused was nothing to the gasp that went up when Lombard – favourite saying, 'Kiss my ass' – blurted out: 'Who the fuck does Norma think she is . . . the house Madam?'

Gable's liaison with Lombard – whom he would eventually marry – had become one of Hollywood's most public romances. They kept their separate residences but, even so, incurred the wrath of moral crusading groups up and down the country. They were not the only ones accused

* The Mayfair Club Ball was an annual event for top movie people. An invitation signified respect and recognition.

of being unmarried husband and wife: Charlie Chaplin and Paulette Goddard, George Raft and Virginia Pine and Robert Taylor and Barbara Stanwyck were among other couples to whom worried studio bosses read the riot act in a bid to head off a puritanical backlash at the box-office.

Though good friends with Gable, Jack was arrogant enough to believe he could lure Lombard into bed. He had made no secret of his infatuation with her in the *New York World-Telegram* and there was little attempt to disguise the fact that he still coveted her. Apparently the attraction was mutual – 'I fancied her and she fancied me,' he confided to Bill Doyle. The price of showing it was a stern rebuke from Gable: 'Keep your eyes off my dame, bud.'

Jack was undaunted. When you have mixed it with some of Europe's finest heavyweights and shown three of your four American opponents the way home, a barbed warning from a mere giant of the silver screen holds few terrors. His mischievous notion to make it with Lombard was more a challenge than anything else and his big moment came when they met by chance in a night-club. Gable had failed to show and Jack and Lombard talked and danced. They had much in common. Like Jack, she loved Kipling's *If* and could recite it by heart. Like Jack she was unashamedly fond of sex, even to the point of finding it therapeutic. And like Jack she rarely wore underclothes – something he would have been certain to discover after she agreed to him seeing her home.

Next day he and Bill were woken from their mid-morning slumber by a loud rap on the door of their room at the Knickerbocker, where Jack was in temporary residence after an altercation with Judith. It was Gable and they could tell he was not best pleased. He had adopted the role of spurned lover and his performance was too true to life for comfort. He considered it monstrous that Jack had taken it upon himself to act as Lombard's escort; he suspected he had used the occasion as an opportunity to get to know her more intimately, and no lame denial from a garrulous Irishman who spoke like he was reciting Shakespeare would make him think differently. He invited Jack to step out in the corridor, doubtless confident that his masculine screen roles and numerous well-practised fight scenes had equipped him with the ability to put his love rival flat on his back – the precise position he was convinced Lombard had assumed for Jack the night before. The two men exchanged blows and Gable was sent sprawling by a right-hand punch, the impact of which when landing with bare knuckles would have been considerably more potent than when cushioned by a leather glove. Mercifully Jack had pulled the punch, or Gable might not have gone on to assume screen immortality in *Gone With The Wind.*

As it was he was able to pick himself up from the plush hotel carpet, a sheepish grin camouflaging his obvious embarrassment. Just one punch had been sufficient to dissipate his anger and restore his rationale. He was his old, amiable self once more, his manner and tone much more conciliatory. He acknowledged he had met his match by offering Jack his hand and the two men later signalled an official cessation of hostilities by getting together for a drink. There was no further contact between Jack and Lombard, according to Bill Doyle. She had no long-term designs on him for the very good reason that she loved Gable to distraction, even if she did find his ears too big and his penis too small.* What matter if, on one occasion, she had found Jack impossible to resist?

Gable was not the only Hollywood star to have traded blows with Jack. Errol Flynn often swapped punches with him, but those occasions were good-natured sparring sessions. The flamboyant Flynn, born in Hobart, Tasmania, liked to boast that he had boxed for Australia in the 1928 Amsterdam Olympics. Aided by the Warner Brothers publicity machine, he also attempted to project an Irish background. Both claims were found to be ficticious. However, in his book *The Life and Crimes of Errol Flynn*, Lionel Godfrey confirmed Flynn had been a contender in the New South Wales state amateur boxing championships in 1927, when he was 'eliminated by a bigger and stronger opponent.'

Jack was everything Flynn would like to have been had he not made it in the movies, namely a giant of an Irish heavyweight who attracted women with effortless ease. He delighted in having Jack put him through his paces, though Jack suspected that this shining star of the Hollywood firmament – who rarely shirked an opportunity to prove his manliness – was constantly attempting to land a sneak knockout punch. In truth a full-powered blow from the swashbuckling Flynn, who sparred just as if he were playing a scene in *Captain Blood*, would not have caused undue inconvenience, whereas one well-timed blow from Jack's right hand could have done Flynn untold damage. But always Jack spared him the indignity of putting him on the seat of his pants, or worse. He was reluctant to spoil the vision Flynn held of himself as the toughest two-fisted slugger in Hollywood.

Flynn and Gable held a considerable respect and admiration for Jack. They knew through personal experience that he was a formidable

* Gable's enormous ears were his dominant physical feature and a popular target for caricaturists. Lombard teased him publicly about the size of what she referred to as his 'sexual equipment'. Gable self-deprecatingly admitted he was dull in bed – 'I can't emote worth a damn' – and Lombard confirmed it, saying: 'He's no Clark Gable at home.' They married in 1939. Lombard died in a plane crash in 1942.

force as a fighter; and as far as looks went, they had nothing on him. In addition, he had a singing voice that could charm the birds from the trees and a speaking voice of such refinement and loquacity that all caught up in his company fell instantly under his spell. The general consensus was that if he were able to weave his magic on screen as in real life, he was destined to become one of Hollywood's biggest heart-throbs.

Jack already knew the truth. He had discovered – like his great idol McCormack before him – that he was no actor. It had hit home during endless weeks on the set of *Navy Spy*, when he was struck finally by the realisation of something he had known inwardly all his life: that he had been born to be a fighter. He had flirted with poetry and philosophy and raised his consciousness to the level where he had felt he was above boxing, but deep down he was still a primitive fighting man who thrilled to the roar of the crowd.

Somewhere along life's uncertain route he had allowed his intellect to rule his heart, and with disastrous results. Mistakenly he had come to believe that singing and acting were more genteel and respectable roles to play, deluding himself that he could take these more pleasant paths to fame. His intellect had been no friend; it had proved an enemy disguised as opportunity. It had led him away from his real vocation with the result that he was now in a no-man's-land of mediocrity, famous neither for his singing nor his acting – in fact, famous for being famous. He had abandoned the one thing that had been responsible for his fame and it in turn had abandoned him. Yet even now it might not be too late. He still had his youth – he was only 23 – his looks and his mighty punch. And he still had Judith, who had proved her love for him by remaining loyal and true through a catalogue of traumas that would have tested the patience of a saint. He had been one of life's inveterate philanderers, having little regard for her needs and treating her with a disdain that bordered on contempt. Judith had been broken, her feelings shattered and her faith in Jack all but destroyed. She had been on the brink of divorcing him, but the very act of instituting proceedings appeared to jolt him into a new mood of penitence. Indeed so earnest was he that Judith had a change of heart and decided to give it another go.

Jack was running out of time and excuses. He had one last chance to save his marriage and his boxing career, and his recent mental catharsis was evidence of a desire to do both. He cabled Dan Sullivan in London and said he wished to return to the ring, his misgivings over Dan's treatment of him in the past overridden by the realisation that there was no one better placed or empowered to help him resurrect his fighting dream. Sullivan responded positively, saying:

> 'Cut out filming and forget the singing and stage work. There is still time for you to justify the great promise you showed at the start of your career.'

He then fixed a meeting with Wembley boss Arthur Elvin,* a mighty entrepreneurial figure who ran regular big-time boxing at the 11 000-capacity Empire Pool arena adjacent to the famous stadium. Elvin considered Jack the greatest box-office draw in Europe and immediately offered him a fight on his first show of 1937 – subject, of course, to a settlement of his differences with the Board of Control. Jack cabled his acceptance and was told to get himself straight over to London to commence training.

There were problems ahead. Judith was not so much worried by Jack resuming his boxing career as dismayed at the thought of him going to England without her. She had a picture, *Telephone Operator*, to finish in Hollywood and could not make the trip until a month later. It would mean spending Christmas at home without him. That, and the prospect of Jack seeing in the New Year in someone else's arms, was more than she could bear. There was a furious row, during which she told him that if he went to England without her the marriage was at an end. Jack insisted he had to go in order to regain his self-respect. He told her it was his last chance as a fighter and that he would be a fool not to take it. Without doubt it was the worst bust-up they ever had, with crockery thrown and blows struck. It ended with Jack defiantly packing his bags and catching a flight to New York, where he took a passage in the French liner *Normandie.*

He reached England on New Year's Eve after an Atlantic crossing so rough that at one stage he had feared the ship might sink. But his heart did not sink; it was lifted by an unexpected message from Judith that made the final leg of the journey a lot smoother than it otherwise might have been. Twenty-four hours before landing he received a cable from her saying she was adopting a 'beautiful baby girl of four months with fair hair and blue eyes.' Judith desperately wanted a child to cement the marriage, but it had just not happened. Now she had taken matters into her own hands and Jack was delighted. It seemed to be her way of saying they would stay together for ever.

In effect it would have been a last-ditch bid to save the marriage, taken in the belief that a child would steady them down, make them less

* *Arthur Elvin* (later to become Sir Arthur) was a former messenger boy from Norfolk. In 1927, at the age of 27, he purchased Wembley Stadium for £122 500 and seven years later built the indoor Empire Pool, now known as Wembley Arena.

selfish and provide a common bond – someone they could both love to distraction instead of tearing each other apart. Jack spoke warmly of his wife's action when he stepped from the train at London's Waterloo Station to be met by Len Harvey, who had since become Elvin's boxing matchmaker at Wembley, and the usual army of reporters. He professed his love for Judith and talked of the 'several mistakes' he had made in his life:

> 'The biggest was when I went to Hollywood, a life of dissipation. Far too much temptation, luxury and licence. One gets soft. All the time I was on the set I was thinking , "This is no life for a boxer." But now I am finished with film work and anything else but the ring. Tomorrow I am going back to Dan Sullivan, the man who bought me out of the Army years ago and began to make a fighter out of me.'

It was Jack's first self-critical remark in public and it hinted at a growing awareness and maturity. Perhaps the revelation that he was now an adoptive father had fostered in him the desire to grow up and recognise the folly of his past indiscretions. It certainly augured well for his future with Judith – if he still had one. Time would tell.

He commenced training at the Star and Garter, once again under the guidance of Fred Duffett. He was to meet journeyman pro Alf Robinson, a Manchester greengrocer, in support of the fight for the world flyweight championship between Scotland's Benny Lynch and Small Montana. He was in good spirits now that his two greatest desires had apparently been satisfied: the resumption of his boxing career (the Board agreed to re-issue his licence after pressure from Elvin) and the repair of his rift with Judith.

Within just a few days his fragile peace was shattered. A cable arrived from Judith stating she had been detained in Hollywood for retakes and would not be coming over to England with their adopted daughter as planned.* She asked for £200 for immediate expenses, which Jack duly sent; he also cabled £5 to a florist for roses for her. But a week later it was announced in New York that Judith was filing a divorce action on the grounds of cruelty, incompatibility and drunkenness, the latter charge borne out by Jack's admission of his 'life of dissipation' in Hollywood.

The news was confirmed in a dramatic one-word cable from Judith which shook Jack down to his size-13s. It said simply: 'FINISHED.' He could scarcely believe it, but after a trans-Atlantic telephone conversation with her he realised it was no New Year hoax.

Bill Doyle, who was staying with Jack at the Star and Garter,

* The existence of the adopted daughter is uncertain. There was never any further reference to her and she may have been a ploy on Judith's part.

remembered well the effect that explosive telegram had on his brother:

> 'I'd never seen him so upset. He was so utterly devastated that he could not sleep. We had beds in the same room and Jack lay awake for nights on end, saying over and over again: "Why is she doing this? I thought everything was all right between us." Apparently Judith had been told Jack was seen with another woman during his stop-over in New York en route to England. Jack could not understand it. He kept repeating, "How can she say that? It's just not true."'

True or not, Judith believed it and nothing Jack was going to say or do could alter that fact. Four days before the fight, he sent her a final dramatic cable appeal:

> 'Don't, Macushla [My darling], I love you. Just one last chance. One wire from you and I will win fight for you.'

Judith did not react, and the following day details of her divorce suit were made public. In it she claimed £20 a week in alimony and alleged that Jack blacked her eye, consorted with other women, ignored her, embarrassed her publicly and threatened her with a pistol. 'Life with Jack was one long series of battles in and out of the ring,' she said. 'Life with Judith constitutes the happiest days of my life,' he responded.

Jack was aghast when told by newspapermen of his wife's allegations:

> 'Judith and I were happy together. If ever I raised my hand to her it must have been in a dream. I would never strike a woman. On the day she says I threatened her with a revolver we didn't even quarrel, so how could I have threatened her? We spent the evening alone and sang to each other. I love Judith and I always will love her.'

Then he began to feel sorry for himself:

> 'She might have waited till after the fight, anyway. It's like hitting a chap when he's down.'

If Jack thought Judith's sense of timing was, for an actress, way off cue, so was the arrival of income tax inspectors at the Star and Garter two days before the fight. They requested the immediate settlement of tax arrears mainly accumulated when he had visited England with Judith the previous year. The problem had to be sorted out quickly in view of the proximity of the contest, and Jack's offer to pay the Inland Revenue from the purses of his forthcoming fights was accepted. The tax liability, coupled with the money he owed the Board of Control and White City, ensured there would be little left of his £1 000 purse.

Predictably, Wembley was packed on the night of January 19, 1937. It had been close on three years since Jack had last fought in England

and that first-round destruction of Frank Borrington had been his only appearance in a London ring since the Petersen showdown way back in the summer of 1933. His last fight of any description, apart from the punch-up with Gable, had been his one-round fiasco against Buddy Baer 17 months previously. He would be creaking with ring-rust, but the familiar buzz of excitement that went round the huge hall in anticipation of the inevitable sensational and explosive content of the fight served to remind everyone in British boxing what they had been missing. As in the past, they would not be disappointed.

Jack's form was a revelation after such a lengthy lay-off. He was hitting with tremendous force and boxing better generally than at any stage of his career. He floored Robinson for six with a right to the chin after only a minute and another count quickly followed. Then, amid a shower of punches as Jack went for the kill, Robinson collapsed in his own corner. Jack was anxious to finish him off and struck another blow in the heat of the moment, whereupon the referee beckoned him back to his corner and called for the ring announcer.

Jack, smiling, was under the impression he had won the fight but the referee, Jack Smith, claimed Robinson had been sitting on the bottom rope with one hand touching the canvas when Jack delivered the final punch. The bedlam that broke out when the crowd heard the decision – Robinson the winner, Doyle disqualified – went on for several minutes. Heated arguments broke out among spectators as to whether it was a foul blow. There was a further extended delay before the world title contestants* could take the ring as the crowd set up a prolonged, 'We want Doyle' chant.

Had Jack 'lost his head' again – as had been conceded after his disqualification against Petersen – or did he deliberately strike Robinson when he was down? To accept the latter premise would be to believe that Jack was fatally flawed, both as a fighter and a man, and that his tough upbringing in the Holy Ground in Cobh, where he had learned at an early age that hitting first and asking questions later was the surest pathway to victory, meant he had never learned to fight fair.

Yet as far as this disqualification was concerned, it is possible to give Jack the benefit of the doubt and accept that the offending punch was the result of over-exuberance after such a prolonged absence from British rings. An additional consideration is that a fighter perched

* Lynch beat Montana on points over 15 rounds. He defended the title successfully with a thirteenth round knockout of Peter Kane, but forfeited it in June 1938 when scaling 8st 6½lb (6½lb over the flyweight limit) for a scheduled defence against Jackie Jurich, whom he knocked out in 12 rounds. Lynch's career and life then drifted into decline. He became an alcoholic and died in 1946 at the age of 33.

on the bottom rope is not officially down and still, therefore, a legitimate target. The question of his protection then becomes a discretionary judgment on the part of the referee, who is duty-bound to step in immediately in the event of his being in no position to defend himself. Whether Jack had noticed Robinson's glove touching the canvas when he hit him for the final time is open to question, but referee Smith must have assumed he had been aware of it. Otherwise there would have been no reason to disqualify him. Robinson himself concedes: 'It was over-enthusiasm on Doyle's part.'

The morning after the fight before, Jack held one of his most improbable Press conferences – stretched out in a barber's chair at a London hotel. Around him were littered the newspaper accounts of his disqualification and he was in no mood for false modesty:

> 'The public wants a killer and that's me – a killer. I knocked Robinson silly. When I knock them down, they stay down. Look at the reception I got. Look at the Press I got. I know, I know – disqualified for hitting a man when he's down. I'm telling you, cross my heart it's true, that he wasn't down. He was balancing on the ropes. You know me. I wouldn't hit a man if he was on the floor. Study the photographs – my conscience is clear. Gee! but I was in fine form last night.'

Jack could not resist going public on the marital bust-up with Judith. He even went as far as to reveal the contents of a private letter in which she had professed her love for him in language as poetic as anything he had read by Kipling.

The fact that he had been disqualified in the first round of his comeback fight seemed to matter little. When a spurned husband is attempting to win back the woman who means more to him than any other, his thinking is not always rational. He said wistfully: 'Oh, everything would be dandy but for this trouble with Judith.' He then pulled out the letter and said to a reporter: 'Read that – the first four lines, mind you. No more.'

Judith would have been mortified to know that her lyrical profession of love for Jack would be plastered all over British newspapers for the consumption of millions of readers. It read, a touch breathlessly:

> 'My Own Darling Lover Man, There is no woman living that draws breath so sad as I, though all things sadden her, and know not what evil thing I have done that life should lay such heavy load on me.'

Jack was in full flow now:

> 'My wife Judith wrote that. She is the one person in the world who matters. I

only got the letter yesterday, yet they say she is finished with me. Someone must have poisoned her mind. She wrote that and I haven't seen her since. Yet when I telephoned her she said she was finished. If only she had been at the ringside last night instead of 6 000 miles away in Hollywood. I think about her all the time – even last night in the ring. It's with me all the time. Gee, I wish we could be reconciled. I do wish that.'

'What do you want most of all, Jack – boxing laurels, a fortune or your wife?' asked a reporter.

'Judith – all the time and every time.'

Jack treated reporters like Trevor Wignall of the *Daily Express* as friends and confidants, appearing always to be at ease with them and never once dodging awkward questions with a discreet 'No comment'. His worries and concerns were willingly shared with the world, and perhaps this accounted in large measure for his popularity.

Judith displayed a similar refreshing lack of cynicism. The Press, who had quite a game with the pair of them, preyed on their problems eagerly and even tried to bring them back together – all in the line of duty, of course, and with an eye to a story. Newspapermen would act as mediators by ringing Judith in Hollywood, relating what Jack had been saying and then reporting on the dialogue that passed between them:

'Judith Allen, sobbing, insists in Hollywood that she is going ahead with the divorce. "Nothing will make me stop now," she said to a reporter over the trans-Atlantic telephone. "I don't want to say if I still love him. I don't think he deserves to know. I think he has behaved very badly, and only he himself knows how badly.

"He wants me back? How can he say that after what happened? I shall never have anything more to do with him."

Reporter: "Jack has become the biggest draw in boxing. He is getting offers from all over Europe."

Judith: "I don't care any more. I never wanted his money anyway. I can earn my own living. I always have; money doesn't enter into it."

Reporter: "Jack says he would rather have you back than win all the boxing laurels."

Judith: Listen. I know very well that Jack has been the idol of the English and Irish people. Good luck to him. I hope he always will be. But he proved conclusively to me that he didn't want either his boxing career or me. He says that someone has poisoned my mind against him, does he?" (Miss Allen laughed tearfully). "If anyone has done that it is Jack Doyle himself."

Reporter (still not giving up): "Your husband says that if you had been at the ringside on Tuesday night the fight might have ended differently."

Judith (sighs deeply, then long pause): "I'm not coming back to him. You tell the English and Irish that – and you can tell Jack Doyle, too." '

With that, she hung up.

Jack vowed not to capitulate. He was committed to one more fight, after which he planned to return to Hollywood and woo her back. His purse from the Robinson bout, withheld while the Board of Control investigated the circumstances of the disqualification, had been returned to him in full. It would be mischievous to suggest that their leniency with him on this occasion was coloured by the fact that, had they confiscated all or part of his purse and donated it to the Board's Benevolent Fund, they would have been unable to dock from it a portion of the money still owed to them and White City.

Jack's next fight would be against Dutch champion Harry Staal at London's Earl's Court Arena. Staal, yet to suffer a knockout after 73 professional fights, was drafted in when the original opponent, Jim Wilde of Swansea, went down with 'flu. It seemed a determined effort was being made to find somebody capable of standing up to Jack's explosive punching, for Wilde had been a tough proposition, an immensely strong fighter hard to put away. The Egyptian Salah-el-Din had him down an incredible 17 times and Wilde not only persisted in getting up each time but went on to win the fight – a feat so extraordinary that it almost defies belief. Jack was unimpressed when told of this, retorting: 'When I hit 'em right, they don't get up.'

The fact that Staal had been brought in when Wilde cried off was a sore point with Welsh champion Tommy Farr, who felt he should have been given the chance to face Jack.* 'Why have I been left out for a Dutchman?' he asked indignantly. 'I haven't lost in two years and have beaten Wilde.'

It is perhaps the greatest disappointment in the long history of the heavyweight division in Britain that a Doyle-Farr match was not made on this occasion and, indeed, never would be. Wilde's withdrawal provided the perfect opportunity to bring the two together, although the vast Earl's Court arena (capacity then 22 000) was five times too small to accommodate the crowd it would have drawn.

It would have been quite a fight – the classic contest of punching power versus skill and durability.

* *Farr* was to be adequately compensated six months later with a world title fight against Joe Louis, in which he would become the first of only three of the Brown Bomber's 25 challengers to last the 15-round championship distance. The others would be Arturo Godoy (1940) and Jersey Joe Walcott (1947).

Chapter 13

Beryl the Peril

Jack's fitness was not all it might have been. His attention had been diverted from the Staal fight by a liaison with the world's leading woman pilot, Beryl Markham, to whom he had been introduced at a party in his smart Carlton Court flat in Hertford Street, Mayfair.

It was an improbable relationship on three fronts. First, Jack was still supposedly pining for Judith Allen; second, he should have been in strict training; and third, Beryl, at 34, was 11 years his senior.

At the time she was enjoying world celebrity status after becoming the first woman to fly the Atlantic solo east to west – a feat previously achieved only by Amy Johnson's hell-raiser of a husband Jim Mollison. But Beryl's record-breaking flight (she crash-landed in Nova Scotia) was considered more meritorious because she took off from Abingdon in Berkshire, whereas Mollison had taken the shorter route from Ireland.

Beryl was a remarkable woman who had been brought up in British East Africa (now Kenya) by her father, Charles Clutterbuck,* an ex-Repton and Sandhurst man who had been attracted there by the Government's drive to encourage white settlers. It was believed that millions could be made by developing and farming the sparsely-populated protectorate, as had happened in India, and Clutterbuck purchased 1 000 acres of land in Njoro, on the slopes of the magnificent Mau Escarpment. Beryl's mother Clara disliked the social isolation of life in the African bush and had no wish to be part of her husband's pioneering adventures there. Also, she was missing her sick son Richard, Beryl's elder brother. He had been sent back three months earlier because the humidity did not agree with him and she

* Captain Charles Baldwin Clutterbuck, then 27 and hunting with the Cottesmore Hounds in his native Leicestershire, had met and married the lovely 19-year-old Clara Alexander – who hailed from a notable, well-to-do Irish family – in 1898, shortly after being kicked out of the Army. He had been forced to resign his commission in the lst Battalion, King's Own Scottish Borderers in mysterious circumstances. In her biography of Beryl Markham, *Straight On Till Morning,* Mary S. Lovell surmises that it was because of bad debts.

decided to go home to Leicestershire, leaving the four-year-old Beryl in Kenya with her father.

Beryl was raised alongside the Nandi and Kipsigis tribes and would later distinguish herself as a successful racehorse trainer and aviator – pursuits not previously graced in large number by women. She would have a well-publicised affair with Prince Henry, the Duke of Gloucester, and immortalise herself further with a remarkable memoir, *West With The Night.*

At the time Beryl was introduced to Jack by Jim Mollison she was separated from the second of her three husbands, the wealthy and aristocratic Mansfield Markham, by whom she had a seven-year-old son Gervase. Domesticity was not her stock-in-trade and Gervase was brought up by his grandmother, Lady Markham.

Beryl had inherited her father's fierce spirit of independence and was obsessed with the desire to push back the frontiers of male-dominated society. She was far more relaxed in the company of men, mainly because they shared her own aspirations of success and achievement in an age when women in the main were programmed for lives of subservience. What an inspiration she must have been to women like herself seeking to prove themselves in a man's world. But a spirit of independence can foster an attitude that holds no respect for customs and traditions and she had little regard for the sanctity of marriage – either her own or, for that matter, anyone else's. The fact that Jack was a married man certainly did not deter her – or him.

Beryl would never have qualified as a glamour girl in the film-star sense, but her tall, slender frame and high cheekbones gave her a classical, noble beauty that was accentuated by clear blue eyes and lustrous fair hair. In addition she was an extremely elegant dresser. Her greatest asset, however, was the sheer force of her personality, and once this formidable woman had set her cap at Jack she was bound to win him – just as with Prince Henry. She was said to have possessed a 'warm sexual appetite' and to have been an undisguised pursuer of the rich and famous, which, presumably, was why she latched on to Jack. In his case the conquest would have presented no particular difficulty in the light of Judith Allen's observation – learnt at first hand and to her considerable cost – that he could not resist sharing himself.

Beryl had no elaborate plan to entice him, apart from letting him know that he alone was the man with whom she would like to fly halfway round the world. She was seeking sponsorship for further remarkable exploits in the field of aviation and hoped to team up with Jack for a record-breaking flight that would 'startle the world'. Beryl coupled her announcement with the news that she would be giving him flying lessons at Hatfield once the fight with Staal was out of the way. Although the Press never hinted at a physical relationship between the pair, those close to Jack knew the score. And it is doubtful if Judith was fooled, even from 6 000 miles away.

When Jack finally found time to resume training at Windsor, the strict daily regimen of running, exercising and sparring brought him down from the clouds and convinced him that the intended venture – the 'secret' destination was believed to have been Australia or South Africa – was in reality a flight of fancy that he had no wish to pursue. The intense sexual partnership with Beryl was another matter entirely; he appeared to be in no hurry to bring that to an end and therein lay the great enigma of the man. Bill Doyle confirmed that Jack was still deeply in love with Judith and making efforts to win her back at the very time he was consorting with Beryl Markham. Perhaps he had been feeling in need of some female company when their flight paths crossed, or perhaps it was as basic as being unable to resist another – and famous – conquest. More likely it was both. But if he really did love Judith as much as he claimed, earning his wings with Beryl was an odd way of showing it.

He had genuinely feared for Judith's life on hearing she had been marooned by floods while on location for her latest film. When news eventually filtered through that she was safe and well, he was determined to hammer Staal into submission for a victory he was confident would bring her rushing back to his side.

Fight night proved as remarkable a spectacle as has ever been witnessed at any boxing event in Britain. Every seat at Earl's Court was occupied – despite it being only Jack's second comeback fight and the disgrace of the first. Indeed there were the familiar scenes of countless hundreds of spectators being turned away and police having to call up reinforcements to prevent the entrances being broken down. It was as if he had never been away.

Jack's reception can only be described as fantastic. Even Jack Dempsey and Georges Carpentier in their heyday were never received so rapturously, said one newspaper report. But the welcome he received when he climbed into the ring was eclipsed by the tumultuous ovation that accompanied him as he returned to his dressing-room after the fight. Dozens of admirers rushed to his corner, men threw their programmes and hats high into the air and evening-gowned women stood up, or in some cases jumped on to their seats, to add to the din with their screams of delight. If Jack had won the world championship he could not have been more of an idol, and only the fact he would not permit himself to be lifted prevented him being carried off in triumph. 'I cannot recall another scene like it,' reported Trevor Wignall.

Jack had started the fight in nonchalant, even careless fashion, as if his thoughts were far away in Hollywood. In the first round he took a swinging blow to the head and then a right to the chin that felled him for eight. There was a gasp as he went down, but Jack had sense enough to stay on one knee until his head cleared. Staal was strong and dangerous, but limited. What little boxing there was came, strangely enough, from Jack, who used his left to good effect. But even his heaviest punches did not succeed in shaking Staal until the fifth round, when the Dutchman began to feel the cumulative effect of the punishment he had absorbed. Even so, he was still menacing in bursts. Jack was hurt by a right hand to the jaw, but soon recovered and went back on the attack. Staal, his face bruised, and bleeding from a cut ear, became a chopping-block for Jack's powerful punches in the sixth. He was reduced to a state of near-helplessness and was staggering round the ring, his hands hanging limply by his side, when the towel was thrown in to signal a Dutch surrender.

Jack had been told beforehand to mind his manners and his punches. Dan Sullivan and Fred Duffett had warned him not to transgress the rules in any way in view of the fact that the referee was once again the prickly 'Pickles' Douglas. He wisely paid heed and was scrupulously fair and controlled throughout. Instead, it was Staal who incurred the wrath of the ultra-strict Douglas for low punching – though Jack had shown no outward signs of distress. Staal was frequently admonished for borderline punches and, in what proved to be the final round, was told in no uncertain terms that the warning then being administered would be his last – the very words the fastidious Douglas had used before throwing Jack out on his ear at White City. However, Jack did not intend giving Staal the opportunity of bowing out with a low blow. The final minute of the sixth saw the Dutchman hanging on the ropes, vainly attempting to escape the powerful punches being rained on him as Jack fought at his most furious. He was beaten to a pulp and it was as much a relief to Jack as it was to Staal when the fight ended.

Jack's victory had raised him to the highest eminence he had yet attained as a pugilist, said one newspaper. The £100 000 that he wished to earn with his fists was now at his fingertips, said another. Not quite. Most of his £1 250 purse from the Staal fight went to the income tax authorities and others with claims on him. Yet Jack was a happy man. He appeared to be more popular than ever with the British public, as evidenced by the remarkable scenes which greeted his victory and the offers that were pouring in for him from all over Europe. These included numerous marriage proposals. One – reputedly from a titled millionairess – stated that within a fortnight of his acceptance of her proposal she would settle £100 000 on him, provided he agreed to retire from the ring. Jack mused over this and several other letters from women of all ages and backgrounds who saw him as their knight in shining armour, each fancying herself the sole object of his desire. But only one woman was the object of his desire and she was Judith – his affair with Beryl Markham notwithstanding. The pain of being parted from his wife for almost two months was more than he could bear; it was driving him to distraction.

The irrepressible Trevor Wignall could not resist playing Cupid following the fight. He rang Judith in Hollywood to give her the news that Jack had won and to discover if her feelings toward him had changed. Her reaction was ambiguous:

> 'Say, did Jackie win? He did? Oh, that's swell! That's grand! He fought marvellously? Oh, this is too wonderful. We may be all washed up but I'm so glad he won. Remember he's still my husband. Naturally, I want him to do well.
>
> I'm working hard and earning plenty. I'll be here quite a time. Then, maybe, I'll come back to England and make a picture there. I love English people.'

Wignall was not to be denied:

> 'Just one question: Do you still love Jack Doyle?'

A long pause – so long that Wignall thought they had been cut off. Then Judith said firmly:

> 'Just right now I'm not prepared to say yes and I'm not prepared to say no. Gee, I've said I'm glad he won – I'm still interested in his career. I'm . . . oh, what's the use . . . ?'
>
> *Wignall*: 'It would cheer Jack up no end if you had a message for him.'
>
> *Judith*: 'No, no, I'm sorry. I just can't. No message. But you can make it known that I'm still alive and kicking after being marooned by floods way out on the mountains. We were out of communication with the rest of the world for four days . . . was it exciting! You didn't think I'd passed away, did you?'
>
> *Wignall*: 'Well, the Continental papers had printed your obituary.'
>
> *Judith*: 'It would have given me an awful kick to read my own obituary in the newspapers. Goodbye . . . and give my love to England.'

But she sent no message of love to her husband.

Jack could stand it no longer. He decided to go to Hollywood in a final, last-ditch attempt to win her back. He knew it was no good sending cables because Judith simply ignored them. He knew it was no good phoning. He had done so on several occasions and usually the calls – costing anything up to £20 a time – ended with her banging down the receiver.

In desperation he sought Arthur Elvin's permission to sail to the United States and straighten things out with Judith. Elvin had already fixed up a Wembley fight for Jack with the tough American King Levinsky, but agreed to the request after receiving an assurance that Jack would be be back in time to complete his training.

Reporters could not resist tracking Jack's every move. They found him packing for the trip on hands and knees in his luxury flat at Carlton Court, a beautiful torquoise ring given him by Judith nestling snugly on his little finger. As a peace offering he had bought her a little white Pekinese and hoped her delight in receiving it would be matched by an equal show of warmth for him.

He headed for Hollywood in good heart. He had cabled Judith with details of his impending arrival and was excited at the thought of her rushing into his arms at Los Angeles airport after the long flight from New York. He calculated wrongly. Judith was not at the airport to meet and greet him; indeed, it was fully two days before she even agreed to see him. During that 48 hours of anxious waiting he bombarded her with flowers and cables until, at long last, she relented.

Judith was cool and distant. She made a big fuss of the little dog in its basket that Jack had guarded like the crown jewels on his journey across the Atlantic, but there was no sign of the affection for which he craved.

He had to come clean. He admitted to Judith he had not played fair. He begged her forgiveness and promised to make amends. He suggested they annul their Mexican marriage and start afresh with a new wedding ceremony in London. He even tried to tempt her to return to England with him in time to see the coronation of King George VI, whom he had met socially on a number of occasions in company with the Prince of Wales, the brother 'Bertie' was now succeeding as sovereign.

Jack's performance might have earned him his much sought-after film contract had the Hollywood top brass been there to see it. But Judith was unmoved by its emotional and dramatic content. She had seen and heard it all before and was perceptive enough to know that Jack was incapable of staying loyal to one woman. She had sacrificed her promising film career for him and all it had brought her was misery and pain. Now she was feverishly attempting to resurrect it and fulfil the lofty words of praise once lavished on her by the mercurial de Mille. In all probability it was too late but, at the very least, she would earn a decent living and have the opportunity of creating a new life.

Jack would not take Judith's oft-repeated 'No' for an answer. He was like a gambler playing for high stakes and hoping his luck would turn with each roll of the dice. His last desperate throw was an offer to take

Judith's younger brother, John Elliot, back with him to London to act as guarantor of his good behaviour. Judith was aghast. John's wife Susannah was expecting a baby at any moment and Judith felt he should be at her side instead of swanning off to England with a husband for whom she had lost her respect if not her love. John proved impervious to pleas for him to stay. He insisted on taking up the invitation, his appetite whetted by Jack's promise to appoint him his personal manager on a variety tour of the British Isles.

Even up to the moment of their departure from Los Angeles to New York on the first leg of the journey to London, Jack hoped Judith would change her mind about him. But instead of being there to see him off, she sent lawyers to bid him *bon voyage* by serving divorce papers on him.

John Elliot's decision to accompany Jack to England whipped up an inevitable storm back home. Cables were sent to him in the *Normandie* requesting his immediate return in view of the condition of his wife, who in fact gave birth while he was aboard the liner. But John had no intention of going back; he preferred to be part of the glamour and excitement surrounding Jack and disregarded all attempts to get him to face up to his responsibilities to his wife and new-born baby.

When Jack stepped from the *Normandie* boat-train at Waterloo Station, he was promptly served with his second writ in a week – this time on behalf of Fred Curran. He had been surrounded by eager, jostling fans and reporters, but the happy smile vanished from his face when a solicitor's clerk, named as Eileen Lawler, stepped forward to serve him with the papers. 'Give them to my manager,' he told her, motioning to John Elliot.

There was further drama when another woman stepped boldly from the crowd, this time to deliver a more friendly welcome – a lover's kiss. She was fair and lissom and striking, and quite what John Elliot was to make of her in view of his role as male chaperone is hard to imagine. Beryl Markham was never a shrinking violet, but her decision to meet and greet Jack in the full glare of publicity must have been a calculated attempt to kill off what remained of his marriage.

Jack's vulnerability to predatory women – the deepest thorn in Judith's side – was never more evident. For an allegedly love-struck husband who had just completed a costly 12 000-mile round trip in an attempt to woo back his wife, his on-going relationship with Beryl was hard to figure. He had, in a manner of speaking, hopped out of bed with Beryl to travel all the way to Hollywood and prove his love for Judith and now would be hopping straight back into bed with her on his return. There appeared to be no sense, no logic to it all. He was quite happy for the two of them to be photographed in the back of the taxi that was soon to whisk them off to Carlton Court while knowing, as he must, that Judith would get the picture in more ways than one.

If he had needed a woman's sympathy and reassurance over the imminent break-up of his marriage, his mother or sisters would have been the natural providers, not Beryl. Clearly he was seeking neither and clearly she was providing neither. Beryl, with her 'warm sexual appetite', would be satisfying requirements of a more physical nature.

She must have been a wonderful provider. Jack did not re-start his training at Windsor for the Levinsky fight until five days after arriving back in England – which left him only eight days of preparation in all. It meant either that he had not taken seriously a 12-round contest against one of the world's roughest and toughest fighters – a man who had twice gone the distance with Primo Carnera, had lasted the course also with Max Baer and Walter Neusel and had beaten former world light-heavyweight champion Tommy Loughran – or, more realistically, he was so besotted with Beryl he could not tear himself away.

The most likely conclusion – apart from a natural desire to live and love dangerously – is that he was unable to resist a basic egotistical urge to sleep with the woman who'd had a long-running affair with Prince Henry, in much the same way he had found it impossible to resist Thelma Furness. The royal connection was important to someone of his background and it provided a stimulating and irrepressible sexual challenge. Not only could he walk and talk with princes, he could bed the same women.

Shortly after he eventually deigned to commence training at the Star and Garter – where brother Bill and John Elliot were also ensconced – it was announced he was injured and that the contest would have to be put back three weeks. A story of spurious content was fed to the newspapers stating he had ruptured a calf muscle in his left leg while skipping in the gym. The only exercise he had taken in recent days was in the bedroom. Although he submitted to an examination by orthopaedic and manipulative surgeons – who considerately encased the leg in plaster for three days – the suspicion must be that, having ignored all earlier pleas to present himself for training, he had realised too late that eight days was not nearly long enough to prepare for Levinsky.

Perhaps it was fate as far as Jack was concerned. In the interim two occurrences were to turn his love life upside down, putting the final nail in the coffin of his moribund marriage, bringing his fling with Beryl Markham to an abrupt end and placing him in the world's super league as a fortune-hunting Romeo.

Chapter 14

Just a gigolo

Act one started with the curtain coming down on Jack's marriage. He had phoned Judith in America one evening with hopes of a reconciliation still strong in his heart, but her frosty tone – 'It's no use Jack; I'm going ahead with the divorce' – finally convinced him he was fighting a lost cause. He had done all a man possibly could do in rushing to Hollywood to see her. As nothing had come of that, and she was still adamant about the divorce, he decided to wash his hands of the whole sad, sorry business. She could continue with the proceedings if it was what she really wanted. He resolved not to contact her again. He, too, was finished.

Act two was the almost immediate curtain-up on an illicit affair that for some days went undetected by the Press. It was to blossom and grow to such proportions that it would cause one of the world's wealthiest families to curse the day Jack Doyle walked into their life.

It had all started innocently enough, with the usual large crowd of admirers flocking to the Star and Garter to witness Jack's training and sparring sessions with George Davis, an 18-stone heavyweight from Banbury. Among them was Horace Dodge Jnr. He was the son and heir of the late Horace Elgin Dodge, one of the most notable multi-millionaires of the century and who, with his brother John, had built the mammoth motor car firm in Detroit that bore their name.

Both brothers died in 1920, after which the entire stock in the company passed to their widows. In 1925, the company sold out to investment bankers Dillon Read for an incredible $146 million. Almost half this sum passed to the former Christina Anna Thompson, who had been a piano teacher in Dundee before crossing the Atlantic and marrying Horace in 1886. He was then a mechanic doing nothing more entrepreneurial than mending bicycles with John in a small shop in Detroit. When the Dodge brothers switched their attention to the embryo motor car industry, business mushroomed so spectacularly that theirs became one of the greatest success stories in American automobile history.

Anna, as she liked to be known, bore her husband two children:

Horace Jnr and a daughter, Delphine. She was said to have been devastated by Horace's death but, being of tough Scottish Calvinist stock, she got over it well enough to be able to remarry six years later. However, her choice of husband second time round was by any standards a strange one – a failed New York actor, Hugh Dillman, whom she met and married in 1926. She divorced him in 1947 after seven years of separation and was to say later: 'Hugh taught me how to have fun with my money.' She must have meant that he taught her how to *spend* her money. He had helped her achieve her dream of becoming a leading Palm Beach society hostess at her magnificent $4 million residence 'Playa Riente', whose sale to her he had helped negotiate. She rewarded him with a commission of $1 million and her signature on a marriage contract. The union eventually foundered after she discovered him in bed with a man.

Anna's hopes that Horace Jnr might follow a similar trail-blazing path to that of his late father were cruelly dashed. He had been only 20 when Horace Snr died, and without his help and guidance could never hope to aspire to anything like the same level of success. He became a miserable failure in life, depressed by his inability to measure up. Being so obscenely rich ruined his mind and destroyed any motivation to high achievement. By his mid-thirties he was a heavy drinker and womaniser. At the time he met Jack he was married to the third, and allegedly most beloved, of his five wives, the former Follies beauty Martha 'Mickey' Devine, and they lived for the most part in magnificent splendour at St Leonard's, a 120-acre estate overlooking Windsor Great Park.*

The Dodge mansion, with its own ballroom, concert room and cocktail bar, resembled a castle. It had more than 100 rooms and separate quarters for the 50 servants employed by Horace. The grounds contained a golf course, a lake, hard tennis courts, stables for six horses, gardens and greenhouses, shooting areas, sheltered nooks and romantic walkways. Yet, touchingly, Horace's most prized possession was an oil painting of wife Mickey in a long white evening gown with red sash that hung in the huge hall. A stark white light shone on it night and day. It was a romantic gesture by Horace, but in reality he was a hell-raising lecher who would have to shell out a hefty £350 000 to extricate himself from his failed marriages. His huge and lavish parties at St Leonard's were attended by some of the most notorious celebrities of the era. A well-known prostitute, Anne Black,

* St Leonard's estate is now the 'Legoland Windsor' theme park.

was a frequent guest. So was weird American-born film actress Frances Day.* Both are said to have given Horace a good time.

Horace may have been a philanderer, but his generosity knew no bounds. He staged spectacular firework displays and exhibition boxing tournaments at St Leonard's, the proceeds of which went to local hospitals. He delighted in using his wealth and influence for the benefit of others. True to his nature, he expressed a desire to help Jack beat Levinsky after observing him at the Star and Garter. The pair struck up an immediate friendship when fun-loving Horace climbed in the ring for a spot of slapstick sparring. An invitation to St Leonard's followed, and what Jack saw there opened his eyes to another world. It was not the grand opulence and immense wealth alone that awakened his powers of perception, but the presence of Horace's cultured, fair-haired sister Delphine on one of her frequent visits from America with 14-year-old daughter Christine. It took Jack no time to catch on. He had been the target of enough women to be able to tune in to the signals the 38-year-old Delphine was transmitting. They were high-frequency messages of instant attraction and desire, and Jack let her know they had been received and understood. Perfectly.

From then on he was sneaking across to St Leonard's daily. Each evening when Dan Sullivan left the Star and Garter to head back to town with his usual circle of cronies, he made sure his Irishman was tucked up safely in bed. According to Bill Doyle, no sooner had Dan departed for London than Jack was up, dressed and off to St Leonard's to canoodle with Delphine. Jack became such a regular visitor that he was invited by Horace to move into the mansion, where he would be free of distraction from back-slappers and women admirers while completing his training.

At first Horace was in ignorance of the sizzling romance between Jack and Delphine. They were careful to hide their feelings for one another for fear he would disapprove. Though Delphine was aware of her brother's extra-marital flings and sexual excesses she was nervous that he, and more especially her mother, would press her to end the affair. Delphine, after all, was a married woman. Like Horace, she had been wed three times. And, again like Horace, true happiness had always eluded her.

Her first husband had been James Cromwell, the son from the first marriage of her mother's best friend Eva Stotesbury, renowned as

* Frances Day (real name Frances Victoria Schenk) was an American revue star who came to London in 1925 at the age of 18. She became well-known in Britain, appearing in several films in the 1930s, 1940s and 1950s. Perhaps the best of them was *Fiddlers Three*, in which she played the part of Poppea. She died in 1984.

the queen of Palm Beach society. She married him in 1920 at the age of 21 and in 1923 bore him a daughter, Christine. In 1928 the marriage ended in a Reno divorce, after which Delphine rewrote her will stipulating that in the event of her death no financial advantage, either directly or indirectly, should accrue to Cromwell. Such acrimony seemed untoward when weighed against the family's indebtedness to Cromwell. He had been instrumental in procuring the $146 million bid for the Dodge Brothers Motor Car Company from Dillon Read at risk of incurring the wrath of his wealthy banker step-father Edward T. Stotesbury, whose company, J. P. Morgan, had offered $95 million. The suave James would not need Delphine's money. In 1934 he wed tobacco heiress Doris Duke – reputedly *the* richest woman in the world – and was subsequently appointed Minister to Canada by President Franklin D. Roosevelt.

Three months after the divorce became final, Delphine married again. This time the man appointed to be Mr. Delphine Dodge was Raymond T. Baker, former director of the US mint. Not content with having printed the nation's money, he acquired a licence to print his own when he wed Delphine, though he was said to be of independent means. They had a daughter, Anna Ray, but their happiness was, literally, short-lived. The marriage had already turned sour and divorce proceedings instituted when Baker died of a heart attack in the Spring of 1935 while Delphine was visiting Horace at Windsor.

Husband number three, and the man currently holding down the position, was Timothy M. Godde. He, too, was rich on his own family's account and had no need to marry Delphine for her loot. But he did just the same. The wedding took place at Bracknell Registry Office in Berkshire within three months of Baker's demise and it united two of the wealthiest families of France and America.

Godde was the son of M. Jules Godde, a well-to-do silk manufacturer and owner of several historic castles in France, one of which – a château near Alsace – was the country's show castle. He had worked in the United States for several years as an import agent, had a property in Rye, New York, and was an outstanding amateur golfer.

Delphine was Godde's second wife. He had previously been married to the former Clorinda Lockhart, but secured the fashionable, almost obligatory, Reno divorce six months before hitching himself to Delphine's star. And what a star. Her reputation as one of the wealthiest women in the world was not without foundation. She was the proud owner of the priceless Romanoff pearls,* said to be the most

* Horace Dodge Snr paid $825 000 for the necklace, which consisted of 389 perfectly-matched pearls strung in five strands. Anna wore it only twice, then gave it to Delphine.

magnificent and perfectly matched in existence and previously the property of the Roman general Pompey and Catherine II of Russia. They had been in the possession of the Romanoff family when they were overthrown. The legend surrounding the pearls is that they bring misfortune to all their owners, and this was certainly true of Delphine. The only real joy she had experienced was in power-boat racing – Horace was also a keen enthusiast – and music, her deep appreciation of which had been passed on to her by her doting mother. Indeed so expertly had Delphine been schooled that she was a pianist of exceptional talent and had given recitals in London and New York.

The extremes of Delphine's two greatest passions gave an insight to her character. The thrill of power-boat racing enabled her to display unusual courage at high speed,* while, in sober contrast, the beauty of classical music gave expression to her innermost being. The quest for excitement and love were inextricably linked; she had found both in recreation and she needed to find both in her relationships with men. In that respect her twin inward desires had to be satisfied not in the mastery of two divergent pursuits, but through one person alone. Delphine was finding success in this area infinitely more difficult to attain.

Timothy Godde, a distinguished-looking man with thick black hair greying at the temples, was no longer Delphine's *beau idéal*. Though a person of great charm and affection, and possessing the great French penchant for romance, he had lost the knack of being able to rouse his wife to passion.

Small wonder, then, that it had been love at first sight for Delphine when she set eyes on Jack. Here was the element of excitement and danger that had gone out of her life. She was captivated by him immediately, the more so when she discovered the brain that went with his considerable brawn. With him she was to be totally fulfilled, both physically and mentally. The fact that their affair had to be conducted discreetly, behind closed doors at St Leonard's, merely added to the sense of drama.

Horace was at first unaware. There was an affinity between them prompted, so he thought, by their common interest in books and music, and Delphine delighted in playing piano accompaniment as Jack charmed the Dodge household with his songs. Perhaps if Horace had discerned some romantic attachment, he might not have agreed to Delphine's request to invite Jack to stay.

* Delphine competed in events at Miami, Port Washington (Long Island) and Greenwich, Connecticut. At one time she was the unofficial world women's speedboat champion.

Luxury such as existed at St Leonard's was, for Jack, like stepping into a world of fantasy. He did not even bother returning to the Star and Garter to collect his belongings; instead a Dodge servant was dispatched there to collect them and brother Bill. John Elliot had long since sailed, disillusioned, back to America to face inevitable family fury for abandoning his wife.

Jack and Bill were allocated their own private rooms and given the run of the house. At their disposal was Horace's huge army of servants – all of them Doyle-crazy. Six horses were available for Jack's use. Often he and Delphine could be seen riding in Windsor Great Park and there was a fleet of chauffeur-driven cars to whisk him to and from the Star and Garter. Little was seen of him in the town, where he had always been such a popular figure in the build-up to his fights. Even his roadwork was done around the secluded grounds. A former maid at St Leonard's, Emily Walpole, remembered seeing him vaulting a gate as he set off on his run around the wooded area of the grounds and chopping wood to tone up his muscles.

Jack spent most of the day in the company of his generous host. Bill Doyle recalled that Horace – once described by a New York paper as a 'middle-aged millionaire with a bad heart, a lame leg, ravaged face and a tendency to mumble in his beer' – liked to start the day with a whole glassful of neat Scotch, which he gulped down in one go. His drinking went on periodically throughout the day to the extent that Jack was moved to express his amazement. Horace was capable of playing a useful game of tennis with Jack each morning, but as the day wore on the whisky began to take its toll and turn him gradually from an affable and likeable host into a surly, argumentative bore.

Toward late evening, after a sumptuous dinner and a sing-song with Delphine at the piano, Jack would retire to his quarters, where he would read and listen to the radio. His favourite book at the time was *Goodbye Mr. Chips*, which he could hardly put down. He carried it virtually everywhere with him – except into Delphine's bedroom. At first he would return to his empty bed well before morning light, searching his way along myriad passages and corridors for his room. Once Horace found out about the affair there was no need for such circumspection. He and Delphine had always been close and her happiness was his prime consideration. If she wanted Jack – with whom he was also particularly taken – then it was her business and he would not interfere.

Jack's stay at St Leonard's constituted probably the most bizarre big-fight preparation ever undertaken. Here was the most celebrated fighter in the land living it up in opulent surroundings and, not for the first time, co-habitating with a woman in the vital weeks and days leading up to a top-of-the-bill contest on a major promotion. Fortunately Jack possessed natural reserves of strength, which he appeared to be able to summon at will during a fight. It was just as well that this was the case, for Levinsky would be a tough and dangerous opponent. The 26-year-old American (real name Harry Krakow) was as much unlike Jack as anyone could be. His chief drawback was that he lacked a sense of humour, though he did raise an unintentional laugh when the Loyal Toast was proposed at a pre-fight luncheon. Everyone stood except Levinsky, who thought the words 'The King' applied to him.

It was evident at the weigh-in that Jack had not completely neglected his training at St Leonard's. He tipped the scales at a trim 14st 8lbs, just four pounds heavier than Levinsky and, surprisingly, 9lbs lighter than when he fought Jack Petersen four years earlier. Advance bookings for the fight had reached £12 000 and a further £3 000 was taken on the day as the usual last-minute rush for tickets ensured Wembley would be packed to capacity. The fact that today the same arena, albeit recently enlarged, is usually half-empty for big boxing events illustrates just how charismatic a figure Jack was in the far from affluent 1930s.

The fight lived up to expectations, with Jack forced to go the distance for the first and only time in his career. He won overwhelmingly on points over 12 rounds and the huge throng of fans loved every second. Almost hysterical enthusiasm greeted each punch he aimed at the American. It was as if the crowd, aware of his limitations in a truly boxing sense, felt they had to will him to victory. Jack had employed his left hand more than usual in training in the knowledge that Levinsky was virtually indestructible and that he might have to settle for a win on points. In addition an unnamed sportsman, said to be keen to see Jack improve his technique, was offering £1 for every straight left he landed.* Jack had good cause to be grateful in the third round, when he damaged his right thumb on Levinsky's iron-hard cranium.

He stuck manfully to his task and throughout the fight the major point of interest was how long Levinsky could survive. In the event the American, though never knocked off his feet, took a fearful hiding. During the last four rounds his lower jaw never ceased quivering. He

* The sportsman – thought to have been Horace Dodge Jnr – stood, by common consent, to lose £178. But Jack, who received £2 300 for the fight, declined to take the money. He asked instead for a small memento as a token of victory.

was badly hurt and his face looked a bloody mess. His left ear was bruised and bleeding from the effects of the incessant pounding he had received in each round from the chopping blow Jack was forced to deliver with his injured right. His mouth was cut, both cheeks were swollen under the eyes and one of the swellings was lacerated. He was in such a state that he clung to the ropes and to Jack and, toward the end of the contest, had to be guided back to his corner at the close of each round by the referee, C. B. Thomas. Whatever Levinsky lacked in skill he more than made up for in courage.

Jack had proved yet again, if proof were needed, that he stood alone in terms of box-office appeal. His 19 fights as a professional, *including* his 12 rounds against Levinsky, had totalled just 45 rounds – statistics that told their own story and accounted in large measure for his unparalleled popularity. He had suffered only three defeats – two by disqualification and the other after being hit low – and his future was brighter than at any stage of his career. But for his injured right hand he would undoubtedly have knocked out Levinsky, one of the most durable men in world heavyweight boxing. At 23, Jack had once more elevated himself to the top of the British heavyweight league. As a showman, he was without equal. He had proved, not for the first time, that he had the power and the majesty to conquer the world.

Tragically, having earned the plaudits of the Press and the unbridled adulation of the public, his self-destructive urge had returned with a vengeance. The love-hate relationship he had with the sport was, by now, plainly apparent. Quite why this most exasperating of men should always have fallen out of love with his tough trade at the very moment it had made him master must forever remain a mystery. Imagine the young Errol Flynn working and scheming and dreaming for years of becoming a movie star and then quitting just as he is about to be offered his greatest roles.

Jack had never wanted to be, and never became, the archetypal boxer. But then his friend Flynn had never wanted to be the archetypal actor. Yet, whereas Flynn was blessed to a degree with the forebearance which enabled him to accept and embrace the disciplines of film-making, Jack could barely countenance the thought of having to prepare for contests for weeks on end. Even in his earliest days as a professional he had abhorred the sweat and grind of daily training; naively, all he had ever wanted to do was get in the ring and fight.

He realised how different his attitude was to that of boxers who had sneered at his lack of dedication and professionalism and who hated him for the success he had attracted with so little effort. He had never hated them – just pitied them. He knew he was unique in a sport that demanded much more to reach the summit than he was ever prepared to give. The method of achieving it was distasteful to him: too distasteful for the end to justify the means. The reflection of himself as the Irish Jack Dempsey had become distorted. Visions of Count John McCormack had often taken over; then images of himself as a great screen lover in the Flynn and Gable mould. Each had transposed the other at various times, only for the former vision to reassert itself. The result was confusion of the mind; he had seen himself in so many diverse roles that he had become a Jack of all entertainment trades and master of none. He had failed to find his true place.

One thing he *had* realised beyond doubt in the aftermath of the victory over Levinsky was that his heart was no longer in boxing. Though he had delighted the crowd and more big fights were being lined up, he had finally become completely disenchanted with the sport which had once filled him with such passion and expectancy.

Perhaps the fact he had been deprived of 50 per cent of his prize-money in his three comeback fights in order to pay back-taxes and legal costs incurred during the Petersen saga had influenced his feelings. He felt as if he would never be free of the burden, and fighting was the toughest method of all of repaying it. He was making the supreme sacrifice by putting his bodily health and mental faculties on the line for – as he saw it – everyone's benefit but his own.

Not least, too, there was his romance with Delphine Dodge Godde. This, not unnaturally, had also caused the fighting embers within him to cool. When one of the world's richest women is a prize within easy reach, motivation in other areas becomes extremely difficult to sustain. Though he was not in love with Delphine – and had confided to Bill that he found sexual relations with her predictable and unexciting – her infatuation with him was like having the key to the Bank of America vaults thrust into his giant paw.

Yet the lure of the almighty dollar, great though it must have been, was not so enticing that it prevented him sharing his affections with other members of the Dodge family. One was none other than Delphine's jail-bait daughter Christine, who, though not yet 15, was a formidable if unlikely rival to her mother for the affections of the man she called Mr. Blarney. The other was Horace's wife Mickey, who found Jack's embraces much more exciting than the fumbling, whisky-induced advances of her drunken husband. The inevitable outcome was that he was eventually asked to leave when Horace, having sensed a more than platonic relationship between Jack and the vivacious Mickey, caught them canoodling in one of the many greenhouses on the estate.

Whether Delphine was made aware of the reason for Jack's hasty exit from the mansion is unclear, but if so it made not an atom of difference. However, the mutual affinity between Jack and her own daughter *did* disturb Delphine. There were frequent rows over him and on one occasion he overheard the precocious Christine telling her mother: 'You'll never marry Jack. He likes me better than you.' That wounding news must have come as a shock to Delphine, but she knew by virtue of her wealth that Jack would never desert her. She had professed her undying love for him between the sheets and although St Leonard's was now out of bounds, he was able to carry on the pretence of loving her at her smart flat in Smith Square, Westminster.* Delphine seemed not to notice or not to care. She was madly in love, and the fact she could have his body but not his soul only added to his appeal in her eyes. He was someone she could buy but never own.

When finally she acceded to her family's repeated requests to return to her husband in America, she did so with a heavy heart. Jack had promised to follow as soon as he could free himself of his fighting commitments and she knew he would honour that pledge – not because he loved her, but because he loved her money. She planned to put it at his disposal if he would agree to marry her in the sure knowledge that it was the only way she could hang on to him.

Meantime, Jack was fighting shy of all attempts to get him back in the ring. The only thing on his mind was to follow the Dodge dollar trail across the Atlantic. Yet the eye to opportunity which many times had persuaded him to abandon his boxing career in favour of stage and film work was once again wide open when he happened by chance to meet up with an old flame in London. She was the alluring American torch-singer Libby Holman, whom he had first met in New York when embarking on that interminable tour of Broadway night-clubs with Goodtime Charlie.

Miss Holman was no ordinary singer: she was a millionairess and head of the giant Reynolds Tobacco Company. She had inherited it – along with £1 200 000 – from her late husband Smith Reynolds, who was found shot dead in mysterious circumstances in his flat at Winston-Salem, North Carolina, in 1932. The suspicion that she may have had her super-rich husband bumped off so she could inherit the company and the cash is irresistible, but the coroner concluded that he had committed suicide.

* According to Mick Doyle, Delphine gave Jack a gold cigarette case on which was inscribed: 'Darling Jack, if only you meant it.'

Libby had been singing her sensuous songs of unrequited love at the prestigious Derby Ball at the Grosvenor House Hotel in London. Jack was not on the bill, but he had put together a lady-killing act for Libby's private edification. One wealthy woman was as good as another as far as he was concerned, but Libby had the advantage of being younger and more attractive than the lean, fair, sharp-featured Delphine. In addition, as a widow, she was more readily accessible.

So successful was Jack's wooing and so persuasive his charm that Libby found herself accepting his proposal of marriage before leaving London for a brief visit to the Continent. He arranged to sail with her to the United States on the *Normandie*, which she would be boarding at Le Havre and he at Southampton. They would wed as soon as he had secured a Reno divorce from Judith Allen.

He confided the details of his marriage plan to two people. One was Trevor Wignall and the other the wealthy Henry Bay, thought to have been a Turkish-Armenian Jew who had made his considerable fortune by inventing the Franco shop and hotel signs. Bay, whose habit of spitting hardly made him an endearing companion, was a man who liked the company of attractive young women; and he was aware that by latching on to Jack he would be surrounded by some of the most beautiful creatures in London, if not the world. He threw lavish parties at Franco Cottage, his home in Maidenhead – the Thames riverside town where Jack had often paid court to the beautiful 16-year-old Peggy Andrews, a member of the Andrews boat-building family. Jack and his great pal Jim Mollison were always at the top of the invitation list, so ensuring a healthy turnout of glamorous girls. Bay was a generous benefactor in return for the provision of such a galaxy of female talent. He volunteered to accompany Jack to the United States and pay the costs of the trip once the nature of the business there was disclosed to him, no doubt anticipating a glut of activity in the night-spots of New York and Los Angeles. Jack was well able to afford the cost of his own trans-Atlantic passage but, once the bountiful Mr Bay had offered to do the honours, it was no contest.

In the meantime Dan Sullivan – blissfully unaware of Jack's impending departure to America – had been busily arranging a fight for him at Earl's Court against the world-rated Finn, Gunnar Barlund. Jack was to get £2 000 for the contest, which was being staged by the National Sporting Club and backed by the Marquess of Queensberry in aid of All Saints Hospital. There was uproar when he pulled the plug on the promotion. He claimed he could not go through with the fight because the right hand he injured against Levinsky was still in a bad way and affirmed his intention of sailing for New York in time to see the Braddock–Louis fight in Chicago.

NSC manager John Harding threatened an injunction to prevent Jack leaving the country unless he submitted his right hand to a medical examination, and the Board of Control requested his presence at an emergency meeting. Jack did indeed attend, his right hand in plaster and his left hand clutching a letter from a specialist which stated that two fingers of his right hand were injured. In the specialist's opinion, he was suffering from chronic synovitis and was 'quite unable to fight at the moment'.

Jack told the Board's Southern Council that his hand went again when he was punching the heavy bag in training. That explanation, and the specialist's letter, convinced them – or, if it did not, they had no option but to accept it. They issued a statement saying they were satisfied he was unable to train and box and that he had done his best to fulfil the contract, leaving Jack free to sail for New York in the *Normandie* that same afternoon.

Typically, as top people did and still do – though *never* fighters – he was 'taking refreshment' in the Ritz when the indefatigable Geoffrey Simpson caught up with him. Simpson was imbued with missionary-like zeal when pursuing a story, especially when it concerned the man who had become an international celebrity since his bold, unambiguous assessment of him at the age of 17 as a 'future world beater'. Even so, had Jack told Simpson then that he would one day be interviewing him in the Ritz instead of at the Victoria Barracks in Windsor it is doubtful he would have believed him.

Jack had come a long way in a short time and was evidently quite at home in such surroundings and in the company of the doyen of boxing writers. It soon became abundantly clear that he had never had the slightest intention of going through with the Barlund fight:

> 'I am sailing in the *Normandie* and cannot meet Barlund. The fact is my right hand is in a bad way. In any case, the match was not on as far as I was concerned. They have a contract, you say? Well, my manager may have signed one but I didn't.'

Sullivan was shocked and mystified and it is difficult not to feel a measure of sympathy with him. He said at the time:

> 'It is true Jack had to pay off his creditors two or three thousand pounds. But he still had £750 for himself after fighting Levinsky. He was to get £2 000 for

meeting Barlund and I had obtained an offer of £6 000 for his next appearance in London. He throws all that away by leaving.'*

Clearly Sullivan sensed there was nothing radically wrong with Jack's right hand, and his and everybody else's suspicions were confirmed when it was revealed that Jack and Libby Holman were fellow-passengers in the *Normandie.* Yet no one was more surprised, or indeed angry, when the news leaked out than Miss Holman herself. She expressed 'amazement' when contacted by Atlantic telephone and told of reports circulating in London that she and Jack were about to be married. 'The report is absolutely without foundation,' she said indignantly, 'and I shall be grateful if you will deny it. I had not the slightest idea Jack Doyle would be in the *Normandie.*'

Libby was apoplectic with rage that the marriage plan had been made public. She had given strict instructions that her name was not to be associated with Jack because she had desired the first announcement to be made in New York to coincide with her return to a Broadway theatrical show. Now that her cover had been blown, she was refusing to speak to anyone. She even went as far as to barricade herself in her state room, with a steward acting as bodyguard outside to prevent anyone seeing her.

No more than half-a-dozen people were aware she was even aboard the ship. When she sailed from Le Havre her name was not on the passenger list and in the revised list she appeared as Mrs Libby Holman Reynolds. Libby was a highly secretive woman, so much so that she was not seen by a soul for the first 24 hours. She then dined in the cafeteria, where there were not more than a dozen people, and was later seen dancing with Jack. Up to then she had not graced the main dining room or any of the other public rooms with her presence. Now she was fuming and in strict seclusion after hearing from her American manager that the publicity given to her proposed marriage was 'very bad' for her career. He asked her to issue a complete denial, and she did so in the plainest possible manner. She refused to accept the frequent telephone calls from the United States and was so incensed that she declined even to see Jack.

* Len Harvey was approached to substitute for Jack at Earl's Court. He was startled when the NSC offered £1 000 for him to fight Barlund. 'That is just half of what you proposed to pay Doyle,' he replied curtly. 'Does that mean you regard him as twice as good a draw as myself, for if that is so, you had better find someone else to help you out. I'll take what you offered Doyle, but not a penny less. If you can afford it for him, you can afford it for me.' But even Harvey was not worth as much as Doyle, and Maurice Strickland, the New Zealander, was brought in to face Barlund. (From Gilbert Odd, *Len Harvey: Prince of Boxers*, Pelham Books, 1978.) Strickland won when Barlund was disqualified in the seventh round.

Trevor Wignall, who was aboard the *Normandie*, claimed he had not given Libby away, though she blamed him among others. Wignall had warned that there would be a sensation on board if the news got out, and already rumours were beginning to mount. Jack felt as if the world had collapsed from under him; he had kissed goodbye to a £1 million fortune just as certainly as if he had tossed it over the side of the ship. Libby had told him in no uncertain terms just what she thought of him and, further, warned him never to cross her path again. She told him so in language spiced with so many choice four-letter words that he was left in no doubt that if he fell overboard and was drowning she would not lift a finger to help.

He consoled himself by doing some singing in the smoke-room, but was a disconsolate figure when the *Normandie* docked in New York. Long after the passengers had disembarked he was sitting alone and forlorn in the lounge, his dash and buoyancy having vanished. Henry Bay, who had been expecting to be best man and who confided to Wignall that he would be building the couple a magnificent house in Maidenhead, had gone ashore feeling rather sorry for himself and stating that he wished to wash his hands of the whole sorry business.

It was just as well for Jack that he missed the verbal knockout delivered by Miss Holman when newspapermen boarded the ship. There were hectic scenes as she frantically denied there had ever been a romance between them. She strongly rejected claims that she had promised to marry him or that she had the slightest intention of doing so. She described Jack as a publicity-hunter whose name she could not even remember until she met him on board ship. Further, she called him all the names she could think of and said she hoped she would never see him again.

'I hardly know the man,' she protested vigorously when a reporter smartly produced a picture of her dancing with Jack. 'That picture is three years old. He asked me to dance with him at a night-club and the minute I was on the floor – boom went his photographers. He must have hidden them somewhere.' As a parting shot, she remarked: 'He's got plenty of brawn, but he should have more brains.'

Jack's arrival in the United States was the least spectacular of his career. As if he had not experienced enough trauma on the journey over, he was faced with additional problems when the authorities refused to recognise his passport and visa – a complication caused by his failure to apply for a re-entry permit on leaving America after his abortive attempt to woo back Judith Allen. He was taken to the immigrants' depot on Ellis Island where, following a Board of Inquiry hearing lasting three-and-a-half hours, he was allowed into the country.

He went ashore attempting to disguise himself behind dark glasses and feeling as if he'd had two big fights in three days, one with Libby Holman – against whom he had been caught amidships and come off a poor second best – and the other with the immigration officials, with whom he had fought an honourable draw. Now he faced a third encounter that, thankfully, held every prospect of being less arduous than the previous two and in which the victory spoils would compensate him handsomely for the loss of Libby Holman. He would be seeking the considerable consolation prize of Delphine Dodge Godde's hand in marriage.

The publicity over Jack's Atlantic escapade had done nothing to dampen Delphine's ardour. She still wanted him desperately and was prepared to go to any lengths to get him. Her principal weapon was money, and lots of it, which she used unashamedly as bait to lure him. Now that she had him on home ground, as it were, she was determined he would not wriggle free to become prey for another Libby Holman. Delphine staked him in Hollywood to the tune of $600 a week and eventually joined him there to discuss the best method of extricating herself from her marriage to Timothy Godde. There was only one way of achieving it speedily – a Reno divorce. The planning was done between bouts of love-making – or, in boxing terms, during the one-minute intervals between rounds. It was decided, perhaps a touch breathlessly, that Jack, with brother Bill still in tow, would stay with Delphine at her home in Calneva, Nevada, in order to satisfy the six-week residential qualification.

There was to be yet a third member of the Doyle travelling circus holed up with them in Calneva – an unlikely fellow-Irishman named Jimmy McIlveen, who hailed from Dundalk and earned his living as a stage-hand.

Like many an itinerant Irishman, McIlveen had gone to America in search of fame and fortune. The nearest he had come to fame was having danced with Joan Crawford, a feat of such moment in his eyes that he dined out on it for many a year. 'I touched her bare shoulder,' he would say with due reverence. 'Franchot Tone was dead jealous.' McIlveen was a brilliant harmonica player and arguably a great mimic. He looked like an older version of Charlie Chaplin and indeed sometimes doubled for him in films. He had appeared also in vaudeville and burlesque, but of late had been finding work hard to come by. In future, generous Jack Doyle would be his meal-ticket; McIlveen would become his camp follower, his court jester and his Man Friday.

Quite how this small, brown-eyed ferret of a man who existed on the periphery of the star scene in filmland could have ingratiated himself when Jack was so preoccupied with Delphine and her millions is difficult to comprehend. But Jack could recognise con-artistry as soon as he saw it and when this was allied to wit and humour he considered it an admirable trait. In essence, McIlveen was an Irishman down on his luck and it is to Jack's credit that he befriended him as much for that reason as for the fact that he got so much amusement out of him. 'Friday!' he would bark, 'Go and fetch the newspapers.' McIlveen, who in later years would be labelled The Rogue with a Brogue, was always sightly in awe of Jack and could never quite make out if he was joking; but he always jumped to it smartly, just in case.

McIlveen became so close to the Doyle brothers that he was privy to everything that went on between Jack and Delphine, right down to the way in which Jack was using her to his own best advantage. Through him it would eventually be revealed that Delphine had offered Jack £200 a week to marry her, paid off £2 000-worth of gambling debts he had accrued in Reno, and promised to sell her magnificent £200 000 house in Washington and build him another in California next to film star Robert Taylor's estate. Delphine in fact advanced Jack a $5 000 dollar deposit – half the purchase price – for a plot of land adjacent to Taylor's residence at Chatsworth in the San Fernando Valley. She even had plans drawn up for a lavish love-nest.

The Reno residential qualification was completed shortly after Jack's twenty-fourth birthday and the announcement that he and Delphine planned to marry within a week brought home forcefully to the Dodge family that her crush on Jack was no passing fancy. It was the love of a lifetime and they had seriously underestimated the depth of feeling she had for the fighting Irishman who wished to be wed to their wealth. Desperate measures were necessary if they were to prevent the marriage ceremony going ahead – so desperate that what happened next was straight out of a Chicago gangster movie. Anna Dodge and Hugh Dillman arrived in Nevada with their lawyers and an unsavoury character doing a very passable imitation of Edward G. Robinson. Jack was told in no uncertain terms to make himself scarce and claimed he even had a gun held to his head to accentuate the point that the Dodges meant business. The distraught Delphine was whisked away under the protective wing of her mother and Jack handed a sizeable cheque by way of consolation – said to be in the region of £10 000 – together with a warning never to contact her again.

*

In 1931 both Louis Armstrong and Bing Crosby had rushed to record a hot new song which later became a 'standard' for every dance band of the thirties:

> 'I'm just a gigolo and everywhere I go
> People know the part I'm playing.
> "Paid for every dance – selling each romance"
> Oh what they're saying!
> But there will come a day and youth will pass away.
> What will they say about me?
> When the end comes I know they'll say "Just a gigolo"
> And life goes on without me.'

Jack must have heard it on the radio and in night clubs but it is doubtful he recognised himself in the lyric. That his youth would pass away was impossible to contemplate.

Chapter 15

The Great Love-Theft Contest

Jack may have been forcibly parted from a multi-million dollar fortune, but he had to be philosophical about the situation. He had lost the big prize on which his heart had been set but, truth to tell, he had not fared badly overall. At one time, shortly before Delphine had been led away sobbing for a tour of Europe that her mother hoped would help get her over her infatuation and bring about a reconciliation with Timothy Godde, Jack had shown Bill Doyle a pillow-case stuffed full of greenbacks. 'It contained thousands of dollars,' said Bill, 'and it was McIlveen's duty to stay in the room and guard it whenever we went out.' His testimony proved that Delphine's wealth had been freely available to Jack as she strove to satisfy his every whim during the six-week stay in Nevada.

Indeed, though Jack later strenuously denied it, she had given him £4 000 with which to gamble and presented him with a cheque for £5 000 as a twenty-fourth birthday present. Together with the plot of land in California and the pay-off from Delphine's mother, he can be said to have come out of it a well-compensated loser.

Poor, rich Delphine. She was mature and intelligent enough to realise Jack did not love her and was stringing her along for her loot, but she had been unable to help herself. She was devastated at having her one big chance of happiness snatched from her when she was old enough to make up her own mind about men. The power Anna Dodge wielded, however, and the respect, even reverence, shown her by the entire family made her a formidable and daunting figure. The statement she issued through her lawyers – 'The romance will not end in marriage' – and Delphine's meek acceptance of the situation – 'Mother thinks it best' – serves to illustrate the matriarchal hold she had over her adult offspring.

Improbable though it may seem, there was a suggestion that Anna had initially wanted Jack for herself. The inference was made some time later in a remark by a black chauffeur he employed and who, marvelling at his hold over women, declared openly: 'Even the old lady wanted you, eh, Jack?' – a comment to which Jack responded by smiling sheepishly and nodding his head in acquiescence. It is said that Anna, then 66 but who was to live another 32 years* and survive both Delphine and Horace Jnr, was as besotted with Jack as were her daughter, her grand-daughter and her daughter-in-law. The story goes that she became affronted when, despite his realisation that the Dodge purse-strings were held and administered by her, he was unable to countenance a physical liaison with someone of such advanced years.

Yet a more plausible explanation for her hostility toward Jack would be that she learned he had been squiring several of the Dodge women – including under-age grand-daughter Christine – and also that she desired the wealth link between the Dodge and Godde families to be maintained. The fact that Jack was a Catholic would almost certainly have been another major barrier. No strict, self-respecting Scottish Presbyterian mother would accept an Irish Catholic for a son-in-law without putting up a fight – especially one who was religiously seeking to lay his hands on the family fortune. Clearly she wanted Delphine to worship the Godde she was married to and not the idol of the ring whom she was convinced was attempting to cash in on his fame. Jack was in a no-win situation from whichever angle he cared to look at it. With Delphine's mother setting herself firmly against him, the Dodge empire was virtually impenetrable.

It is clear why Anna Dodge was held in such awe. She was an imperious figure of whom the entire huge household at St Leonard's, servants and all, were distinctly fearful. In looks she resembled the late Queen Mary with her crinkly curls and she even had the same regal bearing. Her word was law and no one questioned it, least of all Horace Jnr, who was always decidedly uncomfortable whenever she was around and behaved in her presence like a little boy who feared a spanking. Perhaps it was guilt that prompted Horace's uneasiness. He was squandering his mother's money to the extent that he would be £3 million in debt to her when he died in 1963.

The enforced termination of Jack's affair with Delphine was to have such unsavoury repercussions that the carefully-nurtured public respectability of the Dodge family was to be shattered for all time. They must have hated Jack even more than the thought of poverty. He was an ominous dark shadow from which they could not, despite their considerable efforts, distance themselves. If they had thought that spiriting Delphine away and paying him off was to be the last they would

* Obituary notices gave Anna's age as 103 when she died in 1970. According to Caroline Latham and David Agresta in *Dodge Dynasty*, she was 98.

see and hear of him, they were soon to find very differently.

Within a week of being given a one-way ticket to the end of the Dodge rainbow, Jack was front-page news after a young bit-part actress whose attentions he had rebuffed did a dramatic Dying Swan scene by taking poison in his presence at the Knickerbocker.

The girl, Betty Liza Strathmore, was a 22-year-old redhead who had been sitting alone, waiting, when Jack breezed into the restaurant with a high-powered party that included newspaper baron William Randolph Hearst. That he was in such exalted company demonstrated the extent of the celebrity he enjoyed.

Jack had been introduced to Betty at a film studio, but paid her scant attention. She had written to him a few days later saying she was desperately in love with him and must see him again immediately. He did not respond. He saw her on entering the Knickerbocker and remained cool, refusing to acknowledge her. When she told him she loved him, he laughed. Suddenly Miss Strathmore rose from her chair and rushed over to his table, crying dramatically: *'You are the man I love!'* With that she emptied the contents of a beaker down her throat and collapsed to the floor of the restaurant. She was taken to hospital in Jack's chauffeur-driven car, where, after recovering consciousness and a degree of dignity, she told police she took the poison to 'get even' with him because 'he laughed when I said I loved him'.

The incident must have caused acute embarrassment to Delphine Dodge following so soon on the heels of her dramatic break-up with Jack. But it paled into insignificance compared with the bombshell that was about to be lobbed into her lap. No less a personage than Judith Allen had taken the decision to sue Delphine for $1,000 000 for allegedly alienating her husband's affections. In her petition she claimed Delphine

> 'persuaded, enticed and abducted Doyle, offering several hundreds of thousands of dollars for the purpose of creating a life of luxury for him, and giving him many gifts amounting to thousands of dollars.'

True.

She alleged also that Delphine persuaded Jack to abandon attempts at a reconciliation with her and claimed she would still be enjoying the

> 'affection, comfort, support, fellowship, society and assistance of Doyle had not Mrs. Godde campaigned to win him from her.'

Not true.

Judith had made it as plain as any woman possibly could that she wanted nothing more to do with Jack. His wasted three-day visit to

Hollywood when he went down on his knees to beg her forgiveness; the masses of expensive flowers he had sent; the countless trans-Atlantic telephone calls and cables: all had made no impression on her. Judith could not be blamed after all she had been through, but hell hath no fury like a woman scorned – especially one scorned in favour of the immense wealth possessed by Delphine.

Judith stated that although she had filed for divorce, she never intended it to become final. She merely hoped the suit would bring Jack to his senses and claimed it had been serving its purpose – as his passionate letters to her revealed – until he met Mrs Godde. Judith annoyed Jack by making public the letters, in which he had professed to her his undying love in much the same way as she had done in the letter he had made public in London.

The Great Love-Theft Contest, as it became known, dragged on for months, with Delphine proving herself as adroit at avoiding the legal blows coming her way as any boxer. First she claimed Jack was a free agent and that, as such, he was 'prey for any woman'. It was unusually predatory language in the 1930s, but this clearly was a fight to the finish between two sophisticated ladies who could scrap like alley cats in pursuit of victory. Delphine followed up that little offering by promising to fight Miss Allen's action – which broke all known Hollywood records – 'to the last'.

She led Judith's process-servers a merry dance, dashing into her Hollywood hotel apartment with four detectives at her heels and slamming the door in their faces. She barricaded herself in and was under siege for 12 hours. With the apartment surrounded throughout the night, Delphine had no hope of escaping; but she was aware that her pursuers had been unable to get a good look at her and devised a clever ruse to get them off her tail. The following morning the door of her suite swung open and the process-servers were invited in. Thinking it was Delphine they were dealing with, they served the papers and went off happily to get some sleep. But the woman concerned was not her at all; she was a Delphine look-alike, in all probability daughter Christine got up to look much older.

Further games of hide-and-seek with the process-servers followed before Delphine filed an affidavit in the Los Angeles Superior Court denying she had received a summons in connection with Miss Allen's action and asking that the 'love theft' suit be dismissed. She refused point-blank to appear in court and answer questions concerning her relationship with Jack.

Delphine may have been like putty in Jack's hands, but she was tough as old boots when cornered by adversaries. She also showed she could fight dirty by employing even more dubious tactics than those she used when evading attempts to have a summons served on her. This became apparent when Judith had to seek police protection after receiving threats from anonymous telephone callers. Two men and two women, whose voices she did not recognise, had been persistently ringing her with warnings of the consequences if she did not drop her claim for damages against Mrs. Godde. The beleaguered Judith was also under heavy pressure from Hollywood's Will Hays office, which monitored filmland morals. She was requested to withdraw the action because of the undesirable publicity it was attracting.

She fought on bravely, despite the threats to her life and the arm-twisting from the Hays office. Finally, she realised she was beaten when Judge Robert W. Kenny ruled that her suit was 'too vague' as to particulars and that she must file a new complaint if she wished to continue the action.*

Judith may have been forced to abandon her claim but she had succeeded in causing acute embarrassment to the Dodge family and to Jack, whom she declared had hurt her so deeply that she wished never to see him again.

The only option left to him now was to return to England. His marriage to Judith was washed up, his romance with Delphine paid off and his former manager Tom McGovern was pressing him to repay money he claimed was owed him. To say things hadn't quite worked out was putting it mildly. Dejected, Jack moved on to Montreal and sailed home aboard the *Duchess of Bedford*. The snag was that he had burned his boats in Britain, too. Eight months had elapsed since he had beaten King Levinsky and, though he had provided medical evidence that his injured right hand would prevent him fighting Gunnar Barlund, his hurried departure for the United States had left something of a sour taste.

On the music-hall side, too, things looked bleak. His guide and mentor, Fred Curran, had sued in the High Court for £1 622 1s 11d he alleged was due to him as arrears of salary and unpaid commission on Jack's theatrical, film and radio work. He also sought damages for alleged wrongful dismissal. Jack had contested Curran's claim in his absence and it was thrown out. Jack's counsel, Mr. Neville Faulks, submitted he had no case to answer on the ground that Curran had received 12 per cent commission during the three years in question.

On disembarking from the *Duchess of Bedford* at Greenock in Scotland, the first thing Jack did was to contact Curran in an effort to

* Caroline Latham and David Agresta contend that Anna Dodge Dillman's lawyers agreed an out-of court settlement with Judith Allen.

Above left: BIG NEWS – Stacia and Michael Doyle with children Betty, Tim and Mick (right) follow Jack's fortunes at home in Cork

Above right: SOLDIER BOY – Under-age Guardsman Joseph Doyle faces the future with a grin

Below left: STAGE STRUCK – Jack joins Bud Flanagan in the Palladium limelight (1933)

Below right: MOVIE STAR – Jack and Tamara Desni in 'McGlusky the Sea Rover' (1934)

Above left: HEART THROB – The face that broke a million hearts
Above right: RIDING HIGH – Jack and four-legged friend at the Star and Garter
Below left: WEARING OF THE GREEN – Jack is button-holed by manager Dan Sullivan on St Patrick's Day, 1933
Below right: SOAP STAR – Jack gets himself into a lather before the first Eddie Phillips fight (1938)

Opposite, bottom: FROG MARCH – Jack steps out with sparring partners in France (1933)
Opposite, top right: ON SONG – Denise Descamps provides piano accompaniment as father Francois looks on. Inset: Denise Descamps
Opposite, top left: MASTER CLASS – Francois Descamps says, 'Zis eez ow you do eet!'

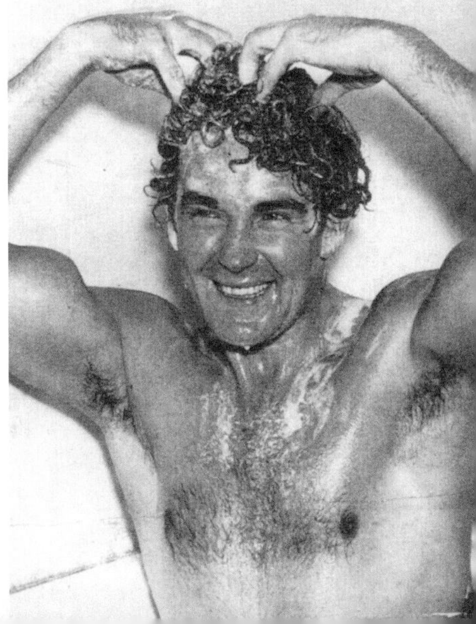

Above left: THE KING AND I – Jack wades into King Levinsky in his only fight to go the distance (1937)

Above right: KILLER BAER – Jack suffers a mauling at the hands of Buddy Baer (1935)

Below: SITTING TARGET – Jack is disqualified after demolishing Alf Robinson (1937)

Above left: PUTTING ON THE STAAL – Jack's famous right hand has Dutchman Harry Staal in trouble (1937)

Above right: WAY OUT – Belgian Jack Humbeeck is heading for a fall (1933)

Below: HIT PARADE – Jack looks suitably miffed after taking a right-hander from Broadway showgirl Elinore Troy. She had caught him whispering sweet nothings in nightclub dancer Michi Taka's Oriental ear

Above left: SHAKE ON IT – Jack and Eddie Phillips are all smiles at the weigh-in for the White City showdown (1939)

Above: IN GOOD HEART – At least Jack was before the fight with Buddy Baer

Left: SEEING STARS – Jack's in a different galaxy as he is counted out against Phillips

Below: IF THE GLOVE FITS – Jack with long-time trainer Fred Duffett at the Star & Garte (1937)

Below: A COUPLE OF SWELLS – Jack (left) with celebrated U.S. sportscaster Ted Husing

Opposite, top left: PUTTING ON THE RITZ – A little light training with brother Bill in Piccadilly (1934)

Opposite, top right: SCREEN GEM – Judith Allen really sparkles in this publicity still

Opposite, below: TEA AND SYMPATHY – A surprisingly chirpy Jack and Movita on the morning after the Phillips fiasco (1939)

GREEN

Maurice Seymour

Above left: COME FLY WITH ME – Flighty Beryl Markham had plans to airlift Jack halfway across the world
Above right: CAMP FOLLOWER – Jack breaks every rule in the boxing book by having wife Judith with him at training camp in the US
Below: RICH PICKINGS – Jack pictured with motor heiress Delphine Dodge in Los Angeles (1937). Inset: Delphine's daughter Christine, who also fell for Jack's blarney

Above left: GOOD LUCK, SON – Stacia and Betty Doyle (left) wish Jack *bon voyage* as he sets off to woo back Judith Allen (1937)

Above right: BIG-GAME HUNTER – Jack looking for a fight on his return from Mexico. Dan Sullivan must have thought he was being taken for a ride

Below left: HEADHUNTED – Jack, on the run in Mexico, is joined by Movita, who raced down from Hollywood to join him (1939)

Below right: LOVE TRAIN – Jack and Movita are reunited at Waterloo Station after Movita's arrival from the US (1939)

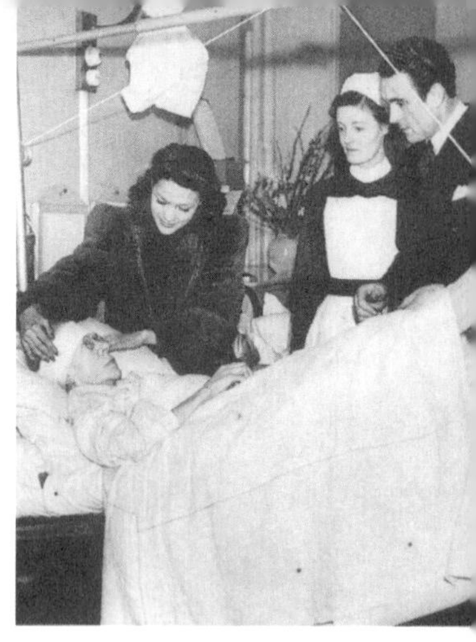

Above left: TUTOR AND TYRO REUNITE – Len Harvey greets Jack at Waterloo Station (1936)

Above right: WAR EFFORT – Jack and Movita do their bit and comfort a hospital patient

Below: GRACE AND BEAUTY – Gracie Fields and Jack with Butlin's bathing belles (1939)

Opposite, top left: DUET IN 'D' – Jack and Movita in perfect harmony on the Dublin stage (1943)

Opposite, top right: MUSCLING IN – Journalist Denzil Batchelor puts the finger on the Gorgeous Gael as he shapes up for his wrestling match with Eddie Phillips (1951)

Opposite, below: BIG TIME – Jack dwarfs 'Wild One' Marlon Brando, iron-man Butty Sugrue and Sophia Loren on the set of the Charlie Chaplin film, *A Countess from Hong Kong* (Elstree, 1966)

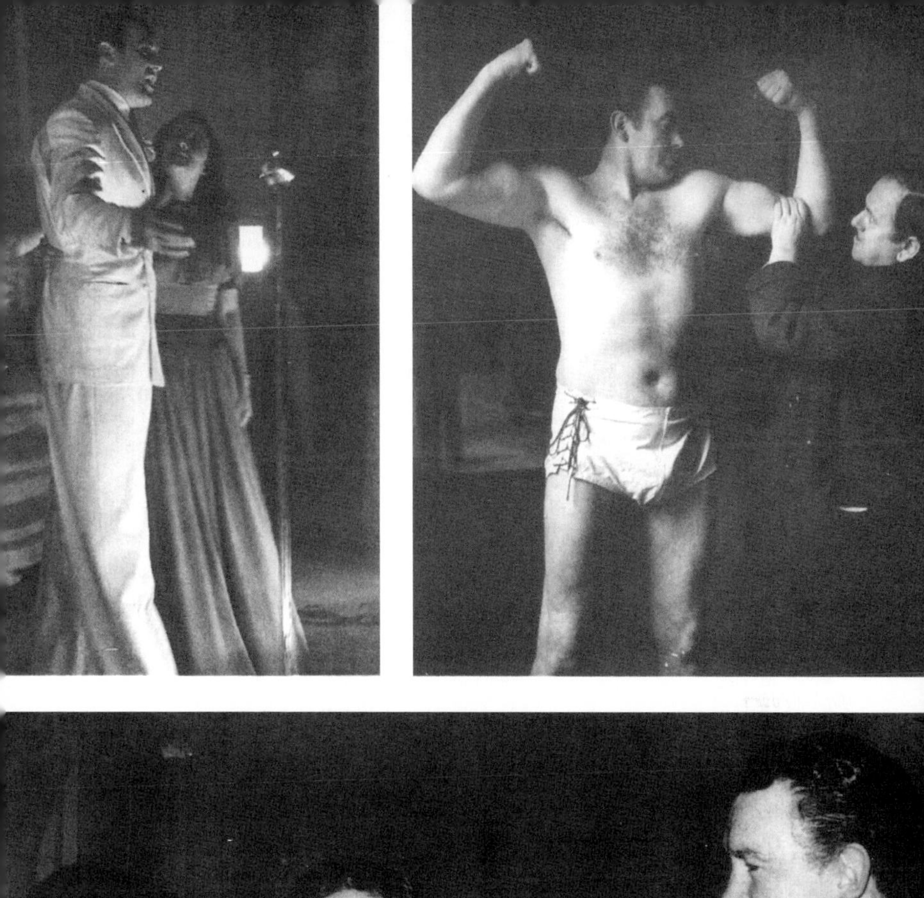

Above, left: OLD STAGER – Jack still in demand in 1972 at the age of 58
Above right: MUMMY'S BOY – Jack and Nancy Kehoe in happier times
Below: ROYAL TOUCH – Jack as ever at home with royalty as he is greeted by the Queen Mother (St Patrick's Day presentation of shamrock to the Irish Guards, Pirbright, 1972)

heal the breach that existed between them. Curran took little persuading. He loved Jack like a son – a prodigal son who had returned to the fold – and agreed immediately to set up a tour of the halls. He was delighted to do so because he knew he would have no trouble getting fees in excess of £100 a day. As far as the British public was concerned, Jack Doyle was still big business. In their eyes he could do no wrong.

Strike up the band – bang the big bass drum. The show was back on the road.

Chapter 16

Fallen hero

The great romance with Delphine Dodge Godde may have come to a swift and dramatic end, but Jack was convinced she would love him till her dying day. An affectionate Christmas Day cable from her served only to reinforce his opinion. As a prelude to his tour of the halls Jack enjoyed himself at the winter sports in St Moritz but on New Year's Day, 1938, a report from Reuter confirmed that Delphine and Timothy Godde had been reunited and were planning a second honeymoon in Cuba. Jack was devastated. He was a poor loser, unable to accept that anyone he had bedded would be anything but eternally devoted to him. The news that Judith Allen had all along been prepared to abandon her outrageous claim against Delphine if only he would return to her indicated that he was not far out in his thinking.

Jack fulfilled his music-hall dates, but became progressively more miserable. Although they were sell-outs, his appearances attracted little national publicity and he longed to be back in the limelight, the talk of the town in London once more.

A return to the ring was inevitable. A fight with South African-born Ben Foord, who had won the British and Empire titles from Jack Petersen and lost them both to Tommy Farr, was arranged for Wembley. Farr was to meet Max Baer on the same bill in an attractive double-header. But the fight with Foord failed to materialise after Jack's chauffeur-driven car collided with a parked lorry just outside London. He suffered arm and leg injuries and splinters of glass penetrated his right eye. The car was a write-off, and only the fact that he was thrown across the car and on to brother Bill, who was unhurt, saved him. Thankfully there was no permanent damage and recovery was swift.

Next came a winner-take-all challenge from Farr, who was so confident of victory that he wanted a £2 000 sidestake – an offer eagerly accepted by that inveterate gambler Dan Sullivan, who had once more picked up the reins of Jack's career. Alas, terms for the fight could not be agreed and the British public was again left to reflect on what might have been.

Jack had decided in the interim to curtail his music-hall activities and go into full-time training in preparation for his return to the ring. Unable to stomach the thought of communal gymnasium training, he rented a huge house in Maidenhead, not far from Henry Bay's residence. Each morning he went on a six-mile run and, after luncheon, was transported to a private gym – The Dolphin in Slough – which had been rented for his exclusive use. In this way Jack felt he was training in the manner that befitted his status. He disliked the everyday company of fellow-boxers and wanted no interference or comment from anyone. He had decided to go his own way as far as keeping fit was concerned and long-time trainer Fred Duffett – whom he loved like a father – could do nothing with him. In fact, Fred was employed more as stop-watch holder and baggage carrier than trainer.

Jack's dream of glory had come back to haunt him, like a ghost in the night. It was something from which he could not escape. It told him he must prove to himself once more that he could still produce the power and majesty that made him a folk hero in his heyday. So back to the ring he came like a wandering minstrel who had found his way home.

Eddie Phillips, the former British cruiserweight champion, was the man chosen for Jack's renewed quest. A more formidable opponent could hardly be imagined, for the useful Phillips, from Bow in London's East End, had been beaten only four times in a 49-fight professional career that stretched back to 1929. Incredibly, one of his setbacks had been a knockout defeat by Bill Partridge a month *after* Partridge had been dispatched unceremoniously in one round in Jack's third professional fight, making a nonsense of claims that Jack's early professional opponents had been pushovers. Partridge had inflicted on Phillips his first defeat in 25 fights. Of the remaining 24, he had lost only to fighters of the calibre of Len Harvey (twice), Ben Foord and Jock McAvoy and had three times beaten the formidable Farr. Phillips, now campaigning as a heavyweight, had since avenged the Foord defeat and was ranked the undisputed number one contender for the British title.

Jack was full of himself as he and Phillips signed contracts for the fight in the London office of promoter Sydney Hulls. Dressed in a white sports jacket and with a red carnation in his button-hole, he sang *Mother Machree* as he put pen to paper. This was Jack the showman at his enchanting, dazzling best. He was the centre of attraction and, at the luncheon that followed the signing, he took command of the convers-ation while the shy Phillips listened intently. There was none of the now almost mandatory 'needle' between the protagonists. Jack, relaxed and confident, was friendly to Phillips and vice-versa. The pleasantries were typified by Jack's aside to Phillips when, after handing Eddie a photograph, he said: 'This is my young brother who has been in Africa for twelve years.' It was a picture of a monkey dressed in sailor's clothes.

Jack accepted an invitation from holiday camp king Billy Butlin to train for the fight at Butlin's in Skegness, on the Lincolnshire coast. It seemed an ideal arrangement and one that would help offset the heavy costs of training. In addition, filling the lungs with bracing sea air each day was considered the perfect tonic for such an important fight.

At first Jack delighted in the surroundings and the adulation he received from the camp's 2 500 holiday-makers. He rode out each morning on horse-back and his open-air sparring sessions with the camp's resident trainer, Phil Fowler, attracted in excess of 1 000 people daily. People stared at him in amazement as he ran around the nearby roads, singing in Italian, French, Spanish and English and wearing a check cap, sweater and ski-boots. Without doubt, he was the most unlikely pugilist ever seen.

Jack had a six-strong personal entourage. There was Fred Curran, who acted as his secretary in dealing with the 100 or more fan letters he received each day; Fred's wife Olive, who had the task of selecting the right food for Jack and helping prepare it; Dan Sullivan, who travelled between London and Skegness to keep an eye on him; Fred Duffett; a chauffeur, Thomas Egerton; and omnipresent brother Bill, who acted as his valet.

Bill was responsible for Jack's incredible wardrobe at Skegness – just as he had been in New York, Hollywood, London or wherever Jack happened to be. Jack had eight trunkloads of clothes with him at the camp, including 25 suits, 25 pairs of shoes and dozens of sweaters. The suits were just a few random samples from his made-to-measure collection of 164, the shoes but a quarter of the number that filled his cupboard. He had brought back more new clothes from his last trip to America than he would need in a lifetime, including expensive riding gear modelled on that worn by Clark Gable.

Jack loved the colour and atmosphere at the camp, but it was probably the one occasion in his life when he became irritated by the demands of women. At Skegness there were more of them than even he could handle and their constant requests for autographs and assignations wore him down. They gazed at him adoringly – particularly in the camp's lounge, where he wanted only to relax. The sight of him in dazzling sports jacket and with a rarely-lit white pipe clenched between his teeth proved too much for them and they let their imaginations soar.

Everywhere Jack went he was followed by dozens of excited women, some young and giggly, others more mature and sexually voracious. They knew of his reputation with some of the world's most desirable women and, as in the States, many beat a hopeful path to his chalet at night. But a man must sleep sometime, and the continual clamour left him feeling completely overwhelmed. The only way he could find peace was for Thomas Egerton to drive him away from the camp to a place where he could look out to sea and be reminded of his formative years in Cobh. It was a therapy to be at one with himself – if only for an hour or so at a time – and he found he was able to calm his mind in concert with the sight and sound of the ocean.

Occasional periods of solitude could not compensate for the seemingly endless signing of autographs and handing out of photographs back at the camp, and Jack was somewhat relieved when Dan Sullivan advised him to complete his training at Slough. The camp authorities had several times requested the hundreds of girls holidaying there not to ask for his autograph, but it was like attempting to halt a herd of stampeding buffalo. They took no notice whatever and after three weeks of it Jack had had enough.

However, he'd have been better off staying on at Skegness, for at least there he had to appear to be keeping to a routine of training. Back in the luxury of his rented home in Maidenhead, he found his enthusiasm for the fight beginning to wane. Soft living, parties at Henry Bay's house nearby and the mad-cap company of Jim Mollison were distractions he could have done without after being absent from the ring for 17 months. Yet Jack was wise enough to hide the evidence of riotous living when he celebrated his twenty-fifth birthday; drinking only milk, he held court somewhat in the manner of a ham actor addressing an audience:

> 'There is nothing unusual in unusualness nowadays. It may seem strange that I, a pug, should steal away from training camp to indulge in a weakness for whoopee. Yet it is neither strange nor quaint if it is allowed that a man is the better for distraction. Fighting fitness may not be the more surely found in the wearisome sameness of a gymnasium nor by imprisoning a man within four walls. I do not claim licence for myself or any fighter to break from the chains of discipline. I have put myself out of bounds by inviting my friends to eat, drink and be merry on this, my twenty-fifth birthday. I seek only mental refreshment, for I react readily to jovial company. There is nothing of the robot in me. I am just a flesh-and-blood man intent upon, but not a slave to, his job.'

Was this a fighter speaking, or a poet? Perhaps it was a mixture of the two – a fighter with a poet's soul. It seemed Jack was again attempting to convince the world, and perhaps himself, that he was too articulate for boxing. The words 'wearisome sameness of a gymasium' summed up his attitude.

In fact Jack had been burning the candle at both ends, and in the middle, and he was in no fit state to go into the ring with Phillips. It came as no surprise therefore when – as before the Levinsky fight – he requested a postponement, claiming this time to have injured his ribs in training. The revised date for the fight, September 27, was fairly immaterial since Jack had made little effort to get himself in shape. He weighed in at 16st 11b, his heaviest ever and almost two-and-a-half stones more than Phillips. 'Has Doyle really trained for this fight?' was a question posed by one newspaper. The answer was a resounding 'No'.

Yet who cared? Certainly not the Great British Public, who signalled their delight at Jack's return to the ring by snapping up every ticket on offer. And the fascination Jack held for women was demonstrated by promoter Sydney Hulls' revelation that most of the top-priced three-guinea seats for the 12-rounder at Harringay Arena had been purchased by the petticoat army. Yet the women thronging the ringside in a state of high excitement were blissfully unaware of a drama which posed a real danger that they might not see their hero at all. Jack, pale and perspiring freely, had arrived at his dressing-room and begun to undress. Midway through disrobing he suddenly had a change of mind, took up his coat and announced to Dan Sullivan and his seconds:

> 'I refuse to step into that ring until I get my money. I am fed up with the game, anyhow. I'm going to get out.'

Jack had been in a state of some agitation in the days leading up to the fight. His only chance would be to win in the first couple of rounds; if he failed, he himself would be knocked out and his return to the ring would end in humiliation. His ego could not accept the thought of it, and so he had hatched out a plan that would involve him losing in a manner which he felt would be less of a disgrace than being battered to the canvas and having the count of ten tolled over him in funereal tones which symbolised the Last Rites being performed on his career. The big problem was that the theatrical scene he had rehearsed in his mind as a last resort would almost certainly result in his prize-money being withheld or even confiscated by the Board of Control.

Jack had been guaranteed £2 000 win, lose or draw – but not if he lost through disqualification. Although his strategy did not involve disqualification – as in the Petersen fight five years earlier – it did mean he would lose in such dubious circumstances that the Board might still impound his purse.

Promoter Hulls and other officials were summoned urgently to Jack's dressing-room. The door was locked and the bargaining began. Jack issued an ultimatum to Hulls:

> 'Either you pay £2 000 to my brother or I won't step into the ring. It makes no difference to me. I'm tired of being kicked around. I'm fed up with fighting, anyway. If you don't pay up, I'll walk right out. I'll do anything – but I won't fight unless I have my money.'

With that he picked up his coat and walked over to the mirror. He patted his hair into place, as if making ready to leave. Hulls and the other officials pleaded and tried to reason with him. They told him he'd get his money – that all he had to do was fight and put up a good fight. But Jack was adamant: no money, no fight.

Eventually a cheque for £2 000 was produced and deposited with Bill Doyle. But that was not good enough. Jack demanded an undertaking that the cheque would be honoured and the celebrated *Daily Mail* cartoonist Tom Webster – who had lampooned Jack on countless occasions – volunteered to act as guarantor. With that Jack grudgingly agreed to go through with the fight.

The scheduled time for the showdown had passed when the lights went down and a fanfare of trumpets and resounding cheers greeted the entry of Phillips. Jack followed immediately. His ovation was breath-taking, generating the kind of atmosphere which guaranteed that the fight would be explosive.

The first round was fought toe-to-toe in the centre of the ring until Jack forced Phillips on to the ropes. The pair exchanged punches with great gusto and Phillips landed one, two, three stinging left-handers. As usual, Jack scorned any pretensions to defence and was out for the kill. He swung his right hand almost from down behind his back and planted a hay-maker close to Eddie's jaw. Phillips shook visibly, but bravely stood his ground and took another right-hander that landed perilously near his chin. In the few seconds that remained until the end of the round, both men fought viciously. It was touch and go in a round of thrills.

They began the second session as they had started the first – like men possessed. Phillips, unusually brazen and arrogant, was ignoring his superior boxing skills to take on Jack in a crude punch-up. He had been caught by two bone-crunching rights to the face and it seemed just a matter of time before one would land flush on the jaw to leave him stretched out on the canvas. But all at once Jack appeared to lose interest in the proceedings, deciding at that moment to vacate the stage by the simple expedient of missing wildly with a left swing that took him clean through the ropes and out of the ring.

He landed on his back on the Press table, his legs shooting up in the air. Time-keeper Joe Palmer's stop-watch was smashed and ringside telephones went flying. In the confusion of it all, Jack, his right eye bleeding, lay apparently dazed. Frenzied efforts were made to get him back in the ring, but to no avail. 'Eight, nine, out.' Referee C. B. Thomas signalled that the fight was over and declared Phillips the winner after 1 min 20 sec of the second round. Jack scrambled to his feet to a mixture of cheers and jeers. He did not climb back in to the ring, where the slightly bemused Phillips – his bespectacled manager Sam Russell screaming and waving hysterically – was being acclaimed the winner. Instead he forced a smile, tossed his head defiantly and strode back to his dressing-room.

Thus Jack had succeeded in making boxing history by becoming the first fighter to knock *himself* out. Was it by accident or design? The inescapable conclusion must be that having pocketed his prize-money in advance and failed to knock out Phillips early as planned, he elected to bring the contest swiftly to an end by projecting himself through the air like a guided missile.

Phillips today is adamant that Jack did not take a dive:

> 'Doyle came out like a bull. We stood toe-to-toe and I stung him with a good right hand. In the second round he threw a punch but I saw it coming, caught him with a left and he went sailing out of the ring.
>
> If he did miss on purpose like they say he did, well, all I can say is that I was a good gymnast and I just don't believe a man of 16-odd stone could have thrown himself like that. From my point of view, I can't see that Doyle would have suffered a defeat against me willingly.'

The late Frank Duffett, son of trainer Fred, thought otherwise:

> 'Fred Curran was staying with Jack in Maidenhead before the fight. He was there to keep an eye on him, but it was a waste of time. Jack used to go missing all night with a bird.
>
> Jack was vastly overweight. I was in the dressing-room beforehand helping my dad and Jack knew what condition he was in. He was walking round saying, "Something has to be done."
>
> Afterwards I said to him as he showered: "You're a great actor. Martin Harvey's got nothing on you."
>
> He replied: "Did it look *that* good?"'

Having disappeared from view by crashing headlong out of the ring, Jack also went missing in the West End after the fight, shaking off reporters anxious to know the name of a 'titled lady' who was expected to become the second Mrs. Doyle. Mayfair was trying to guess her name, but to all suggestions he replied with a shake of the head.

Next morning Jack presented the cheque – and as soon as it was cleared, he headed for Canada. It was his third vanishing act in two days but, just as on fight night, he again had the misfortune to fall among Pressmen while waiting for the ship to sail. Wearing his customary disguise of dark glasses, Jack was seen sitting with brother Bill and Henry Bay in the lounge of the Canadian Pacific liner *Empress of Britain*, bound for Quebec. The labels on his luggage gave no clue as to his identity, and he had booked his passage in an assumed name.

Speculation as to the cause of his sudden departure was rife, but Dan Sullivan was totally baffled. Jack had cabled stating he was rushing to New York to see Delphine Dodge Godde, who was said to be seriously ill. He owed Sullivan his £500 percentage, plus training expenses. There were other liabilities, too, including money he still owed to the Board of Control.

The reason for Jack's hasty exit and his odd behaviour before the fight was a mystery to all but a handful of people here and in the United States. It was hushed up then, and since, due to its unsavoury nature. He had received a disturbing message from America informing him that private detectives thought to have been put on his trail by the Dodge family had discovered he had contracted syphilis during his last visit there. The authorities had been informed and he had been banned from entering the country as a result. There was also the disclosure that Jack's 36-acre parcel of prime land in the San Fernando Valley was being claimed by the Dodge family. His Hollywood adviser and secretary Jack Bac-So had warned that unless he took immediate steps to pay the remaining 5 000 dollars to complete the purchase of the land, he would lose it. This was why Jack had been so desperate to secure his £2 000 for the Phillips fight in advance.

Jack was distressed on the voyage. The nature of his visit was not a pleasant one and he had just thrown the fight against Phillips into the bargain. To add to his misery, his US papers were not in order and consequently he was attempting to enter the country by its Canadian back door. Would he be successful? He did not know for certain, but he had not undertaken a 3 000-mile Atlantic journey to be turned back without accomplishing his mission.

From Quebec, Jack travelled by train to Montreal and attempted to cross the Canadian border at Rouse's Point in New York State. He was refused entry by immigration officials because he did not possess a valid medical certificate.* He returned to Montreal and applied successfully to the US Consulate there for a return permit, conveniently omitting to mention he had been rejected in the first place. Jack then crossed into the United States and flew on to New York city.

He booked into the Waldorf Astoria and was immediately confronted by American newsmen. Their persistent questions as to the reason for his visit again drew the lame response that Delphine Dodge Godde was seriously ill and had sent for him. Delphine, then living on an exclusive country estate at Westchester in up-state New York, vehemently denied Jack's claim and, at the same time, dispelled any notion he might have had that she still held him in some affection:

> 'His ridiculous remarks about my being ill and sending for him are without foundation. I am very much in love with my husband and want nothing more to do with Doyle.'

True or not, there was no comfort or encouragement for Jack in her words. It was clear he had next to no chance of winning her back.

Timothy Godde was livid. He could not even bring himself to utter Jack's name, declaring ominously:

> 'That person has not yet attempted to get in touch with us and will find it advisable not to do so. If he comes here I intend to take drastic steps to put an end to this annoyance.'

It was a dark and almost sinister threat, but Jack paid no heed. He was determined once again to test Delphine's love for him. Meanwhile, the newspapers were having some fun out of the situation: 'Delphine Dodges Doyle' was a typical pun headline.

Nothing loath, Jack hit the Broadway night-spots. On his very first evening in New York he entered the aptly titled Midnight Sun club and ran into a show-girl he had previously met way out west – the statuesque but shapely Elinore Troy, whose figure had been described as 'the most entrancing in Hollywood' and whose name was surely a play on another great figure of beauty and legend, Helen of Troy. This Miss Troy swooned dramatically, Jack proposed marriage almost as a matter of course and she accepted. They were inseparable for all of two days until Jack got bored and turned his attention to a Japanese dancer, Michi Taka. The trouble was that Miss Troy had totally lapped up Jack's line in blarney and did not take kindly to being done down. She exploded

* No medical records are available, but it is unlikely that the Dodge family's allegation that Jack had syphilis was a put-up job. Of necessity, the claim must have been substantiated by written evidence. As a result Jack was *persona non grata* in the United States, although the probability was that the disease had since been successfully treated.

when she found him whispering sweet-nothings in Michi's Oriental ear. She rushed over and slapped him full in the face, screaming: 'Don't you dare fool around with me. We've been engaged for three nights.'

When Jack got back to his hotel suite, he found Miss Troy had invaded it and was staging a sit-in. She was a strong and forceful character and she resisted his pleas for her to leave and let him get some sleep. He had to settle for a comfortable seat in the hotel lounge.

Jack was in for a rude awakening. Into the hotel walked his former manager Tom McGovern, accompanied by a deputy sheriff armed with an arrest warrant. McGovern, alerted by newspaper reports that Jack was in town, was demanding $7 000 for the 'time, trouble and money advanced while acting for Doyle', and finally had his man cornered. He explained to Jack that he had brought the sheriff along to help him collect, but that the arrest was a civil one and he would be free to go if an agreement could be reached.

The three men went up to Jack's suite and found Miss Troy still entrenched there. Jack breezed past her into another room without a word and she meekly acceded to the deputy sheriff's demand that she leave at once. 'I only came to apologise for what I did in the night-club,' she said helplessly, 'and to get an apology from him for standing me up. That's all I want.' McGovern and the deputy relayed the message to Jack, who by this time had become sick of the sight of the woman and wanted rid of her. 'I'm sorry it happened,' he told her without a trace of remorse. 'It was all a misunderstanding.'

Miss Troy left, seemingly happy with her apology, and the three men addressed the financial problem. After much haggling over the precise amount owed, Jack handed McGovern $2 000 (then around £800) and promised to pay the remaining $5 000 within six months. Having secured this gesture of goodwill, McGovern then softened his attitude and stated that all he had really wanted was for Jack to continue his boxing career in the States under his management.

Jack admitted to McGovern that he had let him down badly and agreed that the best way of repaying him would be to return to the ring in a bid to fulfil the rich promise he had shown in his four fights in America. McGovern was overjoyed and signed Jack to a new five-year contract there and then. He put an arm round his massive shoulders, got his pledge not to leave New York State without his permission and vowed: 'Listen, Jack, I'll get you a fight with Joe Louis yet.'

Poor McGovern. Never has one man's faith in another been so callously disregarded. The oral and written agreements meant little to Jack; he was sick of boxing and showed what he thought of the promise he had given McGovern to stay in New York by flying to Detroit the very next day. It was to be the last he would see of McGovern, who finally decided to write off the debt and wash his hands of Jack completely.*

The visit to Detroit lasted one day. Jack went there to test the water in connection with a preposterous alienation suit against Anna Dodge Dillman. Jack named her as the person responsible for wrecking his romance with the motor car heiress and causing him to lose 'several thousands of pounds'. But his attempt to get her to agree to an out-of-court settlement met with no success; she refused even to see him when he visited the Dodge family residence at Grosse Point Farms. In addition, lawyers he consulted advised him that an alienation claim against Delphine's mother would be unlikely to succeed. Convinced, finally, that he could not take the Dodge family for another cent, he flew on to California in an effort to secure his property in the San Fernando Valley.†

Meanwhile, the immigration authorities had rumbled his deft manoeuvre in Montreal and were now hot on his trail. A warrant for his arrest on a charge of illegal entry into the United States was telegraphed from New York and he was detained as he stepped from the plane in Los Angeles.

Jack protested that, if he had misled the Montreal authorities when securing his visa, it had been quite unintentional. He claimed it was due to his ignorance of the immigration laws. His explanation was not accepted. Instead of a warm welcome from his friends in Hollywood, Jack spent his first night back in California in the company of some less desirable associates in the Los Angeles County Jail. It was a shocking experience for a man who had become accustomed to living graciously in the best hotels in Britain, Ireland and the United States, but this was one occasion when he had no say in his choice of accommodation.

Jack complained that he was put in the same cell as a murderer and a man charged with rape. It contained three bunks, each equipped with an uncomfortably hard mattress and a blanket. The heat inside the tiny barred room was stifling during the day and oppressive at night. Jack hardly slept a wink, especially with a killer – who doubled as the prison barber – in such close proximity.

He had gone in on a Saturday and was unable to obtain bail for his

* When McGovern died some years later, his Irish heavyweight dream died with him. The American sports columnist Dan Parker observed wryly: 'Tom went to his grave clutching a bundle of Jack Doyle IOUs.'

† Delphine never got over the enforced termination of the affair. Thereafter she became a virtual recluse and drank herself into oblivion. She died in New York Hospital on June 18, 1943, at the age of 44. The death certificate stated natural causes, but Jack's later claim that she committed suicide over him had some merit. In essence, she had lost the will to live and died of a broken heart.

release until the following Monday. It meant spending two nights in the slammer. His only visitors on the Sunday were newspapermen – hordes of them – and plenty of photographers. They took pictures of him behind the bars of the prison exercise yard, looking thoroughly miserable and feeling desperately sorry for himself. They were splashed on the front pages of newspapers across America. Jack was big news once more, but for all the wrong reasons.

He was released on the Monday morning on bail of $800 and informed that the preliminary hearing against him was to be taken in secret before the immigration authorities in Los Angeles. Inspector Judson Shaw, of the Federal Immigration Department, announced: 'Doyle will be given every opportunity to show cause why he should not be deported.'

Jack was delighted to be free and confident that his unorthodox method of gaining a visa had not constituted fraud. He threw himself into Hollywood's social whirl with all the relief of a man who had been reprieved from the gas chamber. But he had been given only a stay of execution. Deportation still beckoned.

The publicity had made him the hottest guy in town. Everyone wanted to shake his hand. There were the predictable and pointed cracks like: 'How was life in the can, Jack?'

There were other developments, too. Elinore Troy, still Doyle-crazy after all those tears, offered to come to his rescue. She made application to Commissioner Rudolph Reimer at Ellis Island to be declared his legal guardian and guarantor. She told the newspapers she and Jack had become engaged shortly before the night-club tiff over Michi Taka and said she was citing their 'forthcoming marriage' as grounds for her application to be Jack's guardian.

> 'I'm telling the government I have a steady job as a dancer, earning $70 weekly, and am well able to guarantee that Jack won't become a public charge within the meaning of the law.'

Taken at face value it was a 'sweet and generous' gesture, but Jack suspected she was attempting to cash in on his fame. After all, when she socked him in that New York night-club a photographer was conveniently on hand to record the event for posterity. He regarded her offer to fly to LA to marry him and keep him in America as little more than a publicity stunt. The immigration authorities thought so, too, and Miss Troy, her proposal having been rejected on two fronts, faded once more into obscurity. Very shortly Jack would have good cause to be pleased that he did not enter into a marriage of convenience with Elinore or anyone else. First, it was doubtful it would have influenced the immigration authorities into reversing their decision to have him deported; second, within a day or so he was destined to meet the girl who was to be the love of his life.

Enter Maria-Louisa Castaneda.

Book II

MOVITA

Chapter 1
South of the border

The year is 1901 and the location Mazatlan, a tourist town and seaport some 600 miles north of Acapulco on the west coast of Mexico.

Maria Lerma has been wooed and won by the dashing don Adolfo Castaneda, a guitar-playing balladeer from nearby Nayarit.

She is 13 and he 20 years her senior. She hardly knows him, but he is handsome and masterful and she fancies she is in love. He has snatched her from the bosom of her family – almost from the cradle, so to speak – and deposited her with a 'good and decent' family. He issues an ultimatum to her parents:

> 'I want to marry your daughter, but I want to do it properly – with your blessing. If you don't agree I'll take her away with me and marry her anyway.'

The Lermas are wealthy and respectable. Their sons are priests and doctors and lawyers and they are appalled at the fate that has befallen the daughter on whom they dote. They refuse to treat with someone they regard as little more than a common kidnapper. They demand to see Maria, their *niñita.*

Don Adolfo takes them to see her and their worst fears are confirmed. She is indeed smitten by this man who is old enough to be her father, this brash and arrogant stranger who has struck like a thief in the night to disrupt their harmony.

The Lermas face a cruel dilemma. It is the custom for Mexican girls to marry young and they are anxious only for Maria's happiness and well-being. But she is just a child, inexperienced in affairs of the heart, and she is giving herself to the first man she has met. The thought is painful in the extreme.

They are reluctant to give their consent to the union in spite of assurances from their friend don Pancho. He is Maria's godfather and a man of substance, a successful and respected businessman in Mazatlan. Don Pancho knows don Adolfo well and gives the Lermas the low-down on him. They learn that he is a highly-paid engineer supervising work on the oil wells that are gushing all over Mexico. He is also a gambler who plays for high stakes; it is his nature and it directs his thinking. When he wants something he goes for it and lets nothing stand in his way. He is a man of considerable means who has acted honourably toward their daughter.

Still the Lermas attempt to talk Maria round. They warn her she is confusing fascination with love, that her feelings could quickly cool and that, once married, she will have to suffer the consequences if she discovers she has, in haste, made the wrong choice. Maria is adamant and not a little stubborn, like the man she seeks to wed. 'I am in love with don Adolfo and want to marry him right away,' she maintains.

There is nothing more her parents can do. They have tried and failed to get her to change her mind. They give their blessing and Maria Lerma duly becomes the child-bride of don Adolfo Castaneda.

*

Maria settled with Adolfo in Mexico City. A year later, at the age of 14, she gave birth to a daughter, Eloisa, the first of ten children (eight girls and two boys) she would bring into the world. Eloisa was followed by Juana, Adolf, Elothia (Lottie), Petra, Francisca, Rosita (who died from illness as a young girl), Marguerita, Maria-Louisa and Enrique (Kikki).

Maria was happy during the first years of her marriage, though not blissfully. With Adolfo so often away from home working on the oil wells and pursuing his favourite hobby – gambling – life was far from ideal. There were compensations: a comfortable house and servants and the means to be able to send her girls to the same expensive private school as that attended by the daughters of President Plutarco Elias Calles. She was, she realised, far better off than most Mexican wives. Sometimes, after spending weeks away working and gambling, Adolfo would arrive home with an array of valuable jewellery for her; on other occasions he might have won an oil well. Only rarely did he return with nothing.

However, Maria did not delude herself. Mexico was a man's country where women, in effect, were treated as second-class citizens. She did not relish the thought of her daughters living the rest of their lives in such an environment. She wanted them to be free to make their own decisions without being subject, as she was, to the unwritten law of the Latin male that a man is master in his own home, the head of the family whose decisions concerning domestic matters are made arbitrarily and without recourse to his marriage partner. In short, a wife's job was to bear children, run the home and submit to the will of the husband. Of such attitudes women's liberation was born and Maria was way ahead of her time in that respect. She loved her husband and did not blame him for his chauvinistic attitude: it was all part of his Spanish heritage and he had been brought up to believe that it was right. But she resolved to foster a spirit of independence in her daughters.

Her eyes had been opened during a visit to the Scottsdale, Arizona, home of her sister Chenta, a shrewd businesswoman who owned a lucrative complex of cotton ranches. Maria could see that America was a land of opportunity for women, where they shared the decision-making with their husbands. It was a more equitable society where they could secure good employment or carve out fine careers for themselves in business if they so desired.

By this time Maria had eight children, seven of them girls. When she fell for the ninth, she knew there was more than an equal chance that it, too, would be a daughter. She decided she would like the child to be born in the United States and be eligible to enjoy the advantages that American citizenship would bring. Consequently, she obtained Chenta's agreement to her giving birth at her home in Scottsdale.

Maria made the necessary arrangements and, when time was near, set off by train for Arizona. Not wishing to leave her children for longer than was necessary, she had delayed her departure until the last possible moment. But, as the Pullman lurched and rumbled along the tracks that wound their way through the rugged, undulating Mexican countryside, the first sharp pangs of labour told her that she had miscalculated. It was just as well she had taken the precaution of asking son Adolf and one of her aides to accompany her on the long journey north. By the time the train had reached the US border, the baby was fighting to put in an appearance just as hard as Maria was attempting desperately to delay the birth.

The Pullman had to stop at the border while immigration officials checked each passenger's passport and entry permit; carriage by carriage it was permitted to cross into the United States as the papers and documents were cleared. Maria began to regret not choosing a carriage nearer the front of the train but, being experienced in the art of bearing babies, she managed to hold on until at last her carriage was shunted to the US side of the border. Then, almost in relief, she let nature take its course and gave birth there and then on the train. It had been a close call – too close for comfort – but Maria was delighted when excited fellow passengers caught up in the drama told her it was a girl. It meant the whole exhausting exercise had been wonderfully worthwhile. 'At least this one will be free,' she whispered to herself as, cradling the infant in her arms, she was whisked off by ambulance for a post-natal examination in Nogales. So happy was she on this 12th day of April, 1921, that she decided to name the baby after herself.

The child came to be blessed with the same splendid strength of character and natural beauty as her mother. She was nicknamed Maui after the most alluring of the Hawaiian islands – spelt phonetically for ease of pronunciation. Thus Maria-Louisa Castaneda would always be Mawie to her family and friends.

She was to become better known as the film actress Movita.

Chapter 2

Freedom trail

Shortly after baby Enrique was born two years later, in 1923, Maria took the most momentous decision of her life: she would leave Adolfo and head with her family for America and freedom. The first real cracks in the marriage had appeared when Adolfo began lining up husbands for his daughters, who were growing up fast and beautiful. At this time they were still attending their posh all-girls school. Always clean, smartly dressed and with parasols to shield them from the sun, they were terribly spoiled and snobbish. It was the thing.

Adolfo saw it as his duty to guarantee their futures by matching them with fine young men from respectable, well-to-do families. It was more than Maria could stomach. She had endured his lengthy absences from home and his uncompromising attitude over the years without complaint, but was not prepared to tolerate the prospect of the daughters she had reared with such loving tenderness and devotion being forced to marry against their will.

Her eldest daughter, Eloisa, had become the first casualty of Adolfo's arranged-marriage policy. She ran off and wed an out-of-work musician, and a drunkard to boot, because she could scarcely stand the sight of the man her father had chosen for her. Adolfo was furious that his match-making efforts had been thwarted. Maria on the other hand, whilst not approving of Eloisa's choice of husband, was pleased she had at least married for love.

Maria was upset when she learned that Adolfo, undeterred by Eloisa's flight of fancy, was seeking suitable spouses for Juana and Lottie. 'They should marry people they love,' she told him. 'We married for love, so how can you expect your own daughters to marry men they don't love?'

'I can't help that,' he replied. 'I want my daughters to have good homes and a good life.'

Maria wanted only happiness for her daughters, but she knew if she stayed with Adolfo any longer she was condemning them ultimately to a life of misery. Her love for him was still strong after 22 years, but she could never hope to change his mind about arranged marriages; if anything, he was becoming even more dogmatic about it. At 35 she was still a young woman – young enough to start a new life with her sister in America. If she did not go now, it would be too late. Her chance to be free, and to secure the freedom of her children, depended on her being strong enough to leave Adolfo. She knew only too well that it would be far from easy. It was virtually unheard of in Mexico for a wife to walk out on her husband, still less a mother with so many offspring to support – but it was the only way.

The difficulty lay in effecting her departure from Mexico. Maria had been told she could never leave without the permission of her husband, even under the guise of a holiday. So, by the very nature of the prevailing circumstances, she would have to make her exit with stealth and cunning.

Maria had no desire to force the children to accompany her to Arizona; instead, she gave them the benefit of free choice in the matter. It was all done democratically, as if in open defiance of the autocratic family rule imposed by Adolfo. Of course there was never any doubt that she would take little Mawie, then two years old, or baby Kikki, but the rest were old enough to make up their own minds. She told them: 'You can stay with your father and continue to have everything you have always been accustomed to [a comfortable home, servants and good schooling] or you can come with me. It's your decision.'

'No, Mama, we come with you,' said all the girls loyally. Adolf, who might reasonably have been expected to remain with his father, also decided to stand by his mother.

The decision having been taken, Maria then sought advice on how best to make good her escape. She enlisted the aid of a friendly lawyer whom she knew she could trust and the necessary papers and documents were drawn up to enable the family to cross to the United States.

Maria had decided to go while Adolfo was away. She was aware of the difficulties, for her husband was well known and secrecy was of the essence. She realised she would be lucky to get away with it, but the chance had to be taken. She left Adolfo a note telling him why she was going and explaining that he would be able to contact her and the family via Chenta in Scottsdale. The dramatic departure plan was then put into operation.

A friend of Maria's took her and the children to the station in a horse-drawn cart laden with several sacks of vegetables. Maria was dressed humbly, her usual finery discarded for the journey so as not to arouse suspicion. She had been unable to take any luggage: all she had with her was some money, her jewellery and the clothes she and the children were wearing. As extra insurance against being recognised, Maria boarded the train long before the rest of the passengers. Cradling Kikki in her arms, she entered the third-class compartment along with Francisca and Mawie, who were then buried in gunni sacks beneath apples, oranges and other assorted fruit and veg and instructed not to make a sound. Adolf and the other girls, all prim and proper and dressed beautifully, headed for the first-class compartment, where they immediately split up and sat in separate seats in order to be as inconspicuous as possible. They had been given strict instructions not to speak to each other.

The entire family held its breath as the train clattered noisily toward the border, fearful that one false move would wreck the whole operation. When Maria had last made the journey, she was heavily pregnant and hoping against hope that she would reach America before her baby was born; now she was involved in another race against time and with infinitely more serious repercussions. Her main concern was that Adolfo might return prematurely and cable ahead to the authorities, instructing them not to let the family into the United States. In the event her fears proved groundless. He did not arrive home in time to halt their journey and the border officials, having inspected the papers bearing Adolfo's forged signature, allowed them to cross to America and freedom.

Chapter 3

Home of the brave

If Maria and the children had thought life in Scottsdale was to be a bed of roses, they were soon disillusioned. Things worked out reasonably well for about a year but then Chenta, a hard-headed pragmatist and extremely ambitious with it, proved to be as scheming and unyielding as her brother-in-law. She realised her nieces were all young and pretty and highly desirable, that they had been well educated and – despite having servants at home in Mexico City – knew how to sew and cook and run a home. She began arranging dates for them with wealthy ranchers, hoping that suitable marriages would result.

Maria was forced to intervene. She refused even to consider allowing her daughters to become involved in marriages of convenience. 'No Chenta, it cannot be,' she told her firmly. 'We left Mexico to avoid such a thing happening. My girls must marry for love.'

Chenta, like Adolfo, could see nothing morally wrong in ensuring the future security of members of the family. Her own daughter had married well and was enjoying a life of prosperity and she urged Maria to allow her to find similar suitable marriage partners for her girls. Finally, the pressure Chenta continued to exert became intolerable for Maria; she fell out with her in the same way she had fallen out with her husband and decided to leave.

She sold all her expensive jewellery and purchased a small cotton ranch near Phoenix. It proved a disastrous move. Being young ladies of refinement, the Castaneda girls were unused to such back-breaking work and found difficulty in achieving an efficient level of productivity. But they tried – how they tried. They first picked cotton wearing little white gloves to protect their soft and delicate skin – and when those were worn out they covered their hands with stockings, cutting out holes for their fingers. Adolf, at 14, was unable to do much more than the girls, and clearly Maria did not have Chenta's head for business. The result: after a very short time, they lost the ranch.

With no money coming, the family was forced to live in a tent. This was roughing it in a style Maria had never dreamed possible when first she had considered leaving Mexico, but they had to get used to it. The girls made their new surroundings as homely as possible by pinning photographs to the walls of the tent – pictures of themselves with Mama and Papa in happier days. In spite of the financial hardship, they remained close; there was no whining or moaning about their circumstances, no apportioning blame. Maria had made her bed and was now forced to lie on it. The expected bed of roses had turned into a bed of nails.

Chenta, meanwhile, was still hovering in the wings. She was convinced her sister would see the folly of her situation and realise that marrying her daughters into money was the solution. 'It is the only way,' she told her, but still Maria would not yield. 'Suffer then,' said Chenta. 'I will give you no help. You can live in poverty until you come to your senses.'

Maria would rather have starved then compromise her principles. She had immense courage and would never consider asking anyone for assistance – not even her own husband. He, true to his own exalted pride, had resolutely refused to follow his family across the border and plead with them to return. But there had been no bitterness in Adolfo's heart. He understood that Maria was a romantic idealist and inwardly admired the spirited stand she was taking. However, he could never countenance her views: 'It is the way I am,' he told her in a letter, 'the way I was brought up. I cannot change.'

Throughout the bad times they were now encountering, the children were constantly encouraged to write to their father; but they were warned never to mention the situation in which they now found themselves and expressly forbidden to ask for help. Often Adolfo wrote offering to send money, but was always told it was not needed. Pride, or more accurately dignity, was a virtue even dearer than life itself.

Yet clearly something had to be done to rescue Maria and her children from their plight and young Adolf, who now looked on himself as the head of the family, saw the responsibility as resting with him. He decided he would head for America's west coast, to California, where opportunities for work in the Depression days of the twenties were distinctly stronger than in Arizona. He ended up in Los Angeles, a spunky kid searching for a job in a brave attempt to support his family. Finally, after several days of sleeping rough and countless refusals, he found employment at Boyle's Steel Company. He lied about his age, but the boss admired his pluck and gave him a start.

Adolf soon proved his worth. He was conscientious and became a valued employee by learning quickly how to do any job in the factory. He worked every hour he could and saved every cent he earned, and before long he was able to send for his mother and sisters and little Kikki.

He had found an apartment in the tough Mexican immigrant area of east Los Angeles. It served their needs for a time, but when the duplex next door became vacant they decided to take it. Situated behind a drug store on the corner of 4th Street and Gless, the house was small but comfortable, with a long lounge, a kitchen, three bedrooms and a verandah. The girls, their mother and Kikki shared the bedrooms, while Adolf slept on a couch in the living-room.

Adolf was less than enthusiastic about the district to which he had brought his family; it was where the poorer Mexicans settled and it was all he could afford. There were a number of menacing gangs roaming the streets, but he refused to join them. He was not afraid. He just did not want to belong. He earned respect when he told them: 'Look, I'll take on any one of you, one at a time. I don't care which one. I just don't want to join your gangs. It's dumb.' There were no takers and from then on he was looked up to, even feared, by his teenage compatriots.

Initially, Adolf provided most of the family income. The girls had no work experience, apart from picking cotton, but they could sew. They went into linen factories where they earned very little for long hours of labour. Mawie grew up during the Depression:

> 'They were tough times for us all, but Mama never considered remarrying. In fact, she never even went with another man. At the time the US government was helping everyone with food, shelter and allowances. Mama was told that with so many children to support she should be seeking help. But she was a proud person and refused. "It is not my country," she used to say. "I'm not going to sponge on anyone. We did not come here for that. We came here of our own volition. We are not going to be supported by the government of a country that is not ours to start with. We are not going to impose on them. No charity – we'll work." And by God, we did it.'

Mawie attended the local Utah Grammar School, but during the holidays decided that she, too, should do something to help swell the family fortunes. And so it was that in 1930, at the height of the Depression, she borrowed a bra from one of her sisters and stuffed the cups with paper; she put on lipstick and eye shadow to make herself look considerably older than her nine years and went out hunting for a job. The 'disguise' did the trick: she got fixed up in a jam factory, where she was put to work separating the ripe and green strawberries.

The smell was so overpowering that it was all she could do to prevent herself being sick. Mawie was paid by the basket and she was such an industrious worker that there were always plenty of baskets full of ripe strawberries.

She also remembers getting a job cracking walnuts for use in cakes during Thanksgiving and another plucking the feathers from turkeys for Christmas:

> 'They would dunk the turkeys into boiling water and hang them up. I then had to pluck their feathers and squeeze their little butts. It was terrible, the smell and everything. I don't like turkeys now, and I don't care for strawberries or walnuts either.'

At the end of each day, when she collected her wages, it all became worthwhile. She went home worn out and gave the money she had earned – usually a dollar or so – to her mother, who would rejuvenate her frail, aching body with a soothing massage:

> 'Mama was wonderful, really. She realised I was doing it just for her and didn't want to discourage me. She knew I had all this energy. But my brother never knew I went out to work during the school holidays – he would never have allowed it. Neither did my sisters. It was a secret between Mama and me.
>
> My employers realised I was too young, but nobody cared because it was the Depression. Everybody lied about their age then and nobody checked. Any problems and they would say, "Well, she said she was 16." Work was very scarce and you could not survive unless you went out on the hustle. I think they hired me at first because I was so anxious – they must have felt sorry for me. After that they kept me on because I was such a good worker.'

When the circus came to town, Mawie was the first one there. She had always been tomboyish and athletic and particularly good at gymnastic routines such as cartwheels and back-bends. She asked the circus people if she could do a spot on the show. 'I don't want any money,' she said earnestly. 'I just want a free ticket so my little brother can see the circus.' They asked, 'What can you do?'

'Oh, I can sing and dance and do acrobatics – I can do everything,' she said, unabashed. So they gave her a spot on the show. It was a travelling circus, with huge open trucks on which the various artists performed their acts and stunts. They dressed Mawie up in costume and told her what to do – and she did it so well that the circus boss gave her two free tickets *and* a two-dollar bonus.

The circus visited the different neighbourhoods of Los Angeles, with Mawie singing and performing her acrobatics. One Sunday afternoon it happened to pass by her house on the corner of 4th Street and Gless. Mawie could see her sisters sitting on the verandah with their boy-friends. She felt so proud of herself as she did her eye-catching routine that she shouted: 'It's me, it's me, Mawie, Mawie, Mawie.' She was waving and screaming hysterically, but her sisters, self-conscious in front of their boy-friends, pretended not to notice:

> 'They just looked the other way. I felt like an idiot doing my tricks and yelling and shouting like a fool. I wanted them to recognise me, but all I succeeded in doing was embarrass them.'

The Depression continued into the thirties, when a dollar had to go a long way. Food for the dinner-table was plain and functional, with few trimmings, and fruit was a luxury only the well-off could afford. One day Mawie, her eyes and ears open to any opportunity, heard about a market in town where trucks delivered fruit and vegetables from the ranches. She heard also that a lot of the fruit was discarded because it was rotten or badly bruised and would be unacceptable to the posh stores and restaurants. Mawie decided she would go and collect some of the cast-off fruit; if it was smashed or bruised, it would not matter to her. And before she went she promised Kikki she would bring him home some 'big, big bananas' to eat.

Mawie arrived at the market in Central Street full of expectancy. She climbed into the huge bins containing the discarded fruit, rummaged around and selected lots of 'wonderful' bananas – 'There was nothing wrong with them, they were just a little bruised or something.' She placed them in a large box and made her way home, her arms aching and legs wilting under the weight of the bananas, but delighted with her huge haul. Her happiness quickly evaporated when Adolf pulled up in a flash car he had saved for out of his hard-earned factory pay: a beat-up old black Gardner with a canvas top like the ones they used in the gangster movies:

> 'He raised his fist and gave me a look that said something like, "Wait till I get you home." He had some friends in the car and was embarrassed that his little sister had been raiding the left-over bins in the market. I died. I was so frightened that I left my box of beautiful bananas right there on the sidewalk. I should have taken them home because I was going to get whacked anyway, but I was too scared. When I did get home, Adolf was furious and gave me a good hiding. Mama was out at the time, or she would not have allowed it to happen. "How dare you show me up in front of my friends?" he said. He was really upset. As he was beating me, I was crying and protesting, "I only wanted them for Kikki." Afterwards, Kikki kept asking me for the bananas I had promised him. We were both crying, he because he had not got his bananas and me because I had been punished for doing something that I thought was a good thing to do.'

Mawie was so heart-broken that she hid herself in a cupboard and eventually fell asleep. She was there so long that Adolf and the rest of the family thought she must have run away. They called the police, who in turn alerted the city's ambulance service and hospitals. It was confirmed that no girl of Mawie's age or description had been brought in. A big search was mounted, with police cars scouring the neighbourhood amid fears that she had been kidnapped or even murdered.

The mystery of Mawie's disappearance was finally solved when she re-emerged crying from the cupboard and rubbing her eyes to shield them from the light; she had caught fright when she awoke in the darkness and been unable to remember where she was. Instead of pity, all she received was a ticking off from her mother and another whack from Adolf. How unjust the world must have appeared to Mawie then. It seemed she could do nothing right, despite all her good intentions.

The memory of that nightmare in the cupboard has remained with her. She is claustrophobic and has since been unable to sleep in the dark. A small light always burns in her bedroom. Harsh childhood experiences have left their mark.

Chapter 4

Starstruck

As Mawie grew older she began entering talent competitions with her singing and acrobatics. She had received no training; it was a natural talent and she discovered she could perform with very little effort. She was so good, in fact, that she won first prize in every competition she entered. Her *pièce de résistance* was a sad Argentinian song which she sang dramatically, from the heart. She cannot remember its title, but it was her show-stopper and it never failed to impress the judges.

She still has good cause to remember one such competition vividly. It was contest night at one of the theatres on Maine Street. She came out and sang her tear-jerker of a song, during which she always made believe she was a little tramp. Once more it was a show-stopper, the audience applauding so heartily that she was asked to do encores. Again and again the audience applauded, until the judges asked if she could do anything else. She told them she could do tricks. 'Good, do them, do them.' She performed several acrobatic manoeuvres, finishing with a spectacular back-flip. But as she somersaulted in the air, the sight of someone in the audience made her freeze with fear; it was the implacable Adolf, watching impassively with a girl-friend. Mawie was in a state of suspended animation – 'I felt I was in the air for an eternity' – before landing back on her feet and thinking, 'Oh, no. Another whacking!' The applause of the audience rang out around the theatre and inevitably she was awarded first prize: a synthetic pearl necklace and a couple of dollars. Mawie was in no mood to celebrate; she knew she would be in trouble when she got home and she was not mistaken. Adolf ranted and raved about the embarrassment she had caused him and the family. He considered women on the stage to be little more than semi-prostitutes. 'It is no profession for ladies,' he said. 'Good women just do not do that sort of thing.'

Mawie's mother jumped to her defence: 'No, this is the United States – it is different here. She's a good girl and is doing no harm. I am happy for her to continue.' Adolf immediately accepted his mother's viewpoint. He was basically a good, honest, upright young man who wanted the best for his family and desired to see his sisters growing up as respectable young women. In Mexico, solo dancers and actresses were considered scarlet women, with loose morals, and he found it difficult to adjust his thinking along more liberal American lines; but he was also a reasonable person, open to persuasion. 'If you think it's okay, then Mawie can carry on,' he told his mother solemnly.

Having received Adolf's approval Mawie entered any talent competition she could find, her confidence soaring with each first prize she was awarded. She built such a reputation that she came to the attention of a well-known Mexican dance duo, Rosita and Moreno. They were impressed with her singing and dancing and obtained Maria's approval for her to tour with them during the school holidays. They were accomplished dancers, who received neither the appreciation nor the recognition they deserved. Gradually the 12-year-old girl whom they had introduced to their act began, unwittingly, to steal their thunder, capturing the hearts of audiences everywhere as she sang and danced the rumba. Initially, it worked to their advantage and bookings flooded in. However, agents and promoters were not particularly interested in Rosita and Moreno; they could see star quality in the young girl with the enchanting voice and bubbling personality and wanted to engage her separately. But Mawie turned them all down flat, explaining she was part of the act. 'If they don't go, I don't go,' she told them – and because of her loyalty, Rosita and Moreno were in big demand.

Mawie's big break came when the act was appearing at the Orpheum in San Francisco. A group of film producers were in town for a convention, for which they had taken over a night-club. One of the acts went sick and a replacement was quickly sought. Opportunity had slid in through the back door for Mawie. She was asked to stand in and, as this was strictly a one-off, readily agreed to go solo, though normally nobody under 16 was permitted to appear in night-clubs. Her act went down well – particularly with the distinguished Pandro Berman.* He was fascinated by her enthusiasm and her voice. He signed her immediately to RKO studios and she was given a part as a singer in *Flying Down to Rio*, in which Fred Astaire and Ginger Rogers were cast in their first role together.

Flying Down to Rio was a huge success. Mawie, billed as Maria Castaneda, did not have a major role in it because of the appearance as co-star of Mexican actress Dolores Del Rio, but she received plenty of publicity and her future looked bright.

* *Pandro S. Berman*'s most notable films include *Morning Glory* (1932), *The Gay Divorcee* (1934), *Top Hat* (1935), *Winterset* (1936), *Stage Door* (1937), *The Hunchback of Notre Dame* (1939), *Ziegfeld Girl* (1941), *The Three Musketeers* (1948), *Father of the Bride* (1950), *The Blackboard Jungle* (1955) and *The Prize* (1963).

On completion of the picture, Mawie was given a 12-month contract. Her infectious personality and siren voice had won the hearts of the movie men. She seemed set for a rapid rise to stardom when an off-screen incident turned her against a film career and made her resolve to forget all about Hollywood.

One of the assistant producers who had worked with her on *Flying Down to Rio* called her into his office. 'I want to discuss something with you,' he told her. Mawie thought he intended talking to her about a new part, but once inside the office she realised he had other things on his mind. He made a grab for her, but she became frightened and backed away. When he started to kiss her she slapped his face, ran from the office and returned immediately to her family. Her mother forbade her from going back to Hollywood and for months afterwards she ignored countless messages from the studio. 'I had no agent and turned down all their offers of parts. I would have nothing to do with them because of that dirty old man. But they kept sending my pay-cheques every week, because I was still under contract.'

Once the emotional scars had healed, Mawie was to find a man more to her liking. She was just 13 when she met Sam Garrison, tall and handsome with blond hair and blue eyes. He was the brother of Joy Lamont, who, with husband Jack, produced numerous films in America and England.

Sam was in his early twenties when he started walking out with Mawie, who, having been able to pass for 16 since the age of nine, looked and acted far older than her years. They had met at a dance and were soon inseparable. Mawie fancied she was in love with this boxer son of an Irish father and Mexican mother and wanted to marry him right away. After all, if her mother had married at 13, why couldn't she? They could wed in Mexico with their parents' permission, but she knew her mother would not give her consent and allow her to make the same mistake she herself had made more than thirty years previously. So Sam and Mawie did what all story-book lovers do in their position: they eloped. They went to Santa Ana, where Mawie falsified her age, forged her mother's signature and obtained a marriage licence.

The impending union could not be kept secret, for Mawie's appearance in *Flying Down to Rio* meant the name Maria Castaneda was already well-known. News of the wedding was broadcast on radio and caused shock-waves back in Los Angeles. Mawie's mother immediately set out for Santa Ana with a lawyer, but they were too late to stop the ceremony going ahead. They arrived at the registry office just as Sam and Mawie had been pronounced husband and wife. Instead of a congratulatory kiss from her mother, all she got for her pains was a clip round the ear and a long lecture from the lawyer on the possible consequences of falsifying information. Mawie was unable to spend even one night of wedded bliss with Sam. She was immediately whisked home by the irate Maria, whose fury was such that she swallowed her immense pride and contacted Adolfo, asking if he would agree to Mawie staying with him for a while. It was the first time she had contacted him directly since her surreptitious departure eleven years earlier, but she considered she would have been failing in her duty as a mother not to have done so. In her opinion, Mawie would benefit from the one thing she could not give her: a spell of fatherly influence and discipline.

So Mawie was sent back to Mexico City, considerably chastened. The year was 1934 and it was the first time she had seen her father since early childhood:

> 'He was a beautiful person, a wonderful man, tall and slim with lots of black hair and a white moustache. But he was still very old-fashioned; he thought women had too much to say, that they should stay home and look after the children. He had been to Tijuana several times to see my older sisters, but would never cross the border into the United States. He just did not like the country. Mama had always got after us over the years. She would say, "Have you written to your father?" She used to tell us, "Whatever happened was between the two of us, but please feel free to go back whenever you wish. I did what I did for my own reason, and whether I was right or wrong you are at liberty to do whatever you want to do." But my mother and father never met again: they were both too proud. He had offered to take care of the children financially, but Mama always said no.'

Adolfo was resolutely opposed to Mawie going back into films or pursuing a career on the stage, but was soon to find that she possessed the same stubborn streak as her mother. She was determined to accept offers from Mexican producers who knew all about her and wanted her to make movies. There were arguments with her father, who threatened to disown her if she went against his wishes. Eventually he relented and Mawie appeared in several low-budget movies and stage musicals in Mexico City.

Sam Garrison* had followed her to Mexico in an attempt to rekindle the flame of love, but discovered that absence had failed to make Mawie's heart grow stronger. 'It was all over between us. It was very sad, because he was a nice guy and extremely good-looking. But I realised I had made a mistake and that there was no chance for us.'

* *Sam Garrison* became a Japanese prisoner of war. In 1942 he contracted leprosy during the infamous Bataan Death March. He made an apparent recovery but died some years later.

After several months in Mexico, Mawie returned to her mother in Los Angeles. She was immediately asked to do a screen test for *Mutiny on the Bounty*, which was to be shot on location in Tahiti. Hundreds of girls had been tested for the part of Franchot Tone's native sweetheart, but none had proved suitable. Mawie was at first reluctant to go in the light of her previous experience in Hollywood, but changed her mind when a 'little Hawaiian agent and talent-spotter' whom she had met during the filming of *Flying Down to Rio* convinced her she was right for the part and had nothing to fear. 'I'll even go with you to make sure you'll be okay,' he said. So they went, and Mawie got the part. 'Okay, this is the one,' she remembers the casting director saying after just one take.

However, there was a problem over Mawie's age – 'I was 14, and no one under 18 could leave the country unaccompanied by a parent or guardian.' The same applied to Mamo Clark, the half-Hawaiian, half-German actress who was to play the other native girl and who looked so much like Mawie that the two are often mistaken for each other in still photographs from the film. 'Mamo was 17, so she, too, was not old enough to travel to Tahiti.'

M-G-M had already invested big money and two years of work on the film and decided to cut right through the red tape. They approached Maria and asked her to sign a document declaring that her daughter was 19. True to character, she would have nothing to do with it. 'Mawie can go,' she told them, 'and you can fix it whatever way you wish. But I refuse to lie about her age.' Mawie explains how the problem was resolved:

> 'The production manager, Eric Bush, managed to get me a passport on which my year of birth was recorded as 1916, making me out to be five years older than I actually was. I think they had to sign affidavits to do it, but they succeeded. They did the same for Mamo: her age was given as 21. You could say anything and get away with it then, but not these days. Now you would have to produce a birth certificate. That same date of birth is still listed on my passport. When I renew it I have to give exactly the same details.'*

There was another problem for the film-makers to overcome: Mawie's screen name. They considered Maria Castaneda to be too much of a mouthful and after much debate came up with Movita. In the event it captured perfectly the native island image they were seeking and, she claims, gave her the distinction of becoming the first film

* *The Filmgoer's Companion* by Leslie Halliwell (Grafton Books) lists Movita's year of birth as 1915.

actress to be known by a single name. Conjecture abounds as to how 'Movita' was arrived at. Contrary to common belief it has no Spanish origin and may have derived from the words 'Most vital' (*Mo*-st *vita*-l). In all probability this alluded to her looks and body measurements but it must also have been 'most vital' that they came up quickly with a suitable name.

She enjoyed her second taste of the big-time immensely. The stars of the film were Clark Gable, Charles Laughton and Franchot Tone, and they were kindness itself to her on the set:

> 'I worked on the film for a year or so, on and off, and it was a wonderful experience. There was no problem, like the last time. Gable proved a particularly good friend to me and Laughton, whom I had dreaded, was also very sweet.'

Suddenly Movita was a household name – 'I was voted Most Promising Starlet and all that nonsense.' She was put under contract to M-G-M by Irving Thalberg, already a film industry legend after his appointments as head of Universal production at 21 and head of M-G-M at 25. Groucho Marx considered him Hollywood's greatest producer, and he was not alone.

Thalberg resisted feeding Movita the well-worn 'I'm gonna make you a star' line, promising instead that he would attempt to develop her career along conventional lines, building her up gradually with parts that he considered suitable for her looks and talent. But Thalberg was a sick man physically and his career was cut short tragically in 1936 when, at the age of 37, he died during the shooting of *A Day at the Races*.* It was a huge blow to Movita:

> 'Suddenly, I felt lost. Irving had been loaning me out to do 'B' movies for different studios and I was happy because that's how actors and actresses got their training. But after he had gone, I was just there at the studio each day doing nothing.'

Eventually she was offered a contract by Monogram, a small studio which made low-budget pictures. 'It was better than being at M-G-M and kicking my heels,' she says. 'At least I was signed to do four films a year, which I did.'

* *Thalberg* had been responsible for such films as *The Barretts of Wimpole Street* (1934), *Mutiny on the Bounty* (1935), *A Night at the Opera* (1935), the Leslie Howard/Norma Shearer version of *Romeo and Juliet* (1936) and *A Day at the Races* (1937). According to Jeremy Pascall in his *50 Years of the Movies*, Thalberg had resurrected the Marx Brothers (Groucho, Chico and Harpo) from threatened obscurity when Paramount refused to renew their contract following the flop of *Duck Soup* in 1933. For that alone the movie industry has good cause to be grateful to him.

She was, however, to experience once more the heartache of lost love after a chance meeting at a Hollywood party with Jack Dunn, the well-known English skater. Dunn was emerging as a popular figure in America, with a bright career in films before him. He and Movita developed a friendship which blossomed into love and they became engaged to be married. One weekend, when the couple were staying at a California holiday ranch, Dunn went out shooting rabbits. He was bitten on the hand by a fly or mosquito and thought little of it. On the way back to the ranch, some ash from his cigarette blew into his eye. He rubbed it with the hand that had been bitten and poison entered the eye. Within two weeks he was dead.*

Movita was devastated. Her brief nuptial at the age of 13 with Sam Garrison had since been annulled and she had long since forgotten all about it; but this was infinitely more distressing. At first she was bitter and resentful, shutting out even family and friends in an effort to come to terms with her sense of loss. But time is a great healer. As the months slipped by, her anguish eased and gradually she became her natural self once more.

* *Jack Dunn*. Born John Edward Powell Dunn on March 28, 1917 in Tunbridge Wells, Kent. Died July 16, 1938 in Los Angeles (tularemia). Ice skater and screen actor.

Chapter 5

Who wants to be a billionaire?

As soon as it was known she was back in circulation, Movita's name was on every Hollywood party guest-list. She was popular on the social circuit with actors, producers and directors alike. Just about everybody delighted in her lively personality and her infectious humour, to say nothing of her sultry, smouldering Latin looks.

Unknown to Movita, one such person was Howard Hughes. The introverted billionaire businessman and star-maker – then reputed to be among the richest men in the world – had inherited a highly-profitable enterprise* from his father, but his real passions were flying and making movies. *Hell's Angel*, *Scarface* and *The Outlaw* – in which Jane Russell's cleavage was the outstanding feature – were to be among his more notable films. He was at this time an independent producer, though some ten years later – in 1948 – he would pay more than $23 million for RKO, one of the 'Big Five' Hollywood film companies. Hughes was also a superb pilot who set many records, built the world's largest flying boat and put together the international airline TWA.

In the late 1930s, some 20 years before he disappeared from public view to live the remainder of his life as possibly the world's best-known recluse, he was a smart, suave, charming but painfully shy man. He had an office on Romaine Street and was a fascinating and intriguing figure – all 6ft 4in of him – as he moved among Hollywood's beautiful people. As an outrageously rich target for countless aspiring actors and actresses seeking a quick trip to stardom, he must have been hurt, devastated almost, by the realisation that few people liked or cultivated him for his own sake.

As with most men, he would have preferred to make the running where women were concerned in the unlikely hope of encountering someone who just might be more interested in him than his money.

* The Hughes Tool Company, which made oil-well drilling bits.

This type of non-predatory female was rare in his world, and the problem was compounded by the fact that he was never confident enough to make clear his intentions. Instead, like a chess player, he initiated ingenious plans designed to manoeuvre him into a position where he could, with stealth and cunning, close in gently on his prey.

The strategy Hughes adopted in his quest for Movita was to ask an Italian-American film agent, Pat De Cicco, to invite her to a gathering where they might get acquainted. Movita knew the lively, handsome De Cicco socially; she was particularly fond of him and it came as a pleasant surprise when he telephoned asking if she would attend a spaghetti dinner party at his home. She accepted, unaware that the whole thing had been set up by the mysterious Hughes.

In deference to De Cicco, Hughes had insisted on a spaghetti dinner. It was followed by a game of poker in which, again at Hughes' insistence, the guests were expected to throw in their winning hands. The idea was that by being unwittingly allowed to win on practically every occasion, De Cicco would recover the cost of the meals.

Hughes took a particular interest in Movita, though he was careful not to make it obvious. He was as captivated by her as when he had first seen her in *Mutiny on the Bounty*; she looked even more alluring off-screen with her lustrous black hair, olive skin and deep brown eyes, and it must have been hard for him not to show his hand.

More invitations to spaghetti dinner parties followed, all of them following the same pattern: first dinner and then a game of poker, with Hughes always ensuring that De Cicco finished with a healthy profit. This began to puzzle Movita, who realised De Cicco had cottoned on to what was happening and was beginning to become embarrassed by it all.

The charade came to an abrupt end when the impudent 17-year-old, tender in years but tough in mind and spirit, was delivered the hand of a lifetime: a royal flush.* She was determined not to throw it in, even when she got the 'nod' from Hughes; instead, with brazen defiance, she played the hand and inevitably scooped the kitty. Her action later brought her a mild rebuke.

'Why didn't you throw in your cards as I wanted you to do?' asked Hughes.

'I didn't do it because I think it's dumb,' she replied. 'I had a royal flush and I was not going to let it go. It's no fun playing that way.'

Hughes gently pursued the issue: 'You know I'd have paid you whatever you had lost.'

'No,' she countered, 'that wasn't the idea. The money didn't matter.

* A *royal flush* in poker is an ace-high straight flush (ie, cards all of the same suit and numbered consecutively from ace down to ten).

I did not hold on to the hand because I wanted to win the money. It was because I had a royal flush and you just don't throw away a royal flush.'

She was in full flow now: 'This is all very silly. Everybody knows they have to throw in their winning hands. Pat knows it, too, and why you're doing it. It's all so ridiculous. Why don't you just give him a hundred dollars and say, "Hey, cook me a dinner." Then everyone could have fun. We would be able to play our hands and enjoy it.'

'You know, you're right,' said the chastened Hughes. He was unaccustomed to anyone opposing his point of view – especially a slip of an actress. People usually acquiesced tamely with everything he said, but here was a young girl who was not afraid to speak her mind. He was most impressed. Thereafter the poker games were always on the level – but still Hughes had not plucked up the courage to play his hand in the love stakes. He had made no move for Movita, though by this time he had become infatuated with her. Clearly his ideal game was patience, not poker.

Hughes was given further cause to admire Movita's spirit – this time following a meal at a Hollywood restaurant. Several of the men were huddled together over a newspaper, laughing, joking and talking scornfully of the subject of the story that had caught their eye. The discarded newspaper eventually found its way on to the floor of the restaurant and Movita, her curiosity aroused, went across and picked it up. The article that had provoked the outburst of derision was splashed all over the front page: it proclaimed that Jack Doyle, the Irish heavyweight boxer, was behind bars – arrested in Los Angeles for alleged illegal entry into the United States. Movita, her maternal instincts to the fore, felt a twinge of sympathy for the handsome hunk whose picture adorned the story and immediately took issue with her companions: 'My goodness, you're behaving like women – all of you. You don't even know that man. How can you say such things when you don't know someone? How can you be so catty?'

Again Hughes was pleasantly surprised. He was quite taken by her little homily, his admiration heightened this time by her innate sense of fair play and her championing of the underdog. 'That's so true,' he agreed. 'It's ridiculous. We *are* behaving just like women.'

Hughes' simmering passion for Movita had now been brought to the boil. To find someone so young and pretty, so engagingly frank and open and so quick to scold when people were acting unreasonably was refreshing in an unreal world of Hollywood chameleons whose sycophantic fawning over anyone they thought might be of benefit to them was sickening in the extreme. Here plainly was a girl with real character – one who had been brought up always to do what she thought was right and never to be intimidated by company or circumstance.

Movita presented a fascinating challenge and Hughes decided to delay no longer. He had played the classic waiting game – one of hidden intent, of thrust and counter thrust, of manoeuvring and manipulating. Now all the pieces were in place and he was ready for the end game, the winning of the queen. He resolved to make his final, decisive and yet still camouflaged move next evening, when De Cicco was due to host yet another of his now renowned spaghetti dinner parties.

Movita usually drove to the house, as she had no desire to offend anyone who might ask to take her home. This time, however, she received a call from De Cicco requesting her not to bring the car. 'I'll pick you up myself tonight,' he said. Movita was delighted:

> 'I thought, "Great!" because Pat I liked very much. I imagined he was going to ask me for a date.'

De Cicco engaged only in polite small talk en route to the party, which made her think he intended waiting until the homeward journey before making his pitch. Sure enough, after dinner and the mandatory game of poker, Pat sidled up to her discreetly, as if not wishing to alert the other guests. She was filled with expectancy, but her heart sank when he whispered: 'Would you mind if Howard drives you home?'

'No, of course not,' she lied, mortified at the thought of a possible romantic entanglement with the urbane Hughes, whom she fancied not at all. She liked him and considered him a charming and courteous human being. But romance? He was the last man on her mind in that respect. Her mother's homespun philosophy on love and marriage, instilled during early childhood, would never permit her to form an association with a man purely on the basis of financial gain. Yet, mindful of Hughes' well-known rejection complex, she was reluctant to hurt his feelings. She put a brave face on it and began to think she had been spared an ordeal when the young Burgess Meredith, then being hailed as one of the greatest talents to hit Hollywood, rushed up to Hughes as they were leaving the party and asked: 'Would you mind dropping me also?' Hughes, appropriately poker-faced and his tone betraying not the slightest sign of disappointment, replied politely, 'No, not at all.'

Movita lived on Harper Avenue between 3rd Street and Melrose, while Meredith was staying much farther from the De Cicco house at the Garden of Allah, the home of the stars on Sunset Boulevard. She was grateful for the eleventh-hour reprieve provided by Meredith's welcome presence; she would be dropped first, happy in the knowledge that Hughes would never consider asking for a date in the company of someone else. Meredith had no such inhibitions:

'He asked me for my number, but I did not particularly want to walk out with him, either, so I told him I wasn't on the phone yet. I said he could get it from Pat when we got it installed.'

Hughes remained silent, alone with his private thoughts as they purred along in his limousine. But as the car reached 3rd and Melrose he drove straight on, leaving the bemused Meredith to enquire, 'Aren't you dropping Movita?'

'No, I'll drop you off first.'

Meredith must have concluded Movita had turned him down because she was setting herself up for Hughes when, in truth, the reverse was the case. After he alighted, Hughes swung round his huge car and headed for Movita's home. On the way back, he speculated that the reason she had refused to give Meredith her number was because of him. 'Were you trying to impress me?' he asked.

'No. I didn't want to embarrass him by turning him down in front of you, not for any other reason.'

Movita then braced herself for what in Hughes' case would be highly appropriate: the billion dollar question. Predictably, it came dressed as a preliminary to the big question, as a kind of buffer against being rejected. 'Well,' he said, 'if I asked, would you go out with me?'

'Why don't you try me and see?' she replied, confident in her ability to handle the situation and convinced he would ask her some other time.

But Hughes, having received what he considered to be the perfect come-on, seized his chance gratefully. 'Well, would you like to come with me to Palm Springs at the weekend? We'll fly there in my private plane.' Then, without pausing for an answer and as if to reassure her, he continued, 'I'll arrange for a chaperone to accompany us. Everything will be very proper.'

Movita had no desire to go, but had backed herself into a corner. She felt a little sorry for him and decided she had to accept his invitation. Hughes was euphoric, his previous halting uncertainty now replaced by buoyant optimism. He promised to make the necessary arrangements and even call her mother to seek approval. He was true to his word and Maria was highly impressed, considering him to be a perfect gentleman. Indeed he was. There was nothing too eccentric about him in those days.

Jack Doyle, meanwhile, had booked straight into the Knickerbocker on his release from jail. Having been let out on bail, he anticipated having only a few days and nights of freedom before judgment was passed on his suitability to remain in the United States. Not unnaturally, he had wanted to make the most of it and called a film actor pal, Alex D'Arcy, to see what action was available on the female front. Movita, whom Jack recalled seeing in *Mutiny on the Bounty*, was one of several names mentioned. D'Arcy confided that he knew her and, at Jack's request, agreed to play the off-screen role of Cupid.

Was ever Cupid so heedless of consequence?

Book III

JACK AND MOVITA

Chapter 1
Punch and Beauty

Movita was due to leave for Palm Springs on the Saturday morning. Her preparations for the trip were thrown into confusion by a fateful phone call from Alex D'Arcy.*

'Guess who's in town?'

'I've no idea. Surprise me.'

'Jack Doyle.'

The name would have meant little had she not seen the newspaper report of Jack's incarceration a few nights earlier when dining with Howard Hughes and company. She had experienced an instant empathy, feeling he must be 'pretty important' for the others to have been so openly hostile. 'My God, he must be a *very* interesting person,' she remembers saying to herself. Now his very mention aroused her curiosity.

Movita was even more intrigued when D'Arcy revealed he was throwing a party on the Saturday and that Jack had expressed a wish to meet her. 'I'll have to call you back,' she said in some confusion. She wanted desperately to meet this 'big, bad Irishman' who was such a celebrity around town, but how could she let down the sensitive Hughes without hurting him? She realised half the stars in Hollywood would have given their right arms, and a bit more besides, to have been saddled with her problem. To them it would have been no contest – the choice would have been Hughes by the proverbial mile. But her tomboy heart had always ruled her head since the days when she had grafted to earn a few dollars for her mother. This would be no exception. The thought of romantic evenings in the manly arms of Jack Doyle proved to be an infinitely more exciting prospect than a boring weekend in Palm Springs with the stuffy Howard Hughes.

Her mind made up, she got straight on the phone to Hughes. She held her nose as she spoke: 'Oh, Howard, I'm so sorry, I've got this most awful cold. Can we leave it for another time?'

* *Alex D'Arcy* (real name Alexander Sarruf) Born in Egypt in 1908. His arrival in Hollywood sparked a career that would span 50 years and 75 films. D'Arcy had made *The Prisoner of Zenda* a year earlier and was shortly to begin work on *Fifth Avenue Girl.*

Hughes took it better than she imagined. If he had suspected she was lying it was not evident from the impassive tone of his voice. 'Okay,' he said without a trace of the disappointment he must have been feeling. 'I hope your cold clears up real soon.' Movita's emotions hovered between huge relief and uncontrollable excitement. She even had difficulty dialling the number in her haste to ring back D'Arcy and tell him she would be able to attend the party after all.

D'Arcy had met Jack earlier in 1938 at Lake Tahoe and the two men had struck up a friendship. Seated in his favourite restaurant, the Café Casino in Beverly Hills, he briefly recalled their association:

> 'I liked Jack a lot. We were both playboy types in those days, but he was a very charming man. He liked the women and they liked him. He was drinking pretty well, too.'

Movita remembers Jack arriving at the party in a white Cadillac driven by his black chauffeur, a combination which appealed to his sense of style and, doubtless, his sense of humour. When he and Movita were introduced, the vibrations were electric. 'It may sound corny, but it really was love at first sight,' she admits. In effect, she had already fallen in love with him, or rather his picture, a few nights earlier.

She was pleasantly surprised to find the flesh-and-blood man even more enticing than the newsprint version. By the same token he must have found her at least as alluring as the black-and-white celluloid version, for they spent the entire evening together.

Movita felt compelled to voice her disbelief on surveying his slightly *retroussé* nose, which by some miracle had escaped the occupational fate of most fighting men, the absence of scar tissue around those compelling deep brown eyes (though he had been cut against Eddie Phillips) and the even rows of authentic pearly-white teeth – a source of some incredulity, since their regular brushing was never a top priority during his childhood and they had managed to remain intact during his many battles in and out of the ring.

True to her nature, Movita said what was in her heart. 'I cannot believe you are a boxer, being so handsome,' she told him straight out, not minding that he might think her forward. 'Your face is completely unmarked.' Jack smiled. 'While I've got this,' he said clenching his big right fist, 'I don't think I shall ever have to take too many punches.' True to an extent, but he conveniently neglected to mention some of his more unorthodox methods of avoiding punishment in the ring, such as his vanishing act against Phillips the last time he stepped between the ropes.

Movita shook her head slowly in astonishment. She was completely gone on Jack, who towered over her, and it showed. 'I never dreamt I would meet you,' she told him. 'Fancy me seeing a picture of you in prison and then us being together like this.'

The evening ended with Jack stealing the show as usual with a rendition from the McCormack songbook. He knew from experience that, wherever he went in the world, his tenor pipes were guaranteed to turn any hostility – or, worse, indifference – into a wave of popularity. That night he had been feeling especially vulnerable after spending two days in confinement, courtesy of Uncle Sam. It was a difficult time when he needed as much support as he could get in the battle to beat the illegal entry charge that had been levelled against him; and he did so desperately want to impress Movita. He gave it all he'd got, singing from the heart and only rarely taking his eyes off her, to the extent that she felt he was singing just for her. As he finished his last number and glanced over at her once more, he knew she was the girl for him.

Jack's initial scepticism when Movita revealed she had stood up Howard Hughes in his favour quickly vanished as the realisation dawned that she was telling the truth. He felt at first honoured and then faintly amused. It appealed to his perverse humour to whisk her off to Palm Springs for a little light entertainment at the expense of Hughes; he figured it would be a hoot if she turned up there with another escort. Movita was game: 'I really didn't mind. If Jack could stand the embarrassment of it, so could I. Whatever he decided was fine by me.'

Alex D'Arcy wanted to be in on the fun, too, so they all set off in Jack's Cadillac, full of high spirits. As they arrived, the sight of Hughes' light aircraft told them what they wanted to know: he had not called off the trip and must therefore have found somebody else to partner him. They parked up, headed straight for the casino – and almost literally bumped into the great man. Movita recalls:

> 'We were just walking into this beautiful, glamorous place as Howard was walking out with a very attractive girl on his arm. I knew immediately that she was his new date instead of me. He did not show any emotion at all. He just nodded politely, said "Good evening" and that was it. After that, there were no more spaghetti dinner parties or poker games. Howard never called me again and neither did Pat De Cicco* or any of the rest of them. It made me realise that all the dinner parties over the previous few months had been for my benefit. I honestly had no idea at the time. Howard Hughes was the last man on my mind.'

The girl hanging on Hughes' arm at Palm Springs was starlet Arleen Whelan, destined to become a leading lady of the forties. Ironically,

* *Pasquale 'Pat' De Cicco. Born 1910. Died October 24, 1978, in New York (cancer). Screen actor, film producer and theatrical agent. Divorced from artist and designer Gloria Vanderbilt. Appeared in Night Life of the Gods* (1935).

within six months of her date with Hughes she would be married to none other than Alex D'Arcy.

Jack and Movita became virtually inseparable, in spite of Movita's heavy work schedule. She had only recently completed *Rose of the Rio Grande* and was currently shooting *Wolf Call* – both featuring John Carroll.* They saw each other every evening after filming, with Jack's amorousness and attentiveness appealing increasingly to Movita. Telegrams arrived daily, much to her delight and that of her romantically-inclined family. She remembers interminable lines of 'I LOVE YOU, LOVE YOU, LOVE YOU, LOVE YOU, LOVE YOU,' until they filled the whole page, with just the briefest of messages at the bottom saying something like, PICK YOU UP AT EIGHT – JACK. Beautiful, expensive flowers also arrived daily as Jack pursued Movita with relentless vigour. For originality and ingenuity in the art of love and romance, he had no equal:

> 'It was a wonderful time for me. Every day, besides the cables and flowers, he sent my mother chocolates and things. He really was very, very nice – very romantic, I thought.'

Within two weeks Jack proposed marriage and Movita accepted. It was heady, whirlwind stuff and if he feared it was too good to last, he was soon proved right. The court appearance brought him back to reality in no uncertain fashion. He was ordered to leave the country by December 13 or face deportation.

Jack tried everything in an effort to persuade the judge to let him stay, but to no avail. So instead he sought a 90-day postponement of the order to enable him to dispose of his land in the San Fernando Valley. The application was thrown out.

The authorities, clearly wary of his every move, were cracking down hard. They considered he wanted to marry an American citizen solely to prevent his being shipped out of the country. This suggestion clearly rankled with Jack, who felt his motives were being misconstrued. How could anyone know how he felt about Movita except himself? The US Labour Department remained unconvinced. They gave him a final deadline for departure – December 19 – and warned that in no circumstances would they permit him to remain after that date.

Jack had run out of road. There was no possibility of overturning the decision or disposing of his land in the short time available. He had to leave that matter in the hands of Jack Bac-So.

He could hardly bear to leave Movita as she stood sobbing on the

*John Carroll (1906-1979). Real name Julian La Faye, he was a Latin-American leading man and singer.

quayside at San Pedro, watching the 5 000-ton Italian ship *Cellina* carry him off on the first stage of a journey that was to take him down the Pacific coast of South America and then across to Europe. Movita had bought him a St Christopher medal, which she kissed and presented to him as he boarded the boat. The patron saint of travellers would, she felt, aid his safe passage and hasten his return to her loving, waiting arms. In her heart she suspected it was a vain hope. With Jack banned from the States and she having solid film commitments during the months ahead, she wondered when, if ever, she would see him again.

It was to be much sooner than she could have imagined.

Chapter 2

Tijuana without the brass

As Jack stood on the deck of the *Cellina* waving goodbye to the girl he hoped would become the second Mrs. Doyle, he realised it would serve no useful purpose to spend all his time on board feeling sorry for himself: he had to get his mind working on a plan that would bring him rushing back before Movita had managed to get over the tearful parting. Otherwise, with him out of sight and increasingly out of mind, she just might forget about him and pick up with one of those handsome film-star types who were frequently badgering her for dates. He was sure as anyone could be that she would remain loyal and true, but he had known her only a short time and the mind plays disconcerting tricks when you are all alone with your thoughts on a long, lonely voyage of despair.

He had told Movita he planned to travel by way of Italy and France to arrive back in England by the New Year; but, having considered what kind of reception he might expect in London after disappearing with the cash from the Phillips fight, he began having second thoughts. He knew he dare not risk attempting a return to the United States. In addition, the expulsion order had stated that he must not land in any 'contiguous territory' – so, technically, that also ruled out Mexico. It was a problem that would have defeated most men, but not Jack Doyle. As the boat sailed through the beautiful blue waters of the Pacific and along the coast of Mexico – the sun shining brilliantly by day, a soft tropical breeze blowing gently at night – he decided to put his trust in his considerable intuitive powers, vowing to himself that love would find a way.

First the *Cellina* called at Guatemala, the tiny republic south of Mexico, giving Jack the idea that if he were allowed to land there he would then be entitled to enter Mexico, where Movita could join him. His hopes were soon dashed when, because he had no visa and no means of securing one, the immigration authorities flatly refused him permission to go ashore. The liner sailed on, with Jack still aboard. He spent Christmas day on ship – the quietest, loneliest Christmas of his life – becoming increasingly depressed as each passing hour put more miles between him and Movita.

Suddenly, there came the opportunity for which he had been waiting. His mood lightened when he heard the ship's next port of call would be El Salvador. He recalled once meeting that country's president, Maximiliano Martinez, at a social gathering in London. He was General Martinez then, but he would be sure to recall the occasion. Jack cabled ahead, the president was contacted and, yes, he remembered Señor Doyle. He gave permission for him to land and even sent an official to help him through the immigration formalities. Jack was taken to see the president, and shook him warmly by the hand in gratitude. He was told he could stay in El Salvador for as long as he wished, but hastened to explain that he had more pressing business: a reunion with the girl he loved. The president, sympathetic to his plight, smoothed out his visa problems and the very next day Jack was heading by plane for Mexico.

Shortly after becoming airborne, he was beginning to wish he had travelled overland. Most of the flight was over rugged, mountainous terrain and he wondered what would happen if they crashed or had to make a forced landing in the wild, unpopulated countryside below. The flight was different from anything he had experienced. There were several bumps and his head struck the cabin roof: they were beginning to run into a tropical storm and he did not like the way the ground was pivoting every time he looked out of the window. It was as if he were drunk and the world was spinning round, a peculiarity he had experienced many times in the past – particularly after heavy drinking sessions with Flynn and Gable. Yet this was no hangover – he hadn't touched a drop for days. He did not fear death as such, having since boyhood been a firm believer in fate, but surely the Grim Reaper would not come for him before he could be wedded to the girl of his dreams.

The plane was being tossed about in the sky like a kite. Jack gripped his seat and looked down at the mountains, barely visible through thick black cloud, and began to pray like he had never prayed before. Then, as if in answer to his supplication, the tempest subsided. They had flown safely through it and were back in the still atmosphere, where all was peace and calm. He breathed a hugh sigh of relief and, almost without realising it, broke into song. The one that came flooding unconsciously to him was the old Mexican love song *Marcheta*, only he changed the words slightly: 'Movita, Movita, I still hear you calling me, Back to your arms once again . . .'

His fellow passengers stared at him in astonishment, thinking he did not know the right words. He shut up quickly and settled instead for closing his eyes and picturing the moment he would be reunited with Movita.

They got as far as Guatemala on the first day and this time there were no problems, thanks to the travel visa granted him in El Salvador. The second day's flight was without incident. As the plane headed for Mexico City it passed over some of the most breathtaking mountain scenery he had seen, including the majestic 17 887ft volcano Popocatepetl. From Mexico City he travelled to the border town of Mexicali, where he immediately put in a long-distance call to the Castaneda residence in Beverly Hills.

Movita answered the phone – and nearly fainted with surprise when she heard Jack's voice on the line. She was unaware that he had jumped ship and travelled 3 000 miles in three days just to be near her. Instead, she had pictured him still at sea, sailing farther and farther away and perhaps out of her life forever. Hollywood's vitriolic gossip grapevine had informed her he was just a no-good love-'em-and-leave-'em playboy who couldn't keep his mind, or for that matter his hands, off women. 'You'll never hear from *him* again, you can bet on that,' she was told so many times that she lost count. Movita knew all about Jack's reputation and had permitted herself an indulgent smile at such moments. Even so, niggling doubts had existed and there was always the possibility that he had callously used her in an attempt to remain in America. But now? She was deliriously happy, happier than she had ever been. Any lingering fears she might have held as a result of the hurtful suggestions that had been fed to her had been dispelled once and for all. Jack had proved beyond doubt that he loved her.

They talked excitedly, like a couple of children. Movita was amazed at his enterprise and initiative – and it had all been for her. She had still to start work on the last of her films for Monogram, *The Girl From Rio*, and so agreed to rush to Mexicali to join him.

Perhaps impetuously, they decided to marry. Maybe Movita's Catholicism had hastened Jack's ardour in the sure knowledge that there would be no repeat of the disturbing scenes in Ireland which followed his union with the non-Catholic divorcee Judith Allen. The fact that he had, in the interim, pursued the thrice-married Presbyterian Delphine Dodge Godde did not enter his calculation. Had he been joined to her wealth until death did them part, it would have provided the best possible compensation for his inevitable banishment from Ireland.

Jack and Movita would wed in Ensenada, from where Myrna Loy had returned as a bride. Maybe Movita wasn't quite in that class, but the significance was not lost on her. She made a quick dash home to acquaint her family with the news and gather her things together before rejoining Jack in Mexicali. From there they drove through rough, hilly frontier roads to the fashionable Mexican resort some 70 miles from the border.

It was the last day of 1938. When they arrived at the Playa del Ensenada Hotel, the New Year celebrations were already in full swing. They had eyes and ears only for each other as they heralded the start of a new year and a new life together with a pledge to love, honour and obey for the rest of their days – a vow as poignant and meaningful to the young lovers as any wedding ceremony could have been. They married officially three days later in the humble abode of civil registrar and justice of the peace Jaime Pardo. Principal witness was Jose Parado, manager of the Playa del Ensenada. It had to be a quiet, low-key ceremony with Movita forbidden to marry under the terms of her film contract and Jack risking his neck by even being in Mexico. Already the Press had got wind of his disappearing act from the *Cellina*. In order to throw them off the scent he and Movita had booked in at the hotel as Mr. and Mrs. John Beresford, with Jack disguised in dark glasses.

Jack had been traced to Ensenada, but there the trail had gone cold. A reporter from Reuter had called the hotel asking if a Mr. and Mrs. Doyle were registered there, but was given a negative answer. Their cover was finally blown when a call came through from a New York reporter who had managed to locate their whereabouts: 'Movita, I know you are staying with Jack Doyle. Are you married or not? I'm going to print whatever you tell me.'

Movita became nervous. She was reluctant to lie because it would inevitably have meant admitting she was living in sin, the scandal from which could have destroyed her career. 'Yes, yes, we are married,' she blurted – and the news was out.

The honeymoon, such as it was, had to be cut short because of Movita's film commitments. She had to return to Hollywood for *The Girl From Rio* and Jack decided to move to the more accessible border town of Tijuana, where he rented a small bungalow.

Movita travelled down as often as two or three times a week, on some occasions being able to stay only a few hours before having to return for an early-morning appearance on the set. Her sister Francisca, anxious to see love find a way, agreed to drive on the long, wearying journeys, enabling Movita to stretch out in the back for a *siesta*. Even so, the combination of a rigorous work schedule, the learning of lines and the strain of having to concentrate all of her artistic energies on the film made long-distance commuting for love an arduous complication she could have well done without. It exposed their brand new marriage to the severest examination. Movita's devotion to Jack and her strong constitution enabled her to cope.

The enforced absences were tough on Jack, too. He was having to hang around and kick his heels in what then was a tin-pot frontier town, all the while pretending to Movita each time he saw her that he was on top of the world. Being unable to enter the United States meant he was totally stranded – a big enough problem in itself but one which was compounded by an acute shortage of cash. To be a bridegroom on honeymoon without money and without a wife was, he rightly considered, one of the cruellest fates that could beset a man. He could just about pay for cigarettes and bare necessities, but little else. Fortunately, the rent for the bungalow was just a few *pesos* or he might even have found himself having to sleep rough.

His money had disappeared rather quickly, one way or another. He had arrived in Canada with £2 000 in English money from the Phillips fiasco, but £900 of that had been snatched from him almost immediately – £800 of it going to Tom McGovern to ward off writs and a further £100 having been paid in legal fees. Then, of course, came his journey across the States to Hollywood. His detention there for offences against the immigration laws cost him a good deal more by the time he had settled with his lawyers, and then followed his crazy journey to Mexico by sea and air via El Salvador.

He began hanging out at amusement arcades when he realised his money was running low. It helped relieve the boredom – and there was always the chance he could hit the jackpot for a small stake to shore up his finances. He stuck at it for hours on end, spending as much as £10 on fruit-machines and the like before winning the jackpot, only to find there was less in the kitty than he had fed into the machine.

Gambling had always been a weakness of Jack's, as Delphine Dodge Godde had found to her cost in Reno. He could not resist a flutter – especially on the crane with claws that picks up prizes and drops them down the chute in the centre. He was fascinated, hypnotised almost, and it cost him plenty before he was forced to abandon it.

He kept his money worries from Movita. He was unable to bring himself to confide to his lovely bride that his financial embarrassment was such that he was starving himself all week in order to provide food for them both whenever she arrived. It was an agonising predicament, but he considered there was no way out short of shaming himself. The hardest thing of all to bear was the knowledge that Movita was earning plenty in Hollywood and would have been only too pleased to help him out: in fact, she would readily have offered him all she possessed. Yet not once during the long, lonely weeks in Tijuana did he reveal his plight:

> 'I would have given him money, of course. I had no idea he was broke – he never asked me for a cent. In fact he never mentioned money at all. Whenever I arrived in Tijuana he always bought me flowers or a little trinket and had someone cook me a nice meal. I assumed he was well-off, because when I met him he was driving round in a Cadillac with his black manservant and staying at the Knickerbocker.'

But broke Jack certainly was. It was Tijuana without the brass. The situation was becoming so desperate that he knew he would be forced to swallow his pride in one direction or another. After a little thought, he found it not too difficult to decide which way. He dashed off a cable to Dan Sullivan in London saying: 'WILLING TO RETURN. WILL FIGHT ANYONE YOU CAN FIND FOR ME IN ENGLAND SOONEST – JACK.' He disliked doing it, but there was no choice. Being unable to re-enter the States and virtually *persona non grata* in Mexico, a return to the ring was the only way. He hated everything connected with the sport, and yet now, at his lowest ebb and with the tide of fortune turning against him, he had to recognise it was his financial lifeline.

Sullivan had vowed to have nothing more to do with Jack, but the thought of recouping his £500 cut from the Phillips fight and a bit more besides made him most amenable to the suggestion. A few months previously the very mention of Jack's name would have led to him tearing his hair out, had he possessed any, but money to Sullivan was a healing balm that could cure the worst of all ills. He again contemplated, with some enthusiasm, the prospect of his Irishman's magnetic appeal drawing the fans through the turnstiles, and answered: 'THE SOONER THE BETTER. HEAVYWEIGHT OPPOSITION IN BRITAIN VERY POOR.'

Having whetted Sullivan's financial appetite, which he had correctly considered would not be hard to do, Jack then put the remainder of his plan into operation. He sent off another cable, this time requesting his manager to forward the money for his return passage to England. The astute Sullivan could picture Jack pocketing the cash, sticking up two fingers in a defiant Churchillian salute and staying exactly where he was. Dan was too long in the tooth to fall for that one but, if he could persuade someone else to foot the bill, he would be able to sit peacefully at home and await developments without fear of his blood-pressure rising.

He called on Arthur Elvin to see if *he* would be interested in stumping up the cash. Elvin could foresee a clash between Jack and Tommy Farr attracting a crowd of Cup Final proportions to his beloved stadium. He immediately dispatched £200 to Tijuana together with a message expressing confidence that Jack would not let him down. It was a measure of Elvin's expansive thinking that he was prepared to back his judgment by putting his money where his mouth was. The philosophy had reaped him rich dividends.

Jack did not betray Elvin's trust – indeed his financial position was such that he could ill afford to stay in Tijuana any longer. It meant leaving Movita and putting thousands of miles of ocean between them, but he had run out of options. He had to return to London in an attempt to reactivate his still considerable earning capacity. Whether he would be welcome in the city where he made his name was another question entirely, but Movita's promise to join him once she had finished work on *The Girl From Rio* was great consolation to him. With her by his side, he could face anything.

Movita drove with him on that final journey through the rough mountain roads to Mexicali. Once more she bade him a tearful farewell, resigned to the fact that it would be the best part of two months before she would see him again and distraught at the thought of another enforced absence from the man she loved. As for Jack, he was not feeling half as sorry for himself as when he had sailed off from San Pedro. Then he had wondered if he would ever see Movita again. Now he had signed a life contract with her.

One more fight – just one – would clear his debts in England and enable him to start afresh in tandem with Movita. No more, thereafter, the monotonous grind of daily training, of having to satisfy the whims of men he considered to be intellectually inferior to himself; no more the necessity to associate with the coarse boxing breed, whom he now loathed. He would be a free agent once more, able to resume a stage career that would restore him to popular favour.

Jack travelled back to England by plane, boat and train, arriving at Cherbourg on May 17. He hit London the following night, dressed outlandishly; a posse of photographers, flashbulbs popping, captured the sight of this remarkable man garbed in a sandy-coloured riding habit, riding breeches and boots, a bright yellow roll-necked jumper and a cream slouch hat, with an unlit pipe clenched between his teeth. When his picture appeared in the next day's papers, the public could have been forgiven for thinking his flamboyance owed more to the theatre than to the ring. But the feeling among the boxing fraternity that he could no longer be taken seriously as a fighting man was to prove wildly inaccurate in the light of the colossal interest that was to surround his next contest, when the demand for tickets would defy all logic.

Jack's proposed showdown with Farr was scrapped after Elvin agreed to release him for a return encounter with Eddie Phillips at White City. The bill would also feature a contest between Len Harvey and Jock McAvoy that was labelled optimistically as being for the world light-heavyweight title, though it would never be recognised as such.

The renewal of rivalry with Phillips provided a perfect opportunity for Jack to restore his fighting credibility. If so minded, he could turn the tables on Phillips in a manner that would make his critics – one of whom had labelled him the world's biggest fool – choke on their words.

Sadly, Jack was not so minded: all he wanted to do was to get in the ring, put on a show, collect his money and settle with his creditors. As he got down to training at Windsor, he realised his heart was not in it. There was no more glory to be had. He went through the motions and played the publicity game with his usual panache. In fact, so well did he do it that the demand for tickets was soon breaking all records. A typical example of his blarney came when he had finished a run in Windsor Great Park:

> 'There will be no accident like falling out of the ring this time. I'll referee the fight myself with my right hand and after that it's the championship I'm after.'

They were empty words and he knew it. He wanted to win, of course, but in truth he did not have the stomach for the fight. According to Movita he had already decided it would be his last but, as he was on a percentage of the gate, it was vital for him to get as many people as possible through the turnstiles. And Jack could talk a good fight like no one else in history.

Movita, meanwhile, had finished work on *The Girl From Rio* and cabled ahead to inform him she would be arriving in London in time for the big fight. She flew straight from Hollywood to New York – her fear of flying for once overcome by her desire to rejoin her husband. It was the fourth of July, American Independence Day, and Movita had already secured her own independence as she sailed on the liner *Queen Mary* which would get her to England six days later. Her four-film contract had ended with the completion of *The Girl From Rio* and she had asked Monogram for an outrageous sum of money to take up their option:

> 'I knew they couldn't afford to pay me, so they dissolved the contract. I realised it would happen and that's what I wanted, because then I would be free to join Jack in London.'

Newsmen in England, anxious for a quote from Jack's bride,

contacted her on the ship-to-shore phone. They found her refreshingly forthcoming:

> 'I have missed Jack terribly – the boat is not travelling fast enough. I know he has been a bit of a boy – after all he is only 25. But I made it plain to him he will have to reform and when I see him I shall know if he has kept his word.'

Indeed Jack had kept his word, although remaining celibate during the eight weeks he and Movita were apart was an exercise in self-control that had been achieved only with the greatest difficulty and one which he would have no desire to repeat.

He spent the day before the fight travelling up and down the Thames on a steamboat, with Sullivan and brother Bill aboard to keep him company. Bill recalled that in spite of Movita's imminent arrival, Jack was in subdued and reflective mood – obviously preoccupied with the next day's fight and his still precarious financial situation – and confiding that he would end up with virtually nothing from his prize-money.

Just a few hours before the fight, when he should have been resting and settling his mind on the business in hand, Jack was running along the platform at Waterloo to greet Movita. Because of the midday weigh-in he had been unable to travel to Southampton to welcome her from the boat, but at Waterloo he embraced her warmly. As he stooped to kiss her, she reminded him: 'We have been separated for a whole two months!' And to reporters she expressed her happiness at being in London. 'It is fine,' she said. 'I am so excited.'

She was carrying a bouquet of red roses presented to her at Southampton by Jack's mother Stacia – now living in England – and police kept fans at bay as the couple struggled to their car. As they climbed in there were shouts from the crowd of, 'Good luck for tonight.'

Movita's admirable effort to reach London in time to watch Jack box for the first (and she hoped last) time was in vain. She had been looking forward to it eagerly and was disappointed when Jack explained, as gently as possible, that it would be better if she did not attend. He had been warned of the immense crowds expected at White City that night and did not relish the prospect of her being shoved and jostled or, even worse, trampled underfoot.

There was another, more obvious, reason, for his reluctance to let her take her seat at ringside: his concern that unless he could catch Phillips cold he would lose disastrously and present an unedifying spectacle for Movita. She had never seen a boxing match in her life and might just become hysterical if her husband of just a few months was being battered senseless before her eyes.

Jack knew he was in no fit shape to travel 12 rounds. His two years out of the ring – apart from the previous perfunctory exchange with Phillips – had seemed like a lifetime. He was not the man he was, no question about it. Confidence and self-belief, his greatest assets in the past, had deserted him.

Chapter 3

The last hurrah!

The sun beat down mercilessly during that glorious summer of 1939, as if to compensate for the six inglorious summers to follow. The night of July 10 was unforgettable, the heat synonymous with the action to follow as a vast crowd headed for White City. Perhaps they knew they would never see the like of Jack Doyle again. Perhaps they knew they would never attend an event quite like it again. Despite Chamberlain's triumphant return from Munich, the country was mentally and physically preparing for war. Maybe it was a combination of Jack's colossal pulling power *and* a collective desire to celebrate while there was still time which boosted an attendance that remains unsurpassed in the history of boxing.

Every road to the stadium was choked. Cars had been abandoned where they stood. People were alighting from buses and taxis that could move no farther. London was at a standstill. A crowd greater in number than those which attended *both* Dempsey–Tunney fights combined was on its way to a British boxing tournament.

Sydney W. Ackland, editor of *Boxing*, estimated that a quarter of a million people were in and around the arena, a figure later confirmed by police.* No stadium in Britain, no stadium in the world, was big enough to hold such a mass of people. Those locked out became frantic. Once again barriers were smashed down and the main gate stormed. Twenty-five thousand people literally gate-crashed as police reinforcements battled to restore order. Florence Harvey recalled:

> 'Len was in the car immediately in front of Jack, but there was no movement at all – the road was absolutely chocker. Eventually Jack became restless, got out of his car and fought his way through the crowds to Len. "Think I'll walk it – come on Len," he said. Len told him not to be a fool and explained that the police would eventually come to the rescue. But Jack was stubborn – he had never taken Len's advice and he didn't do so on this occasion. How he got through those crowds I'll never know.'

Just as before the Petersen fight six years earlier almost to the day,

* Police monitoring equipment at Hyde Park indicated an unusually large crowd – in the neighbourhood of 250 000 – heading toward White City.

Jack was seemingly ignorant of the risk he was running. He was dicing with death and could easily have been crushed or severely injured by over-enthusiastic fans. Handlers and helpers were forced to carry him aloft on their shoulders to force a route through the throng. The scenes were reminiscent of those at the famous 1923 'White Horse' Cup Final – the first to have been staged at Wembley – and Arthur Elvin must have been bitterly regretting his decision to release Jack to White City.

There was to be yet more drama after Jack arrived in his dressing-room, changed into his boxing gear and had his hands bandaged – a ceremony witnessed by Phillips' manager Sam Russell and Board of Control officials. When it was time for Dan Sullivan to visit Phillips' dressing-room for the same purpose, he left instructions that under no circumstances was Jack to leave the dressing-room. 'Keep your eyes on him,' he said to Jack's brothers Bill and Tim before slamming shut the door.

Tim Doyle, then just 15, was destined to make a name for himself as a crooner in the forties and fifties under the name Tony Clare, singing with the likes of Henry Hall and his Band, Anne Shelton, Betty Driver (now of Coronation Street fame) and Billy Ternent. He related what happened next:

> 'As soon as Sullivan had gone, Jack walked across to where his coat was hanging on a peg. He reached inside a pocket and produced a half-bottle of brandy, the contents of which he poured rapidly down his throat. Sullivan did not need telling what had happened when he returned – he could smell the brandy fumes on Jack's breath. "How the hell can you expect to beat Phillips now?" he raged at him. "Sober you had some sort of chance, but now. . . ." He was absolutely furious, but Jack just smiled his cheeky smile.'

Any apprehension Jack harboured at the prospect of what might happen if he failed to nail Phillips early had now vanished. It was replaced by a cheery defiance which manifested itself in song. The man who was to referee the big fight, Eugene Henderson, recalled in his autobiography *Box On*:*

> 'The White City dressing-rooms were positioned alongside the main roadway. I was in my dressing-room and suddenly heard the sound of singing. I walked down the corridor and asked the attendant: "Who's playing the Caruso record?"
>
> In answer, he pulled open a small window of another dressing-room. Before my eyes was an incredible sight. A magnificent specimen of manhood was standing there in front of a window opening on to the main road, singing in a rich voice, apparently to the empty sky.

* *Box On*, by Eugene Henderson (Phoenix House Ltd, 1959, for the Sportsman's Book Club, for sale to members only).

> That was my introduction to Jack Doyle. But I was wrong about the empty sky. As he finished singing I was astounded to hear thunderous applause and I realised the Irishman was singing to some of the 30 000 spectators who had been unable to get into the stadium.
>
> What a character! Only 20 minutes to go before he was due in the ring – and he was entertaining the crowd.'

Phillips was first into the arena. He climbed in the ring, slumped on his stool and waited impatiently for the appearance of Jack, who did not make his entrance until several minutes later. Jack still had vivid memories of the waiting game he had been forced to play before facing Jack Petersen on the only previous occasion he had graced White City with his presence, and was reluctant to get caught out again.

There is little doubt the delay was deliberate. Frank Duffett, again in attendance with father Fred, recalls:

> 'Jack kept undoing a bootlace, tying it up and then doing the same with the other boot. It was obvious he was keeping Phillips waiting.'

The packed crowd had earlier been patiently watching the Harvey–McAvoy fight, which Harvey won on points over 15 rounds that were frequently punctuated by shouts of, 'We want Doyle, we want Doyle.' With every minute that ticked by after Phillips' entry they became even more vociferous until, just before eleven, a roar went up that must have been heard all over London. Had the open-air stadium been covered by a roof, it would surely have been lifted by the deafening sound that filled the warm night air as Jack presented himself for action.

Eugene Henderson's graphic eye-witness account in *Box On* recaptures the spectacle:

> 'Every light in the huge arena went out. With perfect timing a single spotlight finger-tipped through the darkness to the mouth of the tunnel. Slowly, oh so slowly, there emerged the Matinée Idol himself.
>
> First the black, wavy hair, perfectly groomed and oiled. Then a sun-tanned face, now a dazzling white dressing-gown . . . all combined to make up the magnificent spectacle of this 6ft 5in Irishman. His hands rested nonchalantly in his pockets and he appeared oblivious to the stir he was causing. Never before had I been in on such a scene.
>
> Every woman in the expensive seats seemed wrapped in mink and frothy lace evening-dress creations. They made a whooping, o-ooh-ing dash forward to surround the bold, brave warrior as, in the middle of a 14-strong police bodyguard, he edged his way slowly to the ring.
>
> Doyle kept up his pretence of seeming nonchalance, but several of the police were minus a button or two by the time they deposited the "broth of a boy" in the ring. I even noticed one of them looking vainly for his helmet!'

Over Jack strode, chest out like a king greeting one of his subjects, to shake hands with Phillips, who returned the greeting without looking. The man from Bow, who must have felt like a bit player acting out a supporting role alongside the star of an epic production, then flopped back on his seat and, with head bowed, waited for Jack to pull on his gloves. He did so in leisurely fashion and with an air of utter indifference.

The bell sounded shortly after eleven. Just 2min 25sec later Jack was flat on his back and out cold to the world, the almost regal bearing he presented on entering the ring having been superseded by an unceremonious Lying In State.

In the short time it had lasted, the fight was packed with drama, suspense and comedy. Jack – bronzed and elegant in his green silk shorts – had looked every inch the winner but quickly finished up in the horizontal position with his senses scattered. He had gone off at a tremendous pace, throwing punches of power from all angles and hoping, by the law of averages, that one in ten might land to bring him the spectacular first-round success on which he had based his chance of victory.

Phillips, looking pale beside his taller, heavier opponent, prodded home a dozen straight lefts – 'I just couldn't miss,' he says – but Jack walked disdainfully through them and crashed home a booming right. Phillips went down on one knee, but was up without a count. Desperately he tried to battle back, but Jack charged in and hammered away with both hands. Another right connected and Phillips was on his knees once more, to whoops of delight from Jack's corner. Again Phillips climbed to his feet and again Jack closed in for the kill. But with his man at his mercy, he became careless. The force of his advance doubled the impact of a desperate left thrown by Phillips and he was rocked back on his heels.

Phillips was quick to sense that Jack was in trouble. Perhaps he had also deduced – having come as close to being chloroformed by the brandy on Jack's breath as by his punches – that once toppled (or perhaps tippled) the giant might never make it back to his feet. Topple him he did. Bouncing off the ropes, where he had been under constant attack, Phillips planted another couple of lefts to the chin and down went Jack on his back, his legs shooting into the air as his head cannoned off the ring floor. He lay prostrate, his eyes wide open and staring at the ring lights as the fateful count of ten was tolled, his body motionless apart from the quivering of muscles that refused to obey the counsels of his muddled mind.

Phillips could scarcely believe his good fortune. He was beside himself with joy as his seconds and supporters invaded the ring and mobbed him. Jack was picked up and carted back to his corner, surprised and shaken, but Phillips looked even more startled than his victim. In retrospect, it is not difficult to understand why as he recounts the feelings that were running through his mind after landing what proved to be the knockout blow:

> 'I was standing in a neutral corner and I don't mind admitting that I was praying Doyle would not get up. "Dear God," I said to myself, "don't let him get up." He had hit me harder in that fight than anyone else has ever done. I just wanted it to end, because he had a punch that could knock your head off. He hit me so hard and with so much power that it felt as if my ankles were gripped in iron clasps and someone was shaking the life out of me. I did not even see the punches coming. Can you wonder I prayed that he wouldn't get up?'

Phillips is convinced Jack's good looks were his downfall as a boxer:

> 'He was never capable of doing 12 rounds. He was like a miler trying to run a 100-yard sprint: he wanted to get it all over in just a couple of rounds so he wouldn't get hurt. But he generated more power in those two rounds than most boxers could in ten. He was an amazing specimen of a man and I can still see him now: that angel face and curly hair, very tall and terribly handsome, a brutish man in the ring but a charmer out of it. He was a real showman and the crowds loved him, especially women. Rich ladies used to give him hundreds of pounds, which was a fortune then, and that was part of his trouble: he did not want to lose his looks. They were more important to him than anything else in life.'

When Jack had regained his composure after the fight, he forced a smile as he offered his hand to Phillips. He was smiling still as, head held high almost in defiance, he was escorted by a dozen police officers toward the sanctuary of the dressing-room. As they made their way through the jostling crowd, many of the fans who little more than five minutes earlier had cheered him to the echo were laughing and jeering. This was the hardest blow of all to take – one that hurt far more than the punches from Phillips that had just sent him crashing to the canvas. Now even his faithful public had turned against him as suddenly and as viciously as Phillips had turned apparent defeat into crushing victory.

Back in his dressing-room he had to suffer more scorn – this time in the form of a rebuke from a haughty Len Harvey, fresh from his victory over McAvoy. 'You're a damned disgrace, Jack,' he lectured airily. Jack laughed a nervous laugh. 'One thing's for certain, Len,' he replied. 'I'm never going to work as hard as you for my money.' According to Florence Harvey, that short, sharp exchange summed up the difference in attitude between the two men.

Jack must immediately have regretted his flippant response. Though he had little in common with Harvey, he respected him and would not have wished to offend him. It was easy for somebody as accomplished as Harvey to kick a man when he was down and in that respect he deserved the stinging riposte his unfeeling remark had invited. Had the same fate befallen Harvey, Jack would have been quick to offer his condolences rather than let fly with a caustic comment calculated to add insult to injury.

Jack understood, only too well, that Harvey's prickly attitude was born of resentment at not being able to command anything like the adulation that a loyal and loving British public had always heaped on him in good measure, in spite of his many shortcomings.

Friction had been caused between the two men at the time of Jack's affair with Delphine Dodge Godde. Jack asked Harvey to quit moralising after he had warned him not to do his training in night-clubs. 'Look, Len,' he told him. 'I'm not like you – we've got different temperaments.'

Nevertheless, Jack did have a number of sympathisers on that fateful night at White City. As his taxi attempted to leave the stadium, the large crowd milling around outside surrounded it and refused to let it move until he had given them a song. They even lifted if off the ground to prevent it moving. Jack obliged by climbing on to the roof of the cab, from where he delivered a few verses of *When Irish Eyes Are Smiling*. They cheered him so rapturously that any uninformed onlooker could have been forgiven for thinking that he – and not Phillips – had won the day.

The irony would not have been lost on Jack. He was accustomed to snatching victory of a kind from the jaws of defeat. What the crowd must have realised only too well was that this effectively was the end of Jack Doyle the boxer. The old jibe that he should sell the soles of his boots as advertising space surfaced again and before long this parody of the song *Deep Purple* was in circulation:

'When the deep purple falls
Over old White City walls
And the stars begin to twinkle in Jack's eyes
Through the mist of a memory
Wanders the referee
Counting to ten with a sigh.

In the still of the night
Jack went out just like a light
Eddie can't believe he did it with his paws

> But as long as his heart will beat
> Jack in his dreams will meet
> Ed in his deep purple drawers.'

In Jack's defeat at the paws of Eddie Phillips the crowd had seen the best and worst of him all in one night and his latest fiasco carried a symbolism which would rapidly become apparent. 'In the still of the night Jack went out just like a light' – and the lights were beginning to go out all over Europe, too. The men in the crowd would soon be off to war, many never to return. Ahead lay blackouts, ration cards and casualty figures.

The fight marked the end of an era – for Jack and for the country.

Chapter 4

Home front

It was late July, 1939. For a film actress who had been fawned over in Hollywood, Movita was to have a rude awakening in England. War was about to be declared on Hitler's Germany. She was thousands of miles from her family and, like Judith Allen before her, had abandoned a promising film career for love. She was blissful, innocent and unaware of the difficulties which lay ahead.

Jack and Movita's first measured decision as marriage partners in the flat they had taken in fashionable Devonshire Place was to confirm that Jack's fighting days were over. In spite of much newspaper talk and numerous offers – including one from Arthur Elvin – the theatre would be his workplace and his pleasuredome, just as surely as the ring had become his Valhalla.

Jack's determination finally to rid himself of the boxing leeches he believed had sucked him dry was reinforced shortly after the Phillips fight when he learned the attendance was claimed to be 40 952 and that receipts had totalled £15 501-13s-0d after entertainment tax and promotional expenses.* Although a gate in excess of 40 000 was massive by normal standards, the figure fell woefully short of the 90 000 estimated by newspaper and agency reporters on the night. The well-informed Geoffrey Simpson later put the record straight by revealing the true *paid* attendance to be 82 000. Eddie Phillips' testimony – 'My handlers told me it was the biggest crowd ever' – confirmed that the gate must indeed have been up around the 80 000–90 000 mark.

It follows that receipts would also have been far greater than the figure disclosed to Jack. The normally tight-lipped General Critchley admitted as much when, uncharacteristically, he let his guard slip. He had been drawn into a reply after the great showman C. B. Cochran, staggered by the enormity of the crowd, commented:

* Ticket prices were three guineas (£3.15), £2, 36/- (£1.80), 24/- (£1.20), £1, 15/- (75p), 10/- (50p), 5/- (25p), 2/6 (12½p).

> 'My long-standing record of just over £30 000 for the Carpentier–Beckett fight at Holborn Stadium must be pulverised.'*

Critchley, who had come close to being shut out of his own arena because of the crowd and traffic congestion, acknowledged that this was the case when he said:

> 'In fact we took a good deal more than £30 000, but as Doyle, Phillips and McAvoy were all on a percentage I am afraid it isn't fair to disclose the total gate. It is a commercial secret which we are compelled to keep, even though we'd like to tell you.'

Critchley's comment proves beyond doubt that White City's official £15 000 figure had been a fabrication. The likelihood is that the take was nearer £60 000 than Cochran's record £30 000. As it was, Phillips and McAvoy were each paid £2 200, while Jack received £3 200. Harvey was slightly more fortunate, having boxed for a guaranteed £3 500. White City's manipulation of the figures, in addition to selling the boxers short, would have gained them a significant tax advantage. It is difficult to imagine how they got away with it, not only then but six years earlier with their ludicrously low attendance figure of 24 622 for the Doyle–Petersen fight.

Jack realised he had again been fleeced, but there was precious little he could do about it. His purse, disappointing when weighed against the tens of thousands he had drawn to White City, still paid him at the rate of £1 500 a minute for his brief night's work – but he was left with just £400 after settling up. For a start he had not reckoned on parting with £750 to the Board of Control (the long-standing debt, plus the Board's mandatory five per cent major tournament tax). And as if White City hadn't coined enough already, £800 went to them in payment of their management stipend. By the time Jack had taken care of his training expenses and paid Sullivan and the rest what he owed them, he was left with just the small change. Any top performer who had attracted paying customers to a main stadium event in such record-breaking numbers would have been distressed at ending up with such a pittance. Yet, according to Movita, Jack did not complain:

> 'He was just thankful he had settled with everyone. It was what he wanted to do. He had squared up at last and I think it was a great consolation to him.'

Things started well for Jack and Movita. They rehearsed a novel routine for the stage, following which Jack threw a party at a West End

* Georges Carpentier knocked out the then British heavyweight champion Joe Beckett in the first round at Holborn Stadium on December 4, 1919. He repeated the performance four years later at Olympia.

restaurant in celebration of their forthcoming tour. It was a crazy party, to which seemingly the whole of London was invited. Taxis went round with stickers saying, 'JACK DOYLE'S PARTY ONLY'. Movita recalls hundreds of people turning up and, of course, she knew none of them. Even Jack himself had no idea who half of them were.

The variety show was a huge success, attracting vast audiences around the country. They toured for a time with the much-loved 'Two Ton' Tessie O'Shea, one of Britain's greatest stars of the music-hall era. Tessie, who retired to Silver Springs, Florida, recalled:

> 'In my opinion Jack had the greatest personality, both on and off the stage, of anyone I knew. He was a real lady-killer. We were all crazy about him. I suspect that apart from his handsome looks and his physique, it was his Irish blarney that really got through. Yes, Jack appeared in many of my shows. When Movita joined him we were at the Chelsea Palace in London and there were packed Beatles-type houses for Jack. I wish there were more Jack Doyles in this world. In my remembrance of him, he was a Leprechaun . . . and Charmer. Any other stories I heard and read about him never crossed my path. I only saw and knew the "Little Boy".'

The fact that Jack's stage act included his beautiful new wife gave him even greater appeal, but now it was a very different kind of mass hysteria that greeted his every public performance. Though still one of the greatest sex symbols of his time, his union with Movita had become the standard-bearer for an idyllic and successful marriage. To the public at large this glamorous couple personified all that love and happiness should be. Theirs was a high-profile partnership accentuated by constant media attention and hero worship. To label them the Olivier and Leigh and Taylor and Burton of the late thirties and early forties would not be overstating their popularity:

> 'We could not even go into a restaurant without being mobbed. People would do silly things like grab one of my shoes as I was getting into a taxi. It was just incredible. We were so obvious – big Jack and little Movita. We had all our stage clothes specially made for us, right down to the shoes. I had a dress-maker, Len Pearson from Huddersfield, who used to make some very beautiful clothes. And I had a shoe-maker – such beautiful shoes and lovely turbans I used to wear.'

People from all walks of life were fascinated by Movita. She became a trend-setter in much the same way Princess Diana did several decades later. Fashion-conscious women, even prostitutes, began wearing the turbans that were her stylish signature:

> 'We were very, very popular and highly-paid. We were working extremely hard and Jack was behaving beautifully. There was no trouble until after war

was declared. But even then we were still working as hard as ever and earning big money. Jack volunteered to rejoin his old regiment, the Irish Guards, as either an officer or physical training instructor, but was told, "No. You and Movita are doing more for the war effort by appearing and entertaining the troops." I remember everything so well. We were entertaining the troops for free, entertaining at hospitals and entertaining people in the subways, where Londoners sheltered during the bombing raids. We used to bring them food – fish-and-chips and things – and candy. We also sang for them and signed autographs. We did a lot of that. We did everything that people did during the war – anything to try and help. We were so much in demand that we sometimes did seven shows a day, by God! Two shows a day in the theatre – three when there was a matinée – and the rest was all entertaining troops and sick people. It was really exhausting. We also did a lot of appearances at factories to help boost the morale of the workers. They adored us wherever we went. Everyone used to gather round and mob us. It was almost unreal.'

Shortly after volunteering to enlist, Jack took over The Cartwheel, a roadhouse in rural Buckinghamshire. In addition to it being a place of refuge from his legion of admirers in London, he regarded it as an ideal, easily-run business venture that would occupy Movita and other members of his family while he was away soldiering. He had written to the Irish Guards asking them to take him back because, as a neutral Irishman, he felt he should do his bit for the country in which he had made his name. When told he would not be required, he kept The Cartwheel for a while, doing occasional impromptu cabaret spots there with Movita. They booked in other well-known artists, including the celebrated black singer-pianist Hutch. The Cartwheel, which lays back off the main London–Amersham road, was a charming venue complete with gallery and ballroom. Teas were served in the afternoons and dinners in the evenings, with top cabaret thrown in:

'Jack had fancied a nice, quiet place in Buckinghamshire. It was lovely out there – very picturesque and countrified, with beautiful apple trees all around. But he soon got fed up with it because he liked London, the bright lights and plenty of people around him. He was too fond of the night-life, the glamour, the activity. But he tried, I guess.'

Jack and Movita also rented a riverside cottage in Maidenhead, 'Wynnstay', from the Baroness de Sarigny. They looked on it as their country home and spent as many weekends as possible there during breaks from touring:

'We had a woman servant who once worked for the Royal family. She was wonderful and looked after the place for us. We would go down to Maidenhead and she would have the tea ready for us and everything. But I remember one night, after we went to bed, I awoke and wanted to go to the bathroom. I couldn't get up – I was feeling too heavy and could not lift my body out of bed. I woke Jack and said, "Something's wrong with me. I want to go to the bathroom but I can't get up. I'm too heavy." He said, "Oh my God, so am I." Then I just passed out. What had happened was that we had left the gas fire on and it was leaking. It was the middle of the night and we had almost gassed ourselves. Jack managed to get up, drag me to a window and break it. Had I not wanted to go to the bathroom, we would have been dead. It was a beautiful old cottage, but I'll always remember it because of what happened. We decided not to stay there after that.'

Jack and Movita were happy together during the early part of the war, with hardly a cross word passing between them. According to her they were also earning a considerable sum – around £500 a week – from their popular double act. It was perfect harmony all the way, both on and off stage.

Suddenly, things started to go wrong. First they met with serious financial trouble, allegedly as a result of the activities of their personal secretary Kathleen Look,* described by the late Sir Atholl Oakeley in his book *Blue Blood on the Mat* as a 'Venus' and 'quite the most glamorous woman, outside the Ziegfeld Follies, that I had ever seen'.

Movita uses no such superlatives to describe Miss Look:

'Kathleen came with us wherever we were appearing. We appointed her because she had been a top promoter and her references were impeccable. She handled the finances, paid the bills and looked after everything. Somehow we always managed to get her a room from where she could work. We trusted her completely, but I soon noticed that whenever I happened to buy a fur coat, she would buy one, too. I used to say to Jack: "Kathleen must be well off." We were so naive and trusting that we didn't suspect a thing. Sometimes Jack would say to me: "Kathleen dresses very well, doesn't she? That fur coat must have cost a pretty penny. How does she do it?"

It's funny now, but we just did not realise. She was well-spoken and well educated and her mother was terribly, terribly Oxford. Jack was a trusting person and we assumed Kathleen must have been rich. She was always very smartly dressed when she toured with us. If I bought a dress, she would buy one: it would all go on Jack's bill. Goodness knows how much she spent overall, but it must have been a fortune. He would give her so much to pay bills, but she never settled them. She was with us for a good while and was fiddling all the time. Jack never suspected a thing, so how would I?

She was a thief, let's face it. She wrote all the letters and signed the cheques, so she knew what to do to keep the creditors quiet. The whole mess

* *Kathleen Look* had promoted major wrestling tournaments on a regular basis at Belle Vue, Manchester.

wasn't uncovered for ages because she had been fending off the creditors by paying them so much each week. But eventually they all got together and the pressure became so great that she had to confess. She couldn't do a thing – the game was up. She offered to pay them back at £5 a week, but it was no good. The creditors were pressing their claims and Jack was forced to go bankrupt because he still owed all the people he had already paid, or thought he had paid. He said: "What are we going to do? We can't call in the police because Kathleen will go to jail – and for what?" He did not have the heart to turn her in.'

At Jack's public examination in February 1941 his liabilities were listed at £1 689, with no assets, and he agreed to pay over to his trustees whatever money he could for creditors. It takes only a simple mathematical equation to deduce that he could have cleared the entire debt in a matter of weeks with his and Movita's earning power. Granted he was still supporting his parents – for whom he had bought a new £500 terraced house in Greenford, Middlesex – and his living expenses were undoubtedly high, yet a short period of relative austerity would have salvaged his situation and his reputation.

Bankruptcy signalled the start of a slippery decline which he would find hard to arrest. Movita remembers him suddenly receiving bad publicity and sinister threats:

'The threats came after articles appeared in the newspapers saying Jack had refused to fight for England in the war. It was all so untrue, because he had volunteered to rejoin the Irish Guards and been turned down. And we had exhausted ourselves doing charity concerts to help the war effort. The stories in the papers were followed by anonymous letters saying, "If you appear at such-and-such a venue, you will be shot." We carried on for a while, because at first these threats did not worry him: Jack Doyle wanted to prove he wasn't afraid. But after a while, when they continued, he became concerned. He was scared I might get shot at or something. There were lots of threats – some even by telephone – but he never talked about them because he didn't want to alarm me. He was frightened for me rather than for himself.'

The menacing letters and calls, coupled with the adverse publicity, gradually took heavy toll of Jack. He became moody and violent and it was Movita who paid:

'He began beating me up and associating with other women. He knocked me out once in London and I could not even remember doing the show: I only came to properly after it was over. Things began to get so bad that I was as close to a nervous breakdown as you can get. I must have been like a punch-drunk boxer. I was going through with the shows and not knowing a thing about it afterwards.

We were doubling up at theatres and clubs and earning an absolute fortune. But I was shaking whenever we appeared at night-clubs. I couldn't keep any food down – only brandy and milk. I would just go and do my show, I don't know how, and then I'd collapse. I was as thin as a rake – a real mess. I couldn't sleep. I was just lying there like a zombie while Jack was off with other women: all kinds of women, titled ladies, all sorts, hundreds of them. I've blotted it out of my mind now. He was singing badly, also drinking too much and generally just doing a bad show. He lost all sense of realisation.

He kept getting bad publicity all the time; the papers would never say anything nice about him. I think it hurt him badly. He would stay sober and behave, and then he would get drunk and say, "To hell with everything." He was very self-destructive. It was as if he was trying to fulfil what he thought was his destiny.'

Five months after being declared bankrupt, Jack was again in financial trouble. This time he was sued by a young compatriot, John Muldoon, who received judgement in the High Court for repayment of £750 he had paid to Jack in part remuneration for a proposed fight at Earl's Court with Tommy Farr. Muldoon had been hoping to mark his entry into the fight game by staging a big heavyweight contest – and none came bigger than Doyle v. Farr. Jack had apparently assured Muldoon he would not present the cheque, but then reneged on the promise and refused to return the money when the fight failed to materialise.

According to Movita, Jack never had any intention of making a boxing come-back. Indeed Dan Sullivan had been chasing him for weeks with details of a huge offer he had received for the fight to go on at Wembley Stadium, but his calls were never returned. The suspicion must be that Jack considered any promoter fair game after the way he had been treated in the past. Yet, by Movita's own admission, they were making so much money on the stage that he had no need to take anyone for a financial ride, least of all an ambitious fellow-Irishman of honest intent.

Movita claims she was very much alone when she and Jack were not working: 'He was always going off on so-called business trips and I naturally became suspicious.' On Christmas Day, 1941, she was desperately unhappy after being left alone but cheered up considerably when told by the flat porter: 'Mr Doyle has just arrived outside in a taxi.' She went down to greet him, but on opening the door found a woman in the back of the cab kissing and fondling him passionately. When inevitably Movita erupted in fury, Jack dragged her back in the flat and slapped her till she was unconscious. She says she was pregnant at that time and suffered a miscarriage because of the beating:

> 'Jack tried to explain himself the following day by saying the woman was only wishing him a happy Christmas and I had behaved so badly that he lost his temper, for which he was truly sorry. I was physically sick and disorientated and unable to remember much of the incident at the time. So I accepted his explanation. I even thought he might even be telling the truth about the other woman. That's the sort of state I was in.'

Movita had also miscarried following an air-raid in Blackpool in October 1940. Though she was hauled uninjured from beneath the rubble of a friend's house she had been visiting, the shock of the incident later caused her to lose the baby she was expecting. Her family back home were devastated to read in the Los Angeles newspapers that she had been killed, but distress turned to delight when Movita cabled that the reports were grossly exaggerated.

The incident with the woman in the taxi finally convinced Movita that Jack was still the playboy he had been all his life and the hopes she had entertained of changing him were as far from realisation as ever. Those Hollywood gossips had not been so far wide of the mark after all.

In spite of everything, she was reluctant to leave him. Being a Roman Catholic gave her a strong sense of commitment to marriage and its responsibilities; she saw it as her duty to attempt to get him to mend his ways, however long it took. She was fighting a losing battle. As time went by he seemed to get worse instead of better, hitting her each time he could not explain his behaviour with women or give a plausible reason for not being with her.

Jack had also become resentful of the fact that, as his popularity was declining, Movita's was on the increase. There were several attempts by theatrical agents and promoters to book her separately, but she was loath to agree. However, she did broadcast, record and do solo television shows; and at the tail-end of 1942 she was to make a British film for Pathé, *Tower of Terror*, in which she starred with Wilfred Lawson and Michael Rennie.

With her health and even her sanity at risk, Movita decided to return to her family in Beverly Hills. It would not be as easy as she had imagined. With the war raging in Europe, she found it difficult to secure a passage. Then, whenever she had a chance to leave, Jack was invariably in some sort of trouble and her conscience held her back.

She remembers an occasion when Jack was involved in a street fight with a couple of Dutch naval officers in June 1942:

> 'He tried to defend himself when these giants came at him. He knocked the hell out of one of them and was charged with assault. People used to pick on him like this wherever he went and he began to suspect a plot. As an ex-boxer, he always got the blame. He was not even allowed to defend himself.'

The incident took place outside the Cocoanut Grove Club in London's Regent Street and resulted in Jack appearing at the London Sessions. He was alleged to have 'savagely struck' officer Pieter Egas during a scuffle which started after he was accused of abusing a woman (a Miss Dorothy O'Brien of Sussex Gardens, Paddington), who then attacked him. Miss O'Brien said in evidence that she was not fighting drunk, but struck Jack on the side of the face and kicked him as hard as she could. Two women who were with Jack (Movita was not one of them) then attacked her, and Egas and a fellow-officer became involved in the fracas. Quite a punch-up it was, too. Jack appeared in court limping from the effects of the kick and with one of his eyes blackened, while Egas had his face bandaged. Jack was acquitted and discharged after expressing his regret to Egas – even leaving the dock to shake hands with the Dutchman:

> 'Jack apologised to them and they apologised to Jack. They had been drunk and did not know what had happened. But what was Jack to do when two great big men came at him? Let them kill him? The papers said, "There goes Jack Doyle, in trouble again."'

The build-up of pressure finally became too much for Jack. What with the bad Press over his non-involvement in the war effort and the death threats, life had become hardly worth living. He took the only course he felt was open to him: to quit touring. By removing himself from the public gaze, he hoped the newspapers would stop criticising him and that consequently the threats would cease. It seemed the only way out. In order to make it official he called a Press conference at London's Park Lane Hotel and announced that he and Movita would refuse to accept any further stage engagements until he had cleared his name. He was adamant he would not appear again until he had disproved allegations that he was prepared to sing but not fight: 'I will never take money from the British public by false pretences.'

A reporter echoed what most people were thinking when he asked: 'Don't you think you should be in the Army?' Jack was stung into a somewhat ambiguous reply:

> 'Ireland is my motherland. When the call for freedom goes round the world, I will be ready. I shall answer it eagerly then.'

Movita was mystified by Jack's decision to leave the stage. In view of his frequent outbursts of aggression, she had been more fearful of him than of the possibility of injury or death from a sniper's bullet. As long as she could physically carry on performing, she felt it would be a mistake for them to abandon their hard-earned success:

'It wasn't that there was no work for us, because there was. Plenty of work. We were making an incredible amount of money. I could not understand why he wanted to stop. He had only told me about these threats on one occasion, and then asked: "Do you want to go on?" I said: "Of course. Why ever not?" I was not afraid but as I always went on stage first, Jack thought I might get shot. We both felt Dan Sullivan or the boxing people had stirred up all the bad publicity, the hostility toward us and the threats. Who else could it have been? Sullivan had been annoyed because he had arranged a big-money fight with Tommy Farr and Jack would not return his calls or reply to his cables; he wanted nothing to do with boxing. To this day I still don't know precisely why we stopped touring, because we were doing so well. All I know is that Sullivan was in with a bad crowd [the Sabini brothers] and Jack was fearful of them. I never knew who they were; I didn't know much about that side of it and Jack would never tell me. But he wouldn't have stopped touring for no reason at all.'

In the autumn of 1942 – the curtain having come down on their theatrical appearances – Jack and Movita opened a night-club, the Swizzle Stick, in London's West End. It was situated in Avery Row, a tiny mews behind Claridge's, and the celebrity of the proprietors ensured its immediate acceptance as the in-place for London's smart set.

The Swizzle Stick had three bars – the New Yorker, the American Bar and, upstairs, Alec's Bar, all with their own separate entrances. Clubs such as these were known commonly as Bottle Parties and it was a 'Members Only' establishment. Movita recalls that business boomed:

'The clubs were absolutely packed. All kinds of people used to go there – actors and actresses, society people, British and American officers, you name them. The place was always full. I remember Jack Ford, the film director, coming along too. I had known him since I was a kid, when I used to go on his boat. He spotted me walking to the club through the mews off Bond Street and came in for a drink. He was surprised to see me and I was surprised to see him.

I knew Jack was still associating with other women – I had proof first-hand when phone calls started arriving at the Swizzle Stick. They'd say, "Is Jack there?" I would say, "No, but this is Mrs Doyle. Can I help you?" Then they would say, "Oh, well, he promised to pay my rent and that was two weeks ago. He hasn't been round since." After a while I began telling them, "Honey, if it's any consolation, you're not the only one. Others have been calling, too, so if I were you I wouldn't hold my breath." What else could I say?'

Movita denies, though, that she visited the club early one morning and found Jack having sex with the char-lady – 'I'm just making her feel good.' But she does admit that he was consorting with all sorts of different women, even prostitutes: 'I can't imagine that he paid them. They probably paid *him*.'

She never enjoyed her role as hostess at the Swizzle Stick and did it only to appease Jack, who considered her an asset as far as business was concerned:

> 'I didn't like to go there because I wanted no trouble: I just didn't want to be around the place. Lots of American officers and gentlemen used to go there and proposition me. And I was frightened, because once Jack started drinking heavily he became violent. I used to go to the pictures – anything just to escape when he got like that. Taxi drivers used to take me to hotels, where I would hide. I used to go anywhere just to keep out of his way.'

During this time Movita had the consolation of the companionship of French film actress Mirita Adorée, whose late sister Renée had starred with John Gilbert in one of the most dramatic and powerful movies of the silent era, *The Big Parade*:

> 'Mirita had toured with us before we opened the Swizzle Stick. She was very trustworthy and a good woman and I'm pleased she was around then. She was someone I could always turn to.'

Movita is convinced that Jack's wild and erratic behaviour stemmed from a persecution complex – one that was real rather than imagined:

> 'He seemed to be in trouble all the time and it was trouble he didn't start. It angered him so much that he seemed to go haywire. There was always something happening and it just became too much for him; it was all set up and he knew it, though he never talked much about it. The boxing crowd were upset because he wasn't giving them their percentage. They had demanded a cut from his touring and even wanted a cut from the Swizzle Stick. "You signed a contract," they said. "That means for everything." But Jack refused to cough up because that contract was for his boxing only, not his theatrical work or anything else.'

Unknown to Movita, a considerable number of other pressures were being exerted on Jack – most notably to enlist and help the war effort. In this respect his decision to quit touring had placed him in a paradoxical situation. While he and Movita had been entertaining the troops and making personal appearances at hospitals and factories, all had been well; but having taken the conscious decision to curtail their morale-boosting activities, he learned that he would be expected to contribute in some other way.*

Jack could never understand why he had been turned down when applying to rejoin the Irish Guards. His Army record had been half reasonable – as witness his reference from Lord Gough – and he had

* Under the National Service Act, the Irish in Britain were ordered to dig trenches in a drainage scheme as an alternative to being repatriated to Eire.

helped bring honour and glory to the regiment by becoming the Brigade of Guards heavyweight champion. The decision to reject him, however, had come not from the Irish Guards but the Ministry of Labour, which insisted he engage in more valuable work, like digging ditches. It was something he could not and would not countenance, and understandably so. Len Harvey and other prominent boxers and sportsmen were given posts that befitted their status, such as PTIs, and Jack felt he merited similar treatment. Undoubtedly Ireland's neutrality in the war, coupled with the undesirable publicity he had attracted, contributed to his treatment by the authorities. He courted further unpopularity by proclaiming indignantly: 'Imagine it – a man of my standing being asked to dig ditches.'

Had he been able to bring himself to admit publicly that he had been forced off the stage by death threats, there might have been a greater sympathy for his plight. People would have realised he was no coward. They would have admired him for having kept the threats to himself and performed on stage for longer than was reasonably safe to do so, even manfully shielding the news from Movita until he felt her own life was on the line.

Jack's ambiguous behaviour and paranoid disposition were his undoing. If it was hard then to separate truth from fantasy, and self-justification from guilt, at this distance it is impossible. For there were many other things Jack shielded from Movita and they were not based on so noble a premise. For instance, he did not come clean to her about his association with scores of women, his swindling of John Muldoon or even the fact that he was being pressed into war service. It was to come as something of a surprise to her when she learned Jack would sooner return to his Irish homeland than be coerced into joining the British forces. Having long felt it prudent not to ask questions for fear of antagonising him, she had no idea he had finally been presented with an ultimatum to sign on or get out of the country.

In spite of all she had been through, Movita could not help but feel sorry for Jack. She considered his hard drinking, his womanising and his violence were manifestations of the pressures he had been under since the outbreak of war. To see him now, not yet thirty, broken by the campaign of vilification being waged against him was distressing in the extreme.

Whichever way he turned he faced seemingly intractable problems, for not even a nostalgic return to Ireland presented the prospect of an instant panacea. Jack had to think the situation through carefully and, according to Movita, he had an alert and agile mind on the rare occasions he was off the booze completely. The position he had to ponder in sober contemplation could not have filled him with much cheer; indeed, the outlook was so bleak that he must have felt tempted to reach for the bottle again. He was no longer wanted in England unless prepared to do menial work to help the war effort, and there was no chance of his re-entering the United States. If that was not enough, he had been made an outcast in his own country. There was no alternative but to work out a way in which he could regain the affection of his own people.

As always when he found himself in a tight fix, Jack turned to Movita. The marriage had plummeted to an all-time low, yet he was certain she could be his salvation. Ireland would warm to her as it had failed to warm to Judith Allen, and, in the process, it would warm again to him. As a Catholic, Movita would be accepted wholeheartedly and as a Hollywood film actress she would attract considerable interest in her own right. The fact that she had been married before would not be an issue. It was doubtful anyone would uncover evidence of her annulled nuptial at the age of 13 with Sam Garrison; there would be no digging of the dirt in that connection. There would be a certain pious satisfaction that Jack had rid himself of 'the Allen woman' at last and seen the error of his ways. All would be forgiven.

Jack was aware that Movita had endured a life of lonely isolation in Britain. Her desperation to rejoin her family in Beverly Hills made it extremely unlikely she would agree to accompany him to Ireland. Even in his darkest moments he had to admit that he could scarcely blame her if she never wanted to see him again, still less remain married to him. He appealed to her finer emotions, to the fund of goodwill she still had for him. He begged her to help him regain his popularity. 'With you by my side, the Irish people will welcome me back,' he said, assuring her she could return to the U.S. as soon as he was re-established in Ireland.

Movita was convinced that only more misery lay ahead. She would be going for the sake of appearances, just so that a husband who had made her a nervous wreck could once again walk tall in the land of his birth.

Yet she was aware that unless she agreed, it would inevitably be the end of Jack Doyle; she could imagine him ending up in the gutter, wallowing in terminal self-pity. She had no desire to see that happen. Despite the beatings and the abuse, she nurtured the hope that the happiness and satisfaction he would experience in once again becoming the idol of his people would banish forever the demons that had turned him into a monster. When Jack was feeling good within himself, free of alcoholic influence and evaluating people and events with clarity of thought and generosity of spirit, he could be sweetness and light. Those rare moments were worth savouring; they almost made up for everything that had gone before. Almost, but not quite. Movita realised she would in all probability regret it, but felt there was only one decision she could make: to give Jack the succour and support he would need in order to restore his reputation in Ireland. The agreement was that she would stay for six months in all – long enough to get him back on his feet – and then return to America.

Before leaving for Dublin, Jack and Movita had a harrowing experience when they returned from the Swizzle Stick to their flat at nearby Stratford Place, off Oxford Street, and discovered that thieves had ransacked the place:

> 'The whole apartment was turned upside down. It was obvious we had been robbed, but Jack took one look and said, "Oh my God, the maid didn't come in again." I had to say, "For goodness sake, Jack, we've been robbed." He just didn't realise it.'

Movita is able to smile about it now, but the incident was anything but funny at the time. She lost all her jewellery and her seven furs – 'Minks, ermines, the lot.' They had mainly been presents of conscience from Jack, whose habit of lavishing expensive gifts on her whenever he had behaved badly may give some idea as to the number of items stolen. Movita was not unduly distressed at the disappearance of the furs, which she rarely wore, but was understandably upset over the loss of all her expensive rings, necklaces and bracelets. She may even have become infected with Jack's paranoia:

> 'I was immediately suspicious, because I'd had all our possessions insured before that and the company had refused to cover them for Ireland. Then, just on the eve of departure, when the insurance had run out, the thieves struck. They took everything of value except our clothing and had known just where to look. We must have lost thousands of pounds' worth of stuff. I had to suspect the insurers because they knew exactly where everything was hidden. There was a kind of closet with a special secret compartment for storing your valuables and whoever was responsible went straight to it. There was no liability attached to the company. They did not have to pay out a penny.'

It was hardly the kind of send-off Jack and Movita would have wished, but the robbery was a perversely appropriate epilogue to their life together in England – the symbolic final, destructive act of a drama that had fascinated the public with its emotional appeal and numerous twists of fate.

It was about to open to new audiences in Ireland.

Chapter 5

Disaster at Dalymount

Jack and Movita hit Dublin in some style in the February of 1943, complete with fifty pieces of luggage containing wardrobes of fabulous clothes that the burglars had ignored – her Len Pearson-made dresses and hand-made shoes and dozens of Jack's suits, sports jackets and expensive monogrammed silk shirts and ties.

They might well have topped a competition to find the best dressed, most glamorous couple ever to book into the Royal Hibernian Hotel, but Jack would have been bottom of any popularity poll. It took him little time to discover that the stigma of his marriage to Judith Allen had remained to haunt him in Ireland. Even his union with Movita appeared to hold little sway with the Irish people; it had been effected in a civil ceremony in a far-off country and carried neither the blessing nor even the recognition of the Church.

The path of redemption pointed unequivocally to a sacramental Catholic wedding, but there was the added problem of convincing Movita it was his only chance of success. Her disillusionment was such that she had no desire to remarry a man with whom she did not intend spending the rest of her life. But the cause of necessity and the emotion of the moment prevailed. She allowed herself to go through with it.

They were married at St Andrew's Church in Westland Row, the Dublin street where Oscar Wilde was born. The wedding worked like a charm and the Irish nation accepted the couple with joyful acclaim. The announcement that Jack and Movita would be appearing daily at the city's cavernous Theatre Royal brought a stampede for tickets:

> 'The shows broke all records. We did two a night, plus matinees on Mondays and Saturdays. It went on for weeks and weeks. Crowds were forming as early as ten in the morning and the same people came day after day, or so it seemed to me. It was truly amazing. We were on a percentage of the gate and the theatre, one of the biggest in the British Isles, was packed for every performance. We were earning a fortune, about £600 a week, and that was a great deal of money then. The people were beautiful and Jack was okay, really. He wasn't bad at all; he didn't get drunk too much.'

In light of the Theatre Royal triumph it was perhaps inevitable that a clamour for the greatest heavyweight comeback in boxing history should quickly gather momentum. In Irish eyes Jack would always be fighter first and singer second – it was as a fighter he had made his name and it was as a fighter he had become a legend. The irony was that he had never boxed in his native land and now that he was, semi-permanently at least, back in the old country, the pressure for him to do so was unremitting. No matter how many countless thousands might queue to see and hear Jack and Movita singing *South of the Border** and other assorted love songs, there would be no respite until he had satisfied the public demand to see him back in the ring.

Enter Gerald Egan, a peripheral figure on the fight scene in London and Dublin. The portly Egan was thought to have been smitten by the boxing bug during his early childhood in the United States, where, he ventured, his uncle Tom had acted as matchmaker for that greatest of all promoters, the intrepid Tex Rickard. He returned to Ireland following the death of his father and felt neither the inclination nor the need to conceal his homosexuality, even in the days when it was universally considered repugnant and immoral.

Egan, a native of Cork, liked to portray himself as a big-time operator. He claimed to have brought world featherweight champion Freddie Miller to Ireland and to have promoted such other ring greats as Primo Carnera, Kid Berg and Tommy Farr; in effect, he was a dreamer who was rarely taken seriously by anyone. That Jack was prepared to entertain him as a kind of manager-cum-promoter and confidant served to illustrate the confused level of his thinking.

The artful Egan was nothing if not a chancer. He had been quick to feel the public pulse and bang the promotional drum in the knowledge that Jack would be unable to resist showing himself as a fighting man to his own Irish people. There would be a sizeable crowd to see him although, in view of the fact he was close on 30 and had ballooned to eighteen stones, nobody seriously believed he could recapture past glories. Ireland's best heavyweight of the time, Chris Cole from Mullingar, was deemed the only man capable of giving him a searching test.

It seemed as if all of Dublin had converged on Dalymount Park for the big fight that warm summer night in June. Some were there out of morbid curiosity, a ghoulish desire to witness the final macabre scene of a boxing career that all except the most unswerving optimist must have known was as lifeless as a corpse on a mortuary slab. Others, indeed the

* It is a common misconception that *South of the Border* was composed for Jack and Movita. They had yet to meet when Jimmy Kennedy and Michael Carr wrote it in 1938. 'But they did make the song extremely popular,' said Kennedy.

vast majority, had swarmed to the huge stadium to catch one last glimpse of a giant of yesteryear whose exploits they had only read about in newspapers or heard about on the wireless and who, though well over the hill, was guaranteed still to provide a spectacle of rare excitement and drama. For whatever may have been said or written about him, Jack had been a heavyweight pioneer, a boxing maverick who had carried a torch for them in the boxing rings of Britain and America. He had inspired them with high hope and expectation, most of which had remained sadly unfulfilled. But it had been great fun along the way.

As Jack climbed through the ropes, it was clear the passing years had taken their toll. Gone were the boyish good looks that had captivated London in the 1930s. Gone too was the arrogant air, the cheeky grin, the haughty carriage, the kisses once blown to adoring crowds. He was fuller of face now, thicker in build, a boozer's spare tyre round his middle. The brash confidence of youth had been replaced by a nervous uncertainty that was filled with foreboding. This was not the Jack Doyle of old; this was the ageing shell of a once formidable fighter from whom intemperance had exacted a heavy price.

The portents were significant, the signs chillingly accurate. Jack was battered to defeat inside a round and the great comeback was dead and buried along with what was left of his reputation. He had shuffled forward at the opening bell, as though walking through sand, and thrown a hopeful right hand that was so wide of the mark it nearly hit the referee. Cole, big and brawny, then planted his own right hand smack on Jack's exposed chin. Jack did not go down, but clearly he was dazed. Cole hit him again, and again and again until Jack was battered and helpless. The referee stepped in to rescue him; it was all over inside two minutes.

The spectators were stunned, hardly able to take in what they had seen. There had been something strange about this farce of a fight from the very start – something that did not quite add up. Cole was not yet that good, nor Jack so unbelievably bad, as to warrant such a summary execution; there had to be a hidden reason, an excuse even, for this incredibly one-sided destruction of a Jack Doyle who, if only half fit, could have been expected at least to hold his own with Cole. There had to have been something wrong with him that would account for his lethargy both on entering the ring and during the brief, explosive encounter. A simple explanation perhaps – or something more sinister?

Gerald Egan claimed he had booked Jack into the Shelbourne Hotel for a few hours' sleep on the afternoon of the fight after noting his fraught state of nerves at the midday weigh-in. After four years out of the ring, Jack had suddenly become apprehensive about facing a tough nut like Cole: he had begun to fancy his chances less and less and needed a stiff drink to steady himself.

According to Egan, Jack crept furtively from the Shelbourne and took a taxi to the Dolphin Hotel, a regular haunt of the racing fraternity, and there met an old friend – the handsome, dashing Lord Milton. 'Peter' Milton – full name and title William Henry Lawrence Peter Fitzwilliam, the Viscount Milton – was an old Etonian and ex-Grenadier Guardsman. The only son and heir of the seventh Earl Fitzwilliam, he resided at Fitzwilliam Square, a fashionable part of Dublin owned by his wealthy family, and at the 400-acre Fitzwilliam estate in Coolattin, Co. Wicklow. He was to die tragically just five years later at the age of 38.*

Like Jack, Milton was a lady-killer and keen sportsman. The pair had been playboys together in London when Jack owned the Swizzle Stick and the Dolphin clientèle listened excitedly as the pair related tales of their jaunts round Mayfair.

So compelling was the conversation and so anaesthetising the booze that Jack very soon forgot all about the menacing Mr. Cole. At seven o'clock that evening, the crowds were flocking to Dalymount for the big fight; Irish radio was geared to transmit a live broadcast of the contest; the Press were beginning to take their seats at ringside. Only one person was missing: Jack Doyle.

Egan – 'My heart sank' he says – immediately dispatched Kid Kelly, whom he claimed was a former Irish middleweight champion, to the Shelbourne to collect him, hoping above hope that he had merely overslept. Jack's room was empty. Kelly got straight on the phone to Egan. 'He's missing boss,' he said. Egan blew his top. 'Ask round,' he bellowed. 'Everyone knows Jack Doyle. Make sure you find him. Get him here as fast as you can.'

A taxi-driver revealed that Jack was at the Dolphin; but by the time Kelly got there, he was blind drunk. He bundled him into the cab and they sped off to Dalymount. When they arrived it was eight o'clock. Jack, tottering helplessly, was due to box at nine. He was ushered to the dressing-rooms, where Egan fumed:

> 'This is a disgrace. There are more than 20 000 people out there who have coughed up their hard-earned money to see you fight. But you're in no

* Milton, who was married, had fallen in love with Kathleen Kennedy, favourite sister of future US President Jack Kennedy. The Kennedy curse struck when the couple were killed in a flying accident over France.

condition to stand up, let alone fight. How on earth do you think you're going to beat Cole now?'

He then ordered two pints of black coffee and made Jack drink the lot in a forlorn effort to sober him up; but all it succeeded in doing was to make him so violently sick that the fight had to be put back to ten o'clock.

Egan claimed that the huge crowd felt Jack had let them down with his dismal display. After the first few moments of disbelief they went wild, yelling and swearing in disgust:

'They threw objects into the ring and hundreds surged threateningly toward Doyle. They were out to lynch him.'

Jack, he added, was pushed and jostled by the jeering, abusive fans. He would almost certainly have taken another hiding but for a piece of quick thinking by Movita, who, although almost trodden underfoot in the mêlée, had the presence of mind to take the heat out of the situation by climbing up into the ring. Egan recalled:

'Immediately she did so, the hostility ceased and the fans who just a few seconds beforehand had been baying for Jack's blood became as docile as lambs, chanting, "Movita, Movita." '

A compelling story – but is it true? Movita says not. She refutes every word of Egan's explanation for Jack's abysmal performance on that crazy night at Dalymount. She gives a totally different version of the events that led to her husband becoming the laughing stock of Ireland:

'Jack was very, very "up" for that fight; he really trained for it. He ran hard and kept away from me. We were staying at an hotel while he was preparing for the fight, and we even had different rooms. I remember him telling me: "I'm older now, so I've got to train for this fight." And he did. He really and truly trained. He was prepared.

Jack did not go to the Dolphin. Egan's story is not true because I went with Jack to the stadium and we arrived together. He went to the dressing-room and I went and sat in my seat. Jack was aware. He had told me: "Don't worry: he can't hurt me because he hasn't the experience. And if necessary I'll box him, jab and move. I can do it because I'm in good shape." He was not drunk. Of that I am very, very sure, because this was going to be his big comeback; he wanted to leave a good impression. Jack swore to me that he felt wonderful and that Cole wasn't much of a fighter. He was going to put on a good show and do his best.

But immediately I saw Jack's face as he entered the ring, I was frightened. I remember sitting there and Jack getting into the ring and having an expression on his face that said something like, "Hey, what's happening to me?" The bell rang, Cole came in and hit him a few times and it was stopped; it didn't last any time at all. He did nothing. It was just awful. I was beside myself with grief because Jack did not even try. He was in a daze.

I know they doped Jack and I know who did it. It was a man named Burns, one of his helpers. Jack knew it, too. After the fight he didn't have a clue what had happened – then he got to thinking, "Who could have done this?" He remembered being given a glass of water by Burns before he went on; he realised then that he had been drugged. He told me that when he got into the ring he could hardly lift his arms.

I think Egan must have had something to do with it. Egan I never liked, I'm sorry. He was a con-man. Fat and green eyes. And he knew that I knew what he was like. I hated what he did to little boys – you know, lovely little Irish boys. Of all the people Jack knew, Egan was the worst; he was much too shrewd. After the fight he looked guilty and I knew he had done it, that he had been behind it. He was a very immoral person in every way.

Egan must have been in on it – he was the promoter. He did very well out of it and so did the others – everyone except Jack. His so called friends, they always let him down. Because Jack had been a hot favourite, Egan, Burns and all of them must have bet good money on Cole. The other guy was just a kid – he didn't have Jack's experience.'

The fact that Cole later admitted he had wagered his entire purse on beating Jack reinforces Movita's conviction that the fight was rigged:

'Cole knew Jack would be unable to lift his arms. He was aware of what was happening. He just went bomp-bomp-bomp and the fight was over. It was all arranged.'

Movita claims she knows from personal experience that Jack could not have been drunk, as Egan had suggested:

'If that were true he would have killed the other guy, because when he got drunk and angry no one could hold him. So that's a lot of hooey. Jack Doyle didn't become limp when he was drunk; he was like a lion. If he had been drunk, maybe he would have been better off.'

Movita also remembers vividly the chaotic scenes as she was being led from the ringside:

'It was at the height of our popularity. As I was being taken out there were hands everywhere, feeling me. The men were all grabbing at me. I remember being touched all over. There was nothing I could do about it. It was bedlam. I was taken to the dressing-room and Jack just did not know what had happened. He was not dazed from the punches; he had been dazed before the fight started. And for days afterwards he was like jelly, wondering what had happened. He told me the only thing he could remember was that Burns had given him a glass of water and that he did not finish it because he

> did not want to take in too much liquid. But there must have been enough of the drug in it.
>
> Jack was not a bad person. He trusted everyone. He thought they loved him, but they just used him. I know from my own experience, when I was a rising star, that when you have all those people around you it's very hard not to accept the adulation. You think, "Maybe they do like me." They can make you believe that they're for you, but they're not. They're just using you.'

She considers Gerald Egan came into this category, but regarded Jack's other close associates Jimmy McIlveen – back from America – and his personal secretary, Paddy Lundon, as harmless:

> 'Jack liked having people around him who could make him laugh. McIlveen was a kind of court-jester. He used to do impressions. They were comical, but not very good. He was very untalented.'

Jack's defeat was received with gloating relish back in England. A report in a London evening newspaper, *The Star*, made mincemeat of him:

> 'For a long time we have been telling Doyle that the ring was no place for crooners. But the man who returned to Eire because it was beneath his dignity to dig drains to help the British war effort would not learn. This could not be knocked into his head. Perhaps the bruises he bears today will convince him that he is no boxing champion.'

The bruises did not hurt nearly as much as Jack's wounded pride. The Irish public, too, was disgusted with him. When he took his German Shepherd, Tarzan, for a walk the morning after the fight, an old lady on her bicycle stopped and shouted after him: 'Dogs don't care what they walk with nowadays!'

Jack was worried. His newly-won popularity had taken a dive. He would be unable to face the public again until he had redeemed himself in the boxing ring. He was finished, disgraced, washed up – both as a fighter and stage performer – unless he could erase the memory of Dalymount.

Egan, having in all probability made a killing from the fight, knew it, too. He decided to get Jack back in the ring again as quickly as possible. The public had to be convinced the lapse against Cole was an understandable one – that Jack had merely been caught cold after four years out of the ring. Maybe that was the simple truth anyway – regardless of whether Jack had been drunk or drugged.

The opponent selected for Jack's second – and hopefully less painful – journey down the well-trodden road of his boxing past was one Butcher Howell, a journeyman professional under Egan's management.

According to Howell, the August fight faced an official KO before even a punch had been thrown in anger. From his home in Manchester, in the north of England, he revealed the Irish boxing authorities were intent on banning the contest on the ground that he would concede too much weight. But they were outmanoeuvred and outsmarted by a characteristic piece of quick thinking by Egan:

> 'Egan had heard rumours circulating round Dublin that the fight would be called off because I scaled only 12st 5lb. So before the weigh-in he produced some heavy strips of lead that fitted neatly into the waist-band of my long pants. It did the trick – I weighed in at 13st in those pants. It meant I was a legitimate heavyweight and the fight was able to go ahead as planned.'

In the event Jack won and won well, knocking out Howell in three lop-sided rounds. It was largely a pedestrian performance and it convinced everyone – including Jack himself – that there was nowhere else for him to go as a fighter. There were hopeful mutterings and some talk of tempting Eddie Phillips across the Irish Sea for a third and final showdown, but the war meant there was little hope of importing an opponent from England or the Continent. As a return with Cole was out of the question and there was no one else worth fighting in Ireland, Jack's career, which had started on such a promising note eleven years earlier, was now finally at an end. It had died a painless, low-key death and he did not much mind. If nothing else, the two comeback contests confirmed the truth of a saying that gave him much amusement and which he would often repeat in later years:

> 'A man isn't old when his hair turns grey,
> Nor is he old when his teeth decay,
> But you're on the verge of your long last sleep,
> When your mind makes appointments that your body can't keep.'

Jack missed his appointment in each of those lamentable fights. He realised that with the surplus weight he was carrying – a goodly portion of which had hung down embarrassingly over the top of his shorts – he could no longer move as fast as he once did nor punch with the same authority. Nevertheless, it was some consolation that he had been able to bury the shame and humiliation of his defeat by Cole.

He had managed to go out on a high note. He could stand up on stage with some degree of pride. Credibility had been restored. He tried to convince himself he was a winner again.

Chapter 6

Fast women and slow horses

As boxing became a bad dream Jack and Movita devoted all their vision and energy to their stage act, which they had always considered would be as big a hit in Ireland as it had been in England. Their confidence was not misplaced:

> 'We put on our show in Dublin and, as in England, we called it Punch and Beauty. It really was a spectacular success. Jack had a boxing ring rigged up on stage, with girls in little dresses doing dance routines and acting as trainers while he shadow-boxed and performed exercises. It was all done in the dark, with lovely fluorescent lights illuminating the stage. I thought it was a nice production number, very cute, very clever. We then took the show on tour and called it the Hit Parade, with most of the acts from the Theatre Royal touring with us. Again it was an enormous success; the crowds flocked to see us and you just would not believe the reception we got. The roads were blocked wherever we appeared. We played to full houses all over Ireland.'*

With Jack continuing to be on his best behaviour, things had gone remarkably well. The stage act and the compelling partnership he had forged with Movita had ushered in a new chance of stardom that he thought had gone forever. He grasped it eagerly, gratefully and responsibly. He was back riding the crest of an amazing wave of popularity that would endure for as long as he had sense enough to conduct himself with a certain dignity, for as long as he showed regard for the paying public by performing always to the very best of his ability, for as long as he treated Movita with respect. Alas, it was asking too much of a man who never seemed to know when he was well off and mocked at his own popularity by indulging in behaviour that could not help but destroy it.

It would be convenient to conclude that success the second time round went straight to Jack's head – that in his understandable state of exultation he had failed to recognise it was Movita who had taken the audiences by storm in Dublin and throughout the rest of the country.

* Gay Byrne's brother Ray was the pianist in Tralee.

But it would be a travesty of the truth. Indeed Jack realised only too well that his remarkable renaissance was due mainly to the way in which the Irish people had taken to her. Predictably, he found himself unable to embrace her popularity; he was reluctant to come to terms with the fact that while his part of the show always received applause enthusiastic enough for even the most demanding of performers, hers was received rapturously. During their finalé duets it became apparent to Jack that the audiences were held spellbound by Movita when once they were held spellbound by him.

It was no surprise that the Irish had taken to their hearts this young 'foreign' girl whose head barely reached to Jack's shoulders, this talented actress and singer who had given herself in love and marriage to one of their own. Had Jack been willing to accept that the ovations accorded Movita were largely an emotional response conditioned by a commendable spirit of charity and goodwill, perhaps he would have welcomed her success.

Unfortunately, he was not prepared to see it that way. In his eyes, Jack Doyle was the big name and Movita was stealing his thunder. Even so, he must have known he was back in the big-time only because of her unselfish sacrifice on his behalf. By now he felt he could not live without her. She had become his emotional crutch as well as his wife and lover and the uneasy realisation of it sent him into a deep state of melancholia. Once the celebratory mood which followed the first fantastic tour had passed, he was left feeling isolated and vulnerable. He took refuge in the bottle, with the inevitable result that he became impossible to live with and prone to frightening outbreaks of violence.

Movita is in no doubt that this unhappy period signalled the beginning of the end as far as Jack's stage career and reputation were concerned:

> 'When we decided to do a second tour, it was an absolute shambles. He started getting real bad. I remember being dressed as a nun and doing Gounod's *Ave Maria* with tears streaming down my face after Jack pinched me on stage; he just squeezed my flesh until I cried. I don't know why he did it. I wasn't doing anything to deserve it, I really wasn't.
>
> He just kept drinking and drinking and drinking. On some dates he wouldn't arrive at the show – he would be in the bar or something. In the end he would come on stage drunk and try singing, but all he succeeded in doing was to disappoint the people. It was awful, terrible. It had nothing to do with the people not appreciating him, because at first he had them in the palm of his hand.
>
> But he became impossible. He wasn't singing right, he wasn't trying. He would come out on stage and "Blaaah." It was just no good. He destroyed himself. With Jack it was just self-destruct: womanising and

drinking. It wasn't so obvious on the first tour, but now he was openly drinking and messing around. He behaved very badly and then he just seemed to get worse and worse.'

Jack and Movita were always booked into smart hotels on tour, but between times they stayed at Rocklands, a delightful private house in the Dublin seaside suburb of Dalkey:

'It was a beautiful place with a huge garden that ran right down to the water. The swimming pool was formed from natural rocks and was part of the sea. We used to go out on boats and fish. It was very nice there for a while.'

Movita has other reasons to remember Rocklands and they have little to do with its scenic location. She recalls that while she and Jack were living there, she received a fan letter from a Mexican girl named Maria-Elena:

'She said she was married to an Irishman and was dying to meet me. So I opened up my heart and my home to her, a compatriot in a strange country. She was very pretty and began visiting the house a lot – and soon she became friendly with Jack. On one occasion they started drinking and got tight. I made myself scarce because I knew all about Jack's drunken moods: I always did a disappearing act when he started drinking. I hid in a bedroom, but Jack and Maria-Elena must have thought I had gone out. All of a sudden I heard them coming in, so I dived under the bed: I didn't want any trouble and I just did not care any more. Then they got into the bed and I was forced to listen to every grunt and groan and every squeak of the bedsprings. I was frightened and so embarrassed, but remained there under that bed until they had finished and left the room. It was terrible. I never mentioned it to him afterwards; I was much too shocked and hurt. I was numb. And I was scared of him.'

Throughout her marriage to Jack, Movita was depicted as an archetypal Mexican firebrand who fought tooth-and-nail with him and always gave as good as she got. It is an image of her that Movita insists is totally ficticious:

'Would I have stayed all through that sex session between Jack and Maria-Elena if I had not been scared and embarrassed? If you can take that you can take anything. *I never, never, never fought with him.*'

Gradually their stage success and the remnants of their marriage fell apart, just as Movita had anticipated:

'Jack kept getting drunk all the time and everybody at the house was pinching things from us. Even Maria-Elena was stealing things, but I just did not care. The maid, the cook – they were all at it. There was £100-worth of meat being ordered every week and goodness knows where it all went. We were taken for a ride. They did it all the time. I did not know half of what was going on – and I wanted no trouble.'

Movita remembers an occasion when she left her handbag on her dressing-table. Later she walked in and saw Maria-Elena putting the cash in her stocking. Movita looked into the bag and could see that not all the money had been taken: there was still £10 left. She closed the bag and left the room:

'Like an idiot I was hoping, having let her know I'd seen her take it, that she would put the money back. But when I returned later, the £10 was gone too. I told Jack and he went in and took all the money out of her stocking.

She had told me a sad story about how her husband [thought to have been a barrister] treated her badly. I used to feel sorry for her – give her nice things. I handed her money and clothes and my house was open to her. Maybe the affair with Jack had been going on a long time, because the bedroom incident happened after just a few visits. Then, when we went on tour, she tried to get into the house and pinch things. The police caught her breaking in and she was arrested. I don't know what happened to her after that.'

Although Jack and Movita had been coining it from their stage appearances, wasteful extravagance depleted their wealth. The suite they took at Dublin's Royal Hibernian Hotel after their arrival from England had cost them a hefty £150 a week, and they spent heavily during their stay at Rocklands. Movita's disclosure that they were also being fleeced by the staff tells its own story. In addition, Jack's legendary largesse extended to any hanger-on or dropout who happened to hit him with a tale of woe; he was a sucker for a hard-luck story and shelled out a small fortune on so-called worthy causes and appeals for cash that would have received a less sympathetic hearing from anyone not totally taken by his pet phrase: A generous man never went to hell.

Jack's love of the turf also cost him dear. He purchased a racehorse called Pelorus, a five-year-old chestnut gelding by Sea Serpent out of Dinah's Daughter. Pelorus was registered in his mother's name and trained at The Curragh by the late Paddy Prendergast, a friend of many years' standing. Movita remembers Prendergast phoning to say the horse was 'trying' in a certain race and that Jack should back it. Jack took his advice and had a substantial wager with a bookie called Tommy O'Keefe, a poker-playing acquaintance at Rocklands. According to Movita, O'Keefe would take bets and then cover himself with other bookmakers – a practice known in the trade as hedging:

'Jack had hundreds on but didn't receive a penny when Pelorus won*.

*The race – over hurdles – was at Baldoyle on January 1, 1945, and Pelorus won at 6–1. He won again at 6–1 at Baldoyle on February 10, this time when owned by a Mrs. S. Henry. The Baldoyle course, to the north of Dublin is no longer used for racing.

O'Keefe told him he hadn't got the bet covered, but I don't think he'd have said that if the horse had lost – he'd probably have just taken the money. It was so disappointing for Jack because the horse was costing a fortune to train. After that he just got rid of it.'

O'Keefe lived on the seafront at Dun Laoghaire. He had a conspicuous mouthful of gold-capped teeth which gave him a sinister gangster-like appearance when he smiled. The dispute over the bet soured his relationship with Jack and some years later, according to Movita, he was shot dead in an entirely unconnected gambling feud.

Jack was not a successful punter. More often than not he was fed doubtful information by a whole host of well-meaning people who were supposedly 'in the know' and whose advice he invariably accepted as gospel. Some of these so-called good things won, as on a law of average they must, but mostly Jack backed a succession of losers to lend some truth to another favourite saying of his, oft-quoted in later life: 'Fast women and slow horses – they were the ruination of me.'

Horseracing – and to a lesser extent greyhound racing – were the great loves of Jack's life. When he and Movita took an open carriage to the big meetings at Phoenix Park and Leopardstown, he would delight in emptying his pockets en route, scattering coins on the cobbled streets for impoverished Dublin children to chase and gather.

Rocklands could more accurately have been named Heartbreak House as far as Movita was concerned, and yet all was not trauma and transgression. She did enjoy some splendid moments there which helped compensate for the bad times. A priest of her and Jack's acquaintance, Fr Cyril Kenneally – a genial character with an appealing sense of humour – often popped in for a drink ('Just a wee tot, mind you') and a game of cards. Often he would cheat and then sit back with a twinkle in his eye, as if challenging Jack and Movita to accuse him while knowing all along that they would never dream of doing so. The white-haired, ruddy-faced cleric possessed the knack of being able to put people very much at their ease, have a joke with them and, at the same time, retain the respect his priestly position demanded. He always came armed with a fund of amusing stories with which he would regale the assembled company. No one could be quite certain of their authenticity and Fr Kenneally would never let on; instead, he took great delight in keeping everyone guessing.

For a long time Fr Kenneally was Movita's only true male friend:

'I never had any other friends during that period. They were all friends of Jack's. It was such a frightening situation. Jack used to go missing for days and I did not want to give him any excuse – he was bad enough without having to have excuses. I just had to keep myself to myself.'

She faced an impossible dilemma. She had become lonely and desperate, with nobody to turn to or confide in apart from Fr Kenneally.* But the duty of a Catholic priest is to offer advice calculated to repair a crumbling marriage rather than destroy it, however far down the road to ruin that marriage may have gone. The predictability of Fr Kenneally's homilies, while well-meant and laced with humour, were of small comfort and consolation to Movita, who was becoming increasingly concerned for her safety:

> 'No one could do anything with Jack when he got into these horrible moods. He didn't work – he didn't want to do anything. He was just drunk, drunk, drunk. I didn't know anything about him going with the showgirls; if he wanted to do it he could do it. He was welcome to them as long as he left me alone. I wasn't going to fight. I was so frightened that anything he wanted to do was okay by me. What good was it fighting that sort of thing? I didn't want any trouble: you know from my experience under the bed how much trouble I wanted. On the last Irish tour he would just go into the theatres and fight everybody or throw things around. The audience was out there listening to what was going on – and in some of the smaller venues they must have heard everything. Then he would go out on stage drunk as a lord. If anybody opened their mouth about his behaviour, he would shut it for them. It got to the point where he was just impossible. Poor Paddy Lundon put up with a lot of it.'

Gerald Egan was acutely aware of Movita's plight. His warm and at times touching tribute contrasts sharply with her uncompromising castigation of him:

> 'When Jack became an alcoholic, I warned him he would lose Movita. I told him she just could not put up with any more of his nonsense. Jack was always out drinking with women and his behaviour became so bad that he was barred from most of the more desirable places. When they were on the road touring, he was after every girl in the show – he wanted to have them all. Movita was very honest and decent. She loved a nice, sociable party where everyone enjoyed themselves and she liked a drink. She even sang for the boys as they travelled from show to show. But no one ever touched Movita. There was no way any man could get to her. Never. Plenty tried, maybe they all tried, but she was 100 per cent respectable. Eventually Movita had a nervous breakdown over Jack's behaviour and my mother gave her some good advice. She told her: "You're wasting your time with Doyle. Go back to your family in California." If he'd treated her decently, she would have stuck with him. I heard her tell him: "You're a fool, a no-good fighter. You let Ireland down."'

* Fr Kenneally was attached to St Mary's Church, Sandyford, at the time. He later became chaplain to St Teresa's Home, Blackrock, where he died on November 5, 1976.

Movita tried returning to the U.S. on several occasions only to discover that the ships and planes were taking priority passengers only. The demand was so heavy that it was impossible even to book a passage in advance. She considered going back to England but was unable to get permission while the war was on. Her six-month commitment to Jack had long since expired, but there was nowhere to go. She was trapped.

Chapter 7

The Great Escape

The realisation that Movita was a virtual prisoner in Ireland gave Jack even more ammunition to fire at her. Keith McConnell, who had befriended the couple when they ran the Swizzle Stick in London, later played a prominent role in both their lives:

> 'Jack had Movita in his power and he knew it. She could not get away from him and it meant he could do precisely as he pleased. From then on he was drunk all the time, even during their stage performances. These shows were carried almost entirely by Movita, as very often Jack was utterly incapable of performing. Each time they were together he would fight with her and beat her, sometimes so severely that she could not do the show herself. He was rarely with her at any other time but during a show.'

The tall, fair-complexioned McConnell came from a well-to-do Dublin family. His father owned 40 per cent of McConnell Advertising and ran his own lucrative textile business. Keith was a student at the prestigious west of England public school, Downside, when he first met Jack and Movita. He was such an avid fan that he took a special trip to London to meet his idol and later renewed his acquaintance with Jack and Movita at the Hibernian shortly after their move to Dublin. He had in the interim studied economics at Trinity College before joining the Irish army in 1943. They met again several times, usually in The Buttery after racing at Leopardstown. Jack enjoyed the company of his earnest, engaging, intellectually-inclined compatriot, while to Keith it was a dream come true to be on social terms with a man he had always regarded as a hero. But he confessed that it did not take him long to become disenchanted with Jack when he saw the way he was treating Movita:

> 'I had to go to England for a year to learn the textile business and when I got back, Movita was in terrible shape. She was being beaten to death. I thought, "Jesus – somebody had better help this girl." I must admit I had a yen for her and I think she also liked me, but there was certainly no romantic involvement. I loved Jack but he was demented by this time, absolutely crazed. Movita practically collapsed into my arms and I realised she had

gone through a scene of almost continuous terror. She had even been forced to seek police protection at Dublin Castle.

Movita had earlier attempted to run away, but Jack left the show and hunted her down. After finding her, he knocked her about so much that she was unable to go out for several days. He pulled himself together for a while and behaved very much better, but then went back to his bad old ways. Often Movita would appear on stage with a black eye, a cut nose, a swollen mouth or, as on one occasion, a broken tooth. People began to talk and it got to the stage where Jack no longer cared where he mistreated her. Scenes would occur in hotels, cocktail bars and even on the streets. Decent people would no longer associate with him and he sank lower and lower, frequenting the brothels and dives of Dublin's poorest back streets. For these reasons Movita's popularity grew enormously. The Irish public could feel nothing but pity for her.

Movita had also run away on two previous occasions, each time appealing to the American consul in Dublin to get her out of the country. But he was powerless to help; he required Jack's permission for her to leave and Jack would never give it. She was terrified, as by this time Jack was getting worse day by day.'

Keith felt the key to Jack's violence was his belief that he was being deserted in the hour of his greatest need:

'Objectively he was resigned to losing Movita – he knew it was in her best interests to go. But emotionally he could not bear the thought of her leaving, hence the violence.'

There was no hate in Movita's heart for Jack, only sympathy:

'He used to say to me, "You think you're so great. You want to leave me? I'll give you something to leave me for." It was a sickness. I just used to run and hide. I went to hotels – anywhere. I felt sorry for him but I just couldn't take any more. He probably wasn't hitting me with all his might, but in drink he had bull-like strength. A slap from him was like a full-bodied blow from anyone else.'

Jack had signed an agreement in the Upper Ormond Quay offices of Movita's solicitor, John O'Connor, promising to be on his best behaviour during the last five weeks of the tour:

'But he broke it all the way through. I would go on and he would not appear, which meant I had to do whole shows on my own. It was that bad. He couldn't care less; he just destroyed himself. He wouldn't show up, and even when he did it would have been better if he hadn't. I often had to go on stage on my own and it was very embarrassing. Then I got awfully sick at one venue; I had a cold, I couldn't speak and I told them I couldn't possibly go on – I just couldn't. I said I would have to go back to Dublin and see a doctor. I was so run down from nerves and lack of sleep, my ears were paining and I was running a temperature. By this time we had a lovely flat in Merrion Square and when I got back my eardrums burst and I couldn't hear. Jack had been drunk, but he allowed me to go because he could see I was really sick.'

Keith McConnell urged Movita to leave Jack if she valued her safety and her sanity. 'You'd better vanish,' he advised before whisking her off to the Grand Hotel in Malahide, north of Dublin, where he booked her in under an assumed name. Whether he honestly believed her situation to have been critical or was angling to spirit her away for his own gratification is open to question. If his motives were basically honourable and directed primarily to protecting her from physical and mental anguish, there is no doubt that he had also by this time fallen in love with her.

By the same token, it is possible that Movita was still in love with Jack. She could not rid herself of guilt over his accusation that she was abandoning him when he needed her most. The thought of him attempting to hold things together in her absence and instead alienating audiences by making a complete fool of himself was more than she could bear. She decided to fulfil their engagements, but it was an act of compassion and loyalty that would find no favour with Jack. As the curtain fell at the end of the show at Lucan – a Dublin suburb to the west of the city – he grabbed her hair with such force that huge tufts of it came away from her scalp. His hands closed round her neck and it took the might of four detectives armed with truncheons to force him to release his grip. They were battering him all over the shoulders and arms and still it seemed like an eternity to Movita before they managed to haul him off. A similar situation had occurred after a show in Jack's native Cork. As at Lucan, only a strong police presence prevented a possible fatality.

Whatever had been McConnell's personal feelings toward Movita, the incident at Lucan proves his instincts were right when he sensed she was in mortal danger and that he took the correct action in removing her from Jack's clutches.

For Movita, there now could be no going back. It had become apparent that she was risking her life even by being on stage with Jack:

> 'He soldiered on alone, and of course it was a disaster. He did only two more dates, so obviously he must have ruined the whole thing.'

The Grand Hotel, situated close to the Velvet Strand at Portmarnock from where Jim Mollison had taken off in his Puss Moth at the start of the first east-to-west solo flight across the Atlantic, was not nearly a secure enough place of refuge. Movita was instantly recognisable and it would not be long before word went out that she was resident there. Soon Jack would hunt her down and force her to return to him. He had done it before when she had fled in panic and been taken by compassionate taxi-drivers to various hotels in the city in much the same way that cockney cabbies had been quick to respond to similar emergencies just a few years earlier.

Movita's major problem was that, try as she might, she was unable to leave the country. She could not get over to England nor home to America, despite repeated attempts to do so. Each time she applied for a visa, she was turned down. Also there appeared to be no safe haven for her in Ireland, where she was now such a household name. Although she had been given police protection during and after shows, she was reluctant to request it twenty-four hours a day and, in addition, she had no wish to see Jack arrested. It would have been the final humiliation for him – the public denigration of a famous name.

The outrage at Lucan convinced Keith McConnell that he had to find Movita a more secure hideaway and, eventually, safe passage from Ireland. He decided to risk his friendship with Jack out of concern and a growing sense of duty toward her. He moved her from Malahide to a small service apartment in Pembroke Square, in the heart of the city, where she stayed for seven weeks without once venturing out. 'If she had, she'd have been besieged by a thousand people,' he said. He brought her in food and drink – 'Sex was not on the menu' – and spent every hour he could with her, offering comfort and reassurance in an attempt to rebuild her shattered confidence. It was an uncomfortable, nerve-wracking time for them both.

Jack immediately suspected Keith had whisked Movita away. And when Paddy Lundon arrived at the Wicklow Hotel, where Keith was staying, with the message, 'The Big Fellow wants to see you', he feared the worst. Yet he was bold enough to meet Jack and face up to him, even though he knew that at best there would be a nasty confrontation and at worst he would be given a hiding.

According to Keith, the exchange was short, sharp and very much to the point. 'Where's Movita?' Jack demanded of him. 'If you don't bring her back I'll break every bone in your body. Your family will have to fish you out of the Liffey.'

Keith remained silent, not wishing to say anything that might inflame an already delicate situation. Such a threat would have scared the daylights out of most men, but Keith was astute enough to realise that Jack had no real desire to harm him. The words were calculated to intimidate – to frighten him into returning the broken toy that had been taken from Jack forever. Deep down Jack must have known Keith had done the right thing, the only thing that it had been possible for a sage and compassionate man to have done in such circumstances. It had also been an incredibly brave act, for Jack Doyle when roused through drink was an awesome mountain of a man who had the Dublin police shaking in their boots when they tried to restrain him. Big as Keith was himself, Jack could have crushed him effortlessly had he possessed the inclination.

Keith was adamant that he would not let Movita return. Yet having taken responsibility for her immediate well-being and ultimately her future, he was faced with the difficulty of keeping her in hiding until he could get her out of the country. The possibility of further stage appearances in the Republic was out of the question and he had to think long and hard as to what best to do with her.

It was May 1945, and Movita's enforced stay in Ireland had by this time extended to more than two years. Keith at first ran up against all sorts of barriers in his attempt to get her work outside Eire. The Entertainment Services Association (ENSA) in Northern Ireland refused to take her; and being the wife of Jack Doyle, it was still impossible to get her across to England. Eventually, by dint of native cunning, he managed to get her a spot on the bill in Jack Delino's Big Top in Belfast. In a huge tent bigger than most theatres, she appeared for six weeks in a state of acute anxiety lest Jack should suddenly appear and cause a scene. Then came the break she and Keith had been seeking: ENSA relented and gave her a contract to entertain the British, Belgian, Polish, French and Dutch soldiers still stationed in Northern Ireland. After three months Movita was finally able to transfer to England, where she continued to entertain the troops until her contract terminated. Keith recalled:

> 'I had been forced to wangle the contract with ENSA. They'd always been keen to have her, but had encountered difficulties with the British authorities because of Jack's reluctance to contribute to the war effort. I managed to get her in by impressing on them that Movita did not need the work; she was singing in Jack Delino's Big Top by this time and it was enough to convince them. After that it was easy to bypass all the bureaucracy and prejudice and get her across to England.'

That Jack had not pursued Movita to Ulster in an attempt to force her to return to him signified his acceptance of the situation. He had lost his lovely wife – to all intents and purposes to a man he had considered a good friend – but there would be no violent repercussions. Many men in similar circumstances might have sought out Keith and assaulted him, and it says something for Jack that he did not do so. It says more for him that he finally acknowledged Movita's right to create a new life and a new career.

Chapter 8

Peace making

With the war in Europe over, Movita was keen to project herself as a solo star in England. But she claims to have met with a degree of hostility from certain producers, promoters and agents, among them Lew and Leslie Grade. When she had first appeared with Jack on the variety circuit in England just before the outbreak of war, they had been among the earliest clients of the Grades. The two Jewish immigrant brothers from London's East End, along with a third brother, Bernard Delfont, were destined to make a huge impact on the entertainment industry in Britain. Keith revealed:

> 'The Grades were not particularly helpful. Some other agents took the same view. They felt they would be taking a big chance in booking the wife of Jack Doyle, who was so extremely unpopular, to appear in a show.'

One man prepared to take a gamble with Movita was the well-known West End agent R. G. Blackie, who booked her into the Odeon Theatre at Prestwich, Manchester, for an All-Star charity concert in October 1946. Her appearance was such a resounding success that grateful promoter Max Green, of RKO Radio Pictures, felt moved to record his gratitude in the following letter:

> 'I am writing to thank you for the outstanding performance you gave at my Charity Show at the Odeon Theatre. You certainly scored a big hit with the people in Manchester, and I am sure you will have a very warm reception should you visit this city again.'

Another agent willing to give Movita a solo opportunity was Joe Collins – the late father of *Dynasty* star Joan – who had such fond memories of Movita's previous appearances in England. He signed her up to appear in *Puss In Boots* with Jack Anderson at the Pavilion Theatre, Glasgow. Along with Blackie, who had now placed her on his books, Collins was taking a huge risk. This was reflected in Movita's low billing and her salary of around £100 a week – the lowest wage she had received, according to Keith. However, she was delighted to accept because it offered the twin prospect of ridding herself of the bad name Jack had earned them both while in England and also of re-establishing herself without him. In the event she did both magnificently, proving herself an outstanding artist and going on to appear in a Grand Variety Show co-starring top Scottish comedian Will Fyffe at the Odeon, Dundee.

McConnell claimed Movita earned £200 a week when Blackie booked her into the Opera House, Blackpool, for *Starry Way*, starring George Formby. 'They had come to see Formby, but were enraptured by Movita and her beautiful lyric soprano voice.'

While appearing in *Puss In Boots* in Glasgow, Movita received a letter from her mother in America admonishing her for not having been home in more than six years – a situation, she said, that had caused the family considerable anxiety and distress. Movita had never revealed to her mother the purgatory she had endured in England and Ireland; she had been unwilling to tell her how the man to whom she had given her heart and for whom she had sacrificed her Hollywood career had turned her into a physical and nervous wreck. Any such revelations would have caused untold grief to the mother and sisters and brothers she had left behind. She had been unable to confide in anyone save a lovely old priest who could never quite bring himself to issue the only advice it would have been pertinent to offer in the circumstances: Pack your bags and go.

Keith McConnell had changed all that. He had given her new heart, new hope, new ambition. He had transformed her into a radiant, vibrant woman who had managed to resurrect her reputation and her stage career by virtue of an engaging personality and a delightful singing voice. Now he was determined nothing would shatter the confidence she had worked so hard to regain. The letter she had always wanted to airmail home to her family and which, up to now, she had decided against sending, finally had to be written. There could be no more concealing of the truth and no more protecting of the guilty: the tears in Movita's eyes as she read her mother's reproving words told Keith that much.

He decided to write the reply himself, but it would not go to Movita's mother. He would address it instead to her sister Lottie and her husband Mike, who would be better able to take the shock of contents that he knew would be deeply disturbing to members of her immediate family. They would then be able to reveal to Movita's mother such details as they considered necessary and in such a manner as to cause her the least distress. It would be an unexpected and unwelcome catalogue of shame that sought to place in sharp perspective the events of the past six years.

The letter – written c/o The Pavilion Theatre, Glasgow, and dated

February 13, 1946 – is an emotional account of Movita's life with Jack and refers to her by her old nickname of Mawie throughout. It tells a shocking story, but, even so, shields the family from the worst excesses of Jack's violence. Movita, it appears, went to greater lengths and 'even signed Jack's name on her letters so that you would think he had written them'.

Keith concludes:

> 'All Mawie ever thinks of is her mother and her family and all she wants is to get home to be happy with them once more. I assure you that had it not been for this longing, she probably would not have lived through Jack's awful treatment of her for nearly six years.'

With her life at last revealed to her family and her personal nightmare of the past few years receding, Movita was, nevertheless, still in fear that – with the war at an end – Jack would return to England and spoil everything she had managed to build up. While, as her husband, he still had some kind of hold over her, she would never feel free to conduct her own affairs without threat of interference, to go wherever she wanted and to remarry if she wished. She had written to John O'Connor in Dublin seeking his assistance in obtaining an annulment of the marriage, but was informed that the prospects were bleak.

Her letter of reply sent to O'Connor in February, 1946, emphasises in part her desperation and also gives an insight into the ordeal she had endured:

> Dear Mr. O'Connor
>
> Your letter of 24th January, 1946, received, for which many thanks. As you say, it certainly was unwelcome news to hear that a Dispensation is so difficult. Now I am going home to Mexico very shortly and I want more than anything else to get a Dispensation or Annulment from the Church. I think that I might get this in Mexico; but would it be too much to ask you to send me some sort of document detailing all you have had to do on my behalf, such as the letter you wrote to Jack telling him not to abuse, assault or humiliate me in public, and how he signed an agreement in your office to behave properly for the last five weeks of the tour I did with him and how it was broken in every way all through the tour.
>
> All this I would need and, I am sorry to say, the most horrid details which, as you can imagine, make me feel so ashamed and frightened even to think about. And the thought that Jack, who made this nightmare so real to me, might prevent me in years to come from marrying a good man and being blessed with a family and a happy home, which has been my ambition all my life, which with Jack's treatment was a physical impossibility. It is a terrible thought to me.
>
> As you know, I would never have stood Jack for so long if it had not been

for this; I was always hoping and praying that he would change, but my prayers were in vain and instead he got worse, and unbelievably worse.

I wonder if you could get letters of the same type from Chief Inspector Gantly and Inspector Gill, who have first-hand knowledge of Lucan and Cork, etc. Also one from Mrs O'Reilly,* who has been witness to Jack's behaviour on many occasions and has protected me from him very often and shielded me in her own house; incidentally, her brother Morris saved what could have been a fatal situation in Jury's [a Dublin hotel].

Again I want to thank you with all my heart for all your help and understanding and kindness to me.

With best wishes and God bless you,

Yours very sincerely
Movita

More lengthy correspondence culminated in a letter from O'Connor informing Movita that the Commissioner of Police in Dublin had ruled the affair a civil matter and informed him that a police report could not be supplied. However, O'Connor did promise to submit declarations or affidavits from himself and Mrs O'Reilly to Movita's US lawyer if required, offering the opinion that these, together with Movita's own testimony, would be of more material benefit than a police report.

Movita was still having difficulty securing a passage home, despite the optimistic note struck in her letter to O'Connor. She decided in the interim to accept an offer from Danish agent Martin Rose for personal appearances at the Ambassadeur in Copenhagen. As was usual wherever she played, Movita was a tremendous success – so much so that her contract stretched to seven months and offers poured in from Sweden, Holland and France.

She had been anxious above all to entertain the American troops stationed in Germany since hearing the heart-breaking news from her family that Kikki, the younger brother she adored, had been killed in the war. In addition, American officers in Copenhagen had told her the boys in Germany seldom saw big-name artists and assured her she would be welcomed with great enthusiasm. Consequently she notified Rose that she would accept no civilian contracts, but would go to Germany solely to entertain the US troops.

He offered to make the arrangements for her and she left for Nuremberg on January 2, 1947, with a Danish show under the auspices of USFET (US Forces Entertainment).

* According to Keith McConnell, Mrs O'Reilly was a Cork woman and a good friend of Jack and Movita.

Chapter 9
California here I come

It was a new year and another new start for Movita. She was delighted to be able to contribute to the American post-war effort and by doing so felt closer to Kikki. The shock of his passing was all the harder to bear having not seen him since the summer of 1939, when she had left Los Angeles in a state of high excitement to join Jack Doyle in London:

> 'Adolf volunteered before they called him because he did not want them to take his little brother. Then Kikki volunteered because he did not want his elder brother to go to war. So in the end they each joined on the same day. Kikki was just a boy; he was still at High School at the time, studying to be a doctor. He lied about his age and they accepted him, as he looked older. Because of his medical studies he became a male nurse in the Army, stationed in North Africa. He was in a Red Cross boat that was bombed and sunk. It was all so sad. Adolf, who couldn't even scramble an egg, was made a cook in the Army. He was hit by a bullet while on manoeuvres in the States and eventually died of his wounds in 1952.'

After Nuremberg, Movita entertained the US troops in Munich. She eventually travelled throughout American-occupied Europe, cheering up those homesick servicemen, bringing temporary sunshine into their lives. In view of Kikki's death, she felt she had been called: it was her mission and she set about it with zeal. When it had been completed, she was left with a sense of deep fulfilment. She had made a worthwhile contribution and felt good about herself in a way that she had not done since she was eighteen.

All in all, Movita had accomplished a great deal in the two years that had elapsed since she walked out on Jack. In addition to entertaining US troops she had the satisfaction of knowing that she had restored her reputation in England; she had settled the outstanding bills and had become a star there once more. But she would not be returning to the country that held such bitter-sweet memories for her: all she could think about now was getting home safely to her family. Her sisters would be in their late twenties and early thirties and most of them, she knew, were now married; Adolf would be nursing his bullet wound; her mother would probably be grey. It would be a joyfully happy reunion marred only by the absence of Kikki.

First she and Keith McConnell took a holiday in Paris to help her recover from the rigours of her military tour. They travelled on to Stockholm, where Movita had been told she would be able to get a flight to the United States. She met with no success; for the umpteenth time she was informed that service personnel and their wives had priority and that all planes were fully booked.

They returned to Paris, with Movita despairing of ever getting to America. But sometimes fate has a happy knack of coming to your aid after first kicking you in the teeth – and this time she struck lucky, courtesy of a Colonel Cape. He proved to be a veritable Cape of Good Hope as far as she was concerned. Through his influence, she managed to get a seat aboard a US Army plane that would take her back home to her family in California.

Movita's long ordeal was over at last. She was free to start afresh in the land of her birth.

Chapter 10

He gave you his time and sang you his songs

Keith McConnell was heartbroken to see Movita go. He would be joining her in the States just as soon as he had cleared his affairs in England and Ireland and obtained a civilian flight. The two had become close, but it was a bond that had been forged through necessity rather than compatibility.

There had been a certain inevitability about their attraction to each other, she the hapless victim of a disastrous union with a man who had lost all sense of reason and he initially an onlooker but later an invited guest at a great banquet that had turned into a drunken orgy of violence.

It had given Keith no pleasure to see Jack single-handedly destroy his career, his marriage and his credibility; it had given him no satisfaction that he had been compelled to abduct Jack's lovely spouse in order to save her from grievous injury, possibly even death. It was hardly his fault that he had finally fallen in love with her; but now that he had done so, the die had been cast. There could be no regrets.

Keith loved Jack just as dearly; he loved him like a brother – albeit a wayward brother – who had retreated so deeply into his own private, drunken hell that he could be helped by no one but himself. He had been close enough to Jack to know what made him tick, close enough to observe the pressures that had built up and brought him to his knees more savagely than any blows he had taken in the boxing ring. He understood perfectly every facet of the man's personality – his strengths, his weaknesses, his hopes, his fears, his passions and his aversions. On the whole, his was a generous judgement of his fallen hero, the seeds of whose demise he considered were sown in the early thirties:

> 'There was a lifestyle among an elite faction in London then that was sexually decadent. They got to Jack when he was eighteen and ruined this boy who four years earlier had been humping coal. Doyle realised he had a magnetism that was unique and he became the darling of the upper classes. They spoiled him – Edward and Lady Furness and the rest. He had no

parents to guide him, no family unit, so he became a pleasure-seeker, a hedonist who lived only for today. He was religious to a point, but he never really thought he would pass this way again. Another problem was that he always had sycophants about him who took from him and gave him nothing.

You had to be amused by Jack because he was larger than life – too big a person to be handcuffed to domesticity. He was a prince without a principality, a man who was feted wherever he went. He could walk into any cinema in the dark and be recognised.

Before I met them he and Movita were working like hell, appearing in theatres, doubling up in night-clubs and earning £300 a night. Subconsciously Jack was jealous of Movita because she was starring with him when previously he held the spotlight. Movita was subservient because she felt it was a woman's place; she was dedicated to Jack absolutely. He singled her out for his spite, so perhaps she needled him in some way. I know her jealousy upset him, but you couldn't really blame her. Jack hated her for wanting to leave. He realised she was desperate to see her family, but that if she went she would never return. Sober, he'd try to help her. Drunk, she was the bitch who was deserting him. After the show at Lucan, he nearly killed her; detectives literally had to beat him off her in the dressing-room and backstage. He had to be psychopathic, round the twist from alcohol. He was paranoiac and suffered from a persecution complex. He just couldn't face the fact that he would lose her.

Doyle's cheating in later life, when the chips were down, was, in effect, his old boyhood days coming out – when anything went in the back streets of Queenstown. He did cultivate a kind of righteousness, but when the tide of life started to flow against him he reverted to type. He had two aims in life: self-preservation and self-esteem. They were closely linked, like two sisters, one ugly, one beautiful. The dividing line was thin and he changed from one to another whenever it suited him.

Jack was vastly wealthy, but really he was spoiled by having too much money. I must say he was generous – he'd stand everyone drinks in the bar. He had no mean streaks. He gave you his time and sang you his songs. He was not a pecuniary bastard who counted his change. When he rode the tide, everyone rode it. He was always telling me: "I came from nothing and I suppose I'll go back to nothing." He was fatalistic – he felt it was his destiny. He thought: "When I have it, everyone has it. When I've got nothing, they should all look after me."

Besides being spoiled by wealth, Jack was also spoiled sexually. He could not be satisfied – the conquest was not enough. He used to pick up prostitutes and fuck them. The prostitutes liked him – he was the most propositioned man in the world.'

What is the truth behind the legend? Movita says:

'I haven't had that many men to compare him with, but of course he was well endowed. He was 6ft 5in tall, for goodness sake. I was surprised he was so modest about it. Yes, he was sex mad; in fact I think he was over-sexed. But he was very happy to please – very gentle, a romantic lover. As far as I'm concerned he was. His sex was very healthy. He wasn't kinky with me, although he may well have been with others.'

One woman who knows all about Jack's sexual prowess at first hand is Valerie, Countess de Cadenet, a former 'B' movie and TV actress in England and the United States. The mother of former racing driver Alain de Cadenet and grandmother of TV presenter Amanda, she met Jack in London shortly after the start of the war when she was the star-struck sixteen-year-old Prince of Wales showgirl Karen Scott. No punches are pulled as she explains in graphic detail her encounter with the man sometimes referred to as the Irish Lothario. Her colourful account proves that Jack must have reserved his romanticism solely for Movita:

'I met Doyle in Al Burnett's Pigalle club in Soho in the early part of 1940. At the time I was under-age as a showgirl and doing non-stop revue. That meant six shows a day at the Prince of Wales sitting on a cardboard moon starkers. Doyle was singing in London and out on the prowl every night. Bombs were falling at the time and no one cared. I was in the Pigalle with another showgirl, having a drink, and Doyle was there on his own. He said, "Who's coming home with me?" He was 6ft 5in and so handsome – I ask you: it was like Prince Charming coming. He hauled me off to some shabby room – a real dump – which he used for screwing purposes; in fact I would describe it as his private screwing place. I was captivated by him and didn't even realise he was married.

His claim to fame was a big knob and I must admit I was right and royally done; but in truth it was a lamentable lay. I was very unimpressed. He couldn't have cared less. It was my own fault really; it had just been bravado on my part – I had balled a star. He exuded great charm and said nice things, but once the business was done it was "Out!" I realised then that the performance was unimportant to him – it was just the chase that appealed. He wanted as many girls as possible.

I saw him only once after that. There was no romance: he wasn't interested. He'd already had me, so it was, "Eff off". All he talked about was being introduced to the others. He only liked young girls and he went out of his way to get them. A friend of mine who made it with him later got the clap.

Looking back I'm not proud of being one of 50 000 women who were laid by him. I reckon that if all the women he screwed had lined up together, they'd have formed a battalion. In those days, what you had to do wasn't as important as who you did it with. He was a juicy guy; any sixteen-year-old would have creamed at the sight of him and taken down her knickers. Any woman in England would have done it with him. It was an Honours Day.'

Movita is philosophical about the sexploits that went on behind her back during those early days in London. She suspected it was going on but – as a nervous stranger in the blackout – she was searching for anything but a confrontation with her husband.

She has told the story of her life with Jack Doyle exactly as it happened because that was the only way. It had to be the plain, unvarnished truth or nothing. Much of it is shocking and yet Movita's abiding memories of Jack are unconnected with his drunkenness and his violence. They centre around the appealing side to his complex character – the charismatic side that made him the undisputed people's champion even though he had never won a boxing title; the side that captured a million hearts. Her vision of Jack now is that of the handsome, charming, generous, debonair, devil-may-care young man whom she and the people of Britain, Ireland and America found utterly irresistible:

> 'When Jack wasn't drinking he was very gentle, very romantic – a sentimentalist. He cried easily and was touched by lovely things, like little children. The simplest things would bring tears to his eyes. He was very beautiful and used to write me beautiful things, lovely things. He was child-like with his love letters; they were charming, like young people are. Not sophisticated – and he didn't try to be. Even a little sugary. He was just a pussy-cat.'

Movita admits her romance with Keith McConnell was not in the same league:

> 'With Keith, I appreciated all he did. We just drifted together. I don't know whether I really, truly loved him.'

However, she was undeniably fond of the engaging Dubliner who did so much to help her and whose generosity of spirit was such that, before leaving Ireland to join her in America, he sent Jack the £500 his father had given him 'for a rainy day'. Keith had heard Jack was starting a new tour of Ireland and was keen to help set him up again. Predictably, the tour was an unmitigated disaster:

> 'He used to get blind drunk in little towns and villages and the gardai would be called. "Who's causing the trouble?" they'd ask when they arrived. "Jack Doyle," would come the answer. Normally there'd be at least three of them, but they would say meekly, "What do you expect us to do about it?" They were frightened stiff of him because he was so massive and strong. Jack's behaviour had by this time become worse than ever, if that were possible. At one venue he even pissed on the audience when they jeered him.'

Movita and Keith lived together in the U.S. for three years. Her failure to obtain an annulment of her marriage meant they could not wed. Perhaps it was just as well. The feelings they had for each other after being thrust together by circumstance gradually faded under a hot California sun. They drifted apart, Keith going back to Ireland and his father's textile business and Movita heading for Mexico and a bit-part in *Viva Zapata!*

Keith would be returning to the United States in the late 1950s as a fully-fledged actor, having created a career for himself in films and theatre. He would become best known for his roles as Sherlock Holmes, due in no small part to his uncanny resemblance to Basil Rathbone – acknowledged as the greatest Holmes of all. He would marry a Belgian girl, Diane, and raise a family. And through it all he would remain close friends with Movita until his death through illness in 1987.

Movita was to find new romance on the set of *Viva Zapata!* The love affair with Marlon Brando would span a decade on and off and result in marriage in 1960 when she was expecting their child Sergio, whom she calls Miko (My son). In the meantime, Brando had married and been divorced from Anna Kashfi.

The Movita-Brando marriage* was short-lived. There would be a sequel to it years later in England, with the screen hero and the ring has-been coming face to face at Elstree.

Brando and Doyle: both legends of their time; both having married the same captivating woman; both in urgent discussion over Movita.

* Movita met Brando in 1950: 'He was studying Indian and Mexican culture for *Viva Zapata!* I went to a house where he was eating *borrego*. He started calling me and we got together. Brando was not glamorous like Jack Doyle – he drove a Model T and went round in jeans and T-shirts.'

Book IV

NANCY – and after

Chapter 1

The O'Connell Street Walk

Jack Doyle was a lonely, discredited hero with only memories to feed on and the bottle to cheer him. The realities of the present were too painful to contemplate and he retreated into alcoholic fantasy.

In rare sober moments he sent messages to Movita pledging his undying love. They were never acknowledged. When she was appearing at the Pavilion Theatre in Glasgow, a reporter asked if she had any message for him. Her eyes flashed and her lips hardened: 'I don't want to hear from Jack again. I don't even want to speak about him any more.' There was a softer, gentler tone when Tim Doyle – by this time better known by his stage name Tony Clare – paid her a visit back-stage in Blackpool: 'I love Jack – I'll always love him. I just want to live a little longer.'

At about the time Movita had been re-establishing her career in Glasgow, Jack was going even further downhill in Dublin. Most of the shows he struggled with in her absence had ended disastrously. There was no attempt to maintain a semblance of pride in his performance, no desire to be seen at his handsome, charming, alluring best in front of a public that once worshipped him.

The tour he had embarked on fortified by Keith McConnell's conscience money, as he might have thought it, was the biggest disaster of all. After a performance in Sligo, the six members of his touring party walked out and Jack was forced to abandon the remaining dates. He issued a cheque for £12 in payment of lodgings for the cast, but it proved worthless; he had only a paltry £2.13s.9d in his account. Answering for his action in court he was sentenced to a Draconian four months imprisonment with hard labour – a conviction later quashed by the appeal court in Dublin.

Jack was finished as a stage performer as well as a boxer. To add injury to insult the taxman was claiming his share from the concert tours and the fights with Cole and Howell. He could not pay and was forced to surrender his passport. It was an unnecessarily stringent safeguard. Jack had no money to travel anywhere.

Soon the alcoholic binge that would have put even Brendan Behan to shame took its toll. As a result Jack was barred from pubs and hotels and inevitably fell foul of the law. One incident, for which he was later fined, occurred after he boarded a bus in Naas, some twenty miles south-west of Dublin. When told the bus was full and that he must alight, Jack responded by lifting the astonished conductor in his arms like a baby and signalling the driver to pull away. He did – and his first stop was the local police station.

Jack was in more serious trouble in 1947. This time he would be invited to spend a fourteen day holiday in one of Dublin's best-known guest houses – Mountjoy Jail. He was sent down after an assault on a detective in a pub in Templeogue. In company with two men and two women he had enjoyed an evening's alcoholic consumption of such conviviality that he felt disinclined to leave at closing time. This was the kind of truculent behaviour which invariably surfaced whenever Jack had had a skinful and which was only too likely to spill over into violence if the police were called. They were and it did. Detective Peter McGarry said in evidence that Jack struck him on the chest and lifted a bottle over his head as if to hit him with it when asked to vacate the premises. Jack offered in his defence that he could not recollect the incident. Pleading ignorance was never going to save him from prison, but in all probability he was telling the truth. Only rarely could he recall hitting Movita when, next day, the bruises on her face and body testified to his brutal behaviour in drink. On this occasion his appeal against sentence was kicked out. Judge Shannon described his conduct as 'blackguardly' and assured him he would have had no hesitation in affirming an even severer sentence.

Jack was a model prisoner in Mountjoy, where, in addition to earning two days' remission for good behaviour, he endeared himself to his fellow inmates and any prison guard possessed of a sense of humour by entertaining them to a respectful rendition of *Bless This House*.

His incarceration in Mountjoy, where some of the greatest names in Irish history had languished, convinced him the name Jack Doyle still meant something in one small, enclosed corner of Dublin city. He had eaten and slept better than for a long time and been forced to dry out – a factor that would have helped him kick the drink habit altogether had he felt the slightest inclination so to do. But it took Jack only as long to get back on the bottle as it took him to find the nearest pub to celebrate his release.

There was to be yet more trouble with the police, followed by a further appearance in court, after Jack began consorting with one Mary Spillane, a dark-haired and shapely doctor's wife. Quite why an apparently respectable married woman would wish to associate with a drunken, disgraced, impoverished public figure is difficult to fathom. It seemed Jack still retained a rugged handsomeness, a raffish appearance, a roguish appeal that some women found irresistible. Mary Spillane and Jack moved into an apartment in Lower Leeson Street, but theirs was a volatile, explosive relationship that could not possibly stand the test of time. Its worst aspects manifested when, after a pub crawl round the city, they climbed into a taxi. There was a row and Jack struck her many times before throwing her shoes out of the window.

He was charged with malicious wounding and with stealing from her the sum of twelve shillings and a pair of shoes valued at £3.10s. Mary, her eyes blackened and closed, her face swollen and discoloured, admitted in court that there was an infatuation between her and Jack. If this was infatuation, it should have carried a government health warning. Jack was remanded on bail and the charges later dismissed after Mary refused to press them.

The fiery relationship temporarily at an end, and unable alone to sustain the rent for the apartment, Jack took a dingy room for five shillings a week. Before long he found himself unable to pay even that pittance. The famous Jack Doyle was homeless.

It was the true day of reckoning. Jack had always harboured the fear that his popularity would not last; he had voiced it on many occasions, saying, '*I came from nothing and I suppose I'll return to nothing.*' All the time he was priming his subconscious mind for just such an eventuality, believing more and more in his own affirmation with each piece of 'bad luck' or setback that came his way until now he was down-and-out in Dublin with no money, no influence and no future. Along the way he had hurt, humiliated and finally driven off the women who had loved him and with whose support he would never have sunk so pitifully low.

Of course he still had the loving family he had always cherished and supported. His mother, father and Uncle Joe were living in the house he had bought for them in Greenford. Brothers Mick and Tim, whom he had put through boarding school in Dungarvan, Waterford – when money to him was like so much confetti – were now both on the stage in England and, along with Bill, had superseded him as their parents' dutiful providers. They were vaguely aware that he had fallen headlong into decline since Movita's departure, but never once did he request a helping hand.

Perhaps Jack's most redeeming feature was that he accepted his fall from grace without bitterness or rancour. He realised he had brought it on himself and was never one to whinge, believing implicitly that something would turn up to help him over a temporary difficulty. This cheery optimism in the face of adversity applied only to his day-to-day circumstances. Although he might not have known from where the next meal was coming, he realised he would never starve: there would always be someone around to offer him assistance. He did not apply this blind faith to his long-term future, where it might have done him some good. Instead, he seemed willing to accept his new-found hardship as his lot in life, content just to survive and to enjoy a few drinks and a few jokes with the type of people and in the type of places he would never have frequented in his heyday. Here was a man in his mid-thirties, possessed of good looks and massive build and some intellect, who had settled for being a down-at-heel dropout like those he had once pitied when they successfully appealed to him for a handout. Inwardly he had been convinced he would one day be joining their number. It was a day that had come sooner – very much sooner – than he had anticipated.

Help was close at hand, as he was always so ready to assume. A taxi-driver who knew Jack well offered him rent-free accommodation in the back of his broken-down cab. It was barely believable that a man who had stayed at some of the finest hotels in the western world should find himself having to bed down in a crippled conveyance.

Spike McCormack, the one-time Irish middleweight champion and father of former British champions John and Pat, recalled those desperate days:

> 'The taxi Jack slept in was parked in Henrietta Street and owned by a cabbie called "Tip Boy" Weldon, who also had a stable. Tip was always smartly dressed in a grey suit and a Homburg and wealthy people used to go to him for black-market theatre tickets. I wouldn't mind betting he did very well out of Jack and Movita's shows, for example. He lived in Upper Dominick Street, but operated from a place at the back of Paddy Reilly's pub.
>
> Jack's big-shot friends just blew him out. He moved around all over the city and people would buy him drinks. He was well looked after – everyone knew him. He often went down to the Seaman's Mission on Eden Quay. All the drunks used to congregate at the Mission, including Brendan Behan. He and Jack knew each other well. Jack would go into Daly's bar, also the Scotch House opposite and Egan's bar. He never had any money. People would just come and offer to buy him a drink.
>
> One of Jack's regular haunts was Dolly Fawcett's*, an old run-down cafe in Bolton Street. It opened at ten o'clock at night and you had to bring your own booze. Illegal drinking sessions went on there throughout the night. Although it was a *shebeen* the police never applied for it to be shut down because they could always find people on the run via Dolly's place. She was big, buxom and in her sixties – a very smart dresser. She was also a charitable woman with a heart of gold. She took pity on the down-and-outs and even fixed some of them up with women.

* 'Dolly Fawcett's', as it was known, was officially the Continental Café. It has since been demolished.

Another haunt of Jack's was Tony Tighe's all-night cafe on the Aston Quay. It was the same as Dolly's place, but on the other side of the Liffey. I remember being there at two o'clock one morning. Frankie Welsh, a great lightweight, was also there. A little coloured fellow came in off a ship and Jack asked him for money. The guy said, "No way." So Jack picked him up and carried him outside, placed him in a hole where workmen had been digging and started shovelling earth on him. The bloke got up and ran like a hare down the quay. He was never seen again. He must still be running.'

According to Spike McCormack, Jack still enjoyed celebrity status wherever he went. His every move was a performance:

'Mid-morning he liked nothing more than to stride out along O'Connell Street, where he and Movita were mobbed whenever they so much as took a breath of air. After Movita left, if he had a shilling he would spend it on a red carnation and still do the O'Connell Street walk.'

Dublin sports journalist and author Dave Guiney was another who remembered that famous stroll down O'Connell street:

'Doyle had this great aura about him, even in his down-and-out days. He had a guardsman's swagger – a beautiful carriage. He turned all the heads in O'Connell Street and Grafton Street each day. It was Jack Doyle's Eleven O'Clock Walk and it was almost regal.'

After spending the day and half the night drinking, Jack would ease his huge frame into the back seat of the taxi and grab a few hours' sleep until the hustle and bustle of the city streets beckoned. He would then take his leisurely walk, nodding his head this way and that as the friendly, cheery voices rang out from all directions. 'How are you this morning, Jack?' or just, 'Morning, Jack,' or alternatively from some wags, 'Give us a song, Jack.' His meet-the-people tour completed, he would disappear into a packed and noisy Bartley Dunne's, where whiskies came thick and fast from a host of admirers keen to ply him with drinks but understandably not so keen to invite him into their homes. They loved him, they were good to him, they swapped jokes with him, they bought drinks for him. His glass was never empty. Some would 'lend' him money they knew they would never see again. Jack Doyle had given so much pleasure and excitement over the years that they felt they owed him. It was their way of saying, 'Thanks for the memory.'

After a time he would move on to other hostelries in the city, often being ejected as his behaviour worsened with each passing hour. Most times he would end up in Dolly Fawcett's, where he knew he would always be welcome and where he would drink and play cards until taking to the refuge of the broken-down taxi that had become his home.

Poor Jack. He was missing Movita terribly. Only the brain-deadening effect of the whiskies and brandies he was consuming in vast quantities enabled him to live through the heartache he had endured since her departure. He could never hope to meet another Movita, but there was always the possibility of finding a woman who would love him, care for him and be a good companion. A woman who would help him regain his self respect. Enter Nancy Kehoe. The year was 1947. She almost literally bumped into Jack and Gerald Egan as they barred her way in O'Connell Street. Rather than back down she stood her ground – and Jack was immediately attracted to her spirit and her looks. It was the start of an association that would last twenty-nine years.

Nancy bore a striking resemblance to Hedy Lamarr,* and was predictably tiny in the mould of Judith Allen and Movita. It could hardly have been coincidence that the three women who shared the major years of Jack's life were all as petite as his mother. Her influence in boyhood and adolescence had been necessarily stronger than that of his disabled father and this perhaps was the subconscious thread that bound him to women of similar stature. Indisputably, Nancy inspired an immediate upturn in Jack's fortunes:

> 'At the time we met I wouldn't have described him as an alcoholic, but he was down-and-out and drinking heavily. I don't think it's true that he had nowhere to stay; he just preferred the taxi because he could come and go as he liked. He always had somebody: there was always a friend and he never went hungry. He knew an attendant at the Wicklow Hotel and used to have his laundry delivered there. He wasn't welcome at the Wicklow, so the attendant would let him in by a side-door for a quick wash, shave and brush-up. He'd appear back on the streets looking as if he'd stayed at the Gresham.
>
> You had some good laughs with Jack. I remember there was a wealthy, eccentric old lady named Angela Brady who owned property all over Dublin. She was a scruffy thing and she went round each week collecting her rents; but as she did so, little boys sneaked up and pinched the notes from her pockets. Jack saw her burying the money in the garden of her huge Georgian house in Ranelagh and he dug it up a couple of times. Mostly all the rooms in the house were empty, but she had four Nigerian law students staying there at one time. They were called Coco, Jesus, Semolina and Appia and they were very respectable. Jack used to stay at the house on some occasions and late at night, when he was drunk, he'd shout: "Come out of there, you black bastards. I'll murder the lot of you." All of a sudden four heads would appear over the banister, but all you could see were the whites of their eyes and their teeth chattering.

* *Hedy Lamarr*. Born in 1913, her real name was Hedwig Kiesler. She was an Austrian leading lady of the thirties and forties, and created a sensation by appearing nude in the 1933 Czech film *Extase*. Her name became synonymous with glamour. Her most notable films were *Algiers* (1938), *White Cargo* (1942), *Samson and Delilah* (1949).

Jack just wanted a drink and a laugh, really. He could see the funny side of things, despite his circumstances. Like when he used to drink at Dolly Fawcett's. One of the fellows who went there had a wooden leg. When they were all out of money they'd take this guy's artificial limb over to the pawn shop and get £5 for it. Then they'd have to carry him home.'

Tim Doyle visited Jack in Dublin at around that time:

'I saw him in the Green Bar, opposite the Theatre Royal stage door. He was dressed in riding boots, jodhpurs and hacking jacket. His carnation had given up the fight, but that large whiskey was still in his hand, he had about ten days' growth of beard and there was cigar smoke all over the place. What a sight he looked. Jack had the cheek to sell my return ticket cut-price, but to make up for it he arranged for me to appear at the Theatre Royal. I received £75, and £25 of that went to the pawnbroker to get this chap's wooden leg back. They'd pawned it five times that week.'

Jack gradually pulled himself together under Nancy's steadying influence as he did not want to risk losing her with a repetition of the mindless behaviour that had driven off Movita. One day he informed her quite suddenly and with even a hint of drama: 'I'm off the drink. This is it. I'm going to make a comeback.' He said he would return to London and start afresh as a singer, and Nancy was all for it. With the war over he would no longer be unwelcome in England. Having never officially been served with deportation papers, there would be no official channels to go through, no senior civil servant to deal with in an effort to prove he was now a fit and proper person to live in a country to which he considered he'd paid enough in taxes at the height of his fame to have settled the national debt. Nancy recalled:

'As soon as it became known that Jack intended making a comeback in England, everyone rallied round. Money came in from all quarters, including a donation from a priest called Fr Flanagan, who said Mass for the city's drunks. Extra-quick Masses they had to be, too. I went in to see him with a note from Jack and he gave me £10. Jack had two shirts and a beige gaberdine suit made by Best's, the bespoke tailor in O'Connell Street. They were really lovely. He looked a new man. He had straightened himself out at last.'

Jack Doyle felt reborn. He was ready to conquer Britain once more – this time with Nancy at his side.

Chapter 2

The Gorgeous Gael

When Jack and Nancy hit London in the summer of 1949, the days of sirens and blackouts were a fading memory. The same applied to Jack's war-time disaffection. Bernard Delfont proved more forgiving than his brothers Lew and Leslie Grade were alleged to have been to Movita by booking him for a nationwide tour that would open on the south coast at Brighton and Eastbourne.

Jack attracted crowds of holiday-makers as he ran up and down the sea-front in a futile bid to get back in shape. Bodies abused as his had been by alcohol and indiscipline can never recapture the fitness or firmness of youth, but the attention he was getting all over again made the effort doubly worthwhile. It told him that, far from being finished for good by the hostile publicity that had driven him from Britain, he was still held in popular public esteem.

He would never scale the heights attained in the 1930s, nor command the fees that made him possibly the biggest earner of his generation,* but it was within his compass to re-establish himself in precisely the way Movita had done – with solid hard work and by making the most of every opportunity, however limited.

Ironically, as Nancy recalled, Jack's attempt to resurrect his career and credibility were hampered by a farcical inability to get his act together off-stage:

> 'We could never quite find the venues at which Jack was appearing. He knew the towns he was supposed to be playing, but not the names of the theatres. We used to get in a taxi and tour round looking for them. Eventually we'd see his name up and know we were at the right one.'

Jack's notorious love affair with London was rekindled with predictable regularity on tour:

> 'We travelled back to London nearly every weekend. It was a complete waste of time, money and energy, but Jack lived for London and its atmosphere – he liked to think of it as his home town. He'd spend £100 in a weekend. It

*This statement embraces his combined earnings as boxer, stage performer, recording artist and film actor.

would be drinks all round – everybody in the pub. Owners of Irish clubs literally fought for his services. One St Patrick's Night he was double-booked and the man on the wrong end of the oversight followed him to the other venue in Dagenham. As he stepped from his car, a fight broke out on the pavement between the two club owners. Bookings were always muddled up – and sometimes even the dates. He couldn't apply his mind to anything. He just wanted to sing his few songs.'

Jack had grown older, but sadly not much wiser. Before he had left for Ireland his drinking companions round town had been people of note, like Jim Mollison and Lord Milton; now, at thirty-six, he was content being the big-shot in a pub full of anonymous people:

'When we first came over, Jack stayed at his parents' home in Greenford. Then we got a flat at 32 Pembridge Gardens, Notting Hill. He soon became known in pubs like The Norfolk, The Load of Hay and The Hoop. When Jack was away touring the pubs would be empty – then the word would go round: "Jack's back." And suddenly they would be jam-packed. He brought them great business.

The licensee of The Hoop was a man called John O'Shea. He was so pious that the regulars referred to him as Fr O'Shea. Jack was barred a couple of times when fights started, whether he was to blame or not. Everyone joked that he'd have to go to confession and earn forgiveness from Fr O'Shea but Jack wouldn't do it. "I'm not going back," he'd say. "John will have to come and get me." And sure enough, O'Shea would have to swallow his pride and ask Jack back. He was losing too much business.'

Jack could never bury the past. It kept catching up with him, relived by people unwilling to let him forget his glory days. When it comes to a trip down Memory Lane over a few jars, triumphs on the stage pale into insignificance beside the more stirring deeds of the prize-fighter. And when you are told repeatedly by countless well-meaning admirers that you'd have wiped the floor with today's batch of moderate heavyweights, you begin to believe them. Jack's instincts started to revive, galvanised by the fighting talk with which he was constantly surrounded. He hankered after a return to the ring, believing – or having been led to believe – that he retained the power to bludgeon his way back to the top. Hankering was as far as he got. The Board of Control rejected his application for a licence, rightly deciding that any comeback attempt by a man who had last been seen in action in London a full decade earlier lying prostrate at the feet of Eddie Phillips could prove a distinct embarrassment not only to the Board but to British boxing as a whole.

Jack was hurt by this summary dismissal and indignant that many of those then masquerading as heavyweight boxers would have been unable to withstand even one round of unbridled Doyle aggression. All of his long-standing grievances against the Board gushed to the surface. The confiscation of the larger part of his £3 000 purse from the Petersen fight was still a sore point and would forever remain so; and now the Board had reactivated his sense of injustice. He even threatened to sue unless they could prove the money had gone to a worthy cause, such as the Boxers' Benevolent Fund.

Jack was clutching at straws. Whatever the rights and wrongs of the decision to fine and suspend him after the Petersen debacle in 1933, there could be no questioning the Board's wisdom in refusing to re-issue his licence almost twenty years later. His bloated body would have been used as a punch-bag by aspiring heavyweights seeking to illuminate their records and their careers by beating a big name of yesteryear.

He was forced to accept the Board's decision; but, almost as an act of defiance, he turned his attention to professional wrestling. His aim: to prove to the world that Jack Doyle remained unrivalled as a crowd-puller in any ring of combat. He was convinced he could create a new career as a wrestler; and though his bulky 19 stone frame was no longer in pristine condition, how right he was to deduce that there was still a touch of magic in the name that had twice brought London to a standstill.

Jack knew he was no Gus Sonnenberg: he was better looking for a start. But he had gleaned enough from Judith Allen about her once adoring spouse to realise that good money could be made in the wrestling ring by anyone endowed with more brawn than brain. She had always been quick, however, to correct any impression that Cannonball Gus had been at the back of the queue when grey matter was being handed out. Indeed, anyone who could earn the vast amounts Gus did, and consequently be able to afford the kind of stupendous gifts he bestowed on Judith with loving regularity, must have been pretty smart in her book.

The unlikely Mr. Big of the wrestling world in Britain was the aristocratic Atholl Oakeley, a cousin of the Duke of Atholl and destined in later years to become Sir Atholl by virtue of a baronetcy. Oakeley, a former top-class all-in wrestler, had become the country's leading promoter with shows at major venues like Belle Vue, Manchester, and London's Harringay Arena. He was acutely aware of Jack's pulling power as a boxer and singer, as were the directors of Harringay.* With attendances hitting only the five or six thousand mark in spite of the

* *Harringay Stadium* was owned by White City's parent company, the Greyhound Racing Association.

attraction of some of the biggest names in international wrestling – including world heavyweight champion Frank Sexton of the United States, ex-boxers Primo Carnera and Larry Gains (the former Empire heavyweight champion), and Martinschenok and Georgieff of Russia – the decision was taken to send for the one man still capable of filling the stadium:

> 'The Harringay board called me in one day and said, "Get Jack Doyle. He's the biggest drawing card in the world." Of course I knew all about Doyle: I had heard about him some years earlier when I was wrestling in America. Jack Dempsey told me Doyle was the hardest hitter in boxing and that properly handled he could have been world champion. Dempsey also rated Doyle one of the top five card players in the world. He said Jack could deal himself any card in the pack and that he had learned the trick from a gangster in the US.'

In his book *Blue Blood On The Mat*, Oakeley described his first meeting with Jack:

> 'He was certainly a wonderful-looking man. Six foot five and nineteen stone, he stood straight as a ramrod, as do all the Guards. I felt three foot nothing in front of this magnificent person with the dignity and bearing of Richard Coeur de Lion.'

Oakeley signed him up for a wrestling debut against the fearsome Estonian champion Bucth, known as the Human Gorilla. Oakeley's instincts and those of the Harringay directors were not misplaced. Whereas most of the world's top wrestlers – and even Primo Carnera – had been able only to half-fill Harringay, the astonishing Irishman who just a year earlier had been a washed-up fighter and singer reduced to sleeping in the back of a broken-down Dublin taxi had packed the place to capacity. It inclined Oakeley to the belief that the public at large would have paid to see Jack doing handstands on an ant-hill.

The contest was staged in February 1950. Jack was fanfared in to the ring and there were cheers and jeers as he mixed it with Bucth, whom the spectators understandably referred to as Butch. According to a newspaper report, Jack went charging in head down and eyes closed in the third round. The referee was sent flying, the Gorilla went down and it was all over bar the Irish pipers who played Jack round the ring. The crowd booed as he clasped his hands above his head in victory salute; they booed him when he posed for pictures; and they booed him as he left the ring. Being booed was a new experience for Jack, but it was the easiest £2 000 he had earned. He would be back for more.

Oakeley next decided to pitch Jack in against arch boxing rival Eddie Phillips in a grudge match guaranteed to attract another full house to

Harringay. He described how he spirited Jack away to the wilds of the West Country in order to prepare him for the contest:

> 'When the news was released that the "darlin' bhoy" of the entire British national press was to wrestle for Atholl Oakeley, the storm broke. Everyone wanted to know where Doyle would set up his training camp.
>
> We arranged for a friend to tip off newsmen that he would train in Scotland. But this . . . was a bluff. . . . Accompanied by my six-foot son John Oakeley [later to become an Olympic yachtsman], I took Jack and a sparring partner by train to Minehead. From there we went by car miles out to a lonely farmhouse on Exmoor, far away from telephone, pub or post office. "Nothing but sheep," as Jack said on arrival. I must admit that I have seldom seen anyone so angry as Jack Doyle was when he saw where we had brought him. There was no electric light and I will never forget the sight of this great man in his hundred-guinea suit walking up the stairs holding a candle and cursing like mad.
>
> Finding that he was constantly watched (so as to ensure that he could not try to "escape"), Doyle resigned himself to his fate. We posted a sentry on the hill outside the farmhouse to sound the alarm if the *Daily Mirror*'s Peter Wilson (the only sportswriter who knew Jack had not gone to Scotland) found us. But no one came.
>
> Day after day we practised half Nelsons, wrist locks and all the rest. Every day Jack looked better and became fitter and stronger. We returned him in marvellous shape to London. He looked every inch a champion.'

Phillips, who turned publican after his retirement from boxing, trained for his wrestling debut with the Bow police, who, according to Oakeley, had hundreds of pounds on him to win. Wearing black tights, he entered the ring first. Then, as before their White City fight a dozen years earlier, an interval of several minutes elapsed before Jack made his entrance, a fanfare of trumpets heralding his arrival and a spotlight picking out his burly frame. Phillips was furious at again having to play a waiting game. He decided to steal Jack's thunder by grabbing his dressing-gown, jumping through the ropes and sprinting up the opposite aisle.

Jack, it was said, was caked in enough make-up for Hollywood to have relaunched four Gloria Swansons. His curly locks tumbling over his temples, he climbed into the empty ring with a look of consternation breaking through the pancake. Phillips had comprehensively upstaged him by executing his own disappearing act, just as Jack had done by diving through the ropes the last time the pair had clashed at Harringay. Jack was nonplussed only fleetingly and quickly regained his equilibrium. He turned slowly, as if on a revolving podium, and the crowd screamed their bloodthirsty acknowledgement. He removed his lambswool dressing-gown to reveal a body whose artificial tan was accentuated by white trunks with green piping. Who could have failed to love this most remarkable of showmen?

Phillips finally returned to the ring to dispel doubts that, frightened for his life, he had continued running right out of the arena and all the way back to Bow. He was distinctly apprehensive when the contest started, suspecting – and not without justification – that Jack's monolithic bulk was about to topple from its great height and pin him to the canvas. He was even more wary when he tried a bear-hug and realised his arms would not even stretch round Jack's ample waist. The end came when Phillips was disqualified in the eleventh round after repeatedly being warned for punching by referee Stan Spanner, whose cricket whites added a bizarre touch to the proceedings. Old habits clearly died hard with Phillips, who had continually reminded Jack of their encounters in the boxing ring. Amazingly the 10 000 crowd had been so wrapped up in it all that it might just as well have been a fight to the finish. There was variously roaring, booing, stamping and clapping throughout the contest and the arena erupted in pandemonium when Phillips was ruled out after both men had secured a 'fall'.

Oakeley insisted it had been a genuine match:

> 'How could it have been otherwise? Harringay was packed from floor to ceiling and Doyle would have died rather than lose to Phillips. He received 37 per cent of the takings and was worth every penny.'

Next Jack faced a couple of collisions with one of boxing's biggest juggernauts, 'Two Ton' Tony Galento, the former world heavyweight title contender. Galento's dockside brawl with Marlon Brando in Elia Kazan's timeless epic *On the Waterfront* was still to be captured for posterity on celluloid, but his two battles with Jack in London and Dublin would prove authentically brutal. Oakeley recalled:

> 'There was another huge crowd at Harringay and Galento won when he fell on Doyle, smashing two of his ribs. Jack was in a lot of pain but he took it very well, very courageously. He had to go to St Mary's Hospital in Paddington to be bandaged up. He said that when Galento held him down it was like being under a steam-roller.'

Jack's bones may have been broken, but not his spirit. After all there was more cash on offer for a return encounter in Ireland, where he felt he might gain his revenge. Native support would be like an extra arm against a man who clearly did not know his own strength. Galento had once floored the great Joe Louis* and in his career as a wrestler, had

* The fight took place in New York on June 28, 1939. Louis retained his world title on a fourth-round stoppage.

taken on a black bear. No wonder he had such supreme contempt for Jack, a mere 6ft 5in and human.

Galento's arrogance would prove his undoing in Dublin, where the contest drew 22 500 to Tolka Park. Jack hoisted the American's 'Two Ton' frame on his shoulders and spun him like a roulette wheel, gaining such momentum that both men went crashing out of the ring. Galento's head hit the concrete and he was out cold. Fortunately for Jack, his fall was broken by a chair. He was able to clamber back in the ring before the count was completed to be declared the winner.

That night Oakeley found Jack buying whiskies for the whole of Dublin, or so it seemed. As he walked into the hotel bar, Jack asked for some money to be going on with. 'How much?' asked Oakeley.

'Fifty pounds.'

Oakeley sized up the situation – 'I did not want to see him squandering his hard-earned money' – and handed him a five-pound note. Jack saw the funny side of it. 'You're no promoter at all,' he said. 'You should wear your collar back to front. You're more like the Archbishop of Hamble.' With that he handed the fiver to the barman and said, 'Give the Archbishop a cigar.' Thereafter he always referred to Oakeley as the Archbishop of Hamble – the village near Southampton where Oakeley resided.

There was a mutual fondness between them. Jack would be eternally grateful to Oakeley for conferring on him the title The Gorgeous Gael, an appellation commonly but erroneously believed to have originated during his boxing career. It would strike a chord with the public and become synonymous with Jack through life and death. Nancy recalled:

> 'He absolutely loved being known as the Gorgeous Gael. His chest used to puff out with pride. It summed him up so perfectly. He really was gorgeous. And he was a Gael.'

The Gorgeous Gael was the least bizarre of several preposterous sobriquets bestowed by Oakeley. Among them were: A Gulliver among Lilliputians; God-like in a Gigantic Grappling Galaxy (this, surely, was alliteration gone mad); Idol of Royalty and King among Men; and All Male Film Stars rolled into One, with the looks of an Apollo and the body of Sir Galahad. Jack Doyle, proclaimed the publicity posters and handbills, would Forever be Remembered. Even Jack, a man with a healthy regard for his own grandeur as a human being, must have raised an eyebrow at the sheer outrageousness of it all.

Jack engaged in several more wrestling bouts in Ireland. By far the most novel was his contest with iron man Butty Sugrue at the Puck Fair in Killorglin, Co. Kerry, where, for three days and nights in August of each year, the town's thirty bars never close. Thousands flock from all over the world to see the fun of this incredible fair; they spend a fortune in the pubs and another £200 000 or so changes hands in the horse and cattle market. One of the big attractions there in 1953, apart from the traditional crowning of a large puck goat as King of the Fair, was Jack's set-to with Sugrue, a pocket battleship who enjoyed the reputation of being the strongest man in Ireland. Sugrue's feats of strength were already legendary, but the one destined to earn him most celebrity was his amazing ability to pull along a double-decker London bus with a rope gripped between his teeth. He was also able to lift a chair between his teeth. What made it a superhuman feat was that there would be a heavy man seated in it.

As was to be expected, Jack proved no match for Butty in the strong-arm stuff, retiring graciously after two rounds. The contest took place in a field and Nancy recalled *The People* newspaper's celebrated columnist Arthur (Tony) Helliwell being in attendance:

> 'He lost his famous hat in the commotion and was extremely annoyed. He said he felt undressed without it.'

If Jack was thought to have lacked courage in the boxing ring – and many doubted his resolve – his exploits as a wrestler must have laid those doubts to rest. He may have been fond of his looks but he never had a yellow streak, as witness his efforts against Bucth, Galento and Sugrue. Atholl Oakeley was adamant that none of those bouts was fixed, and the fact that Jack and Galento each suffered injury added credence to his claim.

If it was considered to have taken real guts for Jack to go in against such fearsome opposition, he deserved a Queen's award for bravery for agreeing to take on the ogre lined up for his next outing. To quote Oakeley:

> 'I felt the time had come to find out what Jack Doyle could do against one of my greatest giants. I knew that if a fighter used his brains, he should be able to beat a giant. Anyone who, like Doyle, could spring from little or nothing and earn a hundred thousand pounds could be no fool. So I went off to find the greatest of all living giants. This giant would be the greatest Colossus to appear in London since Angus McAskell appeared before Queen Elizabeth in the sixteenth century – a new giant who would make all other wrestlers and boxers look like children. A fantastic monster of a man of enormous stature and fabulous weight.'

Was there such a person on the planet? Oakeley could be given to colourful hyperbole when it suited his purpose, but he was exaggerating not one iota in his vivid description of Dutchman Kurt Zehe, whom he would christen The Great Gargantua. He had heard about Zehe from

Primo Carnera, who described him as a 'Massive Hercules'. Having thus been alerted as to what to expect, Oakeley was still visibly shaken when first setting eyes on Zehe after travelling to Brussels to sign him:

> 'Zehe's entrance was dramatic. We were all sitting in a hotel lounge drinking coffee when suddenly the door opened and in he came. He had to bend down and turn sideways to get through the doorway! When he stood up I saw at once that this was indeed the greatest of all giants. Here was no Carver Doone [wrestler Jack Baltus, 7ft-plus and 26½ stones], Ivan Georgieff [even taller] or Jim Culley [7ft 7in], but a real behemoth.'

He took Zehe to a gymnasium and weighed and measured him. The astounding result was as follows:

Height	8ft 4 in
Weight	751lbs (53st 9lbs)
Chest	110in
Thighs	3½ft in circumference
Biceps	30in
Boots	Equivalent to size 30
Width of shoulders	3ft

Oakeley, a well-proportioned six-footer, tried on Zehe's jacket. It reached to the ground. He thought, 'This is the man for Doyle. But I wonder what Jack will say when he sees him?' If Jack was only half as clever as Oakeley had figured, he would run a mile at the first sight of him.

A contract was drawn up and arrangements made for the super-giant to fight in London. A double room was booked for him at the only hotel that would take him, the Imperial in Russell Square. Even so three double beds had to be moved into Room 250 for him. Oakeley then got *Picture Post* magazine to take a picture of an eight-year-old boy sitting in one of Zehe's boots, which cost more than £100 a pair to make.

The promoter's comment that Jack was 'not too happy' when he clapped eyes on Zehe was one of his rare lapses into understatement. Jack was scared clear out of his wits! Oakeley went on, 'With his usual Irish courage, Doyle agreed to go through with the match.' By fight night, he was beginning to wish he hadn't. The outcome looked ominous when the giant placed one tremendous foot on the top step leading up to the ring. It broke at once, followed by all the other steps underneath. Fortunately the ring had been reinforced to stand up to more than seventy stones, nineteen of which Jack was convinced would soon be dead weight.

Oakeley included a report of the contest in *Blue Blood On The Mat*:

> 'Gargantua took off his dressing-gown and stood quite still as he literally towered over Doyle. He looked like Ben Nevis. Doyle engaged him and at once, as gently as if he was picking up a little boy, Kurt lifted Jack off his feet and gently put him down. He then lay on him. Time: four minutes.
>
> Jack shouted blue murder. The referee, looking like a pigmy between two dinosaurs, asked Gargantua to stand up. Not tall enough to lift his hand, the referee pointed to him and then raised his own!'

Afterwards, Oakeley asked Jack why he had made such a hullabaloo. 'Glory be, Archbishop,' he replied. 'So would you have made a noise with that damned great Centurion tank on top of you.'

Jack was scheduled to have one more contest at Harringay, against Primo Carnera – a comparative midget at 6ft 8in – but was ruled unfit after a pre-fight medical. Oakeley explained:

> 'He had high blood pressure, with a pulse rate of more than a hundred. He was examined by three BWA doctors. They each confirmed that, although he had not been drinking, he was unfit to wrestle. Thankfully, I had a substitute standing by but it was a great shame because the streets around Harringay were blocked with traffic, as they had been for Doyle's fight against Galento. Jack was the big draw every time.'

The huge crowd at Harringay jeered the announcement that he was unfit to face Carnera, but Jack received sympathetic applause when he climbed into the ring to keep faith with his public.

Shortly afterwards, Harringay Arena closed down for good after being sold and converted to a grocery storehouse. The last had been seen of Jack Doyle the wrestler; another chapter of his multi-faceted career had come to an end. He had tasted briefly his former glory of the ring, though in a different guise. The bonus as far as he was concerned was the easy money he had earned and the satisfaction of knowing he could still pack in the fans. Ironically the most avid among them had been Atholl Oakeley, a delightfully eccentric Clifton College and Sandhurst-educated member of the British nobility. His improbable entry into the notoriously shallow world of professional wrestling had come about as a result of his being beaten up by three thugs while out walking in London one Sunday afternoon. He resolved thereafter to learn to take care of himself – and so began a career that brought him the British, Empire and European heavyweight championships.

He had chosen to turn to wrestling as a result of his fascination with R. D. Blackmore's classic *Lorna Doone*, and particularly the account in it of the fight to the death between John Ridd and the criminal Carver Doone. Oakeley was convinced the story was based on fact, and the profound effect it had on him lasted through to his death in 1987. In later years he had even moved from his 'parish' of Hamble to Lynton

(Devon) in order to be close to Exmoor, the area on which the book was based.

Had the fight between Ridd and Doone been a fist fight, it is possible Oakeley would have become a boxer and so preceded Jack as a heavyweight of some consequence. However, as a wrestling man his appraisal of Jack was equally valid:

> 'No man I've ever seen had the magnetic appeal and looks of Doyle. He was like a Greek god – an Adonis with a sense of humour. In fact he was too good-looking, better looking than any stage performer for fifty years, with great wit and repartee. Women went for him in a big way, but he could not fend them off. They even used to offer money for introductions. He had a hypnotic effect on them with his magnificent sex appeal.
>
> He was an unreliable man, even wild, but I thought him a damned good fellow. He would not take advantage of a friend, but he would of anyone else. He was devious to that extent. Jack was a bit of a fly-by-night. He owed so much money because he always spent so much. He would borrow when he had nothing and then, when he was paid, he bought them drinks and paid them back. Then he'd be skint and have to borrow again and so it went on. He spent thousands of pounds on the Press. I saw him spend £500 in one evening alone on sportswriters. They double-crossed him, but he never sued. They always wrote what they liked about him because they knew they would be safe. I must say I was a great admirer. He was the king – a hero of the Irish people.'

With his wrestling career at an end, Jack returned to the music-hall with Frank Randall's 'Scandals' in Manchester, singing and playing in sketches. The carefree spending and weekend trips to London continued and soon he was in trouble over a tax demand for £960 – a sum deemed sufficiently large for the Inland Revenue to institute proceedings against him.

He travelled down from the north on a third-class overnight rail ticket and agreed at the London Bankruptcy Court that he owed a total of £3 609 to creditors, admitting he first went bankrupt in 1940 and had not been discharged. He blamed his debts on the following: his size thirteen feet, his 6ft 5in height, Carnera and a natural Irish extravagance.

He explained to the court the great difficulty he had over his shoes, which had to be specially made and cost £17 a pair. Because he was so long from neck to waist he had to have his ties made, too, but they were always silk ties and far more expensive than ordinary ones. His suits did not come cheaply, either; it took nearly seven yards of cloth to cover a man of his massive build, just for a two-piece. And naturally, he liked to go to the finest tailors. Only the best would do for Jack Doyle – even in adversity.

Atholl Oakeley spoke loyally on his behalf in court and claimed Jack had to be a heavy spender to get work in the ring or on the stage: 'If he had been fit to fight Carnera, this bankruptcy would not have happened.' Oakeley was attempting to do him a favour, but even if the Carnera fight had gone ahead there is no reason to assume Jack would have squared with his creditors. He'd had opportunities to do so when receiving payment for the matches with Bucth, Phillips, Galento and The Great Gargantua, in addition to his music-hall earnings. Yet still he had failed to settle up. Although generous to a fault, there was something in Jack's make-up that prevented him leading an orderly existence and paying his way in the normal sense. It meant that bills and reminders of bills were ignored until they built up to a point where he would be unable to pay. Even when he had cash at his disposal it would never cross his mind to dash off a cheque in payment of an overdue bill or an unpaid debt. If he had a pound, he would spend it.

Jack's inability to manage his financial affairs meant he would never be in a position to pay off his creditors. The resultant publicity was calculated to do him the utmost harm, with agents and promoters subscribing to the view that he had damaged his image still further. Bookings dried up and he was reduced to singing in Irish clubs and dance-halls, where his name would always retain a certain magic whatever his circumstances. By now he was content to earn what little he could in order to sustain an undemanding lifestyle that was light years away from his champagne days of the thirties. A nondescript bedsit in the heart of Notting Hill bore no comparison with bed and board at The Ritz, but it was home to Jack and Nancy.

Irish dance-hall promoter Maurice Leane, who admitted to being an even bigger drinker than Jack, featured him at venues all over north-west London, including The Stadium and Burton's at Cricklewood and The Carlton at Shepherd's Bush:

> 'When I put Jack on at Burton's, I paid him £15 for his performance – but it cost me £60 for the binge that followed. Jack was drunk for a full three days afterwards. He rarely spoke about Movita or Judith Allen, but I know he was still associating with Mary Spillane in London because I saw them coming out of a pub in the Edgware Road on the eve of the concert at The Stadium. He was also drunk in the dressing-room before his wrestling matches with Bucth and Galento. I know because I was one of the judges. But he had great appeal; he drew them in to the last.'

Jack had retained his devastating appeal to women, as witness his continuing association with Mary Spillane. The flush of youth was fading, but still they could not resist him. When he walked into a room, he was always the centre of attraction. This was never better illustrated than at a showbiz party in a basement house in London's Baron's Court in the early fifties. The young blonde bombshell Diana Dors*, destined to become Britain's answer to Marilyn Monroe, became instantly smitten by him. Family member Ted Doyle, who accompanied Jack and Tim Doyle to the party, recalled:

> 'Diana was a real stunner. She stood out in every respect. She took an immediate shine to Jack and couldn't leave him alone. She was all over him, especially when they were dancing – snuggling close and feeling him. It was an all-night party and everyone did their own thing. Jack and Diana eventually disappeared and I did not see them again until morning.'

The party precipitated a brief, unpublicised affair between Jack and Diana that was never destined to develop into a serious relationship.

Another well-known fifties film actress and TV personality, Katie Boyle, was also rumoured to have had a liaison with Jack. She denies it, saying:

> 'I never had a physical relationship with Jack Doyle. But there was a time when I received several anonymous telephone calls – complete with heavy breathing – accusing me of having done so. They were obviously doing the blackmail bit. I was sometimes woken in the middle of the night by these weird calls and it became quite frightening. I said to my husband Greville Bayliss, "Shall we call the police?" But eventually the calls stopped. I am absolutely intrigued by these rumours linking me with Doyle.'

Jack enjoyed mixing – though it was more rarely now – with people who reminded him of the well-bred, well-heeled company he kept at the height of his fame, when every desire of his heart was within easy reach; when every whim and fancy was catered for; and when, unlike now, he was mobbed like a pre-war Beatle by fans of every class.

Another who enjoyed an unlikely alliance with Jack during the fifties is the former Labour MP Raymond Blackburn:†

> 'I remember an article being published in *The People* that said Jack Doyle used to hang around bars, pick on a chap who seemed to have plenty of the folding stuff, follow him into the Gents and tower over him and say, "I require a gift from you." And in effect obtain money by threat of force. I did

* *Diana Dors* was born Diana Fluck in 1931. She made her screen debut at 14 and became possibly Britain's most glamorous star of the post-war era. She appeared in numerous films, including *Oliver Twist* (1948), *A Kid for Two Farthings* (1955), *Yield to the Night* (1956) and *There's a Girl in My Soup* (1970). Died in 1984.

† *Raymond Blackburn* was educated at Rugby and later studied law at London University. He became a captain in the Army during the war. He won the King's Norton division of Birmingham in 1945 at the age of 32 and became known as 'The anti-porn MP' for his campaigns against hard pornography.

not believe for one moment that Jack had done this (I was a solicitor at the time) and when he said, "Would you please 'do' *The People* for me", I agreed to do so but told him he must leave the whole thing in my hands. I therefore issued a writ and statement of claim against *The People*. Then, about three months later, Tony Helliwell said to me, "Raymond, I think I'd better warn you: we know about your writ, but Jack phoned up and said he'd like some money. So we've settled the whole thing for him and given him some money. We're letting you know this so you don't give him any more, because we assume that out of the generosity of your heart you've given him something."

I said to Jack when I saw him, "Look, what's this I hear about you going to *The People* and getting some money." And he said, "Of course I did. I was short of money and I needed money to drink. You do anything if you need a drink." He didn't show the slightest sign of compunction or remorse – he wasn't put out in the slightest. He thought I would see the funny side of it. And in fact I didn't pursue it with him. That was in 1953. I don't know how much he got in settlement, but it wouldn't have been very much.

In 1951, I had become an independent MP. I crossed the floor of the House to make a speech saying that Churchill ought to be Prime Minister again. Partly because of the feelings about my leaving the Labour Party and more because of the failure of nuclear disarmament, which was my main subject – I produced every debate on that – because of this, and also because of drink, which was a problem, I did things which were a little bit odd. I used to go out drinking till four and perhaps six in the mornings and funnily enough used to meet fantastic people like Gilbert Harding going on from the Gargoyle, where that dreadful Burgess and Maclean and Philby used to meet. Anyway, as a contrast I went out with Jack Doyle all night or took him around with me all night, I should think, and then took him back to my house and gave him a bed.

On one occasion I remember taking him to the House of Commons. I introduced him to Arthur Greenwood, who at the time was treasurer of the Labour Party and had been deputy leader – probably without the booze the ablest man in the Labour Party. I think he should have been the leader, either Arthur or Ernie Bevin.

Greenwood's dead now, but he was a tremendously loved figure in the Labour movement, a very important man. Besides being deputy leader, he served in Churchill's war cabinet. But he was the easy fellow and he and Jack Doyle got on. He liked Jack and I could see that Jack liked him. Doyle got on quite well at the House and he never let me down. The minor MPs then took him on; he looked an interesting chap, he had a sense of humour, he could tell jokes all the time. It was the only time I ever took him there.

The effect of drink is, of course, very important – the extent to which it was responsible for the bad side of Jack. There are many, many signs of alcoholism – one is blackouts, another important one is that it interferes with your work or your family. The particular one that enables you to pick out the alcoholic at a very early stage is the Jekyll and Hyde characteristic. The question of whether Doyle was an alcoholic would not particularly have crossed my mind, because then I would have been asking other unpleasant questions of myself. He had a good mind – that was one thing that attracted me to him. He was not just a bruiser or a boxer and one felt that he could have played many parts. The question is: Was he a rascal only because of the booze or was the real man a rascal? My impression of Doyle is that basically he was a man with a good brain, that he had an excellent sense of humour and, like many Irishmen, he was willing to sacrifice truth to wit and thought wit more admirable than humour, whereas the English think humour more admirable than wit. He tended to go for remarks that were witty rather than for situations that were humorous. Still, you had a very good laugh. I felt also that there was a kindly streak, that he was in favour of the underdog and that he was in a way a tragedy, because he could have done very useful things with all the abilities with which he had been endowed.

My children quite liked him. And I remember him coming to a party I gave right at the end of 1951. Hugh Dalton, who used to be the Chancellor, and Terence Donovan (Lord Donovan), who was a great friend of mine, and all that lot were there. Lord Van-Sittart, another great pal of mine, was also present. Hugh Dalton didn't like Doyle particularly, though he was a big man physically; he wasn't quite as keen on him as the rest. He said, "Why are you hanging about with Jack Doyle?" But he was the only one that did.

I wouldn't say Doyle was one of my closest friends, but the reason I liked him was that he had this marvellous presence and that he had many facets to his character. At the time I knew him he was more or less finished, but he had an open nature which was attractive. It's very difficult to say why you like someone, but I did like him; there was a sort of natural affinity between us. I was a very heavy drinker at the time: my house was in Paddington and I drank in the pubs nearby. If I were meeting someone at Claridge's and Jack was with me I would have been quite willing to take him along and I might well have done – I can't remember. He was dressed quite well on the occasions he met me; in fact, I can't remember any occasion when he wasn't. Most times he would have a carnation in his button-hole. And apart from the libel case, he never tried to sponge on me.

In those days I was behaving in such a way that I would have paid for the drinks. But if he had money he would buy drinks – no question about that. I think once or twice I may have given him something and then saw that he immediately bought everyone a drink in the whole bar. So I said, "Jack, that's bloody stupid." He laughed it off, but the laugh was not exactly the laugh of an Irishman. Jack would usually be short of money, but then if he got some it would be drinks all round.

Doyle always told me he was a coward. Everyone else had told me he was a coward and he said. "Yes, I am." I think he only said that to agree with everybody else*. "They call me a coward," he said, "but I'd like to see some

*That Jack should have subscribed to the popular view as far as his supposed cowardice was concerned was a surprising act of self-effacement. His fights with Jack Pettifer and Moise Bouquillon surely explode the myth that he was a coward. In addition, he had refused to quit against Buddy Baer when taking a hiding. Even against Chris Cole he did not go down.

of them in the ring with these chaps – they'd run quicker than I did." He also told me he did not want to get himself knocked about. Muhammad Ali reminded me of him in many ways.

Ours was a drinking friendship, really. And jokes. And Ireland. He wasn't very good on the subject, but I already liked the Irish. I ended up having more Irish friends than friends of my own country. I've always liked Irishmen tremendously. I don't want to overdo the wit – the man wasn't a Nye Bevan – but I think it is much more important than people realise. He had a nice smile and the situation could be good fun. He never chased women – not while I was around. He was always talking of Movita. He had the time of his life with her. She was more than the great love of his life; she was the great part of his life. The real joy of his life had been this period when he had been with her.

It could have been the liquor that made him knock her about or it could have been a sadistic streak. It's a little difficult because I'm very sensitive on these things and I find it impossible to believe I could have been friends with anyone who was a sadist. He said the great mistake of his life was parting with her; he genuinely thought this. The overriding impression I had was that Movita had meant everything to him.

He can't have been all that bad or Nancy would never have stood for it; he couldn't have been really terrible. He was very fortunate to have that girl. I said, "You must treat Nancy better than you do because she's a jolly nice girl." I felt rather ashamed about that; I didn't know that he knocked her about, although he more or less implied that he did. I was horrified, but he denied it was anything serious. And then he made out that she didn't mind and that generally women didn't mind – and that was rubbish. I think he knew that this would offend me a great deal and he did honestly keep it out of the way. On this one occasion when we did have a discussion [on Jack's attitude to women], I said, "Nonsense! You've got it quite wrong. Women don't like that kind of thing." And I said, "And I don't like it either." And then he said, "Well, let's not take it too seriously." You see, he was very good at sliding away. And then it was "Let's have a drink," and it was on to something else.

He was not a vulgar person or anything like that, or crude. I'm not a prude, but he knew my attitude on the subject and never while I was with him did he ever make remarks that I could object to. I'm not talking about ordinary swearing; I'm talking about material that was clearly and obviously introduced as being salacious and is not funny. Of course, if the thing is funny it's a different matter – then the object of the story is to have a laugh.

To sum up on Jack, it was not only the booze. You knew there was a defect in the character, which I would describe as being lack of serious purpose of any kind. I had the feeling always that he would have been first-class had he remained in the Army.'

Chapter 3
Dearest Mr. Blarney

It was 1959. As London's Irish dance halls throbbed to the beat of showbands, romantic ballads held little appeal for a new, robust generation of expatriates. To them, Jack Doyle was a name from the past. Now in his mid-forties, he was reduced to singing in the pubs around Shepherd's Bush and Notting Hill.

Yet even for a forgotten hero there were to be occasional forays back to the glamorous world he had left behind. He felt wanted again when given the opportunity to cut his first record in nearly twenty years. He had been rediscovered by Cork-born music man Pat Sherlock, who heard him singing at a christening in London's Kilburn and realised the old voice retained much of its charm. He agreed to help Jack get back in the limelight:

> 'I was working for a music publishing company as a professional manager and song plugger. I knew Jack casually and after hearing him sing we got talking. Things weren't going too well for him at the time; he mentioned he'd like to make a record and I agreed to help. He wanted to sing his usual John McCormack songs, but I told him to forget it. Those days were gone.'

Jack proved how seriously he viewed his re-emergence as a recording artist by taking lessons from an Italian tenor, Dino Borgioli. The voice that once enchanted a legion of fans had become deeper and coarser but he wanted to be at his McCormack-inspired best – even if prevented from singing the man's songs.

Accompanied by the twenty-five-strong Wimbledon Girls' Choir, he recorded *On the Shores of Bantry Bay* and *In My Father's House* in a Mayfair studio. Sherlock financed the hire of the studio, the choir and a six-piece and the disc was released through Decca. Jack received no payment, but was on a royalty percentage if the record did well. He appeared on ITV's *Let's Go* and various sports programmes to promote it, but the hoped-for boost the record's success would have given his fading career never materialised. The charts were dominated by American artists like Bill Haley, Elvis Presley, Buddy Holly, Eddie Cochran and The Everly Brothers and by British stars like Cliff

Richard, Marty Wilde and Adam Faith. The rock-'n'-roll era was in full swing and Jack's record never stood a chance.

Sherlock, who has since severed his connection with the music business, concedes there was little expectation of success in terms of sales:

> 'The record wasn't aimed at a specific market or audience. That's not why it was made. The idea was to help Jack secure some stage work and nothing more. It was a gesture – an effort to get him some recognition. I don't really know how things worked out for him after that. I went off to the US to work and we gradually lost touch.'

There were to be yet further excursions back into the world of the rich and famous. In 1964 Butty Sugrue floated the idea of Jack joining forces with the British, Commonwealth and European champion Henry Cooper for a tour of Ireland – ostensibly with the aim of unearthing a new home-grown heavyweight hope. Butty's brainwave of bringing together the two biggest luminaries in British boxing – past and present – was smiled upon benignly by Cooper's shrewd and venerable manager Jim Wicks. He could see no harm at all in Henry being paid handsomely for keeping fit while awaiting his next fight – and having a pleasant time in Ireland into the bargain. He gave his agreement, but not before uttering those classic, time-honoured words, 'Money up front!' It wasn't that Wicks mistrusted Sugrue in any sense, more that he trusted nobody but himself where the welfare of his boxers was concerned.

Though cash had clearly been the prime consideration, it is doubtful he would have agreed to the tour had it involved anyone other than Jack Doyle. Wicks, who had a long association with Dan Sullivan, was one of Jack's greatest admirers and claimed to have been instrumental in his discovery at the Star and Garter in Windsor thirty-three years earlier.

According to Henry Cooper (now Sir Henry, OBE), Wicks and Sullivan were in attendance when Jack sparred with Len Harvey as a young guardsman. Wicks had told him:

> 'Jack hit Harvey on the whiskers and Harvey staggered. When he got back to his corner, I said to him, "What happened there, Len? Was it a slip?" Harvey replied, "Slip? I've never been hit so hard in all my life!" That persuaded us to buy Jack out of the Army.'

The account varies somewhat from the version given by Florence Harvey and confirmed by Gilbert Odd, but this and the many other Jack Doyle stories related by Wicks over the years – 'The Dodge woman followed him all over the world' – meant that Jack had assumed legendary status in Cooper's eyes. Henry had met him once in London

– 'He came into Simpson's for lunch with a lady on his arm' – and he felt he already knew him quite well by the time the tour of Ireland started.

Cooper confesses he was unaware of any supposed search for an Irish heavyweight hope. He says the tour programme consisted of a variety show comprising Irish dancers and six chorus girls, with Jack singing and he and twin brother George – who boxed professionally as Jim Cooper – doing sparring exhibitions and training routines:

> 'It was a good show and it started well. We kicked off with a couple of dates at the Mansion House in Dublin in front of two to three thousand people. Then we did three or four appearances in country places. The guy responsible for the publicity was supposed to go into each town a week or so before our arrival and set things up, but he wasn't getting there until the day before and the whole thing just fell apart. In the end it was a disaster and we all came home. We were well paid, so it made no difference to us financially. Jack was a handsome guy and a lovely fellow – a real character. We got on well with him, but he had a drink problem and he started hitting the bottle when the tour went wrong. As far as his boxing career was concerned, he was a fool to himself. He had a big right-hand punch and could have beaten anybody. But he liked a good time. He liked the ladies too much. If he hadn't been so good-looking, who knows what he might have achieved?'

Jack had again tasted fame, but the trappings of success he once took for granted had slipped tantalisingly beyond reach. They were the unattainable baubles of a bygone age. His slender consolation was the certain knowledge that the heady days of the past would be remembered with affection by those he had known. Delphine Dodge's daughter, Christine Cromwell, was one who would never forget and she wrote him a string of letters professing her love.

Christine admitted that Jack was the first and greatest love of her life and her correspondence bore witness. In 1963 she sent him a colour photo of her and her father inscribed: 'Love to Jack, who has ever been in my thoughts. Christine.' Although twenty-eight years had elapsed since she vied with her mother for Jack's body and soul, the passions aroused in her were such that she had never been able to find true and lasting happiness with anyone else.

In the mid-1960s Christine was a property-owning resident in the British Virgin Islands. She also had a yacht, from which she operated a fishing enterprise with two partners. The first letter to her 'Mr. Blarney' was dated May 1, 1965, and there were shades of Judith Allen's poetic touch enshrined in its breathless message:

'Darling –

My goodness I need you so badly. What twist of fate is it that keeps us apart? Not long now, tho [sic] – My love, dearest Mr. Blarney.'

She signed herself simply 'C.'

It appeared that Christine, then forty-two, was as deeply in love with Jack as ever, although it is doubtful he was of the same persuasion. At this time he would not have been interested in her body and still less her intellect. He would have been after one thing only: her money. This was evident from her second communication, a long-winded missive in which she claimed to have been badly beaten by one of her partners in the fishing enterprise she was running between Barbados and San Juan. It transpired she had been in touch with Jack by telephone and, reading between the lines, the inescapable conclusion is that he had pleaded poverty to her. Her letter read in part:

'My very dearest Mr. Blarney,

Dear God above it was wonderful to talk to you, but my distress as to why I called you this time has made a mercyless [sic] ache in my heart for you. Perhaps some day I can make this up to you just a little bit.

Let me express my very deep hurt for you, and say again I will help you all I can. Please keep good care of yourself for you and for me. Altho [sic] there is a good friend here, my needs have been for you.

My love and affection and my heartfelt sympathy – there's still life for us yet.'

Again she signed off with a simple C.

Whether Christine did indeed render Jack financial assistance is doubtful. Nancy Kehoe could not recall him receiving a sum of money from the Virgin Islands or anywhere else for that matter. She was working as a waitress at the Cumberland Hotel at the time and though she may have been unaware of much of what went on in his life she could not have failed to notice had he become suddenly and significantly better off.

It appears, too, that the ache in Christine's heart was not so 'mercyless' as to send her rushing to Jack's side. Her words had echoed sentiment rather than intent; they were written in recognition of a love for him that was still alive in spirit but dead in practicality. All contact between them then ceased. Whatever feelings they held for each other faded once more into distant memory.

By now Jack was making no attempt to hide the fact he was a kept man. Everyone who knew them realised Nancy was working to clothe and feed him; there was no pretence, no effort to keep up appearances. It highlighted the least attractive side to Jack's nature and character.

Even his trips to the dog tracks were largely subsidised. His beneficiary in this connection was not Nancy but one Adele Foreshaw, an eccentric old lady to whom Jack acted as a kind of escort and who, in her own way, was as besotted with Jack as a 1930s groupie. 'Lady' Foreshaw, as she was known, lived above the White Elephant Club in Curzon Street and was allegedly married to a professor. She was all Victorian-type dresses and jewellery and wore a patch over one eye, though no one could be quite sure if this was not part of her wardrobe. According to Tim Doyle and others, she would pick up Jack in a hired Rolls Royce and transport him to Wembley or White City. She would then seat herself at the bar, buy Jack drinks all evening and facilitate his gambling. Mostly he placed her bets on his selections in the knowledge that if his dog won he could pocket the money and keep quiet about it. When on the rare occasions her dog won, he would offer a plausible excuse about having misinterpreted her instructions – 'I was sure you said put it all on trap six' – or tell her he had been given the wrong tote tickets – 'I must remember to check them in future.'

Lady Foreshaw, who referred to Jack as 'my boyfriend', was up to all his deft manoeuvres. She came to accept the situation with good grace – almost as if she expected to be deceived and would have been disappointed had he behaved differently. It was a little game they played between themselves, but it was not only they who were privy to it. Scores of racegoers witnessed their amusing semi-public charades, which usually ended with Lady Foreshaw proclaiming, 'What a rascal! But he's so sweet with it.'

Jack sometimes visited her at her spacious Mayfair flat. Being well into her seventies, it is said she did not require sex with him but, instead, liked him to lay nude with her on the bed as a kind of love-act without consummation. Jack obliged out of a sense of duty or enlightened self-interest and she considered it to be a sufficient test of his commitment to her. Whenever his visits to her became spasmodic, as was inevitable, she would pretend to scold him, saying, 'Where have you been, Jack? Have you been a naughty boy?'

'No, my dear. I've been entertaining my friends from California.'

'If I find you've been a naughty boy, Jack, I'll kill you, you know that.'

Jack always had a twinkle in his eye at such moments. 'She's good for £20 a week,' he would confide to friends.

Apparently he had been waiting for Lady Foreshaw's husband to die so he could cash in on the fortune he suspected she possessed; but his plan misfired when she was inconsiderate enough to pop off first.

Nancy never minded his association with Lady Foreshaw, having correctly deduced that a physical aspect to the relationship was unlikely. As far as she was concerned it was nothing more than a pleasant companionship focused on their mutual interest in greyhound racing – even if he barely concealed the fact he was taking the old girl for all he could get.

It would not have mattered what Nancy thought anyway: Jack just pleased himself. Her easy-going nature induced him to treat her as little more than a skivvy. He was undeniably fond of her, but the fact she would stand for almost any kind of demeaning treatment in the name of love made it impossible for her to command his respect. One prime example was her apparent approval of his association with Myrtle Rickard.

'Ricky' was formerly a friend of the transvestite April Ashley, who enjoyed brief celebrity during the 1950s after undergoing a sex-change operation. She met Jack in his favourite pub, The Hoop, and shortly afterwards moved into a flat at 32 Pembridge Gardens. Jack and Nancy's furnished apartment in the basement was equipped with a double and single bed and Nancy arrived home one night to find good use had been made of the former by Jack and Ricky, who had fallen into a deep sleep after their exertions. A potentially explosive situation arose when Ricky's aggressive boyfriend came knocking for her at three in the morning. 'Have you seen Ricky?' he asked of Nancy. 'No,' she replied nervously. 'I've no idea where she is.' That diplomatic side-step prevented Jack becoming embroiled in a punch-up that would have woken the whole street.

On the surface, Nancy's acceptance of Ricky was an act of extraordinary generosity; but there was another side to it. Nancy was constantly worried about Jack's well-being and his whereabouts. She never knew from one day to the next quite where he would be or with whom he would be associating. So it came as something of a relief to her when Ricky moved in and began accompanying him on his itinerary of the pubs and bringing him home safely. Nancy settled for that: it took a huge weight from her shoulders. And if, as she had found out, there was more to the friendship than had at first appeared, she turned a blind eye to it in pursuit of a peaceful life.

Surprisingly, Ricky refuted suggestions that her relationship with Jack had been of a sexual nature, in spite of the testimony of Nancy and Jack's closest associates to the contrary. She claimed he merely used her as an alibi in order to meet other women: 'Nancy naturally thought he was with me, but most of the time he was with someone else.'

Ricky was involved in the sequel to Jack's infamous conviction for stealing two pieces of cheese from MacFisheries supermarket in Church Street, Kensington, in the spring of 1966. The incident received widespread publicity laced liberally with predictable anti-boxing propaganda. The theme was a familiar one. It depicted the once wealthy fighter who had been forced to break the law to survive after falling on hard times.

The truth is that the offence was a put-up job from start to finish. It was committed on the strength of a half-promise elicited from the mass-circulation *Sunday Mirror*, which was prepared to run a series of articles on Jack provided he once again became 'newsworthy'. Forgotten ex-fighters down on their luck always make good copy for newspapers, especially one who, as in this instance, had enjoyed unparalleled fame.

Jack's 'I stole the food because I was hungry' line following a £5 fine at West London Court was a thinly-disguised attempt at drumming up publicity for the serialisation and he continued in the same vein:

> 'Listen you rich, famous young buckos. Listen when I beg you: Don't be like me. Don't be mugs. Don't start believing what the fans say. And don't make too many friends. I earned more than a quarter-of-a-million pounds before I was thirty – and they were real pounds, pre-war pounds, worth about six of today's. And now look what has happened to me as a man of fifty-two.'

There is no suggestion that the *Sunday Mirror* urged or even faintly prompted Jack to commit an offence; but having in effect advised him to get back in the news, they could not have been altogether surprised when he was hauled in for shoplifting. The absurd irony of it all was that Jack was forced to report the theft himself after failing to attract the attention of members of staff, even though he was blatantly 'stealing'. Nancy, too, confirmed that he never went hungry: 'I always cooked enough for four.'

According to Scottish former song-and-dance man Dave Rowan, who first met Jack during his appearances north of the border when known by his stage name Eddie Bond and became good friends with him in London in the 1950s and 1960s, the supermarket manager knew Jack well and would never have pressed charges. Others claimed that a Press photographer was in position half-an-hour beforehand to picture Jack being nabbed, though they could not confirm if he was asked to smile and say 'Cheese!' The fact he had more than £4 on him when arrested makes a mockery of the suggestion that he could not afford to pay for the cheese, the value of which was just three shillings and sixpence (the equivalent of 17½p).

Ricky Rickard recalls that the *Sunday Mirror* booked Jack and Nancy into the President Hotel in Central London shortly after the court appearance:

> 'Everything was on the house, including drinks. I was in an adjoining room and the place was crowded with photographers. The next day we all went to

the *Sunday Mirror* offices. They gave Jack £100 spending money, a chauffeur-driven car and a guide and told him to have a pleasant day out on them.'

Dublin journalist Dermot McEvoy claimed that Jack received £200 a week during the running of the story, saying: 'He couldn't have cared less what they wrote as long as he got his money. That was all he was concerned about.'

Chapter 4

Appointment with Brando

The announcer's voice boomed over Wembley's public address: 'Would Mr. Jack Doyle please contact the main stadium office, where a message awaits him.' Jack had been situated as usual in the stadium's Long Bar, holding court in majesterial manner in that unmistakable, rich, resonant Irish voice, so full of authority that it defied dissension. He must have wondered what could have been so important as to warrant contacting him in the middle of a greyhound meeting.

There was an urgent telephone call. Waiting on the line was Marlon Brando, in England to make *A Countess of Hong Kong* at Elstree with Sophia Loren – the first full-length colour feature film to be directed by Charlie Chaplin. Brando told Jack he wanted very much to meet him. There was an important matter to discuss. Would he care to have lunch on the set next day? It did not take much of a deduction on Jack's part to realise the topic of conversation would be Movita. Quite what Brando would be seeking from him or what he would be wishing to impart in connection with her was a mystery, but Jack's antenna was tuned finely enough to indicate that the right answers to the right questions might be distinctly to his advantage. He decided he would take Butty Sugrue along, if only for moral support. Though he would not have been suffering stage fright, Butty was solid and dependable and the right man to have by your side in such circumstances.

Brando was courteous, if a little curious. He had been anxious to meet Jack, not alone to establish what manner of man he was but in connection with certain information he wished to gather. He confirmed he had married Movita in Mexico in 1960 and was now seeking a divorce. In particular he wanted clarification from Jack that the Dublin marriage had never been annulled by the Catholic church – as the desperate Movita had once so earnestly sought – and confirmation that Movita's Mexican divorce had been in respect only of the initial civil ceremony in Ensenada. That being the case, it meant her marriage to Brando would not be officially recognised in any other country – a powerful factor in any future alimony negotiations*.

* Anna Kashfi, whom Brando married in 1957 during an interlude in his relationship with Movita, received a $500 000 property settlement under the terms of her divorce two years later after alleging 'grievous mental suffering, distress and injury'.

According to various sources, Brando made his pleasure manifestly evident by paying Jack $10 000*. Though there is no confirmation that this or any other figure was handed over, such a sum could be considered cheap at the price. Jack's testimony would have been of inestimable value to Brando in enabling him to dictate the terms of any financial settlement with Movita.

It was a pleasant get-together at Elstree, and why not? Brando had been given the news he had wanted to hear. Sophia Loren joined them for lunch and Chaplin expressed his pleasure at being able to renew acquaintance with Jack, whom he first met in Hollywood in the thirties. 'The last time I saw you, you were in bed with my wife,' he said to him. If there was any grain of truth in that remark, Paulette Goddard denied it vehemently when tackled in New York about an association with Jack. 'I hardly knew the man,' she claimed indignantly. 'He took me to lunch once or twice – that's all.'

Though Brando was sweetness and light to Jack at Elstree – and later at a London party attended by both men – in essence he was far from enamoured of him. Movita claims he sneeringly asked her on his return to America: 'How could you possibly have become involved with a man like that? How could you have married him?' She responded by telling him: 'Jack may have gone downhill in the years since we parted, but when I knew him he was the most handsome man in the world.'

Movita claims she decided not to fight Brando for a cash settlement in the US courts in the knowledge that her Mexican divorce from Jack would not have stood up:

> 'What chance would I have had against his lawyers? And besides, I didn't want the publicity to affect my children [she also has a daughter, Rebecca]. So in the end I said to Marlon, "Just do what you want. I don't care any more. Arrange things whatever way you wish."'†

Nancy Kehoe confirmed that Movita had sought Jack's consent to divorce proceedings and that the communication was studiously ignored. It invites the conclusion that Movita was shabbily treated

*Sir Atholl Oakeley revealed that he saw a letter from Brando offering Jack $100 000 if he would divorce Movita. This was in the early 1950s, shortly after Brando had met her. Now, in complete contrast, he was apparently rewarding him for having *not* divorced her.

† Brando obtained an annulment of the marriage in July 1968 at the Superior Court in Santa Monica after a hearing so secret that the court records were ordered to be sealed at the request of both parties. Judge Edward R. Brand granted the annulment because 'Miss Castaneda's husband [Jack Doyle] was still alive and she had not been legally divorced from him.' The closed-door hearing was to protect the couple's children from scandal.

all round. If nothing else, her selfless agreement to the Dublin wedding in an effort to restore Jack's career and reputation deserved a better fate.

It can be said also that Nancy deserved a better fate, as Jack's refusal to divorce Movita meant they would never be wed. Perhaps the issue assumed diminishing significance as the years passed, since the damage had already been done. She had become a two-time loser since teaming up with him. Her family, appalled that she was living with a married man, refused to have anything more to do with her. And life with Jack would bring more misery than happiness.

Nancy considered herself as good as married to him anyway. The words love, honour and obey could not have been more honestly and sincerely adhered to had they been uttered in church as part of the wedding vows. She was a generous, trusting companion who dutifully washed and cooked and provided for Jack in every way until his dependence on her was total.

Nancy was both a saint and a fool for enduring his incessant drinking, gambling and womanising without complaint. She denied that he beat her – as Raymond Blackburn had deduced from his conversations with Jack – but if he didn't, the reason can only be that never loved her with anything like the intensity with which he had loved Movita. Theirs was no union of burning desire and flashpoint jealousy; it was a partnership of convenience based on need. Jack's need. It was also one played out not on the world stage but in the drab solitude of various nondescript flats and bedsits in West London. Though Nancy was some dozen years younger than Jack, he regarded her more as a provider than an equal-sharing partner – more mother than lover. Their relationship was sexual to a degree, but one that served basic requirements rather than one fuelled by mutual desire.

That Nancy performed the role of surrogate mother to Jack may not have been unconnected with the fact that she was the only Irish woman with whom he had maintained more than a passing relationship. She was tiny like his mother, behaved like a mother and displayed all the strengths and attributes normally exhibited by a loving mother cursed with a wayward son: loyalty, protectiveness and reliability, the knack of always being there when needed, despite invariably being used and abused, and finally – and possibly most important – being a provider.

In every respect Nancy was a mother figure*, particularly in the way

* Nancy never became a *real* mother. Jack latterly was unable to father a child – the legacy of syphilis.

she was acutely aware of Jack's shortcomings and deceptions but put up with them without complaint. By tolerating Ricky Rickard because she knew where Jack would be when he was with her, she was behaving precisely like a fiercely protective mother. She was not the 'placid imbecile' she was depicted to be by a former journalist friend of Jack's, but had merely settled realistically for what life with Jack would offer – a companionship of sorts, someone to look after and care for and a feeling of being needed. Nothing imbecilic about that.

Further, she possessed the qualities of humanity and loyalty that are bound up in Irish consciousness and solidarity and which are revealed strongly in expatriates – a fusion of patriotism and friendship which outwardly seems sentimental but is in fact real. To Jack she represented all of this; he knew it and valued it even though he cheated and mistreated her. She was, too, an essential source of support and perhaps even esteem – a memory of his own mother and a link with Ireland. Both must have been important to him or – despite self-interest – he would never have stayed with her.

For a time Jack and Nancy resided at No. 30 Campden Hill Gardens, where Harold Pinter once lived with his former actress wife, the late Vivien Merchant, and from where he was inspired to write *The Caretaker*, *The Basement* and *The Dumb Waiter*. According to George Thomas, caretaker at the premises during Jack's tenure there, he was sometimes visited by the renowned tenor Josef Locke, whom he claimed to have discovered when touring Northern Ireland with Movita. Locke was then supposedly a member of the Royal Ulster Constabulary. The story goes that Jack had been so impressed when he heard the big policeman sing that he made him part of the tour, thus setting him on the road to stardom. Thomas recalled Locke 'kipping down' with Jack at No. 30 and the two men startling neighbours with an impromptu concert while sitting on the steps outside, obviously the worse for drink. Thomas also remembered that after moving out, Jack would often turn up drunk in a taxi late at night believing he still lived there.

Locke, who died in Clane, Co Kildare, in 1999 at the age of 82, disputed the story surronding his discovery by Jack and Movita. He claimed he first met Jack when serving as a young recruit in the Irish Guards at Caterham:

> 'Jack used to come back and visit his old unit. That's how we met. The stories about him discovering me as a singing copper are rubbish.'

As revealed by George Thomas and others, Locke confirmed that he kept in touch with Jack over the years and visited him periodically in

Notting Hill. 'He was on my pension list,' he admitted, which is a way of saying he regularly gave Jack money.

Another well-known figure with whom Jack became acquainted was the late writer and broadcaster Patrick Campbell, a mild-mannered man of great wit and charm who managed to turn a speech impediment to his advantage by making it his trademark on TV talk shows. Campbell often wrote satirically about Jack in the popular magazine *Lilliput*. One such piece bemoaned that fact that he was thinking of leaving the Bayswater area because 'the first person I bump into each morning is Jack Doyle, still drunk from the night before.' According to Nancy, Jack did not see the funny side of it: 'He was very annoyed when he read it.' Campbell, however, was extremely fond of Jack – a fact he illustrated when Jack phoned him saying he required the immediate loan of £200 to settle a dog racing debt. Campbell obliged, knowing full well that he stood more chance of being struck by lightning than getting his money back.

Dermot McEvoy felt Jack was torn between two compulsions – drinking and gambling:

> 'In the end gambling triumphed over drink. Jack was still a reckless spender whenever he got hold of money, but he always seemed able to save something for betting. It was his mania. He had some big wins for small stakes, but he lost overall. And all the time Nancy was paying the rent and buying the food.'

Whenever funds were low, Jack had ways of 'persuading' people to give him money. His favourite was to follow them to the Gents at public houses, put a huge arm round their shoulders and request the loan of a small sum of money – the very conduct Raymond Blackburn had been unable to believe of his friend.* It was as near to demanding money with menaces as you could get, but Jack had perfected the execution of this art to the degree that the threat was contained in the unspoken word and the pseudo-friendly arm that weighed heavy as timber on their visibly wilting shoulders. Such was Jack's size and reputation that few people felt disinclined to cough up, even young Irishmen on The Lump whom Jack regularly strong-armed at The Boilerhouse, a once notorious drinking club in Paddington, and at The Fiesta, a strip-club that was situated beneath the Brigade Club in Notting Hill.

This, then, was the public persona of a man whose behaviour had at one time been the quintessence of charm and civility. Yet somehow he still managed to enjoy celebrity status around those various parts of

* It happened to the late David Thompson – author of *Woodbrook* – who occasionally drank with Jack.

Bayswater that had become his stamping ground; with few exceptions, the locals loved this dishevelled rogue who, in Emerson's words, saw a certain alienated majesty in the life's role to which he was now reduced.

The manner in which he acted out this role was prompted by the knowledge that, wherever he went, people would want to buy him a bevvy and get him to recall his glory days. That being so, all he ever needed when he went to a pub was what he termed his entrance fee – the price of a half-pint of bitter. Having installed himself with this modest tipple in front of him, the drinks would come thick and fast from strangers keen to make his acquaintance and friends who liked to ensure his glass was never empty. Only they never put him up halves of bitter – they sent over Scotches and brandies, and mostly they were doubles. Inevitably, as the evening wore on, Jack would become paralytic – and then the fun would start. He could be amusing or boorish, philosophical or aggressive, sometimes a combination of all four. But it was never a vicious aggression; usually it would take the form of a push or a shove, when he would more than likely miss and keel over on the floor himself. On one occasion when emphasising a point, he brought down his big fist and shattered his glass, cutting his hand to the bone in the process.

Jack's legion of friends and acquaintances are too numerous to mention. There were dozens who enjoyed his company, who watched out for him, who gave him a helping hand when he needed it – which mostly was all the time. They included people like his doctor, Brian Dempsey, a fellow-Irishman whose surname rather than his medical skills must first have persuaded Jack to sign on with him. Ironically, Dempsey was one member of Jack's inner circle who had known nothing of the background to his shop-lifting escapade. Feeling deeply sorry for him, he sent him £20 to tide him over.

There was Michael Mannion, the late self-styled Bard of Kensington; there was TV actor Oliver McGreevy, there was Butty Sugrue, there was old Arthur . . . and there was Gerald Egan, loyal to the last.

Egan so loved Jack that he was still star-struck when the Gael was in his late fifties and early sixties and croaking out his apologies of songs in pubs like The Wellington in Shepherd's Bush, owned ironically by teetotaller Butty Sugrue. As far as Egan was concerned, Jack could do no wrong. To him he was still the amazing specimen of a man who had wooed and conquered London in the thirties; still the ultimate playboy of the Western world whom men admired and women drooled over; still the famous Jack Doyle of everyone's imagination.

He never tired of dreaming up stunts he felt might catapult his hero back into the big-time, where he felt he had always belonged. He even managed to get some decent publicity out of an announcement that Jack was ready to make yet another boxing comeback, with a willingness to take on over three rounds any former professional aged between fifty-five and fifty-eight. Egan arranged a photo-session at Jack Solomons' West End gymnasium and trumpeted: 'It would be a sell-out. Don't forget Jack drew 100 000 to White City in the days before there was TV.'

Jack had remembered how to play the publicity game, vowing: 'It will be a real fight. One of us will end up on the floor and it won't be me.' In truth, talking a good fight was now about the best Jack could do. He sparred a few ponderous rounds with former Irish champion Pat Mulcahy and a useful American, Freddie Mack, and there was even mention of Eddie Phillips, Tommy Farr and Len Harvey as possible opponents.

'Win or lose I'll give the customers a song,' he said, just as in the old days, except these weren't the old days. This was 1970 and Jack was a flabby fifty-seven-year-old has-been. There was no chance of his being permitted to box again. Not surprisingly, the whole idea was labelled a farce.

Jack's mind was making appointments his body couldn't keep.

Chapter 5

Nancy lands the KO

Jack Doyle made more stage comebacks than Frank Sinatra and Dame Nellie Melba put together. While there was breath in his body and an audience willing to hear him, he would never cease to regard himself as one of the great entertainers. There was still no shortage of promoters queuing to cash in on his name in Ireland, perhaps surprisingly so in view of his advanced years and the many disasters that had befallen him. The most recent had been the 1964 variety tour embarked upon in company with Henry Cooper, when it appeared the old name had lost its magic. Now, a decade on, he was being invited back for a new tour that would exceed all expectations by lasting nine months.

Disgraced and in despair he may have been in the aftermath of his stormy marriage to Movita; hurt and humiliated he most certainly was when the Cooper tour took the count. But time heals, time forgives and time retains mostly pleasant memories. Although twenty-five years had elapsed since Nancy Kehoe delivered him from destitution in Dublin, such was the clamour to see him again that sometimes half-a-dozen agents at a time were attempting to book his services. The fact that his voice sounded more like deep baritone than soft tenor made no difference as far as his popularity was concerned; it was as if the people sensed they were getting their last glimpse of Jack in any capacity. As long as he made the effort to sing – no matter how off-key – it was enough to guarantee him a wonderful ovation.

Not a night passed without him being besieged by enthusiastic admirers. Some were his committed fans from the old days; the younger ones were merely curious. But they all wanted to shake his hand, buy him a drink and be able to talk about the day they met the great Jack Doyle. Dave Guiney recalls:

> 'During this tour and the previous short-lived expedition with Henry Cooper, waitresses in hotels greeted Doyle with words like, "Welcome back to Ireland. I remember serving you when you were last here." Doyle would reply, "Of course – I remember you too, dear." It was all false, but he did it with great charm. They were convinced he remembered them.'

The crack was best in Cobh, where, in company with his former boyhood pals, he relived the past through a blissful alcoholic haze, revisiting all the familiar haunts he had once held so dear. Huge crowds followed him from pub to pub, and on entering each he would boom: 'The drinks are on Jack Doyle!' The taverns buzzed with excited talk as the whiskey and the Guinness flowed but, according to Nancy, Jack's big-hearted gestures were never backed up by hard cash. He would leave as quickly and suddenly as he had entered, forgetting all about paying for the huge rounds he had ordered so magnanimously. The landlords and hoteliers forced to foot the bill for his generosity never hounded him for the money; they could forgive him anything and, besides, he had brought them great business.

The old town had changed. Inevitably so. Dear, kind, lovable Tim McCarthy had long since departed for a better world. Mrs. Flanagan, who lived next door in Cottrell's Row and had been such a help to them all, had assuredly gone to the same resting place. Proud Uncle Joe, who had always been more than generous with the Soldier's Duff and latterly lived with Jack's parents in England, was also gone. Nothing stays the same forever. Those of his schoolfriends and playmates in the Holy Ground who were still of this world had, like Jack, grown old as time itself until all they had to feed on were memories.

Perhaps Jack should have stayed in Ireland, where he was known and loved and where there would always be a helping hand in times of trouble. Instead he elected to return to London, a town without pity for those who are down on their luck. He could count on the odd fiver or tenner from his friends and acquaintances in the pubs around Shepherd's Bush and Bayswater, but in other respects the capital could be a cruel and lonely location for a forgotten hero. Yet his love affair with London knew no bounds; it paid no heed to the twin evils of misery and despair. For him it had a magic all of its own. He loved the pace, the cheery street traders, the anonymous crowds, the lovely young girls who – unlike a few decades ago – never gave him a second glance.

On their return from Ireland, Jack and Nancy moved into a £12-a-week basement bedsit at 45 Kendal Street, just off Marble Arch, and once again he became a familiar figure in the area. His patch stretched west from the Edgware Road in Paddington and down through Bayswater to Butty Sugrue's pub, The Wellington. His day invariably started at his new local, the Duke of Kendal. He would then drift down to Notting Hill for a drink at the Prince Albert or The Hoop, collecting his regulation red carnation on the way.

In the afternoons he gambled – a few shillings or, if he was flush, a few pounds on the dogs and horses. Then it was back home to play endless games of patience or sit glued to the television. His day would end with yet another visit to the pubs. The thick black hair that had once been such a striking feature of his youthful good looks was grey now and his fingers stained yellow by nicotine. He smoked constantly – sixty cigarettes a day and, if he could get one, a cigar. Whenever he won on the dogs, he didn't tell Nancy. On one occasion a huge wad of notes fell from his pocket. She saw him counting it – and he had the gall to ask her for more.

Jack gradually lost all semblance of dignity. Even his public house entrance fee had become a thing of the past. On the one occasion he was seen to pass a pound note over the counter at the Prince Albert, it was considered an event of such moment that the publican, Phil Fitzsimons, framed it.

Jack began to draw the dole – and even then Nancy provided everything, including his pocket money. Since the death of his mother in 1965* – he was utterly distraught, according to Ted Doyle – her mother-figure role had become so absolute that he was even calling her 'Mummy':

> 'I tried to maintain his self-respect, but I was fighting a losing battle. The only words I heard each day were in the mornings – "Mummy, mummy, baby", or just "Gimme, gimme." I left my job at the Cumberland for a time in an attempt to keep him on the straight and narrow, but all sorts of drunks started knocking for him and I became frightened. They'd stay all night drinking and in the mornings the place would be littered with broken glasses, broken ashtrays, cigarette butts and spilt beer. I warned Jack that I'd leave him if he started drinking cider, but he took no notice. He went on the Merrydown and that was it. At first I tried to hide it or even give it away. I even tipped it down the drain. But it was no good. There was a yard out the back where all the empties used to be stored and the place began to look like a run-down distillery. By this time Jack was never sober and I just couldn't do any more for him. He was beyond help. I knew then that it was time for me to go.'

It says much about Nancy's selfless love for Jack that she was clearly unconcerned about his feelings for her; whether he still loved her – or indeed whether he had ever truly loved her – was immaterial. Her need was to *give* love and the breaking point had come only when she realised there was no further role she could play in Jack's life. Equally important, she was no longer able to cope. Like Movita, her own sanity had been placed at risk.

Nancy left at the end of July, 1976. She got up one morning and went without a word to him. As a safeguard, she changed her job to prevent him making contact. The break had to be ruthless and it had to be final. There could be no going back. Eventually, she telephoned:

> 'I told him, "I've just phoned to say goodbye." He begged me to return, but I said "No" and put the receiver down.'

* Jack's father had died in 1940.

Nancy's departure signalled the beginning of the end for Jack. From then on the rent was left unpaid and, inevitably, an eviction order followed. Brian Dempsey remembers him coming to the surgery in Pembridge Road and saying, 'Nancy has given me the KO. I've nowhere to go. I'm in a terrible state.'

Help was near at hand in the shape of the immensely powerful Butty Sugrue, a man with a generosity of purpose as rock-solid as the monument of Daniel O'Connell in Dublin which he had once tried to purchase for £500. Butty had provided considerable financial backing for Muhammad Ali's clash with Al 'Blue' Lewis in Dublin in 1972 (Ali won in the eleventh round) and was £20 000 out of pocket when the fight flopped at the box-office. He proved what manner of man he was by bearing his loss without complaint. Now he was about to display qualities of loyalty and compassion by accommodating his homeless friend Jack Doyle.

Sadly, Butty's amazing feats of strength over the years had taken their toll of that big heart of his. He dropped down dead when lifting a heavy fridge during renovation work at The Wellington, where often he had paid Jack over the odds in exchange for songs that could have done little for trade at the rambling, vibrant tavern on Shepherd's Bush Green.* Nancy recalled:

> 'Butty had promised to put Jack up at The Wellington following the eviction order. Jack was due to move out from Kendal Street on the Monday, but Butty died suddenly on the Sunday. It was a great blow.'

Jack was utterly devastated. Within the space of a few weeks he had lost possibly the two best friends he'd ever had – one through default and the other through death. They had stood solidly by him with the big-time gone and his popularity on the wane. Nancy had given him her best years and Butty had helped him more often than anyone would know – even to the point of being prepared to give him a home when nobody else would. Both had shown a strength and humanity that was infinitely moving.

For the second time in his life Jack was homeless, but the situation was far more serious than that which had confronted him in Dublin thirty years previously. He was now in his sixties and quite feeble physically after a lifetime of alcoholic abuse. This time he did not even have a broken-down taxi to use as a home. He was forced to live rough.

Only pride could have prevented Jack contacting his family for help. Clearly, he did not wish to burden them. In the event the Doyles were unaware Nancy had left and expressed dismay that she had neglected to

* *The Wellington* no longer exists.

tell them. For her part, Nancy had been loath to inform the family for fear she would incur their wrath. She had also quite naturally assumed that Jack would break the news to them.*

Friends and acquaintances were reluctant to offer Jack accommodation because of the dossers and winos with whom he was associating. His appearance was unkempt. His hair had become dirty and matted. The sartorial splendour for which he was once renowned had given way to ill-fitting clothes which hung loosely from a body that had become emaciated through lack of food. Dave Rowan bought him a suit and some shoes, but being homeless made it impossible for Jack to maintain a dignified presence. 'He used to kip down in the toilets behind The Swan,' recalls Rowan, 'stoned out of his mind on draught cider and Merrydown.'

It was the final humiliation for Jack. When a man of his self-professed vanity ceases to be concerned about the image he projects, then all hope is gone. He looked like any other tramp now – unwanted, unshaven, uncaring, all semblance of esteem gone, all contact with the real world severed.

Jack found a strange solace in the company of the drunken dropouts who had become his friends. There was no need for pretence – no worries about the present or the future. He had descended to a twilight world with no rules or conformity. It was an escape to a wonderland where the only reality was fantasy. Now he was the changeling of the fairies, floating off to vistas of his own choice and his own making. Brian Dempsey recalls him, 'hanging around with his cronies, drinking Merrydown all day long. It was an absolutely terrible sight. His trousers came halfway up his legs and his John Thomas used to hang out.'

Though barred from most pubs in the area, Jack managed to find his way into The Hoop most nights. In spite of his dishevelled state, there was still a sense of camaraderie. He had not been entirely abandoned. People still warmed to him and they still bought him drinks but there was now a limit to how far they were willing to involve themselves with him. It was friendship at arm's length lest they found themselves being asked for the kind of commitment it would have been impossible to give.

On one occasion when sitting in The Hoop, it could be seen that Jack had lost one of his shoes on his lonely travels round the streets. He had no socks on and the exposed foot was bare. An artist of sorts peddling his wares in the pub took pity on him, removed his paintings from their polythene bag and offered it up to the unshod foot. The humour of the situation was not lost on Jack. He placed his foot in the bag and allowed

* Nancy, who suffered from respiratory problems, died in 1986 after an asthma attack. She was sixty.

the artist to fasten it securely with a length of string. He kept the bag on and was still wearing it when he shuffled out of the pub at closing time.

If Jack had retained his ability to laugh at himself, he had retained also the spirit of charity for which he had been so well known in the past. Of late it had tended to be obscured by the strokes he had pulled on others, but he had always been a soft touch for a hard-luck story. Overall he must have parted with thousands of pounds to people he had never met before and certainly would never see again. Children had also been close to his heart. He could refuse them nothing, so it is especially poignant that an acquaintance at the time, London contractor Jerry Quinn, should speak of this act of generosity:

> 'I knew Jack hadn't eaten for days, so I took him home to give him a good square meal. Just as he was leaving I handed him a fiver, but he refused to take it. Instead, he slipped the money under my little daughter's pillow while she was sleeping.'

Jack must have realised he was on the verge of his own long last sleep when he collapsed at The Hoop and was rushed to St Charles' Hospital in Ladbroke Grove. For a time it looked like the final KO, but in true fighting style he beat the count. Soon his bedside locker was stuffed full with notes of every denomination – fivers, tenners, twenties, even fifties, from friends and admirers who had been shocked to learn of his confinement. His brothers, unaware he had been living rough, made arrangements to put him up immediately he was well enough to leave hospital. It seemed he was destined to live out his last remaining days in comfort, surrounded by those who loved him.

It was not to be. Jack suddenly and surprisingly discharged himself and resumed the life of dosser and drunkard. The key to his reason for doing so had been contained in his rejection of Jerry Quinn's fiver a few weeks earlier: he had finally lost the will to live. Money now meant nothing to him. Neither did the prospect of living once more in comfortable surroundings. It was all too late. The gift to Quinn's daughter as she slept could be perceived as an act of penance that would serve in some small way as redemption for past sins. If so, it would have been bound up in Catholic guilt and all its implications of heaven, hell and purgatory – the three possible destinations of the soul, according to how the life on earth is judged. But it is unlikely to have been the case. Jack never doubted that his soul would be going anywhere but to heaven.

The bell had sounded for his final round. Mainly he dossed down under the stars, but occasionally he was lucky enough to find shelter as the cold winter of 1978 began to bite. A Kensington market security guard, Dennis O'Callaghan, saw him one chilly morning leaving the students' hostel in Church Street, barefoot and hungry. The students were on holiday at the time and he had drawn two beds together in the dormitory. He told O'Callaghan he had been unable to find his shoes. The more likely explanation is that he had none.

If the Hollywood stars with whom he had hob-nobbed in the thirties had seen him now, they might not have believed it. Flynn, Gable and Weissmuller had already passed on, but Cagney and O'Brien and the rest would never have dreamed that the man with whom they shared so many good times had met with such an appalling fate.

Ricky Rickard had seen little of Jack since he and Nancy quit the flat in Pembridge Gardens prior to his last tour of Ireland. One night, as she hopped off a No. 28 bus in Notting Hill, she happened to see him outside the Prince Albert. She sensed he was in a bad way:

> 'I said, "Come and have a cup of tea." Jack didn't answer. He collapsed into the doorway of the pub. I got him a whisky and a cigarette. He was muttering away about his sister, Bridie, but I couldn't make out what he was saying. He had shoes on, but no socks – and he had a lot of money on him. He asked me to get him a double brandy. Then he fell asleep, so I had to leave him. Malnutrition and booze. He had never been the same since Nancy walked out. He'd been asking around for her for ages.'

The following day Jack had gone to The Hoop and it was apparent he needed immediate help. John Sullivan, a railway worker and, like Jack, a native of Cork, took pity on him and offered to put him up permanently. 'You can stay for as long as it suits you, Jack,' he told him. It was a gesture rich in compassion and human decency. Sullivan's selflessness and loyalty to a fellow-Irishman was the obverse of Jack's charismatic qualities. One was perhaps inspired by the other. It takes a special kind of person to put aside his own considerations and take responsibility for a homeless vagabond and wastrel who clearly had little time left to live. Even if his name was Jack Doyle.

Old Arthur, Jack's cockney friend of many years' standing, was in his usual seat in The Hoop* that day. He went home and brought back some blankets to give to Sullivan, who then took Jack with him to his modest second-floor flat in Westbourne Park Road.

Sullivan, a maintenance man on the London Transport tracks, was due to work that night. He set his alarm for nine o'clock precisely. Jack had already gone to bed armed with two bottles of cider and a half-bottle of Scotch. When Sullivan looked in on him, he was fast asleep. He hadn't touched a drop of the booze.

The alarm rang, but Sullivan did not get up. He decided he would

* The Hoop no longer exists.

not go to work that night after all. Perhaps he had a premonition. Shortly afterwards, Jack came into the room. He said he was cold, so Sullivan got him an extra blanket. Suddenly, without warning, Jack started haemorrhaging. In spite of the shock – 'There was blood everywhere' – Sullivan stayed calm. He said softly, 'I'll get an ambulance for you.'

'No,' replied Jack. 'I'll be all right.'

Sullivan insisted. The ambulance arrived within three minutes.

'Sully, get me my shoes,' said Jack.

'It's all right – you won't need your shoes.'

'I don't want to go,' Jack said, almost pleadingly.

The ambulance crew knew their job. They did not prevaricate. Their attitude was one of sympathy allied to an air of authority. 'Come on Jack. 'You know you've got to go.'

It was the last Sullivan saw of his friend. They took Jack down in a wheelchair, a sad old man of sixty-five who knew that Death had again come calling and this time found him in. A few hours later it claimed him at St Mary's Hospital in Paddington. The date: Wednesday December 13, 1978. The time: twelve midnight – the passing from one day to another and, in this case, the passing from one world to another.*

Jack Doyle had fought his last fight. He had sung his last song. He had died as he forecast – a pauper. Would he be buried like one?

* The cause of death was advanced cirrhosis of the liver. According to Dr. Brian Dempsey, Jack had also been suffering variously from cancer of the left kidney, severe gastritis and high blood pressure: 'Heavy drinking was the real killer. How he lived so long amazed me because latterly he never ate.'

Chapter 6

A generous man never went to hell

Jack's body lay unclaimed at St Mary's Hospital. Owing to the suddenness of his death and his recent nomadic existence, hospital administrators had been unable to locate his next of kin. An urgent message was broadcast for members of the family to contact the hospital. There was even a suggestion that the great Jack Doyle would be buried in a pauper's grave.

Police eventually traced Bill and Tim Doyle (Mick was by this time in Australia). They had lost contact with Jack since his unexpected departure from hospital two weeks earlier but would now be making arrangements to have him buried at Greenford, where his parents and Uncle Joe had been laid to rest. But a member of the Irish Ex-Boxers' Association living in London was determined that Jack would be given a hero's farewell.

Joe Fay, a photographer, had good reason to be thankful for Jack's unsolicited generosity forty years earlier, when, as a lad of 17, he had been down on his luck and sleeping rough in Hyde Park. Jack bought him a meal, gave him £10 and paid his fare home to Dublin to visit his sick father. It was a wonderful gesture and he had never forgotten it. Now he was anxious to do something in return.

He contacted an old boxing colleague, Paddy Denn, and the business community in Cobh was alerted. A home-town burial was planned, the like of which had never been seen before. No expense would be spared.

Denn travelled to England with Cobh hotelier Pat O'Shea and undertaker Peter Barry. The family were persuaded to abandon their private burial arrangements. Jack Doyle belonged to Ireland, they were told, and Ireland would give him a funeral fit for a king.

Jack's remains were transported to St Aloysius's Church in Euston for a Requiem Mass, enabling friends and acquaintances in London to pay their last respects prior to departure for Ireland. The church was packed as the seven-foot solid oak casket – draped with Sean O'Casey's Plough and Stars flag and with a pair of six-ounce boxing gloves sitting on top – was shouldered into the chapel.

After the service, the hearse drove into Euston Station. The coffin was placed in a special carriage aboard the train to Liverpool and hundreds lined the platform as it moved slowly out. A lone piper played 'The Minstrel Boy'. Station guards and porters stood to attention. It was a profound, almost regal tribute.

From Liverpool the coffin was ferried across the Irish Sea to Dublin, where the city was waiting to say its last goodbye. Press cameramen, reporters and TV crews were out in force as the huge cavalcade threaded its way slowly through heavy traffic to the Adam and Eve Church at Merchant's Quay for a second Requiem Mass. Peter Barry's hearse then transported the coffin to Cork, where its arrival had been timed to meet the train from Dublin.

Thousands crowded the streets as two schoolboy pipers led the cortège on the two-mile journey across the city and out on to the road to Cobh. Three police motor cycle outriders escorted the funeral procession on the final fifteen-mile journey to the town that had occupied a special place in Jack's heart.

The people of Cobh had declared their own public day of mourning. The roads were blocked and police had to force a way through. As the cortège passed along the waterfront where Jack had worked on the coal boats as a boy, the ships in the harbour sounded a dramatic final salute. Then it was on out to St Colman's Cathedral, where there would be a third Requiem for the heavyweight champion of the people who had been counted out at the age of sixty-five years and 104 days.

His remains lay overnight at the Cathedral. The following day, December 22, the cortège wound its way through the narrow streets to the graveside on the outskirts of town, led by Tom Conway's solemn pipe lament. The coffin was lowered into a grave alongside the mass graves of the hundreds who had perished in the *Lusitania* when it was torpedoed off Cork in 1915. A single red carnation had been placed on top by Tim Doyle. The flower – Jack's essential trademark during life – would be his withering companion in death.

It remained only for trumpeter Denis Twomey, who had played the Battle Hymn of the Republic so stirringly during the Requiem Mass, to sound the Last Post. As he did so I suspect that ex-guardsman Doyle looked down from where all are eternal heroes and nodded approval at the pomp and ceremony that had closed the final chapter of his unique story.

As he had said so often during his lifetime: 'A generous man never went to hell.'

OLD MEN OF COBH

We are old men now and we like to sit
and talk of wind and weather
And the happy days we had in Cobh
when we were boys together

For hours and hours we'd look at the scene
Where else could you see the like?
The white-topped waves and the clear blue sky
and the glorious green of Spike

And old Tom Mac would often say
as boys we were full of pride
We thought we could manage any ship
in the teeth of wind and tide

One day at Whitepoint we boarded a yacht
to sail the harbour round
We hoisted the sails and away we went
and steered for the Holy Ground

In our pride we had no pilot aboard
and a fog from the hill closed round us
Where do you think we ran aground?
Near the Galley Head they found us

For an hour and more we stood on the shore
till our hearts with shame did burn
We prayed to God for pardon
and the tide began to turn

And after that for the rest of our lives
we worked like honest men
The lesson we got at the Galley Head
was never forgotten again

Now the evening of life has come
and our sun is going down in the West
It's time for weary old men like us
to go home for a well-earned rest

But the road to home is long and steep
and old age begins to tire
We'll stop for a minute to take a rest
beneath St Colman's spire

And look again at the peaceful scene
where we spent such happy days
God bless you all old friends of Cobh
Kind friends beyond all praise.

Anonymous

Afterword

I thought I had learned a lot about Jack Doyle from my time at *Boxing News* and from my Irish mother, Ann (Nancy) Donovan. She hailed from Ballitore in Co. Kildare, but was a young girl in service in Dublin when Jack fought his brief but savage battle with Pettifer. She remembers the milkman enthusing, 'We've got a world heavyweight champion in that young fellow Doyle,' and then whistling a cheery tune as he strode purposefully back down the path. His mood was indicative of the mood that prevailed throughout Ireland and indeed the UK, where Jack was already an adopted hero. Simply by *being* Jack Doyle, he lifted the spirit of both nations and even captured the imagination of the United States.

There was great excitement when he was due to appear in my wife Martha's home town of Creeslough, Co. Donegal. Her brother Tom McFadden remembers the moment when Jack's cavalcade was drawing near. 'People were shouting, "Jack Doyle's coming, Jack Doyle's coming." We were little children then and didn't know who he was. We thought he must be some kind of ogre. We became frightened and ran in off the street.'

A *Boxing News* correspondent, Bert Frost, recalled amazing scenes in Windsor in the thirties. Crowds were lining the main street waiting, he thought, to welcome a member of the Royal family. It turned out to be another case of 'Jack Doyle's coming'. He was on his way to the Star and Garter.

It was only when I started researching this book that I discovered truth and legend were inextricably linked where Jack was concerned, as with the children thinking he was an ogre and Bert Frost believing he was a Royal. The Jack Doyle story produced many versions of the truth. Beyond the lovers mentioned in this book, there is a cast-list of film stars, society women – even members of the Royal family – with whom he is rumoured to have had affairs and which I have been unable to verify.

Take the matter of his famous inscribed gold cigarette case. Since he either lost it or sold it, it is not possible to confirm the inscription. Was it a present from the Prince of Wales, as most of the Doyle family believe, or was it, as Bridie believed, a gift from Princess Marina, Duchess of Kent? An affair was rumoured – Jack was said to have been warned off – and certainly the Princess took to the wearing of the green: 'Marina Green', as it became known.

Florence Desmond, formerly one of Cochran's Young Ladies and good friend of Beryl Markham, is said to have been a conquest. 'She didn't know Doyle,' was the terse response from her husband. Irish-born Maureen O'Sullivan – Mia Farrow's mother and Tarzan Johnny Weissmuller's famous Jane – was also rumoured to have been a lover. 'Not true,' she said when contacted in New York. Lady Bridget Poulett was yet another – 'I would very much doubt it,' said her once close friend, the Duchess of Argyle. But of the rumoured suicides born of unrequited love for Jack, at least one attempt is verifiable.

The voluptuous Jane Russell, in Britain to promote a film, was 'extremely keen' on Jack, according to Ted Doyle, who confirmed: 'She liked him and was after him.' That they met is beyond dispute. That they had a sexual liaison is unconfirmed.

Veteran Irish stage and film actor Noel Purcell regaled me with many wonderful tales. Here is a sample:

> 'Louis Elliman, who owned the Theatre Royal, got Jack and Movita to appear. We were doing an excerpt from *Rose Marie*. We were all togged up as Canadian Mounties and the girls were dressed as Indians. It was a fabulous setting and there was a big build-up for Jack. He looked magnificent in his Mountie hat, lariat, red coat and blue trousers. We were all in the same dressing-room (No 1) and Movita came in crying. She had a black eye. We got her pacified, and then in came Jack with scratches all over his face. Their wounds had to be camouflaged with heavy make-up before they could go on stage.
>
> 'Some of the leading ladies were delighted with the service Jack provided. And I heard that Carole Lombard rated him the "best ever". Jack told me Delphine Dodge's husband gave him a settlement of £100 000 to lay off his wife. He claimed he took Lombard to Acapulco and blew the lot on the best "riding" holiday he ever had.'

Truth or legend? Take your pick. But there is still more. Purcell, who has since died, provided yet a further twist to the saga of Jack's incredible fight with Chris Cole:

> 'I went along with Maxie Elliman, manager of the Theatre Royal. We had ringside seats. Elliman heard a story that Cole was under orders to lie down, but would have none of it. Just before the fight he went in to see Jack and Gerald Egan and said, "I want my money now – and this fight's on the level." Jack said: "You can't do that, Chris – you know I'm not fit." Cole got his money and asked his manager to go out and put the lot on him. Jack hurriedly sent someone to get him a bottle of brandy and drank every last drop.'

Dave Guiney heard that Jack was mortified when he realised Cole meant business. Worried about his looks, as ever, Jack is alleged to have said to Cole, 'Not in the face, Chris, not in the face.'

Eugene Barrymore, a member of the famous theatrical family, recalled when Jack and Movita came face to face with Hitler shortly before the outbreak of war:

> 'They were at this beautiful hotel in Berlin when in walked Hitler accompanied by his uniformed lieutenants, all of them bronzed and blond. Everyone stood except Jack and Movita. "I'm Irish – we don't have to stand," he told her. Hitler had electrifying presence, with commanding eyes. He looked daggers at them, so they shot up. When Jack had extended himself to his full height, Hitler was immediately taken by this beautiful hunk of manhood. He was shocked at Jack's size – he was only 5ft himself – and came across to speak to him. When he found out he was Irish, he got one of his soldiers to act as interpreter. Apparently, Jack made quite an impression.'

Another story I encountered was that Jack had fathered a son. I obtained a surname for the mother, but 46 long-distance telephone calls failed to reveal the truth or otherwise of this lead and it, too, must remain part of the legend. It is a neat irony that Miko, Movita's son by Marlon Brando–perhaps the son Jack would have wanted–followed his mother into show-business as a member of Michael Jackson's security staff.

One of Jack's many admirers among the famous was George Bernard Shaw, who, talking of how Britain could settle its war-time lease-lend debt to the United States, declared: 'We should give Jack Doyle to America and call it quits.' The great showman C. B. Cochran, who found Jack, 'a most attractive young Irishman, with the right kind of lilt in his voice,' would rather have sent him to America 'to act, sing and dance in musical melodrama of the type that made fortunes for Chauncey Olcott and a number of Irish-American actors.'

In his paradoxical way GBS hated boxing but loved boxers and explored this idea in his novel *Cashel Byron's Profession*, written in 1882. In a preface added in 1901, he included what could be perceived by some to have been a prophetic portrait of Jack himself: 'A prize-fighter need have . . . courage least of all: indeed there are instances on record of prize-fighters who have only consented to persevere with a winning fight when a mirror has been brought to convince them that their faces were undamaged and their injuries and terrors imaginary.' He also asserts that '. . . the ring, like all romantic institutions, has a natural attraction for hysterical people . . .

'. . . The intelligent prize-fighter is not a knight-errant: he is a disillusioned man of business trying to make money at a certain weight and at certain risks, not of bodily injury (for a bruise is soon cured), but of pecuniary loss. When he is a Jew, a negro, a gypsy, or a recruit from that gypsified, nomadic, poaching, tinkering, tramping class which exists in all countries, he differs from the phlegmatic John Bull pugilist [the very type that Doyle detested] exactly as he would differ from him in any other occupation: that is, he is a more imaginative liar, a more obvious poser, a more plausible talker, a vainer actor, a more reckless gambler, and more easily persuaded that he is beaten or even killed when he has only received an unusually hard punch.'

Since Jack's *actual* death, his memory has been perpetuated in Cobh by a bronze plaque in Kennedy Park unveiled by Ted Doyle and the opening of The Jack Doyle Room in the Commodore Hotel.

When I started work on *Boxing News* at the age of 17, little did I realise that I was commencing a romantic journey through the world of boxing which would lead me to the writing of this book. During my interview with Raymond Blackburn, he fixed me with a quizzical look and said, 'Why are you bothering to do a book on Jack Doyle? There are people who led far more important lives and were of more value to the country.' True. But none was as fascinating. None was as compelling. None drew people to him in quite the same way.

Nancy Kehoe used to tease that I would never finish the enterprise. I must confess there were times when I began to believe her. She revealed that several people had started books on Jack but were forced to abandon them. They had been unable to get to the bottom of him; they had failed to track down the major players in his life. Well Nancy, I did finish.

I went to Cobh, amongst other things, to interview Peter Barry, the undertaker at Jack's funeral. He proved to be typical of those Irish people who so loved Jack Doyle. He got out his records and played them to me. I looked up as Jack was singing *When Irish eyes Are Smiling* to see the tears streaming down Peter's face.

Jack's power to move people was undiminished, even in death.

Doyle the Boxer

(Born Cobh, Ireland, August 31, 1913)

			Venue and Scheduled Number of Rounds	
1932				
April 4	Chris Goulding	Won KO 1	Crystal Palace	10
May 2	Arthur Evans	Won KO 1	Crystal Palace	10
May 23	Bill Partridge	Won (stpd) 1	Holborn	6
July 12	Guardsman Gater	Won (stpd) 2	Wimbledon	6
July 21	Bobby Shields	Won KO 1	Liverpool	6
Aug 13	George Slack	Won KO 2	Swansea	8
Oct 10	Gerard Ghesquiere	Won KO 1	Grimsby	8
Oct 17	Jack Pettifer	Won KO 2	Crystal Palace	10
Nov 10	Moise Bouquillon	Won KO 2	Albert Hall	10
1933				
May 18	Jack Humbeeck	Won KO 2	Olympia	15
July 12	Jack Petersen	Lost (disq) 2	White City	15
	(British Heavyweight title and Lonsdale Belt)			
1934				
Mar 19	Frank Borrington	Won KO 1	Albert Hall	12
1935				
June 24	Phil Donato	Won KO 1	New York	10
July 15	Jack Redmond	Won KO 4	Newark, N Jersey	10
July 30	Bob Norton	Won KO 2	Elizabeth, N Jersey	10
Aug 29	Buddy Baer	Lost (stpd) 1	New York	6
1936 (Inactive)				
1937				
Jan 19	Alf Robinson	Lost (disq) 1	Wembley	8
Feb 15	Harry Staal	Won (retd) 6	Earl's Court	10
April 27	King Levinsky	Won (pts)	Wembley	12
1938				
Sept 27	Eddie Phillips	Lost KO 2	Harringay	12
1939				
July 10	Eddie Phillips	Lost KO 1	White City	12
1940–42 (Inactive)				
1943				
June 11	Chris Cole	Lost (stpd) 1	Dublin	10
Aug 6	Butcher Howell	Won KO 3	Dublin	10

Fights: 23 Won: 17 (13 by clean knockouts, 3 inside the distance and one on points).
Lost 6: (2 by disqualification)

Doyle the Singer

Decca

Catalogue No.	*Recorded*	*Released*	*Title*
F – 3555	28/5/'33	June '33	Mother Machree/ My Irish Song of Songs
F – 3576	1/6/'33	July '33	Little Town In The Ould County Down/ Where the River Shannon Flows
F – 3898	14/2/'34	April '34	I'm Away In Killarney With You/ Ireland I Love You, Acushla Machree
F – 3949	14/2/'34	May '34	My Home by The Wicklow Hills/ Thank God For a Garden (A side)
F – 5128	12/7/'34	Sept '34	Little Irish Girl/The Garden Where the Praties Grow (A)
F – 5129	12/7/'34	Nov '34	Just Pretending*/ That Tumbledown Shack in Athlone
F – 6804	11/5/'38	Oct '38	Danny Boy/Macushla (A)
F – 7199	22/8/'39	Sept '39	When Irish Eyes Are Smiling/ South of the Border (duet with Movita) (A)
F – 7351	3/1/'40	Feb '40	Speak To Me Of Love (Parles Moi d'Amour)/ Romance In Rio (from 'Girl from Rio') (Both duets with Movita)
	1959	1959	In My Father's House/ On the Shores of Bantry Bay (accompanied by Wimbledon Girls' Choir)

Not issued: Ah, Sweet Mystery of Life/Vienna, City of My Dreams (recorded 11/5/'38)

*With Fred Hartley's Quintet. Song written by Jack Doyle (Reviewed in The Gramophone, September '34).

Doyle the Movie Actor

1935

McGLUSKY THE SEA ROVER – Great Britain, 58mins, Cert A (Released in US under title HELL'S CARGO)

Director: Walter Summers (BIP – (Wardour)

Cast – Jack Doyle, Tamara Desni, Henry Mollison, Cecil Ramage, Frank Cochrane, Hugh Miller, Jackie Short.

Summary: Adventure film. Stowaway involved with gun-runner falls in love with Arab girl. (Extract in The Elstree Story, 1952).

1937

NAVY SPY – USA, 55mins, Cert A

Director: Crane Wilbur (Grand National)

Cast – Conrad Nagel, Eleanor Hunt, Judith Allen, Jack Doyle, Phil Dunham, Don Barclay, Howard Lang.

Summary: U.S. Navy thriller. Inventor of noxious gas is decoyed ashore by letter from pretty girl and kidnapped. Secret agent and girlfriend track him down.

1954

THE BELLES OF ST. TRINIAN'S – Great Britain, 91mins, Cert U

Director: Frank Launder (British Lion)

Cast – Alastair Sim, Joyce Grenfell, George Cole, Hermione Baddeley, Betty Ann Davis, Beryl Reid, Mary Merrall, Renee Houston, Irene Handl, Joan Sims, Balbina, Guy Middleton, Sidney James, Arthur Howard, Richard Wattis, Eric Pohlmann, Lloyd Lamble, Andree Melly, Belinda Lee, Jerry Verno, Jack Doyle.

Summary: Comedy. Schoolgirls hide racehorse from gang run by headmistress's brother.

Filmography

MOVITA

1933

FLYING DOWN TO RIO – USA, 89mins, Cert U

Director: Thornton Freeland (RKO)

Cast – Dolores Del Rio, Gene Raymond, Raoul Roulien, Ginger Rogers, Fred Astaire, Blanche Frederici, Movita.

1935 (Reissued 1944)

MUTINY ON THE BOUNTY – USA, 135mins, Cert A

Director: Frank Lloyd (M-G-M)

Cast – Charles Laughton, Clark Gable, Franchot Tone, Movita.

1937

PARADISE ISLE – USA, 73mins, Cert U

Director: Arthur Greville Collins (Monogram)

Cast – Movita, Warren Hull, George Piltz, William Davidson.

THE HURRICANE – USA, 102mins, Cert U

Directors: John Ford, Stuart Heisler (United Artists)

Cast – Dorothy Lamour, Jon Hall, Mary Astor, C. Aubrey Smith, Raymond Massey, Thomas Mitchell, John Carradine, Movita.

1938

CAPTAIN CALAMITY – USA, 65mins, Cert U

Director: John Reinhardt (Grand National)

Cast – George Houston, Marian Nixon, Vince Barnett, Movita.

ROSE OF THE RIO GRANDE – USA, 61mins, Cert U
Director: William Nigh (Monogram)
Cast – Movita, John Carroll, Antonio Moreno, Lina Basquette.

1939

WOLF CALL – USA, 61mins, Cert U
Director: George Waggner (Monogram)
Cast – John Carroll, Movita, Peter George Lynn, Polly Ann Young.

GIRL FROM RIO – USA, 63mins, Cert U
Director: Lambert Hillyer (Monogram)
Cast – Movita, Warren Hull, Alan Baldwin, Kay Linaker.

1942 (Reissued 1949)

TOWER OF TERROR – Great Britain, 84mins, Cert A
Director: Lawrence Huntington (Associated British Pictures)
Cast – Wilfrid Lawson, Movita, Michael Rennie.

1948

FORT APACHE – USA, 128mins, Cert U
Director: John Ford (Argosy)
Cast – John Wayne, Henry Fonda, Shirley Temple, Movita.

1949

THE MYSTERIOUS DESPERADO – USA, 61mins, Cert U
Director: Lesley Selander (RKO Radio)
Cast – Tim Holt, Richard Martin, Edward Norris, Movita.

1950

THE FURIES – USA, 109mins, Cert A
Director: Anthony Mann (Paramount)
Cast – Barbara Stanwyck, Walter Huston, Wendell Corey, Judith Anderson, Gilbert Roland, Thomas Gomez, Beulah Bondi, Movita.

FEDERAL MAN – USA, 68mins, Cert A

Director: Robert Tansey (Monarch)

Cast – William Henry, Pamela Blake, Robert Shayne, Movita.

WAGONMASTER – USA, 86mins, Cert U

Director: John Ford (RKO/Argosy)

Cast – Ben Johnson, Joanne Dru, Harry Carey Jr., Ward Bond, James Arness, Movita.

1951

SOLDIERS THREE – USA, 92mins, Cert U

Director: Tay Garnett (M-G-M)

Cast – Stewart Granger, Walter Pidgeon, David Niven, Robert Newton, Cyril Cusack, Movita.

1952

DREAM WIFE – USA, 99mins, Cert U

Director: Sidney Sheldon (M-G-M)

Cast – Deborah Kerr, Cary Grant, Betta St. John, Buddy Baer, Walter Pidgeon, Movita.

1954

TICKET TO MEXICO – USA, 53mins, Cert U

Director: Lew Landers (Exclusive)

Cast – Bill Williams, Don Diamond, Movita.

1955

APACHE AMBUSH – USA, 68mins, Cert U

Director: Fred F. Sears (Columbia)

Cast – Bill Williams, Richard Jaeckel, Movita, Tex Ritter.

JUDITH ALLEN

1933

TOO MUCH HARMONY – USA, 74mins, Cert A

Director: Edward Sutherland (Paramount)

Cast – Bing Crosby, Jackie Oakie, Judith Allen.

THUNDERING HERD – USA, 57mins, Cert U

Director: Henry Hathaway (Paramount)

Cast – Randolph Scott, Judith Allen, Harry Carey.

THIS DAY AND AGE – USA, 81mins, Cert A

Director: Cecil B. de Mille (Paramount)

Cast – Charles Bickford, Richard Cromwell, Judith Allen.

HELL AND HIGH WATER – USA, 70mins, Cert A
(also titled Cap'n Jericho)

Director: Grover Jones, William McNutt (Paramount)

Cast – Richard Arlen, Judith Allen, Charles Grapewin.

1934

BRIGHT EYES – USA, 84mins, Cert U

Director: David Butler (20th Century-Fox)

Cast – Shirley Temple, James Dunn, Judith Allen.
(Features Temple's classic rendition of *On the Good Ship Lollipop*.)

MARRYING WIDOWS – USA, 65mins, Cert A

Director: Sam Newfield (Universal)

Cast – Judith Allen, Minna Gombell, Lucien Littlefield.

SHE LOVES ME NOT – USA, 82mins, Cert A

Director: Elliott Nugent (Paramount)

Cast – Bing Crosby, Miriam Hopkins, Kitty Carlisle, Judith Allen.

THE OLD-FASHIONED WAY – USA, 69mins, Cert U

Director: William Beaudine (Paramount)

Cast – W.C. Fields, Joe Morrison, Baby LeRoy, Judith Allen.

THE WITCHING HOUR – USA, 62mins, Cert A

Director: Henry Hathaway (Paramount)

Cast – Sir Guy Standing, John Halliday, Judith Allen.

YOUNG AND BEAUTIFUL – USA, 70mins, Cert A

Director: Joseph Santley (Mascot)

Cast – Judith Allen, William Haines.

MEN OF THE NIGHT – USA, 57mins, Cert A

Director: Lambert Hillyer (Columbia)

Cast – Bruce Cabot, Judith Allen, Ward Bond.

1935

BEHIND GREEN LIGHTS – USA, 68mins, Cert A

Director: Christy Cabanne (Mascot)

Cast – Norman Foster, Judith Allen, Sidney Blackmer.

NIGHT ALARM – USA, 66mins, Cert U

Director: Spencer Bennett (Majestic)

Cast – Bruce Cabot, Judith Allen, H.B. Warner.

RECKLESS ROADS – USA, 61mins, Cert U

Director: Burt Lynwood (Majestic)

Cast – Judith Allen, Regis Toomey, Lloyd Hughes, Ben Alexander.

THE HEALER – USA, 72mins, Cert U

Director: Reginald Barker (Monogram)

Cast – Ralph Bellamy, Karen Morley, Mickey Rooney, Judith Allen.

1936

BURNING GOLD – USA, 58mins, Cert A

Director: Sam Newfield (Republic)

Cast – William Boyd, Judith Allen.

1937

BEWARE OF LADIES – USA, 64mins, Cert A

Director: Irving Pichel (Republic)

Cast – Donald Cook, Judith Allen.

BOOTS AND SADDLES – USA, 58mins, Cert U

Director: Joseph Kane (Republic)

Cast – Gene Autry, Judith Allen.

MAN FROM THE BIG CITY – USA, 56 mins, Cert U
(also titled It Happened Out West)

Director: Howard Bretherton (Principal)

Cast – Paul Kelly, Judith Allen, Johnny Arthur, Leroy Mason.

NAVY SPY (See Jack Doyle movie career).

SERENADE OF THE WEST – USA, 73mins, Cert U
(originally titled Git Along Little Dogies)

Director: Joseph Kane (Republic)

Cast – Gene Autry, Judith Allen, Cabin Kids, Smiley Burnette.

MEN OF STEEL – USA, 64mins, Cert U
(originally titled Bill Cracks Down)

Director: William Nigh (Republic)

Cast – Judith Allen, Ranny Weeks, Grant Withers, Beatrice Roberts.

TEXAS TRAIL – USA, 59mins, Cert U

Director: David Selman (Paramount)

Cast – William Boyd, Russell Hayden, George Hayes, Judith Allen.

1938

TELEPHONE OPERATOR – USA, 61mins, Cert U

Director: Scott Pembroke (Monogram)

Cast – Grant Withers, Judith Allen.

PORT OF MISSING GIRLS – USA, 64mins, Cert A

Director: Karl Brown (Monogram)

Cast – Judith Allen, Milburn Stone, Harry Carey, Betty Compson.

1939

THE FIFTH ROUND – USA, 60mins, Cert U
(also titled Tough Kid)

Director: Howard Bretherton (Monogram)

Cast – Frankie Darro, Dick Purcell, Judith Allen.

1940

FRAMED – USA, 60mins, Cert A

Director: Harold Schuster (Universal)

Cast – Constance Moore, Frank Albertson, Robert Armstrong, Judith Allen.

1950

TRAIN TO TOMBSTONE – USA, 57mins, Cert U

Director: William Berke (Lippert Pictures)

Cast – Don Barry, Judith Allen, Wally Vernon.

1952

SOMETHING TO LIVE FOR – USA, 89 mins

Director: George Stevens

Cast – Joan Fontaine, Ray Milland, Teresa Wright, Richard Derr, Douglas Dick (Judith had bit-part role).

Bibliography

BROCKMAN, Alfred: *The Glamorous Years – The Stars and Films of the 1930s* (Hamlyn, 1987)
BRYAN III, J. and MURPHY, Charles J.V.: *The Windsor Story* (Granada, 1979)
BYRNE, Gay: with PURCELL, Deidre: *The Time of My Life* (Gill & MacMillan, 1989)
CARPENTER, Harry: *Boxing – A Pictorial History* (Collins, 1975)
COCHRAN, Charles B. : *Cock-A-Doodle-Do* (J.M. Dent, 1941)
CRITCHLEY, Brigadier-General A.C.: *Critch* (Hutchinson, 1963)
DALBY, W. Barrington: *Come In Barry* (Cassell, 1961)
DEMPSEY, Jack: *The Autobiography of Jack Dempsey* with Barbara Piatelli Dempsey (W.H. Allen, 1977)
DESMOND, Florence: *Florence Desmond: by Herself* (Clarke, Irwin, 1953)
FLYNN, Errol: *My Wicked, Wicked Ways* (Pan, 1961)
GODFREY, Lionel: *The Life and Crimes of Errol Flynn* (Robert Hale, 1977)
HENDERSON, Eugene: *Box On* (Phoenix House, 1959)
HUTCHINSON, Tom: *Niven's Hollywood* (Macmillan, 1984)
KAVANAGH, Patrick: *The Complete Poems* (The Goldsmith Press, 1972)
LATHAM, Caroline and AGRESTA, David: *Dodge Dynasty* (Harcourt Brace Jovanovich, 1989)
LOVELL, Mary S.: *Straight on Till Morning – The Biography of Beryl Markham* (Hutchinson, 1987)
LUCAS, Norman: *Britain's Gangland* (W.H. Allen, 1969)
MARKHAM, Beryl: *West With the Night* (Virago, 1984)
NIVEN, David: *Bring On the Empty Horses* (Hamish Hamilton, 1975)
OAKELEY, Sir Atholl: *Blue Blood on the Mat* (Stanley Paul, 1971)
O'CONNOR, Ulick: *Brendan Behan* (Coronet, 1972)
ODD, Gilbert: *Len Harvey: Prince of Boxers* (Pelham, 1978)
ROBERTS, Randy: *The Manassa Mauler* (Robson Books, 1987)
SHAW, George Bernard: *Cashel Byron's Profession* (1882, Preface added 1901)
SWINDELL, Larry: *Screwball – The Life of Carole Lombard* (William Morrow, 1975)
TORNABENE, Lyn: *Long Live the King – A Biography of Clark Gable* (W.H. Allen, 1977)
TREHARNE, Evan R.: *British Heavyweight Champions* (Avis, 1959)
WALTER, Gerard: *White Ties and Fisticuffs – The Story of Patsy Hagate* (Hutchinson, 1951)
WILSON, Peter: *Ringside Seat* (Arrow, 1947)

Reference Books

BARDSLEY, Geoffrey (Ed.): *British Boxing Records* (National Boxing Association, 1939)
HALLIWELL, Leslie: *Halliwell's Filmgoer's Companion* (Grafton, 1988).
KATZ, Ephraim: *The International Film Encyclopedia* (Papermac, 1982)
MULLAN, Harry (Ed.): *Boxing News Annual & Record Book* (Byblos, 1978)
TRUITT, Evelyn Mack (Compiler): *Who Was Who On Screen* – 3rd edition (Bowker, 1983).

TV Documentary

THE GORGEOUS GAEL (Radio Teilifis Eireann). Reporter: Patrick Gallagher.

Index